Celluloid Soldiers

Celluloid Soldiers

Warner Bros.'s Campaign against Nazism

Michael E. Birdwell

NEW YORK UNIVERSITY PRESS

New York and London

NEW YORK UNIVERSITY PRESS
New York and London

Library of Congress Cataloging-in-Publication Data
Birdwell, Michael E., 1957–
Celluloid soldiers : Warner Bros.'s campaign against Nazism,
1934–1941 / Michael E. Birdwell.
p.   cm.
Includes bibliographical references and index.
ISBN 0-8147-9871-3 (cloth : acid-free paper)
1. Warner Bros. Pictures—History. 2. National socialism and
motion pictures.   I. Title.
PN1999.W3 B57 1999
791.43'658—dc21   98-58058
                             CIP

New York University Press books are printed on acid-free paper,
and their binding materials are chosen for strength and durability.

Manufactured in the United States of America

10 9 8 7 6 5 4 3 2

To the Memory of B. F. Jones—
Friend, Mentor, and Scholar

Contents

Acknowledgments

The completion of this book would not have been possible without the help, cooperation, support, argument, and love of a great number of people. For those of you who were kind enough to let me spend the night at your house, I am forever grateful. Others of you, who listened to me go on and on about all this, thanks for the indulgence. Those of you who made me rethink weaknesses in the argument, I am in your debt. People who ran information down for me (thank God for interlibrary loan and the Internet), I truly appreciate it. And finally, those who offered moral support, meals, or libations, I thank you. The folks listed below know what they did to help, and I wish to thank them (in no particular order) for their indulgence, patience, prodding, and support: Jennifer Hammer; Lois Crum; John Muldowny; Charles Maland; Charles Johnson; Charles Jackson; B. F. Jones; Michael McDonald; Bruce Wheeler; Hack Smith; David W.; Rosemary and Abigail Lee; William Brinker; Michael Martin; David D. Lee; Jeffrey McEwen; Larry Whiteaker; Guy Woodall; Calvin Dickinson; Homer Kemp; Guy Williams; Peter Field; Jeffery Roberts; Lois Clinton; Kriste Lindenmeyer; G. Frank Burns; Justus D. Doenecke; Billy D. Smith; Sue Ellen Odom; Diane, Larry, Hillary, and Vanessa Ragland; Tom, Alison, Christa, Zack, and Rollie Furtsch; Jennifer Williams; Will Schrader; Linda Mulder; Sue Goss; Capt. William Anderson; Jeanette Keith; Patrick Reagan; George Webb; Wayne S. Cole; Leith Adams; Stuart Ng; Ned Comstock; Stuart Galbraith; Andrew Jackson York; George Edward Buxton York; Helen York; Gerry York; Cletis York; Margaret York; Betsy Ross and Howard Lowry; David Woodward; Willie Davis; Peter Rollins; Linda Furtsch; Andy Williams; John Finger; Edna and Rufus Barlow; Dan Webber; W. L. "Buzz" Davis; Rhee Ann Robinson; Lucy York Rains; Leo Hatfield; Jessica Agnew; Steven Denney; Sue McTasney; Chuckles; Lorraine Cargile; Thelma Johnson; John Nisbet; Chris Holmlund; Don Whaley; James B. Jones, Jr.; Steve Rogers; Joe Garrison; Steve Gwilt; J. W. Williamson; Noble Cody; Steve Rains; Eston Evans;

Randy Williams; Kathy Smith; Ernest Buck; Vicki S. Lewallen; Randy Evans; Ernest Buck; Doyle Jones; O. D. Abston; Carol Roberts; Karina Mc-Daniel; Edwin Gleaves; John Thweat; Jon Jonakin; Jim Lloyd; John Lukas; Bill and Phyllis Cronk; Tim Smight; William, Mary, and Brenda Birdwell; Mark Wood; Erika Rittenberry; the Cookeville Breakfast and Noonday Rotary Clubs; the Sergeant York Patriotic Foundation; and the Upper Cumberland Institute.

I would also like to acknowledge the generosity and patience shown to me by the institutions and organizations that house the various special collections that I consulted: the University of Southern California, Los Angeles, where I examined the Warner Bros. Archives and the Jack L. Warner Collection; the Tennessee State Library and Archives; the National Archives facilities in Atlanta and in College Park, Maryland; the University of Tennessee, Knoxville; the East Tennessee Historical Society; the University of Tennessee, Chattanooga; the Chattanooga Bicentennial Library; Tennessee Technological University; Vanderbilt University; the Tennessee Department of Conservation and Environment; the Tennessee Historical Commission; and the Fentress County Historical Society. Special thanks to the Alvin C. York family for allowing access to the papers in their possession.

Time Line

January 30, 1933	Hitler becomes chancellor of Germany.
January 31, 1933	William Dudley Pelley launches the Silver Shirt Legion, a pro-Nazi fascist movement in Asheville, North Carolina.
March 1933	The Nazis open their first concentration camps.
March 4, 1933	Franklin Delano Roosevelt (FDR) is inaugurated president of the United States.
April 1933	The World Disarmament Conference begins and drags on until October; Hitler withdraws, killing hopes of sustained peace in Europe.
	MGM releases *Gabriel over the White House,* a film endorsing fascist techniques to end the Depression.
April 1, 1933	The Nazis boycott Jewish business in Germany.
June 16, 1933	The National Industrial Recovery Act creates the National Recovery Administration (NRA) to promote cooperation among business, government, and labor to end the Depression. Warner Bros., the first studio to embrace the "Blue Eagle," agrees to comply.
June 28, 1933	The Nazis limit the distribution of Hollywood films in Germany.
Summer 1933	Alvin C. York loses control of the York Agricultural and Industrial Institute, and the school's management is assumed by the Tennessee Department of Education.

September 18, 1933	Warner Bros. releases the *Looney Tunes* cartoon *Bosko's Picture Show,* which lampoons Hitler, marking the studio's first attempt at exposing the Nazi threat.
October 14, 1933	Germany leaves the League of Nations.
November 1933	U.S. recognition of the Soviet Union begins normalization of diplomatic relations.
December 22, 1933	Members of Detroit's cryptofascist organization the Black Legion assassinate George Marchuk, secretary of United Auto Workers (UAW).
1934	The Production Code Administration (PCA) under Joseph Breen institutes new self-policing restrictions on the film industry to ensure decency in Hollywood films.
	Nathanael West publishes his satirical novel, *A Cool Million: Or the Dismantling of Lemuel Pitkin,* a send-up of American fascists.
March 15, 1934	Black Legion members murder American Federation of Labor (AFL) organizer John Bielack.
July 1934	*Fortune* magazine praises the virtues and apparent successes of Italian fascism.
July 15, 1934	Warner Bros. discontinues business with the Third Reich, making it the first Hollywood studio to do so.
September 1934	Senator Gerald P. Nye (R-North Dakota) calls for a Senate investigation of the munitions industry, claiming that greed accounted for U.S. entry into World War I.
	Walter Wanger produces *The President Vanishes,* a film about a fascist takeover of the United States.

1935	Alvin C. York preaches a sermon entitled "Christian Cure for Strife," calling for U.S. neutrality and pacifism.
	William Dudley Pelley runs for president of the United States on the Christian Party ticket, espousing a Christian totalitarian state based on the Nazi model.
August 31, 1935	The United States passes its first Neutrality Act.
December 1935	Warner Bros. releases *Black Fury.*
1936	Harry Warner demands that the studio begin filming patriotic short subjects, the *Old Glory* series.
	Fritz Kuhn assumes control of the German-American Bund.
February 29, 1936	The United States passes its second Neutrality Act.
March 7, 1936	Germany violates the Versailles Treaty and reoccupies the Rhineland.
May 1936	Italy annexes Ethiopia and leaves the League of Nations.
May 1, 1936	The United States passes its third Neutrality Act.
May 12, 1936	Black Legionnaires murder Works Progress Administration (WPA) worker Charles Poole, which leads to the vigilante group's undoing.
May 26, 1936	Warner Bros. announces its production of a movie based on the criminal activity of the Black Legion, exposing the threat of fascism at home.
June 8, 1936	The Anti-Nazi League (ANL) is organized in Hollywood.
July 1936	The Spanish Civil War begins.

July 22, 1936	Charles Lindbergh visits Nazi Germany for the first time.
August 1, 1936	Olympic games open in Berlin. Lindbergh attends as the personal guest of *Luftwaffe* Reichsmarshall Hermann Goring.
Fall 1936	Adolf Hitler and Benito Mussolini forge the Rome-Berlin Axis.
October 27, 1936	The WPA's Federal Theatre Project stages an adaptation of Sinclair Lewis's cautionary antifascist novel *It Can't Happen Here.*
1937	Errol Flynn visits Spain in the midst of the Civil War, embarrassing Warner Bros.
January 16, 1937	*Black Legion* opens in New York.
July 7, 1937	The Marco Polo Bridge incident occurs. After conquering Manchuria, Japan continues its war in China.
August 1937	Journalist James Metcalfe interviews Alvin C. York, who says Americans should never again fight overseas.
August 11, 1937	*The Life of Emile Zola* opens in New York.
October 4, 1937	*They Won't Forget* opens in New York.
October 5, 1937	FDR delivers his "Quarantine" speech.
December 11, 1937	The Japanese sink the U.S. gunboat *Panay,* killing three Americans and injuring forty-three.
December 15, 1937	Harry Warner encourages eighty employees to be more politically active and join the ANL.
February 26, 1938	J. Edgar Hoover announces that the FBI uncovered a Nazi spy ring in the United States.
March 1938	Warner Bros. releases *The Adventures of Robin Hood.*

March 13, 1938	Hitler initiates the Austrian *Anschluss.*
March 30, 1938	Warner Bros. shuts down film operations in Austria.
May 10, 1938	Dr. Ignatz T. Greibl, leader of the American Nazi spy ring, escapes to Germany.
June 23, 1938	Warner Bros. negotiates with FBI agent Leon Turrou, who uncovered the Nazi spy ring, to make a movie about the case.
September 29, 1938	Appeasement in Munich cedes Czechoslovakian Sudetenland to Nazi Germany.
October 1938	On Lindbergh's last visit to Nazi Germany, Goring presents him with the Service Cross of the Order of the German Eagle with the Star.
October 28, 1938	Harry Warner is hospitalized with bleeding ulcers.
November 1938	Alvin C. York calls for two hours per day of military training in all Civilian Conservation Corps (CCC) camps.
	Hitler's favorite director, Leni Riefenstahl, visits Hollywood to exhibit *Olympiad* and is coolly received by most denizens of America's film capital.
November 1938	The Roosevelt administration creates the U.S. Film Service to promote the Good Neighbor policy in Latin and South America.
November 8, 1938	*Kristallnacht:* Open persecution of the Jews begins in Germany. The first trainloads of Jews are sent to concentration camps.
December 21, 1938	The Committee of Fifty-Six signs the Declaration of Democratic Independence, asking FDR to take immediate action against Nazi aggression.
December 23, 1938	*The Dawn Patrol* opens in New York.

February 1, 1939	Warner Bros. begins filming *Confessions of a Nazi Spy.*
March 1939	Japan occupies the Spratly Islands.
March 15, 1939	Hitler seizes Czechoslovakia.
March 17, 1939	Warner Bros. announces its impending release of *Confessions of a Nazi Spy.*
March 24, 1939	Madrid surrenders to Francisco Franco's forces.
April 1939	Italy invades Albania.
April 25, 1939	*Juarez* opens in New York.
April 28, 1939	*Confessions of a Nazi Spy,* Hollywood's first openly anti-Nazi film, opens in New York.
July 1, 1939	Alvin York addresses a Christian rally in San Francisco, urging pacifism and neutrality.
July 22, 1939	On Tennessee Day at the New York World's Fair, Alvin York urges nonintervention in the growing crisis in Europe.
July 23, 1939	Nazis begin the Aryanization of the film industry in Czechoslovakia.
August 23, 1939	The Nazis and the Soviets sign the Molotov-Ribbentrop Non-Aggression Pact.
September 1, 1939	The Nazis invade Poland.
September 3, 1939	Great Britain and France declare war on Germany.
	All movie theaters in London are closed temporarily as a precautionary measure.
September 5, 1939	FDR promises U.S. neutrality in World War II.
September 9, 1939	British movie theaters reopen in the countryside, but not in the cities.

September 15, 1939	The Hays Office bans the production of anti-Nazi films in an effort to maintain strict U.S. neutrality.
September 21, 1939	FDR signs the Neutrality Act of 1939, which allows "Cash-and-Carry" provisions for Germany's enemies.
September 22, 1939	*Espionage Agent* opens in New York.
October 1939	Alvin York becomes superintendent of the Cumberland Homesteads near Crossville, Tennessee.
November 4, 1939	The Johnson Amendment exempts copyrighted material from Cash-and-Carry provisions, insuring Hollywood films' ability to make it to their destinations abroad.
February 7, 1940	*Dr. Ehrlich's Magic Bullet* opens in New York.
March 9, 1940	Jesse L. Lasky and Alvin York meet in Crossville to negotiate a possible movie based on the war hero's life.
March 24, 1940	York signs a contract with Lasky and Warner Bros., allowing the production of a movie version of his life.
April 8, 1940	Germany invades the Scandinavian countries.
May 16, 1940	FDR urges Congress to strengthen America's armed forces, calling for the immediate construction of fifty thousand planes.
May 20, 1940	Jack Warner calls an emergency meeting of all studio department heads regarding the war.
May 28, 1940	Belgium surrenders to the Nazis.
June 1940	Harry Warner calls a meeting of all studio employees, encouraging them to prepare for war and use the studio target range.

June 10, 1940	FDR amends the U.S. stance from neutrality to "nonbelligerency."
	U.S. film companies flee Paris.
June 17, 1940	France surrenders to the Nazis.
July 1940	Hungary joins the Axis powers.
	Harry Warner initiates the Warner Club to evacuate children from European war zones and give them safe haven in the United States.
July 7, 1940	Harry Chandlee and Julien Josephson complete the treatment *The Amazing Story of Sergeant York*.
August 15, 1940	Hitler launches Operation Eagle, beginning his war on England.
August 24, 1940	The *Luftwaffe* begins bombing London.
September 1940	The Nazis prohibit the exhibition of Hollywood films in France and Belgium.
September 3, 1940	England and the United States announce the Destroyers for Bases agreement.
September 4, 1940	The America First Committee is established.
September 16, 1940	The United States institutes its first peacetime draft.
October 1940	Japan joins the Axis, signing the Tripartite Pact.
November 1940	Hollywood studios sign a consent decree with the Justice Department, temporarily suspending an investigation of antitrust violations.
November 2, 1940	FDR is elected to an unprecedented third term as president.
December 1940	FDR outlines his Lend-Lease proposal.
1941	Lindbergh becomes the most prominent spokesman for the anti-interventionist organization America First. Alvin York becomes a

	prominent spokesman for the interventionist group, the Fight for Freedom Committee (FFF).
January 6, 1941	FDR delivers his Four Freedoms speech.
February 24, 1941	Representative Lyle H. Boren (D-Oklahoma) calls for a thorough investigation of the motion picture industry for violating the consent decree.
March 1, 1941	Bulgaria joins the Axis.
March 5, 1941	Japan occupies northern French Indochina.
March 9, 1941	Congress approves Lend-Lease.
April 1941	U.S. forces occupy Greenland.
April 6, 1941	The Nazis launch an invasion of Yugoslavia and Greece.
April 12, 1941	The Nazis seize U.S. film offices in Paris.
May 3, 1941	The American Legion supports convoys in the Atlantic.
May 5, 1941	*Meet John Doe* opens in New York.
May 21, 1941	A German U-boat torpedoes the *Robin Moor*.
June 20, 1941	America First holds a rally at the Hollywood Bowl.
June 22, 1941	Hitler launches Operation Barbarossa and invades the Soviet Union.
June 25, 1941	FDR promises aid to the USSR.
July 1941	American ships convoy goods to Great Britain.
July 2, 1941	*Sergeant York* premieres at the Astor Theatre in New York.
July 3, 1941	Alvin York addresses the Tennessee Society of New York and advocates intervention while lambasting Lindbergh and America First.

	The Japanese occupy southern French Indochina.
July 23, 1941	Harry Warner urges FDR to send troops to Britain.
	Wendell Willkie leads the National Unity campaign at the Hollywood Bowl.
	All Japanese assets in the United States are frozen, ending U.S.-Japanese trade.
August 1, 1941	Senators Gerald Nye (R-North Dakota), Bennett Champ Clark (R-Missouri), and Burton K. Wheeler (R-Montana) call for an investigation of the motion picture industry, accusing Hollywood of warmongering.
August 4, 1941	Members of the Motion Pictures Producers and Distributors Association (MPPDA) meet to discuss how they should defend themselves against the Nye-Clark resolution.
August 14, 1941	FDR and Winston Churchill meet and draft the Atlantic Charter.
August 18, 1941	The period of service in the peacetime draft is extended to eighteen months.
September 2, 1941	Former Republican presidential hopeful Wendell Willkie is named defense counsel of the MPPDA.
September 9, 1941	Senate subcommittee investigation of motion pictures begins.
September 11, 1941	FDR's Shoot on Sight address allows U.S. ships to defend themselves in the Atlantic.
	Lindbergh addresses an America First rally in Des Moines, Iowa, attacking the film industry. His speech is inflammatory because some remarks appear to be anti-Semitic.

September 13, 1941	Alvin York says Lindbergh, Nye, and Clark are un-American and should be thrown in jail.
September 16, 1941	The *Montana,* a U.S. freighter sailing under Panamanian registry, is sunk by Germans between Greenland and Iceland.
September 19, 1941	The *Pink Star,* another American freighter under Panamanian registry, is sunk between Greenland and Iceland.
September 29, 1941	Senator Clark declares that *Sergeant York* is not propaganda.
October 17, 1941	U-boats cripple but do not sink the *Kearney.*
October 31, 1941	U-boats sink the U.S. destroyer *Reuben James.*
November 1941	U.S.-Japanese peace talks between Cordell Hull and Kichisaburo Nomura break down.
December 7, 1941	Japan bombs Pearl Harbor.
December 8, 1941	The United States declares war on Japan.
December 11, 1941	The Axis powers declare war on the United States.
July 4, 1942	*Sergeant York* goes into general release.

Introduction

    During the 1930s many Americans avoided thinking about war erupting in Europe, believing that it was of little significance to their interests. Besides, America was suffering from its own myriad problems: the Great Depression, social displacement, political unrest, and burgeoning crime. Bitter memories of World War I and the failure of the Versailles Treaty prompted people from all walks of life to embrace isolationism and denounce any U.S. involvement abroad.

    Challenging the conventional wisdom of the day, Warner Bros. studio embarked on a crusade to alert Americans about the growing menace of Nazism, arguing that the United States could not turn a blind eye to events in Europe and that the Republic was indeed in danger. Polish-Jewish immigrants Harry and Jack Warner risked both their reputations and their fortunes to inform the American public about the insidious threat Hitler's regime posed throughout the world. From the mid-1930s to the early 1940s before Pearl Harbor, the studio produced a number of antifascist films, including *Black Legion, Confessions of a Nazi Spy, The Adventures of Robin Hood, They Won't Forget, Juarez, Dr. Ehrlich's Magic Bullet, The Life of Emile Zola,* and *Sergeant York.* As a result Warner Bros. drew fire from many directions: the Nazi regime in Germany, Benito Mussolini and his Italian fascists, film critics at home and abroad, the Production Code Administration (PCA), the German-American Bund, anti-Semites, isolationists, U.S. political leaders, the Roosevelt administration, and even other members of the Hollywood film industry.

    The story of Warner Bros.'s dogged pursuit is worthy of closer scrutiny, not only because it is a compelling story, but also because it so vividly reveals a state of mind in the United States before World War II. A few Poverty Row studios, such as Raspin and Jewel, along with independent producer Walter Wanger, attempted to make features about the growing threat of Nazism. Every major magazine, whether interventionist or isolationist, regularly informed its readership about events unfolding in

Germany. But the Warner brothers stood virtually alone among the Hollywood moguls in speaking out. Their studio exhibited the most consistent assault on Hitler's Germany and fascism in general to come out of Hollywood before 1942. In spite of the Warners' diligence, interventionists in Hollywood, the American heartland clung to the belief that the growing crisis in Europe was not its affair.

World War I hero Sgt. Alvin C. York had opposed the draft in 1917 but was denied conscientious objector status. The U.S. Army refused to recognize his denomination, the Church of Christ in Christian Union, as a legitimate Christian sect, and the Tennessean reluctantly went to war—to become America's most famous hero. Upon his return, York resumed his pacifist stance, often speaking out against the past war and condemning any future conflagrations.

As tensions mounted in Europe, independent producer Jesse Lasky, who was then working at 20th Century–Fox, approached York in the fall of 1939 about making a film based on his life. York, when he reluctantly signed a contract in March of 1940, demanded that the film emphasize his struggles since the war, not his battlefield heroics. But in the course of his association with Lasky, the studio, and Harry Warner in particular, he slowly altered his views and the pacifist turned interventionist. Typical of the average citizen, York had to be convinced that the events in Europe mattered to Americans, and his conversion to belligerency mirrored the subtle changes in the mood of the American public. Through a score of films produced during the 1930s and early 1940s, the Warner Bros. studio marshaled its forces to mobilize a nation divided over the intervention issue and, along with Alvin York, made one of the definitive statements about the dangers that Nazism and fascism posed for the world.

The purpose of this study is threefold. First, much attention has been focused upon how Hollywood aided the government once war was declared, but little work has been done on prewar calls for intervention. Because Warner Bros. was the only major studio to promote anti-Nazi activity, it begs further scrutiny. A great deal has been written about Warner Bros., but little of it has been very illuminating. The memoirs of movie people who worked there are often woefully inaccurate and anecdotal. They display the vagaries of selective memory and should be read with skepticism. The memoirs of Jack Warner, Jesse Lasky, Mervyn LeRoy, Hal Wallis, Errol Flynn, Howard Koch, John Huston, and others, though entertaining and filled with great stories, are often self-serving in that they embroider the truth or lie outright.

Luckily, the Warner Bros. Archives in Los Angeles are more complete and well cataloged than those of any other studio. Although a number of scholarly works have been written concerning the studio, many of them fall beyond the scope of this inquiry. A few researchers have made excellent use of these documents, adding to our understanding of the heyday of Hollywood. Among them are Rudy Behlmer's *Inside Warner Bros., 1935–1951*, which selectively reproduces primary documents.[1] My scope is narrower, examining only three films in detail (*Black Legion, Confessions of a Nazi Spy,* and *Sergeant York*) while giving cursory discussion to a handful of others, in order to explore more fully how Warner Bros. challenged Nazism before the U.S. entry into World War II. This study pays closer attention to the American sociopolitical atmosphere of the 1930s, in order to provide more context for the reaction of Warner Bros. to incipient fascism.

Second, I argue that more attention should be given to Harry Warner. The studio's patriarch has been overshadowed by his more flamboyant younger brother, Jack. Because he wrote no memoirs, Harry has been eclipsed by the myths created and espoused by his sibling. Most people have never heard of Harry Warner, and those who have often buy into the fiction that Harry was an overbearing, humorless, sanctimonious prude. The documents housed at the Warner Bros. Archives reveal a different story. A highly moral, devout Jew devoted to his family (something of an anomaly among the Hollywood elite), Harry was the company's conscience and its driving force. He held the purse strings and, through his shrewd investments, built the studio into the dynamo it became. It was Harry, not Jack, who led the studio in its fight against Nazism, though the latter usually receives undue credit. In his memoirs, Jack states that he closed down the studio's German operations in 1936 after the Berlin Olympics.[2] This was two full years after Harry had ceased operations there. According to screenwriter Donald Ogden Stewart, Harry possessed more courage than Jack and was the studio's prime mover in its crusade to alert America to the Nazi menace.[3] As a result, Harry is most unusual among the Hollywood studio chiefs, and his correspondence enriches one's understanding of how the studio operated and what its mission was. Harry emerges as a complex and influential person rather than a one-dimensional cardboard cutout.

Third, this work examines the transformation of Alvin C. York from a reclaimed pacifist to a belligerent as a result of his association with Harry Warner and Jesse Lasky. Unfortunately, York has been the victim of what

James W. Loewen calls "heroification."[4] In the process he has been bled of all that made him human and interesting; he has been ossified, nearly deified, and completely obscured from reality. The image most Americans have of York is based almost entirely upon Gary Cooper's corn pone motion picture persona, which bears little resemblance to the savvy, humorous mountaineer. Likewise, most Americans are blissfully ignorant of York's life beyond World War I. It is almost as if he simply quit living in 1919 and disappeared from history. Yet the film, as originally conceived, was to detail his accomplishments since the war; world events intervened, however, and changed the trajectory and intent of the movie.

Biographer David D. Lee lamented that no archive contained the papers of Sergeant York. He doubted that any real cache of documents existed.[5] His biography therefore depended for the most part upon newspaper accounts, government records, and interviews. In fact, literally thousands of documents exist, many of them housed at the Warner Bros. Archives in Los Angeles. It is unfortunate that David Lee was unable to use the material. Because of the material I uncovered there, some of it highly critical, mean-spirited, and contradictory to the party line, the York family granted me carte blanche access to their father's papers. The bulk of them remain in York's Pall Mall, Tennessee, home. The sergeant's papers are fascinating, offering insight into a complex, flawed, and tenacious human being, not some ignorant, cartoonish hillbilly.[6] His reconversion to pacifism after World War I and the slow move back toward belligerence mirrored the shifts in American public opinion. By tracing the trajectory of his own move toward intervention, through his Warner Bros.–inspired opposition to Charles Lindbergh and America First, one can follow America's gradual progress toward another world war. This investigation aims to breathe new life into people's perceptions of Harry Warner and of York and to spawn further inquiry.

1

Warner Bros. and the Opening Salvos against Nazism, 1934–1939

Jack Warner often boasted about his aversion to Nazism, even though his brother Harry had worked more vigilantly to make the American citizenry aware of the approaching war in Europe while the United States was officially neutral. The Warner brothers had reason for concern regarding the ominous events in Europe in the 1930s. Harry had been born in Poland, during an anti-Semitic pogrom, and Jack was a first-generation Polish American Jew. Their parents, Benjamin and Pearl Warner, both born (in 1857) and raised in Krasnashiltz, Poland, had to hide to study the Torah and the Talmud. After living in fear of being discovered practicing their religion, they emigrated to the United States in 1883 with their children Harry and Anna to escape a pogrom. They traveled through Virginia, North Carolina, and Canada, settling in the Polish quarter of Youngstown, Ohio, where Benjamin opened a cobbler shop and taught his sons the trade. By that time his family had grown to include Jack, who was born in Canada, and sons Sam and Albert ("Abe" or "Major"). Three children, Cecilia, Henry, and Fannie, died in infancy. Benjamin's bustling store evolved into an all-purpose enterprise, selling kosher food, making and repairing shoes, and even fixing battered bicycles.[1]

It was Sam Warner who, in 1903, first took a job connected with the movies, as a projectionist for the Chicago concern Hale's Tours. He returned to Youngstown when the company booked a limited engagement at the Idora Amusement Park and soon had the entire family entranced by the possibilities of the new medium. The brothers—Sam, Harry, Albert, and Jack—worked for the Duquesne Amusement Supply company from 1907 to 1909, when the Edison Trust, which virtually monopolized

the fledgling industry, drove them out of business.[2] Disgruntled and intimidated by Edison's thugs, they were forced to quit temporarily. They
returned to it by importing foreign films that the trust had no control
over, but that offered them little security or room for creative expression.[3]

In 1912 Sam and Jack followed independent producer Carl Laemmele's lead and moved to the West Coast to avoid the trust and further
explore the possibilities of film. Laemmele headed the Independent Motion Picture company (IMP) and later organized Universal Studio. By
1916 Harry believed that the brothers should produce and distribute
their own films rather than rent them. In 1918 they unveiled their first
successful motion picture, *My Four Years in Germany,* based on the autobiography of the U.S. ambassador to Germany, James W. Gerard.[4] The
choice of material is interesting because it exploited many of the same
themes that would define their anti-Nazi films—senseless brutality by a
megalomaniacal dictator, the importance of liberty, and a plea for tolerance. After years of struggling and false starts, Warner Bros. Pictures was
officially founded in 1923 with Harry as president of the corporation;
Sam and Jack became vice presidents in charge of production, and Abe
assumed the role of company treasurer.[5]

Harry and Jack possessed different personalities and work habits. A serious and industrious man who seldom smiled, Harry was the most religious Warner brother.[6] Benjamin Warner's personal devotion to Judaism
manifested itself in his desire for his sons to worship freely and without
fear. He urged Harry to learn Hebrew, and the elder Warner brother duti-
fully came to appreciate the Scriptures. Mastering Hebrew by age seven,
Harry regularly pondered the Talmud and loved to quote proverbs
throughout his life. Intense devotion to Judaism made him the moral
conscience of the studio, and he "could be tirelessly and often tiresomely
messianic about racial and religious prejudice. . . . [; he] realized he could
use the movies to promote tolerance and justice."[7] *Fortune* magazine ran
a feature about the studio in 1937, noting that Harry Warner had "two interests: business and morals."[8] He quit drinking and smoking while a
young man and advocated a healthy lifestyle. Relishing the refuge of family, Harry was devoted to his wife, Rea, and a doting father to his four
children.

> He never succumbed to the temptations that were available to him as pres-
> ident of Warner Bros. He didn't even like to be in the company of stars, and
> was ill at ease around the studio's sensual leading ladies.[9]

Remembering him fondly, his daughters considered him a kind, sentimental man. Betty remarked, "My parents were religious but never forced it on us kids. But I was Jewish. I never felt for a moment that I was not Jewish."[10] Harry also believed that a businessman owed a debt of responsibility to his community and to those who were less fortunate.[11]

The Warner brothers ran the most economical and efficient studio in Hollywood in the 1930s, largely because of Harry's business acumen. Jack remarked, "[W]ithout my brother Harry's wizardry we would not have had the cash [to keep the studio afloat]. He had the toughness of a brothel madam, and the buzzing persistence of a mosquito on a hot night."[12] In spite of his strict manner, Harry won the respect and admiration of most employees. Unlike Jack, he was even-tempered, rarely raising his voice. While Jack strutted around the Burbank studio like a Bantam cock, crowing orders to employees, Harry wielded the true power from his New York office. As a devout Jew, Harry believed the company should make heartwarming films with strong moral statements supporting the sanctity of family.[13] Jack, on the other hand, tried to distance himself from his Jewishness and to assimilate into California's WASP society.[14] An inveterate joker who wished he had been able to pursue a career as a comedian, Jack was a loud, brash, self-conscious man whose attempts at humor compensated for his notorious insecurity. Jack Benny said that "Jack Warner would rather tell a bad joke than make a good movie" and preferred yelling to conversation.[15] Employee Lee Katz remarked, "Jack was not too truthful and, correspondingly, not too trustworthy. If Harry said something, you could depend on it."[16] On the other hand, John Huston considered Jack "anything but pretentious, and seemed to be constantly laughing at himself, but he was certainly a canny, astute individual when it came to his own interests."[17]

Jack relished the glitter and glamour of Hollywood. He admired men like Errol Flynn, who bedded women with abandon. Lacking the charisma of the stars, he used his position as studio chief to seduce a bevy of women, thereby spreading the notoriety of the casting couch.[18] "Jack Warner bragged about his conquests as if they were trophies."[19] His disregard for propriety and his indiscreet infidelities drove a wedge between him and his family, leading to divorce from his devoted Jewish wife, Irma, who was well loved by his extended family. Jack's actions, as he essentially abandoned his first family, strained his relationship with Harry, who believed that family was sacrosanct. He never approved of Jack's embarrassing second marriage to his former mistress, the superstitious and vain starlet Anne Paige.[20] She was a shiksa and pathologically devoted to her astrologer. Anne tended to flirt with other men, annoying Jack to the point of distraction. Harry supposedly told Jack that he was glad their parents were dead and did not have to witness his reckless, insensitive behavior. Neal Gabler, Aljean Harmetz, and Bob Thomas argue that Jack's sexual shenanigans led to a complete breakdown between them, making them grow to absolutely hate each other.[21]

Unlike Harry, Jack hated to read and boasted about his virtual illiteracy. Studio scenarists boiled scripts down to one-page synopses for him; if it was longer than a page, he rarely read it. Harry and Abe Warner, however, regretted the fact that they never completed high school or had the opportunity to go to college; they constantly worked at improving their minds.

Sam Warner introduced the possibility of talking pictures to his brothers, and on June 25, 1925, Harry signed an agreement with Western Electric to jointly develop the process. Naming the new company Vitaphone, they appointed Sam studio liaison.[22] Their first film to exploit the process and the most expensive feature that Warner Bros. had produced up to that time, *Don Juan,* starring John Barrymore, contained only a musical soundtrack and no talking. Enthusiastically received when it opened on August 6, 1926, it encouraged the brothers to gamble on more adventurous sound projects, a decision that forever changed the course of motion picture history.[23] In 1927 they released *The Jazz Singer,* the first feature film to employ spoken dialogue. Though it is often regarded as the first talkie, the majority of the movie is silent. The studio's first all-sound feature, *Lights of New York,* debuted on July 28, 1928. Sound was here to stay, and Warner Bros. earned the grudging respect of the industry at large, which had previously tended to regard the studio as a low-rent operation.[24] Unfortunately and sadly, Sam Warner did not get to enjoy the triumph that he had been so vital in achieving. He died the day before *Don Juan's* premier and was buried on the eve of Yom Kippur. Losing him was a great distress to the family; the brothers never fully recovered from his death. Harry took Sam's daughter Lina into his family and raised her as his own.

For most of their careers, the Warner brothers supported the Republican party; Jack Warner even tried to persuade Calvin Coolidge to run for reelection in 1928.[25] During the 1932 campaign they switched loyalties, fully supporting Franklin D. Roosevelt and California Democratic senator William Gibbs McAdoo. (One possible reason for the change in political affiliation could be that Harry disapproved of Herbert Hoover's sanctioning a Senate investigation of the stock market after the 1929 crash.) The brothers stumped tirelessly for Roosevelt and guaranteed him the votes of most of their employees on both coasts. FDR compensated Jack by naming him Los Angeles chairman of the National Recovery Administration (NRA). Jack later said that FDR offered him a diplomatic post overseas, but Jack Warner, Jr., denied his father's claim.

> I heard him say he wished it were true, but his old presidential pal never came across. My father was jealous of Louis B. Mayer, who, rumor had it, was offered the ambassadorship to Turkey by President Hoover.[26]

Harry's celebration of Roosevelt's victory was interrupted by the death of his only son, Lewis, the heir apparent to the studio dynasty, who died as a result of an infected jaw after dental surgery. During the war that ensued, twenty-two Red Cross ambulances were dedicated by the studio in Lewis's honor.[27]

With new-found capital and a strong market share as a result of the success of sound, Harry began building up the studio and its ancillary holdings. By the end of 1930, Warner Bros. had shed its "Poverty Row" image and owned 51 subsidiary companies, 93 film exchanges, 525 theaters, and 2 studios.[28] The studios were the old First National studio in Burbank, which became the main center of production, and the old Warner Bros. studio on Sunset Boulevard, which after 1934 housed the B-unit under the direction of Bryan Foy.[29] The purchase of Vitagraph in 1925 added extensive foreign offices to the Warner empire. Harry diversified the company's holdings and purchased radio stations, advertising firms, musical recording studios, and a publishing house. Wishing to gain a stronger footing in the European market, he rented the Teddington Studios in London in 1931 and three years later purchased it outright.[30] In 1935 Harry acquired the seven-hundred-acre Calabassas Ranch in the Simi Valley north of Burbank; it became the studio's principal site for location shooting. Harry bought a home in Los Angeles, moved his family from New York to California, and divided his time between the two cities. By 1937 *Fortune* magazine regarded him as the second most important man in the film industry, second only to Nicholas Schenk of Loews/MGM.[31]

In spite of the deepening depression, Warner Bros. continued to grow, suffering only minor setbacks as the economy worsened. The period 1934–35 proved the most intense for the company. Fire destroyed much of the Burbank studio; Benjamin and Pearl Warner both died; Jack married Anne Paige; and Harry, along with representatives from Paramount and RKO, was indicted by a federal grand jury in St. Louis for conspiracy to violate the Sherman Anti-Trust Act. He rejoined the Republican party as a result of the indictment and did not support FDR again until after his exoneration in 1940.

The tenor of Hollywood during the Great Depression revolved in part around entertaining a downtrodden population whose economic woes appeared insurmountable. Eight major studios at the time competed for the few dollars that were available. They were the "Big Five": Metro-Goldwyn-Mayer (MGM), Radio Keith Orpheum (RKO), Paramount, 20th Century–Fox, and Warner Bros., each of which owned its own theater chain; and the "Little Three": Columbia, Universal, and United Artists, which did not. A series of smaller companies, such as Republic, Monogram, Raspin, Jewel, Roach, and Disney, were known as "Poverty Row." The eight majors symbolized Hollywood to the world and churned out mostly escapist fare. Warner Bros., too, made its fair share of schlock, but a number of films defined the studio more concretely after the advent of sound. Although Warner Bros. earned a reputation for frugality bordering on outright cheapness, it also pioneered films with a social conscience. The studio depicted injustices inherent in the bosom of the American dream and railed against class conflict.[32] "[T]he detritus of Depression America . . . were Warners' heroes and Warners' films demonstrated an unusual—unusual for Hollywood—sympathy for these people and their plight."[33]

Warner Bros. willingly tackled topics most studios avoided—the Depression, crime, racism, religious intolerance, prostitution, southern chain gangs, drug abuse, and the mistreatment of World War I veterans—and argued that Americans must be responsible to their fellow man if the ideas that supposedly made America unique were ever to come to fruition.[34]

This production trend was the legacy of former Warner Bros. scenarist and producer, Darryl F. Zanuck. Originally a hack who cranked out stories for the studio's first star, Rin Tin Tin, Zanuck became production chief in 1930 and revamped the studio's output for the transition to sound. He made the studio more efficient by requiring all departments to submit production reports daily; studio memoranda bore the legend "Verbal messages can be misunderstood. Please put it in writing." It was Zanuck who ripped stories from the headlines, fashioning from them hard-edged thrillers, a tradition that remained long after he left Warner Bros. for 20th Century Pictures and was replaced by Hal B. Wallis.[35]

Many Warner Bros. features rooted for the "little guy" who tilted at the windmills of bourgeois convention. The studio was the only one of the majors to regularly depict working-class people and construct plots around ordinary people's workaday lives.[36] Warner Bros. heroes and heroines—Humphrey Bogart, James Cagney, Errol Flynn, Bette Davis, and others—"demonstrate what one can accomplish against all odds. . . . They exalt the small rather than the outsized, the people at the margins rather than those at the center."[37] As a result, "Warner pictures are . . . as close to real life as Hollywood ever gets."[38]

Warner Bros. tackled a variety of controversial topics from gangland slayings in *Little Caesar* (1931) and *Public Enemy* (1931) to homeless youth in *Wild Boys of the Road* (1933). Therefore, it was only natural for the studio to become interested in the brewing troubles in Europe and compose cautionary tales for an embattled population. John Davis observed, "It is generally assumed that no Hollywood studio took the role of enlightening public opinion more seriously than did the Warner Brothers," and noted that they always displayed an interest in American foreign policy.[39] The studio's output from 1918 on exhibited their commitment to foreign affairs. *My Four Years in Germany* was followed by a host of films denouncing German militarism in World War I, including *Beware* (1919), *Lilac Time* (1928), *Noah's Ark* (1929), and *The Dawn Patrol* (1930 and 1938).

In their zeal to caution the world about growing Nazi aggression, Warner Bros. ran afoul of the nascent fascist organizations in America, isolationists in and outside of government, and the industry's own in-house censorship organ, the Production Code Administration (PCA). In his annual report issued May 28, 1938, Will Hays warned the industry to resist propaganda.[40]

Jack Warner boasted that while visiting Berlin in 1928, he "saw the first goose-stepping evidence of the coming Nazi march."[41] Though it is doubtful that he recognized the budding Nazi menace that early, Jack did witness some of the Nazis' shenanigans. Beginning in the early 1930s, after Jack's remarriage, Jack and Anne took yearly vacations to Europe and even bought a villa in Monte Carlo. These sojourns heightened the awareness of Nazi aggression in the normally oblivious Warner brother, and by 1938 he was convinced that war was imminent.[42]

Although Harry Warner cooled toward Roosevelt in the mid-1930s, the studio reflected the ideology of the New Deal more than any other in Hollywood; but the Warner brothers' social conscience predated that of the federal government.[43] The Warner Bros. studio generally touted liberal causes, which in no way ensured the respect of fellow members of the industry.[44] In spite of disagreements with other studios and members of Roosevelt's administration, the Warners remained zealous in their attempts to influence American foreign policy by encouraging citizens to support a strong defense at home, while recognizing Britain's importance to American security. In the meantime, Roosevelt's New Deal created as much animosity as it did reverence, causing critics to label it as either Communistic and fascistic, because of the growing intrusion of the federal government into the everyday lives of ordinary citizens.[45] As the Depression wore on, many people lost faith in FDR's programs, while others believed he wanted to establish a dictatorship in this country.

During much of the Depression, Hollywood dominated cinema throughout the world. American cinema created a hegemonic structure that distinguished the Hollywood product from its European counterpart. Through the magic medium of film, American moviemakers exported their distinctive style and interpretations of American culture.[46] American cinema informed the world about the habits, customs, thoughts, and aspirations of the "average" U.S. citizen.

> [I]t displayed American cars and American homes . . . the American West; and it interpreted in its own peculiar fashion, the American way of life. The motion picture was the main channel . . . for spreading information about, as well as the popular myths of, America.[47]

After World War I, Hollywood lured stars and directors away from studios throughout the world, including such luminaries as Greta Garbo, G. W. Pabst, Fritz Lang, Ernst Lubitsch, and Emil Jannings.[48] Not all émigrés found Hollywood to their liking, however: G. W. Pabst left Warner Bros. and returned to Germany, eventually making his peace with the Reich's propaganda minister, Josef Goebbels.[49] An international business, by the mid-1930s Hollywood counted on receiving 30 to 40 percent of its gross revenues from foreign distribution. As late as 1939, approximately 150 million Europeans watched Hollywood films each week.[50]

Warner Bros. was no different. The studio depended on foreign receipts to keep it competitive and had a significant stake in the German market before Hitler rose to power in January of 1933. Warner Bros. had to compete with movies produced both at home and abroad. One of Germany's most prestigious studios, Universum Film A. G. (UFA), held the exclusive rights to distribute Warner Bros. films, as well as those of Paramount and MGM, in that country. UFA essentially dominated the cinema in Germany throughout the twenties because of the quality of its domestic productions and its distribution of American features.[51]

Harry Warner wanted to eliminate his competition in Germany and was able to negotiate a lucrative deal with Western Electric in 1930 that granted Warner Bros. exclusive rights to distribute sound films in Germany, resulting in a short-term monopoly. Meanwhile, Harry entered into negotiations to purchase UFA, in hopes of diminishing the influence of other American studios in Germany. Since German sound technology seriously lagged behind that of the United States, Harry wanted to take advantage of the situation.[52] Thomas J. Saunders argues, however, that the introduction of sound actually hurt American producers, leading to a general decline in the popularity of Hollywood films precisely because spoken dialogue posed a barrier to understanding that silent films never suffered.[53]

With his director of foreign distribution, Sam Morris, Harry Warner traveled to Berlin in 1932 to close the deal, but the trip dulled his desire to acquire UFA.[54] Though Adolf Hitler had yet to formalize his power, his handiwork was visible throughout the German capital. Anti-Semitic slogans, ubiquitous Brown Shirts and Black Coats, and the general tensions evident among the German populace frightened the normally unflappable Warner. He ordered an abrupt end to the negotiations to buy UFA and returned to America.[55]

Throughout 1933 American journalists focused their attention on Nazi Germany. Journalist Waldo Frank issued a call to arms encouraging Jews everywhere to flaunt their Jewishness and stand up to the Nazis.[56] He recognized the threat the Nazis represented but underestimated the horror to come when he wrote:

> The lesson of Hitler in offering the Jew as the traditional scapegoat for the accumulated rage of a bewildered people is bound to be learned; already we have our little Hitlers, profiteers of stupidity and blindness. The Jewish people are going to suffer. And for those who are individually and innocently hurt, and who know not why, there can be no soothing words.[57]

Adding to the fears of Harry Warner and Waldo Frank were Hitler's own words. The Fuhrer declared that Americans had no right to criticize the

Reich or its racial policies because the United States practiced similar discriminatory acts. Hitler smugly informed James G. McDonald, president of the American Foreign Policy Association, "What we are doing to the Jews is just what you would like to do in the United States. You ought to be grateful to us for showing you the way."[58] But Warner and Frank represented the exception rather than the rule regarding the reactions of American Jewry to the Nazi pogrom. Most American Jews assumed that protesting the situation in Europe would create problems for Jews in the United States. Although anti-Semitism rose dramatically in America during the Depression, pretending that nothing could be done about the situation looked more like cowardice than prudence in Harry's opinion.[59]

New York Herald Tribune reporter Leland Stowe spent September and October 1933 in Nazi Germany and wrote a book about his experiences entitled *Nazi Means War*. A sober-minded observer, Stowe predicted exactly what Hitler's regime would be like and tried to open Americans' eyes to the holocaust to come. After carefully reading *Mein Kampf*, he argued that all one had to do was peruse the book to understand that Hitler wanted war. "[I]t would be folly," he cautioned, "to take Hitlerism at anything less than its own words and deeds."[60]

Witnessing burgeoning Nazi militarization, Stowe was most alarmed by the rigid indoctrination of children in the Hitler Youth, which he said numbered around 1.5 million.[61] He also observed how effectively Hitler and Goebbels used the radio to disseminate the Nazi ideology. German citizens' unquestioning conformity disturbed him, causing Stowe to conclude that the masses could be mobilized for war with no difficulty whatsoever.[62]

The Third Reich proved hostile to foreign journalists who questioned its intentions or criticized its policies. As a means of controlling information, Goebbels purposely leaked false or inaccurate stories to the Associated Press and Reuters. Once the erroneous reports were published, the German Ministry of Information and Propaganda promptly presented the "corrected" material, forcing the foreign press to print retractions that undermined their credibility. Journalists found it difficult to pursue their craft because of censorship, limited access to information, and intimidation.[63]

By contrast, most Hollywood studios believed the Nazis to be merely a temporary economic inconvenience, no substantial threat to either the industry or the world. In 1934 MGM studio chief Louis B. Mayer sought out friend and publishing giant William Randolph Hearst, asking him to talk to Adolf Hitler and persuade him to keep the studio's German film interests alive. Hearst met with Hitler and then assured Mayer that the Fuhrer's "motives were pure"; MGM need not worry about the Nazis.[64] Genuinely impressed by Hitler because of his virulent anti-Communist stance, Hearst launched his own crusade, his primary targets being the New Deal and academia. FDR had moved too far to the left for Hearst's tastes, and he insinuated that Roosevelt intended to Sovietize America.[65] As the world moved steadily toward war, Hearst broadened his targets by denouncing the British and encouraging Anglophobia in his newspapers.[66]

In 1933 Hearst's production company, Cosmopolitan Studios, in conjunction with MGM, produced *Gabriel over the White House*, starring Walter Huston, a film that essentially advocated a fascist dictatorship in America. It depicted the relentless despair the Depression wreaked on the heartland and was one of the first films to accept it as fact.[67] Focusing on the beleaguered Bonus Marchers, it used the World War I veterans' cause as a catalyst. In the film, through sheer force of will after a near-death experience that caused the angel Gabriel to enter his body and resuscitate him, President Judd Hammond (Huston), like Hitler, purges most of his cabinet, declares a state of national emergency, and rules by fiat. After assuming total control of the federal government, President Hammond single-handedly saves the country. Even though the film endorsed fascist tactics, it stopped short of endorsing a permanent fascist dictatorship, because Gabriel departed Hammond's body after order was restored, and Hammond then died. The film toyed with the idea of subverting the Constitution in order to end the Depression and questioned the validity of the American political system, arguing that civil liberties stand in the way of successful governance. William Troy, film critic for *The Nation*, observed that the film's "all too evident purpose is to convert innocent American movie audiences to a policy of fascist dictatorship in this country. The only difficulty is that those audiences may not be so susceptible as Mr. Hearst."[68] In spite of its harsh criticism of democratic republicanism, the film was reasonably well received at the box office.[69] Shortly after that, however, in 1934, Hearst and Mayer had a falling out and Hearst moved his Cosmopolitan operation to Warner Bros. As the world situation worsened, predictably, the relationship between Hearst and the

Warners deteriorated as a result of their political differences. He terminated his business with them in 1939.[70]

Louis B. Mayer's production chief, Irving Thalberg, visited MGM's German operations in 1934 to assess the situation. When he returned, Thalberg informed Hollywood that things were tense in Germany and "a lot of Jews will lose their lives"; however, "Hitler and Hitlerism will pass; the Jews will still be there."[71] Though Thalberg believed that it was unfortunate that German Jews were endangered by the official anti-Semitic stance of the Nazi government, he considered the situation to be temporary. He declared that German Jews should not try to fight the Nazis, nor should Jews in Hollywood interfere in any way. Thalberg's assessment of Nazism, while galling and incredible, typified the attitude commonly held by most Hollywood moguls: Hitler represented something of a problem, but Hollywood Jews could continue doing business with him. Likewise, during the 1930s the American public generally believed that the troubles in Europe had little, if any, bearing on their lives; the Warner brothers were part of a distinct minority with their early plaintive call for vigilance and intervention.[72]

Anti-Semitism was not limited to Nazi Germany: throughout the 1930s Jews suffered persecution in the United States. One result of the swelling tide of anti-Semitism at home and abroad was that Jewish characters were portrayed with less frequency on movie screens. Although some argue that the disappearance of Jewish stock characters had more to do with the conscious efforts of moguls' attempts at assimilation, the fact remains that Jewish filmmakers considered it prudent to avoid obvious Jewish themes and stereotypes in this ever-more-hostile environment. *The Jazz Singer,* for example, had centered on the tensions between a Jewish cantor and his son who had forsaken his heritage in search of fame— something with which many of the Hollywood elite could easily identify. Because such stories had no hope of being exhibited in either Germany or, later, in most European theaters, American studios consciously avoided them.[73] One studio executive stated while defending that practice, "Jews are for killing, not for making movies about."[74] Another reason for the wholesale removal of Jewish characters from the screen was the twisted fact that most studios considered the German market indispensable to their survival. As the Nazis spread their influence across Europe, they placed restrictions upon the importation of American films. Most studios agreed, however reluctantly, to comply. According to Stephen J. Whitfield,

At the very moment in Western history when an entire minority people was being designated for destruction, was being singled out as a fantastically powerful incarnation of evil, Jews were disappearing from the screen, their vulnerability unnoticed, their victimization unrecognized, their pain and grief unassuaged.[75]

In contrast to other studio heads, Jack Warner, at his brother Harry's urging, refused after 1934 to conduct business with Nazi Germany. One of his most outrageous apocryphal stories about the treatment of Jews in Nazi Germany concerned a nonexistent employee, Joe Kauffman, who died at the hands of the Nazis. While visiting producer-director Max Reinhardt in Salzburg, Austria, on vacation in 1936, Warner noted:

> I got the sickening news that Joe Kauffman, our man in Germany had been murdered by Nazi killers in Berlin. Like many another outnumbered Jew, he was trapped in an alley. They hit him with fists and clubs, and kicked the life out of him with their boots, and left him lying there. I immediately closed our offices and exchanges in Germany, for I knew that terror was creeping across the country.[76]

There are several things wrong with this story. Not only did no one by the name of Joe Kauffman work for Warner Bros., in Germany or America, but Kauffman's supposed murder, which the Warners would have willingly publicized, never surfaced in the press, raising doubt about the authenticity of Jack Warner's claim. The supposed event took place in 1936, during the Nazi-sponsored Olympics, two full years after Warner Bros. had ceased doing business in Germany. And even if the accusation had been true, Jack Warner lacked the authority to suspend operations overseas; that authority resided with the company's president, Harry Warner.[77]

Christine Ann Colgan noted that although the Kauffman myth may be important to studio folklore and to the patriotic heritage of the Warner studio, a more sober interpretation of the story is entirely plausible when one examines the dramatic changes that took place in Germany beginning in 1933. When Adolf Hitler assumed power in January, he embarked on a systematic program to rid Germany of its "Jewish problem." One of the first stages began on April 1, 1933, with the boycott of all businesses owned or operated by Jews. By demonizing the Jews, Hitler foisted all the problems associated with Weimar Germany and the worldwide depression squarely on their shoulders. This included foreign Jews doing business in Germany, directly affecting the way the Warner Bros. conducted its business there.[78]

Warner Bros. did have a Jew named Kauffman stationed in Germany in 1933, Phil Kauffman, who fled Nazi Germany and took up residence in London. From that safe distance he oversaw the studio's interests in Nazi Germany, Scandinavia, and Central Europe. He died suddenly of natural causes in December 1933. When writing his memoirs thirty-odd years later, Jack Warner may have remembered some film operative in Germany named Kauffman who died in the 1930s and from that thread fabricated his fantastic story about the loyal employee's brutal slaying at the hands of Hitler's Brown Shirts.[79] The myth fit neatly with the reputation the Warners earned as staunch anti-Nazis and, though untrue, personified the studio's willingness to oppose Nazism.

As the Nazis consolidated their power, they placed more limitations on American films. Goebbels, who loved movies but resented the Jewish dominance of Hollywood, seized control of the entire German film industry, producing simplistic pap that deified Hitler and the Third Reich.[80] To encourage domestic viewing of German films, Goebbels imposed a severe code of censorship on all foreign imports. As early as June 28, 1933, the Nazis issued a decree stipulating restrictions on the distribution of foreign films in German markets. Any films deemed detrimental to Germany would be confiscated and destroyed. German officials could also revoke distribution rights if American studios refused to abide by the decree.[81] Hollywood films had to promote the ideology of the Third Reich both politically and morally, or they would not be shown. Furthermore, American film companies had to agree not only to cut objectionable material from movies slated for exhibition in Germany, but also to distribute the Nazi-approved version throughout Europe.[82] As the Nazis occupied more territory, they extended their control over cinema into each new region. The German public, to Goebbels's chagrin, continued to demand Hollywood features, and critics often compared the clumsy pro-Nazi films produced in the Fatherland unfavorably with the more aesthetically pleasing Hollywood product. Goebbels reacted by imposing a decree banning film criticism on November 27, 1936.[83] When the Germans moved into Austria on March 13, 1938, they restricted the distribution of American films; as a consequence Harry Warner ordered an immediate halt to the Warner Bros. operations there.[84]

A few members of the Jewish community rightly criticized moguls who continued to kowtow to Goebbels's demands and traffic with Nazis.

"Fascism tipped the European applecart," Helen Zigmond lamented, "and Hollywood, instead of crying out against the bunglers, still scrambles for the fruit."[85] Most studios argued that abandoning the Nazi market would bankrupt them, and they continued to acquiesce to German demands. By 1940 only three American studios were allowed to export their product into Germany—MGM, Twentieth Century–Fox, and Paramount, and they lost that "privilege" in September of that year.[86]

With these conditions in mind, representatives of the Reich Federation of Moving Picture Exhibitors informed American film offices operating in Germany that they must fire all German-Jewish representatives then working there, even if they had converted to Christianity. It was racial extraction, therefore, not religion, that motivated their dismissal. For a short time non-German Jews remained unaffected. Offended by these capricious restrictions, Harry Warner announced that his studio would immediately discontinue its business in Germany.[87] Paramount considered following his lead but decided, along with the other six major studios, that it could not exist without the lucrative German market. They opted to remain and to abide by the regulations imposed by the Nazis.[88] Due to prior contractual obligations, Warner Bros. was forced to remain in Germany until July of 1934, when Harry Warner ordered all operations there to cease. Although the studio faced a short-term economic loss by canceling its German operations, it made a courageous stand against anti-Semitism and Nazism at a time when no other film folk were doing so.[89] It should be noted that United Artists also closed their German offices shortly after the Warners pulled out, but they continued to exhibit films in Nazi Germany through other distributors.

An indignant Harry Warner told the world of his determination to expose Hitler and Nazism for what they truly were as early as March 27, 1933, when he announced that Warner Bros. intended to make a movie on the subject.[90] Although no overtly anti-Nazi feature film reached the screen until 1938, the Warners held fast to their convictions, and in so doing they battled not only Nazism but also the Hays Office, the PCA, the federal government, and fellow heads of Hollywood studios. Jack Warner worried that Harry's stance might upset William Randolph Hearst, whose approval of the studio Jack deemed essential to its survival. Harry forged ahead and made good on his promise to expose Hitler. On September 18, 1933, the Warner Bros. animation unit released the *Looney Tunes* cartoon *Bosko's Picture Show.* A parody of the *March of Time* newsreels, it depicted "Pretzel, Germany," ruthlessly governed by a buffoonish, lederhosen-clad

Adolf Hitler. The cartoon marked the first appearance of Hitler in an American film other than newsreel footage.[91]

The PCA presented a troublesome obstacle to producing a feature because the Production Code seal was needed for distribution, even to a studio's own theater chain. PCA chief Joseph Breen wanted to avoid movies dealing with Nazism. He thought they might not be entertaining, on the one hand, and might make matters worse on the other. In 1938 he put the quietus on RKO's proposed film adaptation of Bruce Reynold's tract about Hitler, *The Mad Dog of Europe,* arguing that the film would backfire and perhaps lead to an anti-Semitic pogrom in America.[92]

It is sadly ironic that only Warner Bros. among the eight major studios recognized what Nazism meant for the fate of Judaism. All of the film studios except 20th Century–Fox were headed by Jewish immigrants, and all but Warner Bros. operated under the delusion that they could continue to do business with the Nazis.[93] Between 1933 and 1940, for a number of reasons, Hollywood studios avoided political controversy in their films. Harry Warner, who professed his opposition to the anti-Semitic outrages in Europe, was often the sole exception.[94] The 1937 *Fortune* article about Warner Bros. observed, "Harry is so violently anti-Nazi that his incalculable influence could be all too quickly enlisted in America if the democratic nations should go to war."[95] It would be inappropriate to suggest that the other studios simply ignored the problems in Europe. Many moguls agreed with Joe Breen that drawing attention to the crisis would backfire and incite a domestic pogrom. Rare attempts at making anti-Nazi films emerged at Poverty Row studios such as Jewel and Raspin, but they had no theater chains of their own. Though *Hitler's Reign of Terror* (1934, Jewel) and *Are We Civilized?* (1934, Raspin) were actually filmed, they were never distributed. German ambassador Dr. Hans Luther protested the exhibition of *Are We Civilized?* to Secretary of State Cordell Hull, who prevailed upon Nicholas Schenk of Loews/MGM to cancel its distribution. That dampened the desire of both the majors and the minors to tackle the subject matter.[96]

It looked as if the Warners might not be alone when, in 1935, MGM bought the rights to Sinclair Lewis's antifascist novel *It Can't Happen Here.* Unfortunately, the studio quickly abandoned the property because of fear that it might offend audiences at home or abroad. Lewis, in turn, was offended by MGM's hesitance and accused Louis B. Mayer of caving in to censorship imposed by Will Hays. So he told the *New York Times:*

> Any film version of *It Can't Happen Here* has been categorically forbidden by Will Hays . . . [who] actually says that a film cannot be made showing the horrors of fascism and extolling the advantages of liberal democracy because Hitler and Mussolini might ban other Hollywood films from their countries. . . . Democracy is certainly on the defensive when two European dictators . . . can shut down an American film. . . . I wrote "It Can't Happen Here," but I begin to think it certainly can.[97]

Lewis's comments prompted Nazi and Italian fascist officials to praise the MGM's abandonment of the proposed film, making it appear as if Hollywood and the federal government had bowed to their whims.[98] MGM's timidity regarding *It Can't Happen Here* seems rather curious since the novel had already been dramatized and repeatedly performed by the Federal Theatre Project (FTP). More than twenty-two separate productions of the theatrical version had been staged in eighteen different cities, including two Yiddish adaptations and one Spanish-language version, all of which had proved popular.[99] It should be noted, however, that the FTP appealed to a smaller, more elite audience than the cinema, and at the same time it gave artists greater leeway than filmmakers had, because of the lack of oversight by any organ similar to the PCA. Most plays, such as Lillian Hellman's *The Children's Hour,* that made their way from Broadway to film had to be toned down and approved by the Breen office before they could be shot.

It was not Will Hays who was responsible for the failure to film Lewis's best seller; rather, Mayer killed the project on the recommendation of PCA chief Joseph Breen. Expressing his opinion that the material was dangerous, Breen cautioned against the production. As the head of the PCA, Breen was supposed to make Hollywood's product as "safe" and unobjectionable as possible. A devout Catholic and a former public relations director for the Peabody Coal Company of Illinois, Breen was also a rabid anti-Semite. When he assumed the role of chief censor in 1934, he took the job seriously. He believed movies should avoid sexuality, criticism of American institutions, adultery, and politics. Jewish moguls absolutely irked Breen, and he considered them unregenerate "lice," pariahs who corrupted the morality of American moviegoers.[100]

By the mid-1930s many Americans were increasingly aware of Nazi excesses because of eyewitness accounts by reporters, emigres, and others who had visited Germany.[101] Unfortunately, the caution exhibited by most studios in presenting anti-Nazi activities was endorsed by the State Department. At the 1936 Inter-American Conference on Peace held in

Montevideo, Uruguay, the twenty-one member nations adopted a resolution intended to muzzle the film industry by prohibiting the production
or exhibition of any feature that might offend another nation or romanti-
cize war. Though Will Hays attempted to keep Washington out of the
movies by granting the federal government certain concessions, the State
Department often warned the Hays Office about potentially offensive
films, thereby making an already nervous Hollywood act even more cau-
tiously. *New York Times* film critic Douglas Churchill railed against the
policy:

> Hollywood dare not make an important picture to which Turkey objects,
> nor can American audiences see a major film that is offensive to the Minis-
> ter of Education and Propaganda in Germany. . . . What cannot be shown
> in Rome or Berlin can generally not be shown in Omaha or Detroit.[102]

So Hollywood features, in the main, offended no one by providing safe,
escapist fare that would not threaten their market share or profits
abroad.[103]

In 1936 the Nazis attempted to broaden their influence closer to the
United States, namely in Central and South America. More than 1 million
persons of German extraction lived in Brazil, Argentina, and Chile, and
many of them harbored a degree of animosity toward both the United
States and Hollywood.[104] In spite of Hollywood's attempts at promoting
FDR's Good Neighbor policy through showcasing Latin American talents
like Carmen Miranda, critics argued that Hollywood belittled its Latino
neighbors and perpetuated unflattering stereotypes. In an attempt to
curry favor with the nation's southern neighbors, FDR's administration
created the U.S. Film Service in November of 1938; Hollywood helped in
the campaign.[105]

Evidence of the deterioration of relations between the United States
and countries to the south could be seen at the Pan-American Conference
of 1938 held in Lima, Peru. The Nazis, who sent an official delegation to
strengthen trade relations with Argentina, Brazil, Chile, and Peru, used
the occasion to propagandize their cultural and intellectual ties to Latin
America.[106] Paraguay organized a nationwide Nazi party in 1937, and
Hitler saw Mexico as the solution to many of Nazi Germany's problems.
He said, "Mexico is a country that cries for a capable master. . . . With the
treasure of Mexican soil, Germany could be rich and great! Why do we
not tackle this task?"[107] In addition Peruvian imports from Germany increased 400 percent and exports to Nazi Germany jumped 300 percent,

leading to a degeneration of U.S.-Peruvian relations.[108] In such an atmosphere, Hollywood producers tried to avoid offending their Latin neighbors. By openly condemning Nazism and Hitler's Germany, therefore, Warners faced opposition not only from Nazi Germany but also from other countries that supported or sympathized with Hitler's policies or sought not to antagonize Hitler.[109]

Increased tension in Europe only served to exacerbate the situation. The invasion of Poland in 1939 led to the unanimous acceptance of the "Declaration of Panama," brainchild of Undersecretary of State Sumner Welles. It proposed an incredibly silly plan to create a gargantuan security zone around the Western Hemisphere, forbidding any belligerent acts within it. Impossible to implement because it would require a fleet four times that of the U.S. Navy at its peak during World War II, the plan was derided by critics as the "Pan-American Chastity Belt." Its futility was made manifest in December 1939, when the German pocket battleship *Graf Spee* sank eight British cargo ships in the South Atlantic and then steamed to Montevideo. Although Hitler acquiesced and ordered the ship scuttled, the incident heightened anxiety about the Nazi threat at home.[110]

Sociologist Leo Rosten, who visited Hollywood in 1939, approved the courageous stand Warner Bros. and independent producer Walter Wanger took: "It will be to Hollywood's credit that its anti-Fascist activities predated the swing in American public opinion and diplomacy. It will be to Hollywood's credit that it fought the Silver Shirts, the German-American Bund, and the revived Ku Klux Klan at a time when few realized their ultimate menace."[111] It is significant that only Warner Bros. and Walter Wanger were singled out by Rosten.

Although hostile to Germany, Warner Bros. did not immediately discontinue its business with Mussolini's Italy nor regard the Italian fascists as an imminent threat. Anti-Semitism was not state policy in Italy, and over ten thousand German and Austrian Jews were granted safe haven there. Unfortunately, Mussolini caved in to Hitler's demands in 1938 and enacted a series of anti-Semitic laws, although he did not stringently enforce them. As long as *Il Duce* was in power, no Jews were deported to concentration or death camps. It was not until the Nazi occupation of Italy in 1943 that any were shipped to the camps; by that time only some forty thousand Jews remained in Italy.[112]

Mussolini, like Goebbels, adored the cinema and was determined to create an Italian counterpart to the American goliath. To successfully build a market for Italian film and to foster a distinctive style, he believed American influence had to be curbed.[113] To that end, in 1936 Mussolini followed the Nazi lead and imposed economic sanctions on American film producers, allowing only 25 percent of the income earned in the Italian market to leave the country. The 75 percent that had to remain in Italy could be spent only with the Italian government's approval and was used to finance Mussolini's new studio complex, Cinecitta.[114] Balking at the restrictions, Hollywood filmmakers negotiated a deal that allowed Americans to continue film distribution in Italy; they promised to invest in and produce films in Italy. In April 1937 Italian and German film industries forged a partnership placing further restrictions on Hollywood.[115]

Politicized by the growing tensions in Europe, the Warners, both Harry and Jack, wholeheartedly supported efforts to provide relief to European Jews. The studio supported United Jewish Appeal, raised money for German refugees to resettle in Palestine, and sponsored 108 displaced children during the Spanish Civil War.[116] Employee Harold Rodner helped find jobs for refugees and homes for orphans, while keeping Harry abreast of his progress.[117] In 1939 Warner Bros. produced the short subject *The Nine Million*, which addressed the refugee crisis. It begged American audiences to increase immigration quotas, allowing safe haven for refugees fleeing fascism.[118]

As they grew more politically active, the Warners encouraged the creation of a series of patriotic features and short subjects that celebrated the uniqueness of America. Many of these movies, centering upon the importance of the military and preparedness, were musical comedies. Attempting to combat the suspicion much of the public held toward the military after World War I, films like *Miss Pacific Fleet* (1935, with Joan Blondell), *Sons o' Guns* (1936, with Joe E. Brown), and *The Singing Marine* (1937, with Dick Powell) tried to humanize the military and were often made with the full cooperation of the military. Though light hearted, they emphasized the importance of teamwork while justifying the necessity of the armed forces. Surprisingly, most of these were produced at the studio by Hearst's Cosmopolitan company.[119]

The *Old Glory* series of patriotic shorts, a brainchild of Harry Warner's launched in 1936, lionized positive events in American history and perpetuated the mythology of the American Dream. Directed by some of the studio's top directors and starring its best talent, the twenty-nine-minute "featurettes" were given "A" budgets and shot in the expensive new techni-

color process. The patriotic shorts almost always lost money, but they were praised by the American Legion and the Daughters of the American Revolution, garnered four Academy Awards for Best Short Feature, and earned Harry Warner a special achievement Oscar.[120] By March 1940 they had lost $1.25 million. In spite of that, Harry Warner remained committed because he considered the *Old Glory* series necessary to safeguard America's uncertain future.[121] The studio produced fourteen installments in the series between 1936 and 1940.[122] Generally based on factual material and incorporating the texts of actual speeches made by the participants, the action-packed series dramatically sold patriotism to the American public. As war threatened, Harry Warner stepped up their production, and the featurettes made in 1939–40 preached military preparedness. Warner wanted American citizens to prepare against the Nazi menace while ferreting out fifth columnists at home. True Americans must not let down their guard, for the burden of American security resided in the responsibility of the individual citizen to do his or her part.[123]

Harry Warner's mission extended beyond the patriotic shorts and armed service comedies. It manifested itself in Warner Bros. six-minute cartoon classics, *Looney Tunes* and *Merrie Melodies*. Porky Pig, Daffy Duck, Elmer Fudd, and Bugs Bunny were mustered into service to do their patriotic part. Audiences identified with the cartoon characters—the frustrations of Daffy and Elmer, the perseverance of Porky, and the sheer audacity of Bugs—which made them excellent conduits for Warner's preparedness message. For example, in the 1939 cartoon *Old Glory*, Porky Pig cannot remember the Pledge of Allegiance, falls asleep, and is taken on a whirlwind tour of American history by none other than Uncle Sam.[124] Between 1937 and 1941 the Warners' animation unit at the "Termite Terrace" produced twenty-three cartoons that dealt directly with the war in Europe, the peacetime draft, and preparedness. When America entered World War II, Warner Bros. cartoons did, too. The wartime cartoons number among the most creative and hilarious of the entire repertoire. The animation unit created a cartoon series for the U.S. Army, *Private Snafu*, written by future *Cat in the Hat* author Theodore Geisel. Because the studio was virtually alone in its call for action, it "dominate[d] both in overall production and in social consciousness through 1941."[125] Warner Bros. cartoons often parodied its feature films that dealt with war themes and played off their titles, such as *Meet John Doughboy*, *The Fighting 69th and 1/2*, and *What Price Porky?*

Besides their antifascist pictures, the Warners supported organizations such as the Anti-Nazi League (ANL), which was organized in June of 1936. Typically, Harry and Jack were the only studio heads who supported the league. Other members included Mervyn LeRoy, Melvyn Douglas, Robert Benchley, Howard Koch, Boris Karloff, Dorothy Parker, Alan Campbell, Dudley Nichols, Eddie Cantor, Ernst Lubitsch, Donald Ogden Stewart, and Paul Muni. The league's mission was to inform the public about the danger the Nazi regime represented and to provide a rebuttal to the fiction disseminated by Goebbels's mendacious Ministry of Propaganda. They monitored the activities of fascist movements in this country, fought for the release of political prisoners in Germany, and offered assistance to refugees. ANL members organized boycotts against German and Japanese goods, raised relief money, and published a bimonthly newspaper, *Hollywood Now,* exposing the horrors of Nazi Germany.[126] On August 5, 1937, ANL celebrated its first anniversary. The only film folk of authority to attend other than Harry Warner and his son-in-law Mervyn LeRoy were Charles Russell of Universal and, interestingly, PCA director Joseph Breen.

The league, in cooperation with the American Legion, produced the twice-weekly radio program *America Marches On,* for which Warner Bros. donated free air time on its KFWB affiliate. Screenwriter Donald Ogden Stewart noted, "Harry kept letting us use his radio station, KFWB, once a week. Jack wasn't quite as brave as that." Stewart considered the actions of the ANL to be "Hollywood's finest hour. We were trying to prepare America for an understanding of what was going on in Germany and Italy."[127] Each program was hosted by Dr. John Lechner of the American Legion, who echoed Harry Warner when he signed off every broadcast, saying, "Americans are opposed to Nazism, Fascism, and Communism."[128] The ANL understood the power of radio and intended to use Goebbels's own propaganda techniques against the hypocrisy and terror of Nazism.[129] The show remained on the air until 1938. It was canceled because it was accused of being a Communist front by Representative Martin Dies of Texas and the House Committee on Un-American Activities (HUAC), which investigated domestic subversion before World War II. When HUAC continued after the war, it played a crucial role in the Cold War witch hunts of the late 1940s and early 1950s.

In mid-December of 1937, Harry Warner dined with some eighty-odd employees and prevailed upon them to become more politically aware and socially responsible. He argued that Nazism threatened not only Jews but all races and creeds. He pleaded with them to assist refugees coming to the United States. Alone among movie moguls in encouraging his employees to be politically active, Warner reminded his listeners that his father had come to this country to escape the same kind of pogrom that Hitler had imposed in Germany.[130] Although most studios frowned on such behavior and discouraged politicization among their employees, many screenwriters supported Warner, for they presumed that Harry wanted to mobilize the forces of cinema to combat the Nazi menace, not merely entertain a passive audience with flickering images of beautiful people.[131]

In 1937 the ANL boycotted Vittorio Mussolini's visit to Hollywood. *Il Duce*'s son traveled to Tinsel Town with a twofold purpose: to learn more about the Hollywood mode of production and to finalize a coproduction deal between Cinecitta and Hollywood comedy mogul Hal Roach. The intended joint venture was to be called RAM—Roach and Mussolini—but anti-Nazi elements in the film community pressured Roach to suspend negotiations.[132] The industry press hounded young Mussolini, and journalist Ella Winter applauded the Anti-Nazi League for driving "the boy who had called war 'the most beautiful of all sports' out of town."[133] The notoriety of his actions during the Abyssinian campaign caused ANL members to denounce him as "a friend of Hitler's and an enemy of democracy," and his cold reception in the film capital led to further deterioration of relations between Italy and Hollywood.[134]

Before the establishment of Cinecitta, Hollywood produced approximately 80 percent of all the films shown in Italy. After Vittorio's visit, his father imposed further restrictions, which reduced the American market to about 20 percent. In September of 1938 Warner Bros. announced that it could no longer operate under such conditions and would pull out of Italy altogether.[135] Other studios threatened to do the same but, characteristically, dragged their feet, unwilling to relinquish their dwindling share in the anorexic Italian market.

As the Nazi noose tightened around the neck of the free world, Warner Bros. grew more hostile. On March 31, 1938, Jack Warner sponsored a dinner in honor of Nobel laureate novelist and refugee Thomas Mann, whose books had been among those burned in the famous Nazi bookburning frenzy of May 10, 1933.[136] Since his exile in the United States, Mann had been an outspoken critic of the Third Reich, begging Americans to wake up to the impending doom that Hitler represented. Jack's sponsorship of the Mann dinner reinforced the studio's reputation for social consciousness and "marked the first time a studio head organized and participated at the forefront of an anti-Nazi activity."[137] Warner's openness in supporting Mann and condemning Nazism won the grudging admiration of some in the film business for the studio's commitment to a controversial cause.[138]

In addition to ANL activities, the Warners supported the American Committee for Anti-Nazi Literature and the interventionist group known as the Committee of Fifty-Six.[139] Taking its name from the fact that fifty-six patriots had signed the Declaration of Independence, the group composed a manifesto intended to persuade FDR to sever all ties with Nazi Germany. Like the Declaration of Independence, it proclaimed the intentions of the signees and listed the abuses of the enemy. Copies of the document were circulated, and supporters were asked to sign a petition letting the president know that Americans had had enough Nazi nonsense.[140] The lengthy declaration, reproduced in its entirety in *Hollywood Now,* said in part:

> We accuse the leaders of Nazi Germany . . . of "a design to reduce the world under absolute despotism." They deny the rights of man. They destroy the Freedom of Speech, Freedom of Worship, Freedom of the Press, and the Right to Peaceful Assembly. They wantonly persecute defenseless minorities; they imprison ministers of all religions; they enslave labor; they victimize their own citizenry. . . . They defy International Law; violate treaties, repudiate Covenants of Peace; they bring chaos and disunity into sovereign nations and then seize and dismember them. They send their agents to spy upon us. . . . They exalt Error above Truth, Superstition above Science, Oppression above Justice, and War above Peace.[141]

The manifesto hit hard on several issues. By invoking freedoms deemed sacrosanct by the Constitution, it called upon the president to defend American principles. Although isolationists and Nazi sympathizers labeled the group "Communist," the campaign collected over 5 million signatures.[142]

Harry and Jack Warner also supported the Jewish People's Committee for United Action against Fascism and Anti-Semitism. The organization praised Harry's efforts in battling Nazism. The group petitioned American Jews, asking them to take a stand against "the Nazi government's 'cold, official pogrom' with its sly, tongue-in-the-cheek legality," which sanctioned the persecutions and deaths of innocents.[143] Disgusted by the Nazi treatment of all Jews, adults and children alike, the group argued that young people who survived the persecution would suffer most because they had "the brand of pariah seared upon their sensitive young souls, and . . . from birth [were] condemned to exist as the living dead."[144] The organization urged Jews to take action because "there is no place in American life for the vulgarity and moral leprosy of race-hatred."[145] Because of their willingness to support such anti-Nazi causes, Harry, especially, won the respect and admiration of Jews throughout America. Helen Zigmond of the Jewish Telegraphic Agency considered him an "inspiration to all Jewry."[146]

Vittorio Mussolini was not the only fascist filmmaker to receive an icy reception in Hollywood. In November 1938 director Leni Riefenstahl, "Herr Hitler's emissary-in-skirts," visited the United States to showcase her documentary *Olympiad,* chronicling the Nazi-sponsored 1936 Olympics.[147] Since Riefenstahl was the guest of MGM, the ANL bore down on MGM as a studio that continued to do business with the Third Reich and the woman who deified the Fuhrer in *Triumph of the Will.* They accused MGM of hiring and harboring Nazis at home and abroad. Significantly, the only film executives outside MGM to welcome Riefenstahl were Hal Roach (who obviously had learned nothing from the Mussolini affair) and Walt Disney, who, along with Henry Ford, admired Nazi Germany. Disney also supported the anti-interventionist organization America First and often attended meetings of the American Nazi Party with Gunther Lessing.[148] But Hollywood in the main wanted nothing to do with the woman believed to be Hitler's lover.[149] Riefenstahl disingenuously denied accusations that Nazis abused Jews and feigned disbelief about the treatment she received in Hollywood. She blamed the ANL for Gary Cooper's cancellation of a date with her, while lavishing praise on Walt Disney. She said he was one of the few people who greeted her warmly.[150]

Harry Warner's rabid anti-Nazism took many forms over the years; one of the most controversial involved his policy regarding newsreels. Since the studio had no news unit of its own, it subscribed to the services of other companies that produced them. He issued an order in 1936 stating that Warner theaters would not exhibit newsreels glorifying Adolf Hitler, would excise Nazi material from news shorts the studio rented, and even would ban some newsreels (such as those depicting goose-stepping storm troopers and cheerful Germans heiling Hitler). Employee Harold Rodner had the task of combing through the newsreels for profascist material; he found Paramount and Fox, two companies that continued to distribute their films in Nazi Germany, to be the biggest of-fenders. In 1936 alone, Rodner cataloged fifty-seven newsreels that could be construed as glorifying Nazi Germany.[151]

Furthermore, Warner Bros. forbade the exhibition of footage from the 1936 boxing match in which Joe Louis was defeated by the future Nazi paratrooper Max Schmeling, because Warner considered it an en-dorsement of Aryan racism.[152] German publications, such as *Der Weltkampf*, regarded the defeat of Louis not only as a triumph of Aryanism over an inferior and mongrel race but also as a testament to the superiority of Nazism.[153] Schmeling's victory served as a corrective to the embarrassing fluke of the Berlin Olympics when African Ameri-can sprinter Jesse Owens defeated Hitler's track stars and won three gold medals.

Harry Warner's anti-Nazi stance intensified when he refused to allow any Warner theater to show the March of Time Newsreel *Inside Nazi Ger-many* (1938), which he regarded as sympathetic to Nazism.[154] This earned the studio a great deal of adverse publicity, even from his supporters in the ANL. Harry's own daughter Doris disagreed, saying that *Inside Nazi Germany* was not pro-Nazi. She assured him that she still supported his efforts and encouraged him to assemble "all anti-Nazi, Pro Liberty groups in America to teach in schools Tolerance and principles of Democracy . . . and to show the horrors of Fascism."[155]

Even though politics played a major role in Warner's attitude, there were also economic issues to consider. Since the Warners subscribed to the March of Time, Movietone, Pathe, and other news services, to deny 275 theaters access to the March of Time newsreel cut deeply into the newsmaker's profits. Henry Luce, president of Time, Inc., lashed out at Harry and argued that by not showing *Inside Nazi Germany,* Warner Bros. actually supported the Nazis.[156] Unfortunately for Harry's cause, Fritz Kuhn, the Bundesfuhrer of the German-American Bund, also argued that the newsreel should not be exhibited. Kuhn had allowed newsreel re-porters to shoot footage of himself and the Bund offices but was outraged when his group looked silly rather than menacing. After seeing the film, Kuhn raved, "If Hitler sees this film, I will be ruint [*sic*]."[157]

To add fuel to the fire, anti-Nazi *New York Daily Mirror* gossip colum-nist Walter Winchell jumped into the fray, defending Warner Bros.[158] He reminded readers that the Warners were staunchly anti-Nazi and the only studio with the courage to close their operations in Nazi Germany.

Winchell said, "Harry Warner is the leader of the fight to get the other major companies to discontinue doing business with them [the Nazis]."[159]

Like Harry Warner, Walter Winchell had followed Hitler since the early 1930s, and as the dictator grew bolder, Winchell used his column to try to convince Americans that intervention was necessary. By 1938 he advocated a massive domestic military buildup in preparation for what he believed inevitable—war.[160] Winchell criticized Montana senator Burton K. Wheeler for his isolationism and called Montana Representative Jacob Thorkelson the "mouthpiece of the Nazi movement in Congress."[161] In 1940 he began running a regular feature, "The Winchell Column vs. The Fifth Column," which attacked nativist groups, cryptofascists, and isolationists as Nazi sympathizers.[162] In Winchell, an egocentric pioneer of tabloid journalism, the Warners found a powerful ally whom they could depend upon.

Throughout the 1930s, as the Warner brothers sought to alert the country to the dangers of fascism, there were inconsistencies in their campaign. Though they considered Hitler evil and threatening, they were unafraid of Mussolini. Likewise, they were largely ambivalent concerning the Spanish Civil War and uninterested in Japanese attempts to create the Greater East Asian Co-Prosperity Sphere. Jack Warner saw the Spanish Civil War as a struggle to defeat the forces of Marxism, and his sympathies, if forced to choose, were with Franco, whom he considered the lesser of two evils.[163] The studio discouraged discussion of the Spanish Civil War and suffered embarrassment in 1937 when swashbuckler and rake Errol Flynn visited Spain, setting off rumors that he was fighting with the loyalists. Upon his return a chastened Flynn denied rumors about his possible Communist leanings or fighting in Spain and wrote an article for the *Hollywood Reporter* explaining his behavior.[164] Livid about Flynn's escapade, Jack Warner forced him to make a formal statement renouncing the Spanish Civil War and to claim that he cared not one whit which side won.

Jack did not share the zeal of his brother's righteous rage, and he urged Harry to slow down and not try to fight the Nazis single-handedly. He feared that Harry's zealousness might engender a variety of repercussions, saying, "[T]he less you, I or any Warner talks at this time, the better."[165] It would be better, he argued, to leave such things up to the president because he had more access to the public and because "he isn't a Jew, even though the German agencies say he is."[166] Warning Americans about the possible threat the Nazis posed to them eventually took its toll on Harry Warner. Obsessed and virtually alone among the moguls, Warner empathized with the biblical pronouncement that a prophet is rarely recognized in his own country. By 1938 he had developed ulcers, and as the world crisis worsened so did his health.[167] Even though Jack Warner made an extraordinary effort to shield his brother from bad news, newspaper reports provided Harry with enough bad news to keep his stomach perpetually upset. The fact that Jack tried to keep such unpleasant facts away from Harry challenges the claims made by Neal Gabler, Aljean Harmetz, and Bob Thomas that the brothers hated each other. To try to alleviate both his physical and mental distress, Harry created a cottage industry, writing letters criticizing people whom he believed sympathetic to the Nazi cause or letters of praise to those in his own camp.[168] In late October of 1938, Harry collapsed and was hospitalized for treatment of his ulcers.[169]

In spite of Harry's weakened health, he continued to speak out against Hitler and Nazi aggression, though many members of the industry struggled to hang on to the dwindling German market. Amazingly, on June 20, 1939, MGM hosted ten Nazi reporters touring Los Angeles, rolling out the red carpet for them. Among them was Carl Cranz, the editor of the German-American Bund's newspaper, *Völkischer Beobachter*. As a result Louis B. Mayer's studio incurred the wrath of Harry Warner and other politically active writers and artists. Warner complained to Sam Katz that he had tried to talk sense into Mayer a number of times but considered it a waste of time to discuss anti-Nazi activities with him any more.[170] The lateness of the date of the visit illustrates MGM's continued belief that it could go on doing business with the Nazis and keep German profits rolling in and that the Nazis posed no threat to America.[171]

Despite some ideological disagreements between the Warner brothers, both men staunchly supported the British and believed that American security was inextricably tied to the success or failure of England. Anglophiles, they considered England the inspiration of American democracy and an important arbiter of culture and good taste.[172] As war approached, Warner Bros. was forced to take stock of its English holdings. In August of 1939, Harry Warner sailed to London to plan for the inevitable. He consolidated the distribution of Warner Bros. and First National into one unit, in case the bulk of the staff should be drafted. On September 3, 1939, the day England declared war on Nazi Germany, the

British government officially closed all movie theaters because of their vulnerability in the event of air raids. The closings were temporary, however, and movies were marshaled to action to help boost domestic morale.[173]

When the Battle of Britain began, the brothers launched a campaign to assist the Royal Air Force (RAF). They raised enough money for Great Britain to purchase two Spitfires for the RAF and named the planes *The President Roosevelt* and *Cordell Hull.* Warner's Teddington studio also produced *London Can Take It,* one of the most important documentary/propaganda pictures filmed while the battle raged.[174]

This ten-minute film represented a new approach for the British Ministry of Information (MOI) to alert Americans to the urgency of war. Assuming Americans in the main were pro-British, they believed a depiction of the daily terrors encountered by Briton in the blitz would convince fence-sitters to favor U.S. aid to England.[175] Careful not to repeat the mistakes of World War I, the MOI cultivated relationships with American producers and distributors and with Warner Bros. in particular.[176] *London Can Take It* marked the first British

> propaganda film made exclusively for American distribution [and] signaled the metamorphosis from a policy designed to ensure implicit cooperation, or at least benign neutrality, to one aimed at soliciting greater aid and involvement.[177]

The film followed the directives of the MOI and stressed three themes that all British propaganda films should follow: it explained why Britain was fighting; how the British fought; and the need for sacrifice in order to win the war.[178] *London Can Take It* also involved the new policies drafted by the Foreign Office in February 1940, intended to curry support from abroad. That policy stressed that other countries should be convinced that Britain would win the war and, more importantly, should convince other countries that Britain *should* win the war.[179]

Pieced together in September 1940, the documentary depicted one night during the blitz, illustrating how average London citizens coped with being bombarded. By focusing on common people rather than military or political leaders, the film subtly drove home the point that Americans could suffer a similar fate. Incorporating gritty black-and-white photography, the film was narrated by the well-known American journalist Quentin Reynolds.[180] The matter-of-fact narration informed American viewers that the current war affected the citizenry as much as, if not more than, the military and that normal people had to somehow go on about their daily lives under abnormal conditions.

Warner Bros. willingly distributed the film in the United States. Because most theater chains avoided exhibiting documentary shorts other than newsreels, Warner Bros. ended up being the sole U.S. distributor of the film and, true to form, they were willing to screen the picture at a loss.[181] Luckily, the film earned twenty-five thousand dollars, which Harry and Jack donated to the British Spitfire fund.[182]

As the blitz continued, Americans grew strongly divided over what the U.S. role regarding the European War should be. Two groups typified the polarized sentiments of a concerned nation—the America First Committee, organized in 1940 to combat intervention; and the Fight for Freedom Committee, which championed American aid and, if necessary, intervention.

Though Harry Warner had announced as early as 1933 his intentions to produce a film exposing Hitler, it was 1939 before the studio could do so. Restrictions imposed by the MPPDA, the PCA, and the state department made it difficult to produce anti-Nazi films before 1939, so Warner Bros. had to look elsewhere for cautionary material. The studio exercised two options to warn the country about the growing menace. It turned to historical allegory in the form of biopics and costume dramas as one means of exposure. But because of the rising tide of fascism at home, it also turned again to the headlines.

2

Black Legion
Fascism in the Heartland

Although Harry Warner announced in 1934 his intentions to expose Nazism through a number of hard-hitting features, pressures placed on the film industry from within and without made it impossible to make good on his promise before 1936. Hobbled by the federal government and the PCA's restrictions against violating American neutrality, Warner had to find another way to fulfill his promise to expose Hitler. He opted to examine the burgeoning fascist threat at home and found inspiration when a news story broke in Detroit concerning a Works Progress Administration (WPA) worker who was murdered by clandestine crypto-fascists, the Black Legion. Exposure of a secret organization that terrorized citizens convinced him that Americans were equally vulnerable to the hate-mongering invective of Nazi wannabes. The Warner Bros. film *Black Legion* became the perfect vehicle for exposing the horrors attendant on Nazism by sounding the clarion at home.

Because of American neutrality, the PCA and the State Department discouraged the production of movies dealing with conflicts abroad. On August 31, 1935, the United States passed the Neutrality Act, placing an embargo on the shipment of contraband materials to countries at war and restricting American ships from carrying cargo into war zones. Its first application coincided with the Italian invasion of Ethiopia in October; but as the Spanish Civil War erupted, the Japanese resumed their conquest of China, and Hitler instituted *lebensraum,* the United States further restricted American economic and social involvements abroad. A second Neutrality Act was passed February 29, 1936, broadening the embargo, forbidding investment in belligerent countries except Central and South America. On May 1, 1936, a third Neutrality Act banned travel to belligerent nations. A fourth Neutrality Act, passed after the invasion of Poland in November 1939, lifted the embargo but forbade U.S. merchant ships to enter the war zone.[1]

Harry Warner kept up with Nazi activities throughout Europe and their cheap counterparts in America. He monitored the rhetoric of William Dudley Pelley, the Black Legion, the German-American Bund, Father Charles Coughlin, Henry Ford, and many others by collecting their publications and by his voluminous correspondence with employees in the field.[2] Harry urged his employees to be vigilant and encouraged them to keep him abreast of any news concerning Nazism in the United States. Private detective William J. Burns informed one of Harry's operatives that "there is no doubt but what there is going to be a concerted movement against the Jews in this country" and said that Jews with influence should band together and expose the threat.[3]

Hundreds of right-wing groups sprang up out of the despair caused by the Depression. Bound together by common fears and spurred on by scapegoating leaders, the various groups wrapped themselves in the flag, claiming to be true 100 percent Americans. But their twisted view of America trampled civil liberties underfoot; excluded foreigners, Catholics, and Jews; and called for pogroms at home to purge the American heartland. The enduring economic crisis midwifed an American-born anti-Semitic movement, with Jew baiting becoming a national pastime for some U.S. citizens.[4]

The nativism that came to prominence in the 1930s emerged as a by-product of the nineteenth-century Populist tradition, counting among its ranks midwestern farmers and benighted, downtrodden whites of the New South. It also grew out of the rising tide of postwar fundamentalist and charismatic Christian movements, which promoted an intense pride in America while fostering an anti-alien bias. Cryptofascists often invoked the name of God, claiming that their mission was Christian. As the Depression wore on, disgruntled white Americans, already susceptible to rumor, believed that immigrants were largely responsible for the Depression. American fascist groups exploited that fiction while invoking patriotism and religion for their own, often insidious, purposes.[5] Nativists believed the canard that immigrants—Catholics, Poles, Jews, Central Europeans of various origins—took jobs away from loyal 100 percent Americans.[6] The message also appealed to some veterans of World War I, especially former Bonus Marchers. Feeling powerless, many joined quasi-fascist organizations like Art J. Smith's Khaki Shirts or William Dudley Pelley's Silver Shirt Legion.[7] In one bizarre instance, a Jew named Cohen joined the Khaki Shirts. When he was discovered by a visiting Nazi agent of the North German Lloyd, the unflappable leaders informed him,

"[T]his Jew is a real go-getter who is of great service to the cause and, besides he will be kicked out . . . as soon as we get a big enough membership."[8]

American fascists looked for someone or something to blame, rather than searching for viable solutions to the socioeconomic morass that plagued them. Appropriating a Neo-Jacksonian distrust of monetary institutions, people of prestige, and the role of government, they declared that the Depression was a fiendish plot hatched by Communist-Jewish "banksters" who reveled in the chaos they wrought.[9] Commingling economic straits, current events in Europe, and memories of the recent war, the situation encouraged a host of reactionary movements.[10] Journalists J. B. Matthews and R. E. Shallcross observed presciently in 1934, "No country on Earth has a richer assortment of hatreds which are available for demagogic exploitation for political purposes."[11]

The Jews in Hollywood had ample cause for alarm. As the Depression lingered on, Jews and Hollywood became the target of a number of attacks from several different quarters of the American population. Many Americans knew that Jews played a prominent role in the film industry and believed they controlled an entertainment-information monopoly. MGM's Louis B. Mayer, the Cohn brothers of Columbia, and Carl Laemmele of Universal downplayed their Jewishness, trying to assimilate into American society. The last thing they wanted was for Harry Warner to purposely draw attention to the Jewishness of the film community; they opposed his desire to expose Nazism abroad, much less at home. Some American anti-Semites attacked Hollywood because they believed movies promoted the supposed international Jewish-Communist conspiracy in subtle, even subliminal ways. The Pacific Coast Anti-Communist Federation distributed a particularly vicious handbill that read:

> Christian Vigilantes Arise! Boycott the Movies! Hollywood is the Sodom and Gomorrah where INTERNATIONAL JEWRY controls VICE—DOPE—GAMBLING. Buy Gentile. Employ Gentile. Vote Gentile.[12]

The film industry was frequently targeted as an alien pariah by Father Charles Coughlin, Rev. Gerald B. Winrod, and William Dudley Pelley.

Father Charles Coughlin reached millions of people through his radio broadcasts and his periodical *Social Justice*.[13] The radio priest used the pulpit to fulminate against the Jews, spreading the harmful fiction of an evil international Jewish-Communist conspiracy intent on world

Fig. 1. One of the many examples of anti-Semitism and demonization of movies that were distributed during the 1930s. Courtesy of Warner Bros. Archives.

domination. Members of his Christian Front organization shouted at one rally, "Send the Jews back where they came from in leaky boats."[14] In a notorious November 1938 broadcast, Coughlin defended Hitler's bloody *Kristallnacht* pogrom, which set the Holocaust in motion. Nazis burned and looted over three hundred synagogues and stores, then rounded up about twenty-five thousand Jews who were then shipped to work camps.[15] When war broke out in Europe, Coughlin blamed the Jews for starting it. He argued that America should imitate Nazi Germany and remove all Jews from the Civil Service as a precaution against America's entry into the conflict.[16]

Coughlin and other like-minded demagogues attacked Franklin D. Roosevelt as a Jew-lover or worse. Critics attacked Roosevelt's administration as a government held hostage by the nation's Jewry, causing many to label his New Deal relief programs "The Jew Deal," while other critics said that democracy had been replaced by "Jewmockracy."[17] Some, like Silver Shirt leader William Dudley Pelley and Gerald B. Winrod, argued that FDR was a Sephardic Jew whose real name was Rossocampo-Rosenvelt.[18] Pelley loathed Bernard Baruch, Henry Morgenthau, Felix Frankfurter, and other Jews in the government and frequently attacked them in print.[19]

Kansan Gerald B. Winrod organized a quasi-fascist group called Defenders of the Christian Faith and stirred his followers up through his periodical, *The Defender*. It attacked not only the Jews but also a curious list of offenders and offenses, including Darwinists, alcohol, Friedrich Nietzsche, smoking, nudism, loosely defined modernism, the Illuminati, Marxism, birth control devices, Christian Science, Freudians, dancing, immodest dress, Zionists, divorce, and, of course, the movies.[20]

The Depression encouraged backsliders to smoke, drink alcohol, gamble, and worship sports and movie stars instead of God. Winrod preached Jeremiads against Hollywood and the men who led it. Lewd entertainments like prize fighting, professional baseball, and the "Sin-e-ma," spurred on by profit-seeking Jews, constituted a growing anti-Christian decadence engulfing middle America. Women emulated the whore of Babylon, wearing short skirts and bobbing their hair. Hussies in the heartland painted their faces with makeup like the temple prostitutes of the cult of Diana or, worse, the starlets of Hollywood. Movies popularized filth and brainwashed passive, indefensible audiences who absorbed the screen's flickering images, which would no doubt lead to aberrant, sinful behavior.[21]

Like the Catholic Legion of Decency, Winrod and a host of Christian groups found fault with movies. Clara R. Paige wrote, "[T]he vast majority of movie pictures are anything but 'clean.' If they do not actually portray immorality they suggest it."[22] She argued that movies made vice attractive and ridiculed "right living." Young people watching the screen soon had their passions so worked up after gazing upon a smutty and salacious play, [they would] drive away from a theater only to park their car in some secluded lane where virtue and self respect are forever lost. . . . Hollywood is a hotbed of sex vice.[23]

To protect good Americans from the immoral filth that oozed out of Hollywood, she called for a nationwide boycott of films.

One of the most prevalent and successful of the homegrown fascists who irked Harry Warner was journalist William Dudley Pelley. Stationed in Vladivostok with the YMCA during the U.S. occupation of Siberia in 1917, he met a mysterious "Dr. Toisler," who introduced him to the "virtue" of anti-Semitism.[24] Upon his return to Vermont, Pelley pondered Toisler's pronouncements and began to accept the notion that Jews represented the evil nemesis of Christian democratic capitalism. He advocated a pogrom to expel all Jews from political office.[25]

Pelley actively pursued a journalistic career, contributing regularly to a number of publications, including the *Boston Globe,* the *Saturday Evening Post, Philosopher Magazine, Colliers, Good Housekeeping, Redbook,* and more.[26] Possessing a rather cockeyed vision of the ideal America, he hated Sinclair Lewis's satire of small-town life, *Main Street,* and published his corrective novel, *The Fog,* in 1921. Moving to California in 1928, he began publishing his own magazine, *High Hat,* and submitted scenarios to several film studios. Warner Bros. optioned his novel *Drag,* and earlier, in 1923, Metro Pictures produced a faithful film version of *The Fog,* which fared well at the box office.[27]

Life in Hollywood confirmed many of his preconceived notions. A sexual prude, he considered Hollywood the new Babylon, an immoral enclave peopled with whores and satyrs. Worse still, the "fleshpots" of Hollywood were owned and operated by the scourge of the earth—Jews. The studio heads were, in his estimation, largely illiterate, boorish men with heavy accents who virtually enslaved the artists toiling for them. Considering himself superior, he hated working for them because he believed Jewish moguls incapable of appreciating his talents.[28]

On April 29, 1928, Pelley suffered a near-death experience that added to his growing eccentricity, causing him to believe that he had been reincarnated several times.[29] He enthusiastically reported the experience in an article, "Seven Minutes in Eternity: The Amazing Experience That Made Me Over," in the March 1929 issue of *American Magazine.* This out-of-body experience convinced him that he had received a divine calling, and in 1930 Pelley moved to Asheville, North Carolina, and established the Galahad Press and Galahad College to proselytize his erratic mission. His so-called college offered instruction in a "superior form of Christianity," while providing a rather twisted curriculum that included such topics as "Spiritual Eugenics" and "Cosmic Mathematics."[30]

Pelley argued that Jesus was not Jewish but had actually been birthed and raised by immigrant Gauls. Likewise, he doubted the divinity of Christ and argued that the fear of God was actually a holdover from one's fear of parents. Because of his criticism of the Jews, Pelley claimed that Jesus Christ was a Silver Shirt ahead of his time.[31]

In April 1931 Pelley expanded his operation by establishing the League (or Fraternity) for Liberation, which created its own church, the Church of Christian Democracy, appointing himself as its High Priest.[32] He proclaimed that all the material he published was divinely inspired and that his messages "were received 'clairaudiently' via the Psychic Radio, from Great Souls who have graduated out of this Three-Dimensional world into other areas of Time and Space."[33]

In the meantime, he grew fascinated by Adolf Hitler and the Nazi movement. His fourth novel, *Golden Rubbish,* displayed his curiosity about Nazi ideology and laid the groundwork for the political philosophy at the heart of the Silver Shirt Legion.[34] He said that the rise of Adolf Hitler represented the fulfillment of a prophecy, and on January 31, 1933, the day after Hitler assumed the chancellorship, Pelley, who wanted to be America's Hitler, launched the Silver Shirt Legion in Asheville, North Carolina.[35] He wanted to recruit "Christian American Patriots" to populate his "American Aryan Militia," which would purge the nation of Jewish vermin.[36]

Like other cryptofascists, Pelley appealed directly to World War I veterans who he believed had been hoodwinked into fighting in 1917 by an international Jewish conspiracy. He authored a pamphlet, *Dupes of Judah: The Inside Story of Why the World War Was Fought,* which he sent to members of the American Legion, hoping to persuade them to join his group. Among those who received a copy of his revisionist causes of the World War was hero Sgt. Alvin C. York. Like Pelley, York had grown disillusioned over the U.S. role in the war and often spoke out against intervention and for international peace.[37] Pelley berated the American Legion for failing in its duty to provide veterans with a voice to air their grievances. Because, in his view, the American Legion had disgraced the country, Pelley was forced to create his own organization "that should actually *do* what the American Legion *might* do, or should be doing."[38]

So he organized a crowd of "virile Americans," unlike the flaccid, carping veterans who continued to let their country down.[39]

Pelley charged that Secretary of State Cordell Hull was besieged by Jewish pariahs who clamored for intervention in the current European crisis.[40] "I know for instance," he declared, "that with the 'kikes' swarming into the Federal Administration thicker than midges in flytime . . . [they] give Roosevelt and his White House Sanhedrin precisely the opportunity they wanted to heat us to war fever anew."[41] Pelley raved on:

> According to the Jewish Statistical Bureau there were only 4,228,029 Jews designated as residents of the United States in 1927. . . . But in 1937, *ten years later*, the number had jumped to 12,046,648—an increase of 7,818,619. That's an increase of 15,000 Jews a *week* in this country, every week for ten years! Have they got any right here?[42]

The "Jewish cockroach" had invaded the country, and there was an unending wave of the vermin destined to flood American shores, intent on taking the jobs, food, and dreams away from patriotic Americans and sure to do so unless defensive action was taken immediately. Leo Ribuffo argues that Pelley insisted "that anti-Semitism was twentieth-century Americanism."[43] Though he advocated a policy reminiscent of Hitler's final solution, Pelley did not initially call for the extermination of the Jews. He first advocated two potential exceptions to the "Great Extermination": (1) segregation of all Jews into ghettos he called "Beth Havens" or "Jew Zoos," and (2) sterilization of Jews to prevent the continuation of the race. Otherwise, "the sole available alternative was death."[44]

Pelley hoped to take over the federal government and control economics, politics, the military, the media, and the nation's culture. New government officials would be an army of right-thinking people who possessed what Pelley considered "good Christian values." As in Nazi Germany, the products of all motion picture producers, journalists, radio stations, and clergy would be censored to preserve state values.[45]

As the 1930s wore on, Pelley's attacks on Hollywood grew more strident. Like Winrod, he praised the Catholic Legion of Decency for the pressures it placed on the industry, resulting in the enforcement of the Production Code of 1934 and the creation of the Breen office. PCA chief Joseph Breen, like Pelley, hated Jews; therefore, Pelley applauded the fact that an avowed Christian had been given the commission to censor movies.[46] But as far as Pelley was concerned, Jews still controlled the most effective propaganda medium in America. Jews used film to poison the minds of millions of patriotic citizens every week, celebrating violence, licentiousness, and a general disrespect for authority. To underscore his feelings, Pelley wrote a series of anti-Semitic film reviews that reminded readers that he had once "toiled in the fleshpots" of Hollywood under the "hooked schnozzles" of the "kikes" who "ravished pure Christian women."[47] Enlarging on negative stereotypes, Pelley salaciously informed his readers, "They [Jewish movie moguls] have a concupiscent slogan in screendom: 'Don't hire till you see the whites of their thighs!'"[48] Hollywood Jews practiced white slavery and preyed upon helpless Gentile women. For the sake of white womanhood and Christian society, therefore, it was necessary to usurp Jewish control of Hollywood.

Not surprisingly, Pelley and his Silver Legion attracted the attention of Hollywood and its writers. Screenwriter and novelist Nathanael West wrote a scathing satire of the movement in his 1934 novel *A Cool Million: Or the Dismantling of Lemuel Pitkin,* an American *Candide.* The novel skewered the fascisti, spoofing the various shirt organizations of the 1930s through its depictions of the neo-Luddite National Revolutionary Party, better known as the Leather Shirts. Their uniform consisted of a coonskin cap, a deerskin shirt, blue jeans, moccasins, and a squirrel rifle.[49] By the novel's end Lemuel Pitkin is martyred and fascists are successfully taking over the United States.

Considering all the interest in fascism in America, it is not surprising that Hollywood also turned its attention to the subject. Prior to the Warner Bros. film *Black Legion,* independent producer Walter Wanger released *The President Vanishes* (1934), a feature film about a paramilitary group, the Grey Shirts, modeled after Pelley's Silver Shirt Legion. Lincoln Lee, the Grey Shirts' leader, conjoined images of the American Civil War and two of that conflict's most highly regarded heroes. Lee calls for reunification of America against a common enemy that knew no geographical boundaries and included bankers, lawyers, publishers, and lobbyists, people who wielded power without being elected to office. He offers absolution for the schism that continued to cause distrust between the North and the South if all would turn their anger against the aforementioned enemies and unite to destroy them. A new galvanized America would rise from the ashes. Lee's Legionnaires shout jingoistic platitudes like "Save America's Honor" and imitate the Nazi salute while ejaculating "Union!"[50] The Grey Shirts are portrayed in a quasi-complimentary light, and *The President Vanishes,* unlike *Black Legion,* could be mistaken as a profascist film.

Not surprisingly, Warner Bros. became interested in the American fascists and the shirt organizations as potential film subjects, but initially the Warners feared that making a film about homegrown Nazism might backfire. Public reaction to *The President Vanishes* and *Gabriel over the White House* convinced them that the uninitiated moviegoer might mistakenly believe that such films were intended to glorify the hate groups they portrayed.[51] That changed when news about the terrorist activities of the Black Legion filled the national media.

The Black Legion represented a more virulent strain of nativism in the American heartland. The product of four midwestern states (Michigan, Ohio, Indiana, and Illinois), it sprouted out of the so-called "new" Ku Klux Klan (KKK) of the 1920s.[52] Led by Dr. William Jacob Shepard, former Grand Cyclops of the Bellaire, Ohio, Klan, it was a more fearsome vigilante organization than the new Klan.[53] Shepard tried to distance himself from the KKK; his group replaced the ghostly white robes of the KKK with more ominous black ones bedecked with embroidered skulls and crossbones and called itself the United Brotherhood of America, or the Black Legion.[54] Forsaking the pointed hoods of the KKK, Legionnaires wore black tricorn pirate hats. Self-appointed guardians of white Christian values, the Black Legion policed the sexual and social habits of fellow citizens. The role of morality police was ironic to a fault, however, because Dr. Shepard gained infamy for his willingness to perform illegal abortions.[55]

Persons who joined the Black Legion were subjected to a fearsome initiation ceremony meant to mortify would-be night riders. In the dark of night, initiates were blindfolded and escorted into the wilderness, where hooded, black-robed Legionnaires tested their loyalty. Potential Legionnaires were asked if they were native-born, white, Protestant, Gentile Americans and whether they would break the law to support the Black Legion. Initiates swore an oath of allegiance to the Legion upon pain of death. They agreed to perjure themselves in a court of law on behalf of the Legion; vowed to rid Christian America of African Americans, immigrants, Jews, and Catholics; promised to arm themselves as quickly as possible; and supported the speedy, unforgiving justice of the lynch law.[56] They recited the oath on their knees while full-fledged members held loaded guns to their heads; a chaplain solemnized their initiation.[57] To further dissuade new recruits from betraying the Legion, initiates were promised agonizing ritualistic torture before their summary execution.

After completing the entrance rites, initiates learned the secret hand-shakes, passwords, and other clandestine rigamarole that separated Legionnaires from ordinary men. This tactic often had deleterious effects: since many of the recruits' loyalty was based purely upon fear, that fear had to be constantly maintained by threats.[58] The Warner Bros. version, given the strictures placed upon the industry by the PCA, did not do justice to the real horror of Shepard's ceremony.

The Black Legion began to expand in 1931, when Virgil H. "Bert" Effinger of Lima, Ohio, centralized the power of the clandestine terrorist group.[59] Described as "a ponderous, big-nosed salesman with a fog-born [*sic*] voice who quotes extensively from the Bible, [and] addresses everyone as 'Brother,'" Effinger visualized a national syndicate of underground militia cells bent on the political overthrow of the current establishment, saving America from "Communism, fascism and any other ism."[60] A humorless, equal-opportunity hate-monger and self-professed visionary, Effinger nudged Shepard out of the picture and divided the United States into thirteen districts under the direct command of appointed "major generals."[61]

Effinger's Black Legion would save Depression America from all the ills that beset it. Legionnaires would institute a pogrom punishing the Jews and the Communists for creating the economic chaos, cast out Catholics who perverted "true" Christianity, persecute African Americans, and purge liberals and radicals from the public sphere.[62] Like Hitler and Stalin, Effinger rewrote history to fit his needs, claiming that the Legion was as old as America itself. It was Black Legionnaires, he declared, who had staged the Boston Tea Party and had filled the ranks of the famous Minute Men of the American Revolution.[63]

Unlike Pelley, who wanted to take over the government through legitimate means, Effinger advocated a coup d'etat with Legionnaires violently seizing Washington.[64] Having made one foray into legitimate politics when he ran for sheriff of Allen County, Ohio, Effinger was convinced that the political process was irredeemably corrupt. He wholeheartedly agreed with Shepard, who had once said,

We regard as enemies to ourselves and our country all aliens, Negroes, Jews, and cults and creeds believing in racial equality or owing allegiance to any foreign potentate. These we will fight without fear or favor as long as one foe of the American liberty is left alive.[65]

Americans needed a dictator willing to rule with an iron fist, and Effinger's Black Legion would institute a new efficient, authoritarian, brutal, revolutionary state under his direction.

The very clandestine nature of the organization, however, worked against its ability to effectively recruit new members, and the much desired revolution was postponed. This led to internal dissension, personality conflicts, and disorganization in the ranks.[66] Because loyalty was always suspect, most of the activity of local chapters involved spying on their own members and meting out "justice" to offenders from within. For example, Major Dayton Dean was demoted to the rank of private and beaten after Legionnaires discovered that he had raped his twelve-year-old stepdaughter in a drunken stupor. Roy Pitcock of Wyandotte, Michigan, married a Catholic woman who had lived with a policeman out of wedlock. She had two strikes against her, according to the Black Legion morality police, who ordered him to divorce her. When he refused, frustrated Legionnaires flogged, then lynched their brother-in-arms.[67]

Between 1932 and 1935, Effinger's Black Legion grew in strength and number. The people he liked most to recruit were paramilitary types—policemen, security guards, National Guardsmen, and World War I veterans—people already accustomed to rigid discipline and not put off by violence.[68] Although the Black Legion cultivated men of violence who reveled in meting out pain and bloodshed, it also attracted a number of would-be politicians anxious for power. In some cases the police protected the Black Legion and their raids.[69] Journalist George Morris, who covered the Legion, observed that

> The Nazis, like the Black Legion, attracted with their appeal an element of morons and various types of degenerates. Those who could not think for themselves but allowed themselves to be impressed as blind dupes, the cowardly, sadist types, were candidates for the Nazis as for the Legion.[70]

On December 22, 1933, Black Legionnaires shot and killed UAW secretary and labor organizer George Marchuk. On March 15, 1934, a Black Legion death squad murdered AFL organizer John Bielack; his violent death was meant to be a warning to other labor leaders.[71] On another occasion, Maj. Dayton Dean took the life of African American World War I veteran Silas Coleman because he wanted to know "what it felt like to kill a nigger."[72] By 1934 the Black Legion's violence became more political, leading to a series of bombings and burnings of Communist or "radical" bookstores and recreation centers.[73]

Obsessed with taking over the country, Effinger continued plotting revolution. Like terrorist organizations of the 1990s, the Legion explored the possibilities of biological warfare and considered unleashing typhus on Detroit's Jews.[74] Their scheme was simply to inject typhus into the milk and cheese delivered to the city's Jewish customers. They also toyed with other ideas. They considered creating poison "death needles" that could be shoved into various enemies in crowd situations, cyanide canisters that could be activated and forced through keyholes, cigarette bombs, stink bombs, and other simple explosives.[75]

As the Black Legion grew more fanatical, it also grew more careless, and it was Maj. Dayton Dean's personal appetite for violence, rather than the political aspirations of Bert Effinger, that resulted in the group's undoing. Charles Poole, a Catholic and a former auto worker employed by the WPA, was married to a Protestant woman who was pregnant with their second child.[76] She was related to one of the Black Legion's thugs, unfortunately for Poole; the Black Legion member despised the fact that his cousin had married a Catholic. He lied to Dean, saying that the evil Papist regularly beat his cousin. Stirred by such an accusation, Dean and sixteen other Legionnaires kidnaped Poole on May 12, 1936, drove him west of Dearborn, and shot him five times with a .45 automatic. Legionnaire Urban Lee shot Poole three more times and left the corpse in a ditch.[77] Poole's murder backfired on the Black Legion. Because he was *not* a radical, a Jew, an African American, or a labor organizer, the police doggedly pursued clues surrounding the murder and followed the bloody trail to Dayton Dean.[78] Bert Effinger eluded capture, however, and tried to revive the organization in 1938, under the new name of the Patriotic Legion of America; this legion admitted Catholics.[79]

Dean turned stool pigeon and coward when confronted by the incriminating evidence and implicated all his coconspirators including Ray Ernest, a Jackson State Prison guard.[80] Dean's evidence led the Michigan State Police to reopen a number of murder and suicide cases that had been ruled insoluble, and the ensuing trial revealed that the Black Legion had been involved in fifty-seven murders or attempted murders over a six-year period.[81] It was Dean's testimony that drew the attention of Warner Bros., causing the studio to bring the sordid story to the screen.[82]

The studio initially encountered a number of problems when planning the film. Producer Hal Wallis wanted the movie to star Edward G. Robinson, but that choice was vetoed because some personnel feared that he did not look American enough. Robinson, star of such films as

Little Caesar and *Five Star Final,* had earned a reputation of playing for-eign types; and given the nature of the film, a more pointedly Anglo-Saxon-looking actor was needed for the lead. The studio finally settled on Hollywood newcomer Humphrey Bogart.[83]

The PCA presented the Warners with another problem, because it demanded that the screenplay tone down the anti-Semitic bias of the Black Legion. This forced the scenarists, Abem Finkel, Robert Lord, and William Wister Haines, to focus on Poole's murder as the film's central conflict. In spite of the PCA's proscription, the completed film made the xenophobia and racism of the Black Legion obvious. Finkel, who went on to write *Sergeant York* with Harry Chandlee, Howard Koch, and John Huston, emphasized the threat of fascism to America.

Finkel also collaborated with Robert Rossen on another 1936 domestic antifascist film, *Marked Woman.* In that film Bette Davis portrayed a prostitute forced to work for a mafiosi patterned after Lucky Luciano's. The film argued that organized crime, like fascism, represented a form of domestic slavery enforced through brutal totalitarianism. Fascists and Nazis, therefore, were criminals. Several critics noted that Nazis came to be depicted in film in much the same way that criminals were. Though he received no credit, Finkel later collaborated with John Huston on the in-terventionist film *Juarez,* which criticized totalitarianism and celebrated democracy.[84]

During the filming, producer Hal Wallis fretted over the safety of the individuals involved in the film, fearing retaliation from the Black Le-gion's cadres or other hate groups. Though director Archie Mayo told *Va-riety* that he was not afraid of the Black Legion or their threats, Wallis beefed up security at the studio.[85] The legal department expressed its concern as well and anticipated a raft of lawsuits from Legion members not incarcerated. The studio was sued, but not by the Black Legion. The Ku Klux Klan charged in Atlanta, August 17, 1937, that the studio had copied their uniform without permission. They sued for $113,500 for patent infringement for illegally using the KKK logo.[86] The case was thrown out the next year, and the judge ordered the Klan to pay the court costs.[87]

The screenplay underwent considerable revision as filmmakers at-tempted to bring the story to the screen while earning the PCA seal of ap-proval. Robert Lord's original treatment, the one suppressed by the Breen office, forcefully confronted anti-Semitic/anti-Catholic sentiment and concomitant red-baiting. It traced the history of the Black Legion from its inception to its unraveling after Poole's murder. Lord's treatment depicted a fairly direct parallel between the Black Legion and Nazism, cautioning Americans, as Sinclair Lewis had, that it *can* happen here.[88] The PCA informed Warner Bros. that if they went ahead with Lord's original screenplay, the film would be denied the PCA seal of approval. Joseph Breen wanted filmmakers to avoid topics with any taint of controversy. Though *Black Legion* dealt with real events people could read about in a number of periodicals, he cautioned strongly against the production of such films. The screenplay for *Black Legion* was deemed "unacceptable" because the subject matter raised the "provocative and inflammatory subjects of racial and religious prejudice."[89] *Black Legion's* toned-down final screenplay subtly demonstrated the seductive nature of fascism, emphasizing the fact that average, normal Americans, not just the lunatic fringe, could fall prey to its rhetoric. No one, the film argued, was safe from the ever-spreading tentacles of fascism.

Humphrey Bogart portrayed an affable, "all-American" factory worker, Frank Taylor, who is well liked by his coworkers and appears to be next in line for promotion to shop foreman. When the audience first meets Taylor, he is a devoted husband to his wife, Ruth, a hard worker, and a father who dotes on his son, Buddy. His initiation into the Black Legion, however, causes him to undergo a dramatic, Dr. Jeckyll–to–Mr. Hyde transformation. Unlike Robert Louis Stevenson's tormented protagonist, who uses science to play God, turning into a monster in the process, Frank Taylor's metamorphosis could clearly happen to anyone.

Neither Frank Taylor nor his neighbor Ed Grogan is depicted as a perfect male specimen. Ambitious, Taylor wants to be shop foreman and lets his inflated estimations of his own abilities cloud his judgment. Grogan initially fails to recognize that Betty, the boarder living with his family, is the ideal woman for him; he often carouses with a fallen woman, Mrs. Pearl Danvers. When confronted with choices that are key to moving the plot along, however, Grogan makes the right choice, abandoning the floozy to propose to Betty. Frank Taylor, however, chooses badly, sacrificing family and friends for a fraternal brotherhood of evil.

Too smug in his conviction that he will be awarded the promotion, Taylor is passed over when it is granted. The man who earns the position, Joe Dumbrowski, is a dedicated, hard-working, Polish American immigrant who attends night school, hoping to earn his share of the American

Dream. Because he takes the action as a personal insult rather than a reward to the more qualified party, Taylor's mood darkens, and so does the tone of the movie.

When Taylor goes home that evening to break the news to his wife, she shows compassion and understanding. Ed Grogan also tries to console Taylor, explaining that Dumbrowski invented a self-oiling mechanism that saved the factory thousands of dollars. Brooding, Taylor demands to be left alone and turns on the radio. During this moment of self-pity he surfs through the channels, stopping to listen to a speaker fulminate against foreigners and anti-American forces. The cadence and pitch of the speaker's voice sound eerily similar to Father Coughlin, and the invective is reminiscent of the radio priest's own diatribes.

When he returns to work, Taylor pouts, making no attempt to perform his job well. After he breaks three bits on his drill press, Dumbrowski offers him assistance and kindly advice, but Taylor mistakes his coworker's concern for harassment. Embittered, Taylor blames the "dirty foreigner" for his own troubles and gradually becomes a hateful, vengeful man. Overhearing his complaints, fellow worker Cliff Summers encourages Taylor to attend a Black Legion meeting.

Somewhat reluctantly, Taylor goes to the meeting, which is held in secrecy at a local store. In order to gain entry, Taylor must give the clerk a password. He descends a dark flight of stairs into a dimly lit basement filled with gaunt men reminiscent of Dorothea Lange's stark portraits of Depression Americans. As they listen to the impassioned hate-mongering of the Legion recruiter, the desperate men appear eager to jump at any quick solution to their problems. They listen intently as the demagogue denounces swarms of foreigners who have descended on America like a plague of locusts, having no regard for the American way of life. With an evangelical zeal, he urges the listeners to take their country back by force. Foreigners have refused to assimilate; they "have clung tenaciously to their alien doctrines, foreign faiths, and un-American morals."[90] Through his ranting, Warner Bros. was able to inform audiences, without using the word *Jew* or *Catholic,* that the Black Legion hated foreigners and non-Protestants, while satisfying PCA guidelines at the same time. The tone of the harangue would have reminded viewers in 1936 of the 100 percent American campaigns that raged during World War I, the Red Scare of the early 1920s, and the hysteria the two engendered. The film asked audiences if they were willing to live in such a state of fear and paralysis again.[91]

As the recruiter continues, he argues that foreigners are "poisonous vipers" who fatten themselves on "the bleeding bosom of our country."[92] Frank Taylor smiles; the words are music to his ears. Looking for easy answers to his personal problems, Taylor pays rapt attention to the hate-filled message. The intensity increases: the recruiter argues that good Americans have been duped and cheated by foreigners, and in words echoing the invective of Coughlin, Winrod, and Pelley, he says,

> Now, enriched with jobs they have chiseled away from Americans and drunk with the omnipotent power of their stolen prosperity, they are openly plotting to seize control of our government . . . and subjugate the American people to their own dastardly designs.[93]

There is a solution to this problem, however, and the Black Legion will gladly share it with any and all who care to join. Taylor, who lost his promotion because of a man he considers a dirty, chiseling, self-important "Polack," is ready to enlist. Fully caught up in the spirit of the meeting, Taylor agrees with the recruiter when he continues, saying:

> [I]f we unite with the millions of other red-blooded Americans under the banner of the Black Legion we are invincible. With fire and sword we'll purge the land of these traitorous aliens and trample every deadly scheme, till once more our beloved stars and stripes will wave over a united nation, a free, white, one hundred percent America.[94]

Frank Taylor is elated, filled with new-found confidence, and aware that he is not alone. He cannot wait to join the Black Legion, and he sacrifices reason for emotion.

The next sequence involves Taylor's initiation, and the screenplay incorporates the actual oath of allegiance used by the Black Legion. On his knees before a coterie of black-robed thugs with a pistol pointed at his head, Taylor recites the oath in the flickering light of a bonfire. Legionnaires promise to torture and kill him should he betray them. After completing the initiation, he is told that he must buy a uniform and a gun as soon as possible.

A large silhouette of a man holding a gun fills the frame in the next sequence. No longer small in his own mind, Frank Taylor admires his enormous shadow on the wall and then examines himself in the mirror. He is no longer a put-upon worker overlooked for promotion; he is part of a secret organization intent on the purification of America. He believes that he is a bigger man now that he owns a weapon. His reverie is interrupted by Buddy, who is fascinated by the pistol, and Ruth, who is alarmed that Taylor squandered the family savings to purchase it.

Now a member of the clandestine group, Taylor has to prove his willingness to perpetrate violence. He also has to fabricate stories to justify the time spent away from his family; he tells Ruth that he has joined a lodge. Under the cover of darkness, Taylor skulks out of his house, dons his black robes, and joins his comrades. In his first terrorist act, he participates in the arson of the Dumbrowksi farm, an act of vengeance upon the man who earned the promotion to shop foreman. After destroying the farm, Legionnaires truss up Dumbrowski and his father and put them both on a cattle car headed out of town. Proud of their accomplishments, Taylor and his new friends proceed to a bar to get outrageously drunk, celebrating their victory over two defenseless men. He returns home drunk at four in the morning, finding his wife still dressed, waiting up for him. Annoyed by her concern, he yells and abuses her.

Finally awarded the promotion he believes he deserved, Taylor goes on a spending spree. He buys gifts for the whole family—a new car, a vacuum cleaner, and a Louisville Slugger. All is not bliss, however, because Taylor spends more and more time pursuing Legion activities at work rather than doing his job. His devotion to duty dwindles as he becomes more involved in terrorism. Montage sequences, interspersed between scenes at work and at home, catalog the destruction caused by the Black Legion—lootings, bombings, arson, and floggings. Taylor attempts to recruit Ed Grogan, who declines, saying that secret organizations are "for half-wits."[95]

Recruiting Legionnaires on the job ultimately results in his being fired, making the point that the Legion, like quicksand, drags people down and destroys them. Ed Grogan's father, Mike, replaces Taylor but takes no comfort in his new position. Angry and at loose ends, Taylor complains to the Legion. Calling upon Mike Grogan late at night, Taylor is clearly heard saying, "telegram." Mike Grogan then opens his door to be accosted by a host of Legionnaires who take him out into the countryside and flog him.

Unemployed and embittered, Taylor finds his life further deteriorating. He abuses his wife, neglects his son, begins drinking heavily, and is seduced by Pearl Danvers. Ruth and Buddy leave him. His self-neglect is depicted through slovenly dress, a staggering walk, and an unshaven face.

In a drunken stupor, Taylor tells Grogan about his involvement in the Black Legion. Threatening to go to the police with the information, Grogan tries to get Taylor to see the error of his ways. Taylor argues that there is no way out of the Legion and tells Grogan, "I swore a solemn oath." To which Grogan counters, "Yeah, you swore a sacred oath to Ruth, too."[96] Afraid Grogan will turn him in, Taylor calls Cliff Summers for help and they decide to frame Grogan, like real-life Charles Poole, as a wife-beater. Taylor assists in Grogan's kidnaping, and in the ensuing events he shoots Grogan in the back four times, killing his friend and neighbor for the sake of the Black Legion.

The film's final sequences portray the trial and conviction of the Legionnaires. Lawyers employed by the Legion urge Taylor to testify that he killed Grogan in self-defense in a fight over Pearl Danvers. Willing to perjure herself for money, Pearl's testimony presents a tawdry love triangle gone sour. Initially eager to go along with the ruse, Taylor comes clean when he takes the witness stand. Struck by the silent courage of his estranged wife, who sits in the courtroom, he confesses to those assembled all about the Black Legion and fingers his coconspirators.

As the judge passes sentence on the convicted, he launches into a soliloquy dogmatically driving home the point of the film. He condemns racism and religious bigotry as un-American and diametrically opposed to the Constitutional guarantees associated with this country. The Black Legion, no matter how well-intentioned they believed themselves and their actions to be, pervert patriotism and make a mockery of the American Dream; for, as the judge proclaims:

> Your idea of patriotism and Americanism is hideous to all decent citizens. . . . We cannot permit racial or religious hatreds to be stirred up, so that innocent citizens become the victims of accusations brought in secrecy. We cannot permit unknown tribunals to pass judgments nor punishments to be inflicted by a band of hooded terrorists. Unless all of these illegal and extra-legal forces are ruthlessly wiped out, this nation may as well abandon its Constitution, forget its Bill of Rights, tear down its courts of justice, and revert to the barbarism of government by primitive violence.[97]

As hard hitting as the judge's speech may have been, the rough cut of the film had a tougher edge. The preview version shown to test audiences was cynical and depicted the Black Legion not only infiltrating the courtroom but even sitting on the jury. Audiences found such a miscarriage of justice too uncomfortable, and the final version was watered down. The film that went into general release portrayed upstanding citizens in the jury box instead, willing to mete out justice to the "Michigan anti-social, secret society."[98]

Black Legion graphically portrayed what happened to so-called good Americans who swallowed the vitriolic pap of the Black Legion. Frank Taylor joined the Legion initially reveling in the sense of power it gave him, but gradually the Legion took over his life. His home life deteriorated, his job performance grew sloppy and slipshod, and he lost the respect of his former friends and neighbors. Participation in such organizations offered only brief respite from life's real problems, dehumanized its followers, and erased any sense of conscience.[99]

The emotional impact of the film was enhanced by the lighting, the music, and the camera angles. Family and work scenes were highly lit, but as Taylor's descent into the nether world of the Black Legion deepens, so do the shadings of the film. All Legion activities occur at night. All scenes depicting the destruction of Taylor's life likewise occur at night. It is evening when he slaps Ruth. She leaves him on a bus in darkness. It is in the dark of night that he has his assignation with Pearl Danvers. In darkness *and* in his black-hooded robe, he kills Ed Grogan. It is in the full light of day, exposed on the witness stand, where he unburdens himself. His coconspirators look less threatening without their hoods or the cover of darkness. There is no good reward for Frank Taylor. He will go to jail for the rest of his life and live it in the company of his newfound friends.

Many shots are photographed from a low angle, making the black-robed thugs more menacing. Close-ups during violent sequences portray the horror of the victims. Process shots and slow dissolves add to the film's tension by juxtaposing images of Legion members and the objects of their rage. The initial music is upbeat and reflects the popular music of the day. There is a contrapuntal distinction between the music underscoring home/work and the activities of the Legion. Whereas the music associated with home and work is generally light and melodic, the militant music that accompanies Legion activities is fast-paced, staccato, dissonant, and generally driven by a heavy bass line.

Black Legion won accolades as a critical and courageous film. Praised for its topicality and its semidocumentary style, the movie was marked by realism that testified to the studio's research and its commitment to fighting social injustice. Several reviewers celebrated the fact that Warner Bros. pulled few punches, resisted a happy ending, and made a film that was both thought-provoking and entertaining in the process. *New Republic* film critic Otis Ferguson praised *Black Legion* for its courage. He lamented that, because of the strictures of the PCA, "the wisdom teeth have been pulled."[100] Though he feared that the film might suffer because Warner Bros. refused to tack on a happy ending, Ferguson applauded the decision to close the picture honestly, "not only [with] gloom but without much clear satisfaction either way."[101]

Time celebrated the film as "one of the most effective in Warner Brothers' series of industrial problem plays."[102] The unnamed critic praised the honesty of the film and its background research. "Black Legion makes no effort to mollify its message," he declared. Praising Robert Lord's screenplay, the reviewer noted that the film "investigates the Legion from three angles: its effect on Taylor, its purpose of making money for a crew of cold-blooded organizers, and its own mob activities."[103]

The Warner brothers refused to be intimidated, proving that filmmaking could be both socially responsible and entertaining. "In 'Black Legion' Hollywood grows up," declared the *Literary Digest*.[104] The film criticized not only the Black Legion but also the conditions that made such organizations possible.[105] Like Otis Ferguson and others, the *Literary Digest* critic praised the somber ending. "The hero-villain, after exposing his comrades, gets no reward for turning State's evidence. He shambles off to prison with the rest of them."[106] *Black Legion* stood as a firm indictment of pseudopatriotic groups who used fear and intimidation as a tonic for the woes of the Depression. It stands as a daring film, given the societal and industrial strictures placed upon it. *Black Legion* unflinchingly examined how decent people can be transformed for the worse when they fall prey to poverty, fear, irrational hatred, and jealousy. Once in a state of despair, they grab for any hope they can find, demonizing others, resorting to terrorism, and doing violence, all in the name of some twisted form of patriotism.[107]

The film's conclusion not only demonstrated that good people could be corrupted by the contagion of race hatred and lose everything dear to them—their family, their livelihood, and their freedom—but it also reassured the audience that the American justice system worked. The institutions established to preserve order in this country really do protect its citizenry, and the system does its best to protect against incipient radical movements at home.[108]

Another Warner film from the same year, *Black Fury*, compared resistance of organized labor to fascism. The film resonated with world events, for when Hitler assumed power he outlawed unions and the right to organize. Corrupt policemen do the bidding of the mine owners and suppress the work force. *Black Fury* centered on another Polish American, a coal miner (played by Paul Muni) who, like *Black Legion*'s Joe Dumbrowski, wanted to improve working conditions for his fellow workers and persuaded them to strike.[109] Like *Black Legion,* it was based on a real event and the screenplay was written by Abem Finkel. It explored how unions were manipulated by corrupt outsiders who preyed upon the workers. Also like *Black Legion, Black Fury* provides no happy ending for the miners involved.[110]

The next series of films the studio produced not only dealt with the Nazi threat at home, but for the first time called the nation's attention to the global Nazi threat, which was slowly undermining America's officially neutral position vis-à-vis the rest of the world.

3

The Road to *Confessions of a Nazi Spy* and Beyond

Benito Mussolini's desire to produce films rivaling those made in Hollywood and Paris led to the creation of the Cinecitta Studio and, in 1932, the advent of the Venice Film Festival, the world's first international competition.[1] Jack Warner entered *The Life of Emile Zola* in the 1937 festival as his studio's prestige picture. The importance of the film had already been recognized: the French government had awarded Warner Bros. the Legion of Honor for its depiction of the crusading novelist. Centering on the infamous Dreyfus case, the film questioned the illogic of anti-Semitism and race hatred. That message, however, caused the cancelation of its screening, which upset Jack Warner because the Nazis ruled the day at the Venice Film Festival that year. Propaganda Minister Josef Goebbels personally accepted the grand prize for the best picture.[2]

While in Italy Jack renewed his acquaintance with Countess Dorothy di Frasso, who had an odd assortment of friends: Mussolini, gangster Ben "Bugsy" Siegel, and several members of the Nazi high echelon, including Goebbels and Hermann Göring. Bristling under what he considered unfair treatment at the film festival, Warner confessed his disappointment to the countess and Siegel. Recalling the event much later, he claimed that Siegel offered to "liquidate not only Goebbels but Hermann Göring as well, but I talked him out of it."[3] Warner boasted to them that the studio was currently preparing a picture called *Confessions of a Nazi Spy,* which would hurt the Nazi elite far more than a political assassination because it exposed their nefarious attempts at espionage in the United States.[4]

A few nights later, supposedly, the countess took Warner aside, telling him that she had discussed the Nazi spy picture with Goebbels, who offered to play himself in the proposed film. Not only that, but Goebbels said that he would work for free.[5] This story smacks of outrageous fabrication since Warner Bros. quit its business with the Nazis in 1934, and news about a Nazi spy ring operating in the United States did not break until July of 1938, nearly a year after the 1937 film festival. Furthermore, why would Goebbels volunteer to perform in a film hostile to the Nazis or try to renew business ties with a studio known for its hostility toward Hitler's Germany?

This whole scenario is dubious at best, but Jack Warner used it in his memoirs to outline the difficulties that filming *Confessions of a Nazi Spy* created. Warner Bros. received numerous threats during the filming and maintained tight security, since it ran counter to the U.S. formal neutrality policy and the proscriptions of the PCA.[6] If completed, the film was guaranteed to generate controversy. Addressing the Reichstag on January 30, 1939, Hitler blamed Hollywood for the deterioration of relations between the two countries:

> Our relations with the United States are suffering . . . under the pretense that Germany threatens American independence. . . . We all believe, however, that this does not reflect the will of the millions of American citizens who, despite all that is said to the contrary by the gigantic Jewish capitalistic propaganda through the press, radio and films, cannot fail to realize that there is not one word of truth in all these assertions.[7]

The German-American Bund protested the production, and the German consul general in Los Angeles appealed directly to PCA chief Joseph Breen, asking him to quash the picture.[8] If the PCA passed on the film, which the Germans deemed hostile propaganda, they would have no recourse, he threatened, but to counter with official sanctions against the motion picture industry.[9]

In addition to the Warners' proposed *Confessions of a Nazi Spy,* three antifascist projects were announced by other producers—*The Exiles* (Goldwyn), *Personal History* (Walter Wanger), and *Blockade* (Walter Wanger/United Artists), all of which suffered their own share of criticism. *Blockade,* which dealt with the Spanish Civil War, was the only film completed. *Personal History* and *The Exiles* were aborted midproject due to myriad difficulties, including intervention by the Catholic Legion of Decency and the PCA, canceled budgets, threats of intraindustry blacklisting, fascist threats, and the fear of retaliation against relatives living in Europe.[10]

The German-American Bund, under the leadership of Bundesfuhrer Fritz Kuhn, spread pro-Nazi and anti-Semitic propaganda in America while imitating the lifestyle of Nazi Germany.[11] The Bund was often critical of movies, considering Hollywood decadent and a threat to Aryanism. Though the Bund tried to appeal to all German Americans, it was successful primarily in New York, New Jersey, and the upper Midwest.[12]

German Americans who originally followed the Nazi ideology in the United States first christened their organization Teutonia, later changing the name to The Friends of New Germany. Led by a bogus clergyman, Heinz Spanknobel, they disseminated Nazi literature, sponsored Nazi youth indoctrination camps, and promoted the superiority of Germanic culture to all others.[13] The Friends, and later the Bundists, spread vicious rumors that Jews had created organized crime.

Internal dissension caused a schism in 1934, giving rise to the new organization, the German-American Bund, under the more powerful leadership of Kurt Georg Wilhelm Ludecke. A true believer, Ludecke hoped to Nazify America and rid the country of all Jews living there; "If we are coming near our goal there will be no Jew left in these United States. . . . Here is our toast: TO THE LAST JEW!"[14] When Bundists met, they greeted one another with the slogan, "*Sterbt ein Jude*" [Let a Jew die].[15] In 1936 Fritz Kuhn, a naturalized American citizen, replaced Ludecke as Bundesfuhrer and begged the German American community to support Nazi Germany, while promoting American neutrality in Europe.[16] As events heated up abroad, the pro-Nazi activities of the Bund increased.

Since the release of *Black Legion*, Warner Bros. had made other films urging Americans to wake up to the specter of Nazism, such as *The Life of Emile Zola* (1937). The Warners continued producing installments in the *Old Glory* series, making the featurettes available free of charge to any school, church, or American organization.[17] In 1939 the studio won an Oscar for the best short feature with *The Sons of Liberty*, starring Claude Rains and directed by Michael Curtiz. The film, though ostensibly about the American Revolution, focused on the little-known story of a Polish-Jewish immigrant, Haym Salomon, who helped finance the fledgling Continental Congress. The parallels with Harry Warner were striking. Harry was a Polish-Jewish immigrant who saw his adopted country in a time of need and who would willingly and selflessly assist it in its hour of impending peril. The film also provided a tonic to the rising tide of domestic anti-Semitism, for it assured viewers that Jews were as patriotic as Christians and loved their country just as dearly. Harry Martin wrote, "[The short] will serve as a reminder of America's indebtedness to the

Jewish people at a time when this proud race is being harassed by the Nazi maniacs."[18] Haym Salomon, then, could easily be interpreted as a filmic embodiment of Harry Warner.[19]

As the persecution of the Jews increased in Europe, some people wondered why Hollywood said little about it. Emblazoned across the cover of the *Hollywood Spectator* in November 1938 was the following: "A Plea to the Jews Who Control Our Films to Use the Mighty Voice of the Screen on Behalf of the Jews Who Are Victims of Maniac of Germany."[20] Gentile editor Welford Beaton berated the industry for not standing up to Nazism or speaking out in defense of the Jews who suffered under Hitler. Why, he asked, did the moguls sit silently while thousands died? "Do not let us forget the crime of Germany!" he demanded. "The screen must keep it alive until some form of punishment is inflicted and the world is guarded against its repetition." Beaton recommended that moguls ignore the admonitions of Will Hays, their "paid pussy-footer," and do something courageous; otherwise they were as guilty of the mayhem as Hitler and the Nazis.[21]

Though that stinging indictment of Hollywood should have come as music to the ears of Harry and Jack Warner, it did not. For the very next article in the same issue condemned a project under way at their studio entitled *Concentration Camp*. The story was to graphically depict life under Nazism and the brutality of the work camps. Beaton, who had just begged Jewish moguls to do something about Nazism, condemned the Warner Bros. project, demanding, "Put a stop on the Warner effort to capitalize the tragedy."[22] Beaton, the skittish Hollywood studio heads, and the PCA prevailed, and pressures were placed on Warner Bros. to abandon the project. The film would have been timely, for after the war a fiction circulated that the United States knew nothing about the Holocaust, concentration camps, or other Nazi atrocities, though dozens of contemporary authors informed Americans about those very things. Furthermore, several Warner Bros. films made during the war explicitly mention concentration camps, including *All Through the Night* (1942) and *Casablanca* (1942). Freedom fighter Victor Laszlo, it should be remembered, escaped from a concentration camp before arriving in Casablanca.[23]

By 1937 news filtering out of Nazi Germany grew more ominous. Americans who thought Hitler was a benign dictator grew more wary after the Nazi-sponsored Olympics and Axis involvement in the Spanish Civil War.[24] Reporters informed Americans about the intensity of the racial hatred made state policy by the Nuremberg decrees and about the pall of fear that permeated German society.[25] Such events caused Warner Bros. to step up its condemnation of Nazi Germany's tactics through the production of several ostensibly historical dramas. *They Won't Forget* (1937), based on the infamous 1905 Leo Frank case, used Jim Crow and lynch law in the American South to criticize government-sponsored race hatred and propaganda. *The Life of Emile Zola* (1937) exposed a deep strain of anti-Semitism inherent in the French military. Significantly, both films condemned all racial prejudice.

Not wanting to alienate its southern audience, while wishing to draw parallels between the racial intolerance of the American South and Nazi Germany, Leo Frank was transformed into a Gentile school teacher from the North named Robert Hale, who moved to an unspecified southern hamlet. In reality, Leo Frank was a Jewish manufacturer in Atlanta who came to the aid of a black employee accused of raping and killing Mary Phagan. Many viewers could remember the infamous case, which resulted in a gubernatorial pardon but ended in the subsequent lynching of an innocent man. Interestingly, *They Won't Forget* arrived in theaters during the trial of the Scottsboro Boys, a case that drew considerable attention to the racial injustices in the American South.[26]

Like *Black Legion*, *They Won't Forget* effectively portrays the dangers of corrupt officials in the government and the debilitating effects of bigotry. Race hatred, the film argues, is official policy in the American South, just as it is official policy in Nazi Germany. The state imposed and enforced racial segregation, foisting a caste system upon a particular segment of the population, denying them their civil rights. Such policies, condoned by people in authority, invited fascism to take root in this country.

In *They Won't Forget,* the South represents a benighted region influenced by demagogues who prey upon people's basest fears and prurient interests. Claude Rains portrayed the corrupt southern district attorney Andy Griffin to smarmy perfection. The screenplay, based in part on journalist Ward Greene's novelization of the Frank case, *Death in the Deep South,* exposed the routine mockery of justice inherent in the South under Jim Crow. Southern officials kept citizens in a constant state of anxiety while blaming all the region's problems on outsiders and African Americans. The screenplay, however, purposely drew parallels to Nazi Germany, for as Hitler singled out the Jews as the bane of Germany's existence, southerners demonized blacks and "Yankees" for similar reasons.[27] Set during the Depression, the film demonstrates how emotions could be easily manipulated while it also captures "the sense of boredom and frustration that makes lynching a perverted form of entertainment."[28] The murder of the fictional Mary Clay was purposely enigmatic, for the audience, like the film's jury, never discovers who killed her. The murderer's identity is immaterial because the movie intends to illustrate how race hatred and mass hysteria can transform ordinary citizens into monsters.[29] The insidious nature of bigotry relentlessly pervades the film, arguing that the fascist mentality already has its own counterpart well established in this country.[30]

The film also examines the role of the press in manipulating public opinion. The capricious media distort facts to fit the whims of district attorney Griffin. Corrupt, malevolent, and propagandistic, the press whips up people's emotions, eventually leading to Robert Hale's lynching. Thus, as in Nazi Germany, a compromised press in collusion with a corrupt government can turn a group of otherwise decent citizens into a destructive mob. To heighten the tension, director Mervyn LeRoy presents the events in a harsh, glaring light. Most of the sequences appear to be overlit, driving home the notion of the South in the summer as actors constantly wipe their sweaty brows. No one looks comfortable except the cool and calculating district attorney, Andy Griffin. Unlike *Black Legion,* where the vengeance of the gang occurs at night, *They Won't Forget* has the mob acting in the full light of day.

Although some contemporary critics saw no need for Warner Bros. to alter the facts of the case, most praised the unflinching portrayal of racism and irrational fear. *Time* extolled the film as the "most devastating study of mob violence and sectional hatred the screen has yet dared to present" and considered the courtroom scene riveting: "for bleak, malevolent drama, the screen has never achieved a better one than the trial of Robert Hale."[31] *Newsweek* applauded screenwriters Robert Rossen and Aben Kandel for their faithfulness to Greene's novel.[32] *Literary Digest* considered the examination of racism and hatred as the studio's "most daring attack thus far."[33] The drama of the film lay in its matter-of-factness and the ease with which ordinary people can be made to do evil. "*They Won't Forget* is a naked, clinical account of how a man gets lynched in this country. It exposes every detail with blinding clarity, it leaves nobody a hero, it trumpets no pompous solutions. It is shockingly there—a simple statement of a thorny American problem."[34]

With the production of *They Won't Forget,* the studio subtly examined anti-Semitism, mob violence, and racism of all stripes. Although Frank was transformed from a southern Jew into a northern Gentile, the associations with the source material implicitly connected themes of anti-Semitism and race hatred. The South of *They Won't Forget* served as a dark mirror reflecting the seamy underbelly of the American heartland. Clearly, what had happened to Frank/Hale could conceivably happen anywhere in this country. No moviegoer could smugly point a finger at the screen and announce that the events depicted "can't happen here." The film brilliantly examined how emotions can be manipulated, while making it clear that impartial justice is not always served in the American courts of law.

The film's message remains as relevant today as it was in 1937. The filmmakers chose not to compromise the ending of the film, nor offer any assurance that good ultimately triumphs over evil. Rather, in *They Won't Forget*, evil succeeds and is rewarded, not punished. Film historian Nick Roddick considers *They Won't Forget* as "Warners' most emphatic social document" of the second half of the 1930s and places it alongside *Black Legion* and *Confessions of a Nazi Spy* as prime examples of Warner's fight against fascism and social injustice.[35]

The Life of Emile Zola represented an allegory of the events in Europe, condemning jingoistic militarism, racial discrimination, and intolerance. The biopic, starring Paul Muni, provided the studio with the latitude it needed to address a potentially combustible topic; and the utilization of a historic figure, placed in its contextual setting, allowed the filmmakers to discuss topics normally deemed taboo. By focusing on the venomous anti-Semitism that surrounded the Dreyfus affair, Warner Bros. could subtly point out the parallels between France at the fin de siecle and the current Nazi regime.

Dreyfus, the first Jew in the French General Staff, was framed by anti-Semitic factions in the military that forged documents and accused him of selling state secrets to the Germans. Indicted, court-martialed, and convicted by a kangaroo court, he was sentenced to Devil's Island in 1894. Emile Zola questioned the legitimacy of the Dreyfus affair and protested the proceedings. His actions resulted in anti-Jewish riots in Paris and the wholesale burning of his books. When the forgery was finally discovered and Dreyfus was released from prison, France split into two factions—the Dreyfusards, who supported Dreyfus and embraced the ideas of republican government, human rights, and justice, and the Anti-Dreyfusards, who advocated monarchy and elitism. The Dreyfus case, therefore, offered contemporary parallels, reminding viewers of the Nazi "night of the long knives," purges of the German civil service, burning of so-called decadent books, and the Reichstag fire.[36]

Not everyone was overjoyed by the decision of Warner Bros. to produce a motion picture about Zola and the Dreyfus case. The studio's European representative, Robert Schless, contacted French Premier Leon Blum and informed him about the intended film. To Schless's surprise, Blum discouraged the production, fearing the film might exacerbate the current political situation in France. Blum could well remember the anti-Semitic violence that erupted around the Dreyfus affair, for he had worked with Zola to reopen the case. Part of his reasoning was personal; as an assimilated Jew, Blum saw no reason to dredge up the sordid Dreyfus affair and possibly endanger his family or other French Jews.[37] To accommodate Blum and the PCA, Warner Bros. opted to remove overt references to Dreyfus's Jewishness. The word "Jew" appears only once in the film, when the General Staff is looking for a scapegoat and chooses Dreyfus because his religious affiliation is Jewish.[38] Some critics chastised Warner Bros. for downplaying Dreyfus's Jewishness and toning down overt anti-Semitic themes. Mark Van Doren wrote, "Rightly or wrongly the direction has seen fit to suppress the anti-Semitic theme . . . one certainly never learns that the case, at least until Hitler, was the high water mark in European history of agitation over race."[39]

Meanwhile, the German-American Bund grew and chose a number of targets to attack. In September of 1937, Bundesfuhrer Fritz Kuhn addressed eighteen thousand Bund members at their retreat, Camp Nordlund, New Jersey, calling for a boycott of Hollywood films, which were the creation of ignoble Jews. Kuhn called for all German Americans to torture the Hollywood Jews where they would hurt most, their pocketbooks. Hollywood films poisoned the minds of good Americans and needed to be silenced.[40] Bund activity received an even bigger boost after the Austrian *Anschluss* and the Czech crisis, when Hitler announced in July of 1938 that all Germans, whether living in Germany or not, were citizens of the Third Reich. Many Bund members gladly embraced the pronouncement of the Fuhrer.

By the summer of 1938 the world was put on alert that a crisis might be imminent, one that might profoundly affect the film industry. Several British actors belonged to the reserves, and if England went to war, Hollywood could lose some of its favorite stars.[41] In the midst of the 1938 crisis, Warner Bros. began filming a remake of *The Dawn Patrol*, starring Tasmanian Errol Flynn and Englishmen Basil Rathbone, David Niven, and Donald Crisp, with sixty-four additional British actors in supporting roles. Though somewhat cynical, the film depicted the courage of patriotic British pilots in the face of crushing odds. The message was clear: Warner Bros. detested war, but the studio would, if necessary, endorse it to stop the largest aggressor nation in the world, Germany.[42]

Also in 1938 Hitler stepped up his persecution of the Jews. New regulations restricting property rights, and laws that limited Jews' mobility in Nazi-held territories, made all Jews under Nazi occupation *personae non gratae.* Papers identifying them as Jewish had to be carried at all times; likewise, passports were reissued indicating that the bearer was a Jew. Forced to wear a yellow Star of David on their clothes in public, Jews were easily identifiable. Jews whose names did not sound Jewish enough were forced to change them, making them more obviously Jewish.[43]

As a result of the more strident policies, Harry Warner broadened his attacks on the Nazis, hoping to influence public opinion. Advocating that the current situation required sacrifice and patriotism, the elder Warner approached the American Legion as a possible ally. Although the Legion was divided over what role America should pursue, he found many supporters in their ranks.[44] On September 19, 1938, Warner addressed the American Legion Convention in Los Angeles and challenged the Legionnaires to join him in the struggle against Nazism. Appealing to their vanity, he said that the American Legion represented the apotheosis of true Americanism and assured the assembled veterans:

> I tell you this industry has no sympathy with Communism, Fascism, Nazism or any "ism" other than Americanism. . . . Certain bigots representing mal-contents [sic] who want to ruin what they cannot rule, whisper that Hollywood is run by "isms." They Lie! . . . Drive them out from their insidious propaganda machines, drive out their bunds, their clans and Black Legions, the Silver Shirts, the Black Shirts, and Dirty Shirts. Help keep America for those who believe in America.[45]

His rhetoric might have reflected the very groups he condemned—those who tried to co-opt Americanism as their exclusive province—but Warner hoped he was preaching to the choir. A milder version of the speech was incorporated into the final version of *Confessions of a Nazi Spy,* applauding the American Legion's role in securing and preserving the country's liberty.[46] To further capitalize on this message, Warner had 150,000 copies of the speech printed up and distributed to film exhibitors, newspapers, and American Legion Posts throughout the country.

Fig. 2. Harry Warner, the conscience of the studio, vowed to do all in his power to stop Nazi aggression at home and abroad. Courtesy of the Alvin C. York family collection.

Harry Warner was not the only person alarmed by the growing Nazi agitation at home. *Nashville Banner* journalist David Lawrence offered a possible solution to the worsening crisis. Noting that the State Department's quota for Jews was a paltry twenty-seven thousand, though six hundred thousand European Jews had applied for asylum, he suggested, Why not "trade U.S. Nazis for Jews?"[47] Upset by Bundists and pro-Nazi sympathizers, Lawrence argued: "Since these pro-Nazi enthusiasts are so fond of the Nazi form of government, it may be they would prefer living in Germany, whereas there must be an equal number now in Germany who would be glad [to move here]."[48] Unfortunately for thousands of Jews, the State Department failed to significantly increase quotas and make it possible for them to reach safe haven in the United States.[49]

Recognizing that the United States was not the only country in the Western Hemisphere vulnerable to fascism, Warner Bros. appealed to Mexico and Latin America to help fend off the Nazi scourge. One vehicle was the production of *Juarez*, starring Paul Muni. *Juarez* upheld the New

Deal's Good Neighbor policy, while condemning foreign dictatorships. By focusing on the well-known tragedy of Napoleon II and his mad wife Carlotta, who tried to impose their rule on Mexico, the studio found a hero in the Mexican Indian who resisted them, Benito Juarez. The film stressed four themes: democracy is superior to dictatorship, sovereign nations should have a right to self-determination, racial intolerance is untenable, and the Western Hemisphere should stave off foreign intervention at all costs. Like *They Won't Forget* and *The Life of Emile Zola*, *Juarez* espoused the importance of racial equality and tolerance. Mexico was a country of Indians, half-breeds, and immigrants who recognized the impossibility of racial purity, and Americans could do well to learn by their example.[50]

In an article he penned for the *Christian Science Monitor,* Harry Warner made it plain that though *Juarez* was a historical epic, its relevance to the current international situation was intentional. "The struggle of the remarkable Mexican to save his nation for its own people," he wrote, "is so surprisingly paralleled by world events today that the timeliness of the subject matter is obvious."[51] Straightforward as usual, Harry made his position firmly known. Just as Juarez stood up to a dictatorial regime for the good of all Mexicans, Americans should guard the United States against unwelcome foreign aggression.[52]

The crusading Warner vowed that the motion picture industry was obliged to inform its audience about the threats posed by outside forces. Movies should depict proper ethical standards, civil liberties, and patriotism. In this mission to bolster pride in America, "the motion picture producer shares this obligation with the schools, the churches, the service organizations of all kinds which stand for tolerance, for decent thinking, and fair relations with the rest of mankind."[53] It was Hollywood's duty to preach to the world, as well as U.S. citizens, those values all people should hold dear in a democratic republic. Unabashed in his candor, Warner made his mission plain. He would continue to speak out against intolerance in hopes that other movie producers would do likewise. His article was a call to arms for both the general public and the film industry. In his estimation there was

> an ever present duty to educate, to stimulate, and demonstrate the fundamentals of free government, free speech, religious tolerance, freedom of press, freedom of assembly and the greatest possible happiness for the greatest possible number. To that end our company and, I believe, our whole industry, stands pledged—now and for the future.[54]

In a world careening toward destruction, Harry Warner refused to twiddle his thumbs and do nothing.

Meanwhile, his studio looked for other parallels to Nazism, and medieval England provided ample grist for its interventionist mill. The Errol Flynn swashbuckler *The Adventures of Robin Hood* used the mother country's past as an allegory for modern concerns. *The Adventures of Robin Hood*'s evil Prince John, the Norman pretender to the throne of England in Richard the Lion-Heart's absence, abused his Saxon subjects just as Hitler did his own people. John's onerous tax policies kept his countrymen impoverished and frustrated. Actress Olivia de Havilland (Maid Marian) remembered the parallels when filming the movie: "I suppose, unconsciously, we were preparing for another terrible conflict, because there really were the good guys and there really *was* a bad guy—and that was Hitler . . . and anyone who fought him became a kind of Errol Flynn."[55]

John's followers, Sir Guy of Gisbourne and the sheriff of Nottingham, represent humorless brutality and carping cowardice. Lusting for power, the Norman invaders try to impose their form of order on Saxon England. Robin's followers, by contrast, represent the ideal democratic community—the Merry Men—who work together and love life in spite of its hardships. Film historian Ina Rae Hark considered the sequence in which Prince John's henchmen capture Robin and display him chained from head to toe as a symbol of freedom in bondage; it pointed to the possibility all humanity faced if fascism were allowed to continue in the world unchecked.[56]

As the world situation heated up, tales of Nazi activity in America increased. Aviatrix Amelia Earhart's husband, publisher George Palmer Putnam, ran afoul of Nazi sympathizers in 1939 when he published an anti-Nazi novel, *The Man Who Killed Hitler*. He claimed that he was threatened by "the arm of Greater Germany," who ordered Putnam to suspend the book's publication immediately or else.[57] The publisher received threatening phone calls and letters and a bullet-ridden copy of the offending novel. Sensing the potential sales the controversy could garner, Putnam staged his own kidnapping. Authorities found him bound and gagged in a house under construction in Bakersfield, California, where he claimed to have been brutalized by Nazis.[58] The hoax Putnam perpetuated to boost book sales did not, of course, diminish the reality of the Nazi threat in America.

Harry Warner addressed the Ancient Order of Hibernians on Saint Patrick's Day in 1939 and officially announced his intention to produce *Confessions of a Nazi Spy*. During this time of conflict, citizens of the United States should work together. "You are not presenting yourselves as Irish-Americans," he told them. "You are Americans. I am not accepting your hospitality as a *Jewish*-American. I am here as an *American*."[59] Likewise, Christians and Jews should put away their grievances in the face of a common enemy, Nazi Germany. In such a tempestuous climate, Hollywood should make a concerted effort to use film as a means of "exposing the plots against the United States, and of glorifying and sustaining our love of country and pride in its institutions."[60] Professing his love of America, Warner swore that his studio would complete not only *Confessions of a Nazi Spy* but also more films in the same vein. Threats could not dissuade him, he declared, and those who found his stance uncomfortable or belligerent must realize that his sole purpose was to champion the cause of American liberty.[61] In a world hurtling toward destruction, Harry Warner refused to sit idly by. Convinced that Hitler had to be stopped and that the film industry could play some role in thwarting the dictator, Warner stood committed to donate his time, energy, and the resources at his disposal. As Christine Ann Colgan so aptly noted:

> Warners had committed itself heart, body, soul, and money to the project and had begun rolling cameras on 1 February 1939; before the dissolution of Czechoslovakia (14 March 1939); before Madrid surrendered to Franco (24 March 1939); before Mussolini began his attack on Albania (April 1939); before Japan occupied the Spratly Islands (March 1939); and before Roosevelt sought a modification of the Neutrality Act (September 1939). *The Warners did not need these events to be persuaded to break the silence.*[62]

The announcement of Warner Bros.'s intentions to produce a movie about a Nazi spy ring caused tension within the industry because many studios continued doing business with Nazi Germany. Although Warner Bros. could claim the high moral ground, most studios believed that they could not compete without the German market. Jack Warner exploded when fellow Jews tried to rationalize their continued relations with the Nazis. Reflecting on the period, he fumed:

> Hurt what? Their pocketbooks? Listen these murdering bastards killed our own man in Germany because he wouldn't heil Hitler. The Silver Shirts and the Bundists and all the rest of these hoods are marching in Los Ange-

les right now. There are high school kids with swastikas on their sleeves a few blocks from our studio. Is that what you want in exchange for some crummy film royalties out of Germany? I'm going to finish this picture, and Hitler and Goebbels can scream all they want. And so can guys like you![63]

Prominent among the Warner studio's politically active talent was Edward G. Robinson, and when Harry and Jack Warner professed their determination to bring *Confessions of a Nazi Spy* to the screen, he requested inclusion in the production. He wrote Hal Wallis saying, "I want again to express a strong desire to appear in the International Spy Ring story you are going to do. *I want to do that for my people.*"[64] Like Harry Warner, Robinson was a member of the ANL and the Committee of Fifty-Six. A proud Jew, he wanted Hitler stopped as soon as possible.

Confessions of a Nazi Spy, like *Black Legion* and *They Won't Forget,* was based on actual events. On February 26, 1938, FBI chief J. Edgar Hoover announced that the bureau had cracked a Nazi spy ring at work in this country and that it included members of the German-American Bund. Unfortunately, Hoover's remarks were premature since not all the spies had yet been arrested. Among those missing was Dr. Ignatz T. Greibl, leader of the American Nazis, who escaped to Germany on May 10, aboard the passenger liner *Bremen.*[65] An unnamed reporter for *The Nation* observed that though the Nazi spies "appeared to be rather stupid and amateurish," it did not preclude the fact that the Nazi threat to the internal security of the United States was indeed serious.[66]

The G-Man who broke the case, Leon G. Turrou, wrote about his exploits in the dramatic bestseller *Nazi Spies in America* (1938), which was first serialized in the *New York Post.* An outraged J. Edgar Hoover fired him for writing the book. Federal charges were leveled against Turrou for possibly prejudicing the jury's opinion in the case and undermining the Nazi spies' constitutional guarantees to a fair trial. The charges were later dropped.[67] Warner Bros. quickly optioned the rights to the story and employed Turrou as an advisor on the project. Although a deal was finalized in June of 1938, Warner Bros. had to guarantee the federal government that it would not release the movie until after the spy trials ended.[68] *The Nation*'s aforementioned reporter feared that dramatization of the Nazi spy activities would numb the American public to the real danger they represented and he warned against the production.[69]

As a result of such conditions, preproduction occurred under absolute secrecy because of fear of repercussions from the Bund or the federal government.[70] Federal officials at that time launched an investigation of motion picture distribution that eventually led to the infamous *United States v. Paramount* (1948) case, which caused studios to divest their theater chains. Harry Warner wrote FDR in September of 1939, asking him to suppress the antitrust investigation for the good of all studios who had suffered the loss of overseas markets, and the Justice Department issued a consent decree in June of 1940 suspending the proceedings. Detlef Junker made the specious argument that the antitrust investigation was a ploy to coerce the studios to follow Roosevelt's interventionist policies. Such an argument overlooks the stance Warner Bros. had assumed since 1934. If Junker's argument were valid, the administration would have omitted the studio from the antitrust investigation and rewarded them for their action.[71]

As soon as Warner Bros. made it known that they were committed to the production of *Confessions of a Nazi Spy,* numerous groups began pressuring the studio to cease and desist. Dr. Georg Gyssling, the German consul stationed in Los Angeles, launched a campaign to disrupt the project. Prevailing upon Joseph Breen to keep the German consulate informed about everything the censor knew concerning the production, Gyssling badgered the PCA to do the Third Reich's bidding.[72] Not above physical intimidation, Gyssling threatened actors and technicians (including both Harry and Jack Warner and producer Hal Wallis) who participated in the film. Wallis declared that Gyssling had received direct orders from Hitler to sabotage the movie.[73]

The studio beefed up security and kept the names of the cast secret as a precaution for those with families in Europe. Some cast members' names were altered in the film credits as an added precaution. Pages of script were meted out on a daily basis to prevent their being leaked to unfriendly third parties. For a time, the studio considered releasing the film without any credits whatsoever, but a compromise was reached, and the credits ran at the end of the film.[74]

Warner Bros. prudently chose to wait until after the trial had ended with the conviction of three spies before it sent a preliminary screenplay to the PCA. Joseph Breen sent Jack Warner his analysis of the script on December 30, 1938; although he considered the film questionable, and although the initial script violated a section of the Production Code concerning "National Feelings," Breen did not wholeheartedly condemn the project. Rather, he decided that

> since the screenplay was based on fact and sworn testimony presented in the New York trial, it did not as such represent Germany, its institutions, or prominent individuals unfairly.[75]

The PCA chief cooperated with the studio rather than with Gyssling, and Warner Bros. provided Breen an extensive bibliography and copies of research materials that the studio had collected to illustrate their willingness to accurately portray the events that occurred in the film.

Studios that tried to hang on to their dwindling German market regarded the plans of Warner Bros. as selfish and disrespectful of the welfare of the industry. Afraid that the movie would hurt the few American films that still found a German audience, Paramount's liaison, Luigi Laraschi, complained bitterly to Breen. In an exercise in incredibly twisted logic, he wrote, "Warners will have on their hands the blood of a great many Jews in Germany" if they go through with the project.[76] Not only is Laraschi's argument illogical, but it also represented placing craven cowardice and the love of box-office receipts over concern for the safety of his fellow man.[77] Leon Turrou was surprised by the various studio heads' attempts to warn Warner Bros. off the picture. He noted, however, that the "Warner executives were fearless and willing to risk their own lives and property" to warn the world about Nazi aggression. Nevertheless, MGM, Twentieth Century–Fox, and Paramount could somehow, in good conscience, rationalize continued business with the Third Reich as it carried out routine discrimination of the Jews. Likewise, they blamed the Warner brothers' expression of righteous rage as being somehow responsible for the fate of European Jewry.

Rather than cave in to the threats and accusations, the Warners dug in their heels and fought back. Jack Warner told the *New York Times:*

> Our fathers came to America to avoid just the sort of persecution that is taking place in Germany today. If we wish to keep the United States as the land of the free and the home of the brave, we must do everything we can to destroy the deadly Nazi germs of bigotry and persecution. I consider this picture our greatest contribution and we shall produce it regardless of the consequences, regardless of the threats that have been pouring in on us, regardless of the pressure that has been brought against our organization by certain forces, even within the industry, which have an interest in seeing the picture abandoned.[78]

In spite of the studio's desire to remain firm, they had to make some compromises. Because the film depicted living persons and real events, releases from those parties to be portrayed were legally necessary. The German-American Bund was in no mood to cooperate with a Jewish-owned and -operated studio bent on depicting them unfavorably. Characterization of the Nazi spies, therefore, underwent considerable rewriting in order to make the specific people involved less recognizable. Thus, in the interest of getting the story to the screen, the names of all the principal American spies had to be changed to prevent a raft of lawsuits from inundating the studio. The studio faced similar problems when bringing *Sergeant York* to the screen and was plagued by numerous lawsuits during and after that film's release.[79]

The film not only utilized the factual account of a story taken from the headlines and the G-Man who put it there, but it also capitalized on the talents of the émigré community, many of whom had witnessed the atrocities of the Third Reich firsthand.[80] Director Anatole Litvak wanted the film to have the authentic look audiences associated with newsreels and therefore incorporated a quasi-documentary format to heighten its verisimilitude. As a result, the studio had to eat some crow because of its inclusion of newsreel footage in the montage sequences. Harry Warner's campaign against newsreels depicting Nazis came home to roost when he attempted to get permission to use those very clips. To heighten the drama, Litvak incorporated footage of Goebbels and other Nazis, as well as clips from the German-American Bund's rally at New York's Madison Square Garden and from Leni Riefenstahl's *Triumph of the Will.*[81]

The film opens with a voice-over and the narrator in shadow. The camera pulls back to reveal the courtroom where the Nazi spy trials occurred, then segues to the story of Nazi activity in America. It ominously depicts the Nazis not only as Teutonic thugs but also as seemingly unassuming ladies with braided hair. In short, Nazis are everywhere, even in the most unexpected places and among the most innocent-looking folk. The film displays happy children dressed as Brown Shirts being indoctrinated to hate by smug adults, and draws direct connections between the Nazis and cryptofascist movements in the United States. Dr. Kassel (Paul Lukas), the film's antagonist who was based on Dr. Greibl, instructs the members of the German-American Bund to say that they believe in "America for Americans" and promote U.S. isolationism, just as the real Bundists had.[82] The audience is invited to loathe Kassel for his easy hatred, his manipulation of people, and the fact that he is a philanderer.

When Dr. Kassel addresses members of the Bund, his speech and mannerism are eerily similar to those of Adolf Hitler. He tells members that America was founded on German blood and culture and that they should believe in a German destiny for America. Therefore, Germans must save America from the "chaos of democracy and racial equality."[83] When the craven, money-grubbing Kurt Schneider (Francis Lederer) asks Franz Schlager (George Sanders) for a job as a Nazi spy, Schlager remarks to Bund members about him, "Americans are very simple-minded people. Who needs a wolf when a weasel will do?"[84]

Warner Bros. appropriated the pseudopatriotic verbiage of the Bund to draw a direct connection between *Confessions of a Nazi Spy* and *Black Legion*.[85] Goebbels informs Dr. Kassel, "There is to be a slight change in our methods. From now on National Socialism in the United States must dress itself in the American flag. It must appear to be a defense of Americanism."[86] Just as the Black Legion, the Silver Shirts, and other reactionary groups had perverted American patriotism to do their bidding, so too did the Bund. When an American Legion member played by Ward Bond accuses Kassel, the Nazis, and the Bund of intentions to trample upon American civil liberties and subvert the Constitution, he quotes Harry Warner, saying, "We don't want any isms in America but Americanism." His remarks lead to a brawl where he is dragged from the rally, presumably to be beaten.[87]

The film depicts the violence inherent in Nazism. Bund members live in fear of their lives. They are spied upon by their peers and everything they say is suspect. When members discover that Gruetwald has been critical of the Bund and of Nazi Germany, he is forcibly detained and deported to Nazi Germany. Though the viewer never knows what happens to him when he gets there, one can assume the worst.[88]

Just as *Black Legion* had argued that good, honest people could be duped by the forces of hate, *Confessions of a Nazi Spy* informed audiences that America was under siege. Even so, the film toed a very fine line and tried to distinguish between good German Americans and Nazi-sympathizing German Americans.

It is due to the bungling incompetence of Schneider and his wild attempt to secure fifty blank passports that the spy ring is uncovered. After thirty minutes elapses the star of the show, Edward G. Robinson, finally appears as the fictional counterpart to Leon G. Turrou. Schneider is a whimpering weakling, easily broken by the G-Man. Though Kassel attempts to escape, he is forcibly taken back to Germany, where he will suffer a worse fate than American justice, and the audience can get some satisfaction in that.

Like *Black Legion*, the film's denouement occurs in a courtroom. Drawing heavily from the actual trial transcripts, the final sequence once again features an officer of the court pontificating about the dangers of fascism. The oration pointedly singles out isolationists; criticizing their unwillingness to face unpleasant facts. District Attorney Kellogg (Henry O'Neill), says:

> [T]here are some who will say there is nothing to fear, that we are separated by vast oceans from the bacteria of aggressive dictatorships and totalitarian states. But we know . . . this bacteria can slowly poison the organism of our civilized society and dull its common sense and reason, working insidiously through its Bunds and training camps . . . But ladies and gentlemen, America is not simply one of the remaining democracies, America *is* democracy![89]

Because America represents the last bastion of freedom and democracy in the world, Americans must be more diligent in guarding against further fascistic inroads. The success in uncovering the spy ring presents a glimmer of hope that the United States could resist other such onslaughts in the future.

The filmmakers consciously parroted documentaries and newsreels stylistically to heighten the drama of the film. The intercutting of actual newsreel footage with staged scenes often made it hard to discern the line between reality and fabrication. The film also employed "voice of God" narration by an unseen commentator who presided over the events in the manner of a newsreel commentator. The set crew faithfully reproduced the New York courtroom where the trial occurred. The research department scoured hundreds of photos, which were passed on to the crews to reproduce authentic costumes and makeup and to assist in the lighting design. The use of actors who bore more than a passing resemblance to people in the public eye (such as Goebbels) enhanced the film's verisimilitude. The soundtrack incorporated music associated with Nazi Germany such as *"Deutschland über Alles,"* increasing the emotional impact of the film. In such ways it was perhaps too successful: it looked too much like a documentary rather than a typical Hollywood feature. After the final cut of the film was assembled, it was presented to the PCA. Though Breen continued to harbor reservations about the film, fearing repercussions could rock the entire film industry, after a number of revisions the PCA reluctantly granted its seal of approval. Breen considered the affair to be a questionable subject for entertainment.[90]

The movie, which opened April 28, 1939, was the first major Hollywood production to openly point an accusing finger at the Nazis. It was the first feature film to directly mention the Nazis, Hitler, and his infamous henchmen.[91] Nazis were presented as humorless, maniacal, efficient, and officious. The cold, calculating sadism of the Hollywood Nazi stereotype pioneered by Warner Bros. continues to influence how filmmakers portray the Nazis to this day.[92]

Upon the film's release, the studio braced itself for repercussions. They were not long in coming, for the film angered audiences both at home and abroad.[93] Irate German Americans in Milwaukee burned down the local Warner theater after the film opened.[94] Father Coughlin attacked it as an example of the Communist-Jewish conspiracy run amok. Fulminating against the Warner brothers and Edward G. Robinson, Coughlin reminded readers of *Social Justice* that all three were Jews, unworthy of trust. "The sponsors of *Confessions of a Nazi Spy*," he harangued, "need not wrap themselves in the American flag and pose as patriots. Their patriotism is only as deep as their hatred of Hitler."[95] Throughout the country movie houses were picketed, exhibitors threatened, and in some cases violence erupted, causing a few squeamish exhibitors to refuse to show *Confessions of a Nazi Spy.*[96]

The German charge d'affaires stationed in Washington, D.C., complained bitterly to Secretary of State Cordell Hull. Nazi authorities banned the film throughout their occupied territories and tried to suppress its release elsewhere, including Latin America. *Confessions* was prohibited in Norway, Sweden, Denmark, Holland, Switzerland, Hungary, Iraq, South Africa, Chile, Argentina, and Ireland. Brazilian theaters refused to show the film. Brazil, which continued to do a healthy business with the Nazis, saw no need to agitate its economic partner. To make matters worse, the Brazilian war minister and the army chief of staff were decorated by Hitler for their service to the Reich.[97]

Nazis threatened the State Department, saying that German filmmakers would counter *Confessions* with a series of quasi-documentary films exposing life in the United States and prove that America was a nation of greed, corruption, crime, and general discontent.[98] Jack Warner stated in his memoirs that he learned that Hitler, Goebbels, Ribbentrop, and others saw *Confessions of a Nazi Spy* at Berchtesgaden. The film supposedly so infuriated Hitler that he placed Warner on "his extermination list."[99] Several theater owners in Poland lost their lives; they were hanged in their movie houses for exhibiting the film. The Warner Bros. managing director in Poland, Boris Jankolwicz, escaped the terror by walking more than three hundred miles to evade Nazi reprisals for showing the film.[100]

The film opened in this country to mixed reviews. Franz Hoellering praised the film in *The Nation*. He considered it an excellent blend of detective story, thriller, and current events with chilling and memorable scenes. "Taken as pure cinema," he wrote, "'Confessions of a Nazi Spy' is first-class . . . blending documentary information and common story so perfectly that almost a new style results, a kind of movie journalism."[101] The film did have its drawbacks. Hoellering considered some of the Nazi material heavy-handed and preachy.[102]

Otis Ferguson blew hot and cold. He considered the film the "most vivid, matter-of-fact, unescapable induction into Nazi principles and practices that the majority of people have ever been given outside a concentration camp."[103] Although he found the film sensational storytelling, he considered it a dangerous enterprise. "The film is a hate-breeder if ever there was one," he lamented.[104] The unnamed critic writing for *Time* was less flattering. He said the film was about as "undiplomatic as an artillery bombardment" and woefully simplistic.[105]

The German propaganda ministry wasted no time in retaliating. They chose several methods to undercut the charges of anti-Semitism and the official racial policies of the Nazi government by pointing accusing fingers at the United States. Nazi publications declared that America advocated a double standard, and in reality its views were more sympathetic to Nazi ideology than most Americans wanted to admit. Using the same argument Warners espoused in *They Won't Forget,* the Nazi leadership asked: How were the Nazi racial policies against Jews any different from the anti–African American Jim Crow laws of the American South? Hitler expressed his admiration for the antebellum South and congratulated the New South for its suppression of African Americans. At the same time, the S.S. journal *Schwarze Korps* complained that if lynchings had occurred in Nazi Germany with the same frequency as they did in the American South, the entire world would condemn them; yet the United States claimed to be morally superior in its own racial policies. Many southern newspapers took offense at the comparison, pointing out that lynchings were illegal, whereas anti-Semitism was state policy in Germany. Nazis were unpopular in the South, as were pacifists or noninterventionist groups like America First.[106]

Variety reviewed *Confessions of a Nazi Spy* in May of 1939, just four months before the fateful invasion of Poland, and rightly observed:

> The world is outwardly at peace. Actually there is a war going on. A war of nerves, of bluff, of propaganda and counter-propaganda. The bullets may come later. Decades from now what's happening may be seen in perspective. And the historians will certainly take note of this daringly frank broadside from a picture company.[107]

Confessions of a Nazi Spy did poorly at the box office.[108] Perhaps people had seen more than they wanted in the popular press or in newsreels and did not want to be reminded of the Third Reich in a feature-length film. In spite of its paltry showing, the Warners continued looking for ways to alert people about Hitler and his evil program. The brothers made it clear that they would continue in their resolve to displace the dictator whether they made any money or not.[109] The studio even re-released the film in 1940, adding new scenes and more recent newsreel footage to keep abreast of the changes in Europe.

The desire of Warner Bros. to create more anti-Nazi pictures ran afoul of MPPDA director Will Hays, who declared that in keeping with America's officially neutral stance, no studio could produce any more anti-Nazi films and receive the PCA seal. From September 15, 1939, until January of 1940, American studios were forbidden to develop films with an obvious anti-Nazi bias. The ban was imposed in part in reaction to an editorial by *Nashville Banner* editor and American Newspaper Association president James G. Stahlman.[110] Another factor was the fear of external censorship and government intervention. On September 29, 1939, Senator Elmer Thomas (D-Oklahoma) urged Congress to prohibit the manufacture or distribution of any films, newsreels, or radio broadcasts dealing with the European war in order to ensure American neutrality.[111]

Confessions of a Nazi Spy meant a great deal to those involved, however, and it even inspired a *Looney Tunes* homage, *Confusions of a Nutzy Spy*, released in December of 1942. In it the ever-vigilant and intrepid Porky Pig tracks down the spy and saboteur, Missing Lynx, as he sets out to undermine American security.[112] In spite of the film's poor financial showing, it made a substantial impact on the film community.

In 1940 Columbia paid homage to Warner Bros.'s daring by releasing a Three Stooges short feature, *You Nazty Spy!* Written by Clyde Bruckman and Felix Adler, the comedy tipped its hat to *Confessions of a Nazi Spy*, while depicting Hitler as a talentless buffoon. To avoid a run-in with the

PCA, the film opened with the disclaimer, "Any resemblance between the characters in this picture and any persons living or dead, is a miracle."[113]

Set in the fictitious country Moronica, the film features Moe ("Hailstone"), a paper-hanger who is prevailed upon by three scheming European ministers to engineer a coup and establish a dictatorship. Because of the economic straits the country faces, the ministers believe: "There's no money in peace. We must start a war."[114] The stooges oblige when told that being dictators will entitle them to beautiful women, plenty of food and wine, and no work.

While thinking the proposal over, Moe accidentally gets a piece of black gaffer's tape stuck on his fingertip, which he unknowingly transfers to his lip. He runs his fingers through his hair as he muses, and the transformation from stooge Moe Howard to a Hitler look-alike is complete. The ministers agree to make Curly ("Gallstone") the field marshall of all armed forces and Larry ("Pebble") the minister of propaganda.[115]

This short feature took several opportunities to remind the American public of Nazi Germany's sordid history by referring to the Beer Hall Putsch, book burnings, and concentration camps. But the most pointed comparisons were made in the film's satire of the Munich conference. Moe threatens the assembled foreign delegates that if they do not adhere to his demands, he will initiate a "Blintz-Krieg."[116] Recalcitrant ministers accuse Moronica of unwarranted aggression, but the stooges stand (Moe holding an umbrella) and chant in unison, "Peace! We want Peace!" To which one minister replies, "Yes, a little piece of this country and a little piece of that country."[117] In an overt reference to the cession of the Sudetenland, Moe announces, "What we want is a corridor through Double Crossia into the Bay of Window."[118] The film degenerates into the usual slapstick silliness the stooges were famous for, but the spoof let Warner Bros. know that they no longer stood alone in Hollywood against Nazi aggression.

When war erupted in September 1939, the studio scrambled to keep abreast of events. On September 13 Jack Warner canceled travel plans so that he could oversee the conversion of the studio to wartime operations. He apologized to East Coast liaison Joseph Hazen for his inability to come to New York and added, "[Y]ou may pick up any paper or tune in on any radio and hear Adolf Hitler just shot himself, or someone just shot Hitler. I hope they both happen."[119]

The reality that war had arrived caused the studio to reassess its priorities, and on May 20, 1940, Jack Warner called a meeting of all department heads to plot strategies to contend with the situation. All vacations were canceled, budgets for feature films were pared down to conserve materials that might have to be rationed, and production of prestige pictures were postponed temporarily. They also drafted some rather peculiar orders: radios were banned because they feared the worsening news might have a deleterious effect on the morale of studio employees. More ominous, and reminiscent of World War I's anti-German hysteria, was Jack Warner's order forbidding anyone to speak German at the studio.[120]

When Paris fell in June 1940, the U.S. film industry in France collapsed and many American film representatives fled the country. On April 12, 1941, the Nazis seized all American film offices in France.[121] As European markets crumbled, Warner Bros. resolved to continue production at Teddington, whereas MGM, Twentieth Century–Fox, Paramount, and RKO rapidly put an end to all overseas ventures. The irony of the situation was not lost on Harry and Jack Warner—the last studios out of Nazi Germany were the first to abandon Great Britain.[122] The brothers intended to continue producing films at Teddington and purchased a large share of the United Kingdom's Maxwell Theatre chain.[123] Production there continued the best it could until July of 1944, when a V-2 rocket destroyed the studio and killed Jack Warner's friend and former in-law Doc Salomon.[124]

Wartime reality inspired the studio to look backward for themes to remind viewers about the importance of vigilance and solidarity. In 1940 the studio released *The Fighting 69th,* loosely based on the famous Irish-American unit that fought in World War I's Meuse-Argonne offensive. The film starred James Cagney as a tough Brooklyn punk who withers under fire, causing the deaths of some his fellow combatants. Pat O'Brien dons his priest's collar once again and acts as Cagney's counselor-confessor. Convinced that he could overcome his cowardice, Cagney returns to the front lines, throws himself on a grenade, and saves his detachment.[125]

Though the film may have lacked credibility, the snappy dialogue and realistic battle sequences made it a box-office hit. The chemistry between Cagney and O'Brien moved the plot along and allowed the chaplain to pontificate upon the special merits of American life, democracy, and freedom. Cagney ultimately became a martyr for all who enjoyed the fruits of democracy. Even cowards, the film argued, could find redemption and achieve true heroism because of the intrinsic values associated with Americanism. It was no accident that the film was shot and released in 1940, for Warner Bros. was at war whether or not the rest of the country followed suit.[126] Daniel J. Leab argues that the message of the film was muddled and tried to pacify both isolationists and interventionists.[127]

In February of 1940 the studio released *Dr. Ehrlich's Magic Bullet,* ostensibly about the scientist who created Salvorsan, the first workable cure for syphilis. Screenwriter Norman Burnside and German expatriate producer Henry Blanke saw in Ehrlich's story a potential anti-Nazi cautionary tale. It was Burnside's idea to develop an anti-Nazi film using Ehrlich because "he happened to be a great humanitarian and a German Jew."[128] The message was clear: the Nazi pogrom deprived the world of people whose talents could change life for the better. By persecuting the Jews, the Nazis marched backward toward the superstition, fear, and privations of the Middle Ages. Burnside wrote producer Blanke explaining how Ehrlich's story could be used to fight Nazism and criticized Hollywood moguls who refused to face facts:

> Continued unemployment, continued unrest, continued Nazi propaganda, continued Ford-financed Coughlin propaganda are nudging the American masses toward the pit of fascism and anti-Semitism in its sadistic stages. . . . Nazi hooligans in the streets were slugging rabbis and women and children. *And the Jewish movie producers for the most part hid their heads like ostriches.* . . . There isn't a man or woman alive that isn't afraid of syphilis— and let them know that a little Kike named Ehrlich tamed the scourge— and maybe they can persuade their hoodlum friends to keep their fists off Ehrlich's co-religionists—in spite of the political Spanish Fly spat out by Coughlin, Winrod, Ford and others.[129]

Wanting to capitalize on the Warner Bros. reputation for social conscience, Burnside saw the Ehrlich biopic as an opportunity to make a strong moral stand against anti-Semitism. Unfortunately, Hal Wallis did not share his passion and ordered the Jewishness of the film toned down.[130] Infuriated, Burnside blamed cowriter John Huston for the changes instead of Hal Wallis.

One of the most passionate films the studio produced arguing for aid to Britain was the Errol Flynn swashbuckler *The Sea Hawk* (1940), written by Howard Koch and Seton I. Miller. John Huston secured a job in Hollywood for his friend Howard Koch after the splash he made in scripting the famous Orson Welles Mercury Theatre *War of the World* broadcast of 1938. Ostensibly a film about the defeat of the Spanish Armada, *The Sea Hawk* stressed that England was a tiny island nation under siege by a larger, more belligerent, totalitarian state. King Philip's Spain mirrored

Nazi Germany, and critics recognized the parallels. The attack of the Armada was no different from the Nazi blitz, and as a critic for the *New York World Telegram* observed:

> the authors have written in to [*sic*] the character of King Phillip [*sic*] of Spain an arrogant Hitlerism and a determination that the Spanish conquest will cease only when the entire world is under his domination.[131]

Film historian Christine Ann Colgan argued, however, that contemporary film critics missed a more subtle point in screenwriter Koch's depiction of fascism. The small English vessels sail under the power of the wind, whereas the Spanish galleons depend upon galley slaves chained to oars; therefore, totalitarianism equaled slavery and England represented the last bastion of freedom in Europe.[132]

Warner Bros. also employed Bryan Foy's B-Unit in their fight against Nazism. One of the most successful offerings centered on the Brass Bancroft secret agent series starring Ronald Reagan. One installment, *Murder in the Air,* "favorably portrayed the young House Committee on Un-American Activities, warned of internal subversion from spies and saboteurs, and contained veiled criticism of those who would hinder American preparedness."[133] Unspecified spies who use phrases reminiscent of those that fascists used in *Black Legion* and *Confessions of a Nazi Spy*—"100 percent Americanism" and "America for Americans"—steal a U.S. secret weapon intended for peace.[134] The "Inertia Projector" emits something like the electromagnetic pulse associated with a nuclear explosion, which renders all motorized and electrical equipment powerless. America intends to use it as a defensive weapon, so Bancroft pursues the evil thieves to prevent its being used offensively. Lobby cards promoting the film depicted Brass Bancroft with Charles Lindbergh, in an effort to sell the film's patriotic message.[135] As a peculiar irony, Lindbergh, perhaps more than any other American, came to represent nonintervention to the nation and became the most visible representative of the America First movement.

In June 1940 Harry Warner called a meeting of all 3,411 studio employees and their spouses and read to them from the Nazi publication *Defilement of Race.* The monograph spelled out how the Third Reich intended to rid the world of both Jews and Christians. He reminded his employees that none of them had ever been asked what their religious affiliation was and that all faiths were respected by his company, although he professed his pride in being a Jew.[136] If Nazis took over this country,

he cautioned, one of their first targets would be the motion picture industry.[137] "Can you imagine the American motion picture industry
under the iron hand of a Goebbels?" he asked. Everyone associated with
the industry would be forced to make pictures solely for the purpose of
propaganda, and anyone who protested could expect "a concentration
camp, or worse!"[138] Harry reminded his employees that his parents came
to America to escape the same kind of persecution Hitler currently endorsed; he declared, "We don't want anybody employed by our Company
that belongs to any bunds, communistic, fascistic, or un-American organization."[139] He wanted them to know that Hitler posed a threat to
everyone, and to facilitate his employees' preparedness, he encouraged
them to join the studio's Rifle and Pistol Club and suggested they use the
studio's target range to improve their shooting skills. He asked for assistance in seeking out "fifth column" activities in Hollywood. At his own
urging, Harry's wife was not in attendance, because she feared for his life
every time he spoke publicly against the Nazis.[140] The speech was printed
up and sent to all Warner Bros. employees and distributors, FDR, the
American Legion, certain members of Congress, and Martin Dies of
HUAC.[141]

The speech earned Harry quite a bit of press, and he received a flurry
of letters praising the oration. Employee Peter Colli, in charge of distribution in Cuba, was a Christian raised by a Jewish family and a member of
the Beth Israel Temple in Havana. He considered Harry's stance courageous. "[N]o one," he wrote, "should be ashamed of being a Jew, as the
Jews *have faith* also."[142] Harry's tenacity should be emulated by others, because "you had a vision to foresee over a year ago, even before the declaration of war in Europe, all what Hitler was after."[143] The letter informed
him that *Confessions of a Nazi Spy* had been banned in Peru, Guatemala,
and Costa Rica. Likewise, Helen Zigmond enthusiastically supported
Harry's efforts, reminding her readers, "It is well known [that] Harry
Warner is at once a staunch American and a fervent Jew."[144]

Warner Bros. continued its policy of humanitarian aid to the civilians
in war-torn Europe. Harry personally donated $25,000 to the Interna-
tional Red Cross to purchase twenty ambulances for hospitals in Britain
and France.[145] In July of 1940 he initiated a program to rescue the children of Warner employees in Britain from the blitz. In an incredible out-
pouring of largesse, arrangements were made to transport two thousand
children to the United States, where they would be cared for in the homes
of Warner executives and employees. Not only that, but Warner Bros.

agreed to pay for their education and guaranteed all other financial needs.[146]

By December 14, 1940, Warner Bros. employees had donated $5,200 to the British Relief Fund and over five hundred items of clothing. On March 30, 1941, Harry sponsored a fund-raiser at the Sunset Bowling center that featured 104 celebrity bowling teams. The studio also raised $70,000 for the Red Cross. Abe Warner's wife donated their fifty-foot yacht, *Restless Too,* to the U.S. Navy.[147] In June 1941 Harry's daughter, Doris LeRoy, acquired a Messerschmitt downed by the RAF from the British Air Ministry. With help from the wives of Ernst Lubitsch and Milton Bren, she arranged a traveling display of the wrecked plane to raise more money for British relief; the effort garnered $72,000.[148]

By 1940 more and more Hollywood filmmakers finally cast a hostile gaze upon German expansion in Europe. By the end of that year all American studios had been forced out of the European market, as the Nazis not only controlled the German film industry but also assumed control of the highly lucrative and influential French studios. Hitler wanted Nazis to create their own films and corner their own market devoid of Hollywood's influence.[149] In 1941 Italy followed suit and banned the importation and distribution of all Hollywood films for the duration. As Mussolini slowly forced American films from the Italian market, his reasons for exclusion became more capricious. He banned all Marx Brothers films from Italy because they were "exemplars of the full flower of anti-fascist culture."[150]

Two British expatriates in America decided to make movies, drawing attention to the European Crisis—Charles Chaplin and Alfred Hitchcock. Chaplin worked furiously on a film initially titled *The Dictators,* which eventually became the interventionist classic *The Great Dictator.* Critic Frank S. Nugent reported that "although it will be a comedy, most certainly [it] is inspired by Chaplin's personal philosophy."[151] The film used humor to debunk the excesses of Hitler's Germany; the horror lurked beneath the comic facade. Hitler had stolen the Little Tramp's moustache, and Chaplin used the similarity of the Fuhrer's physiognomy to satirize him. Hitler and Mussolini were caricatured as "Hynkel, the Phooey of Tomania" and "Benzino Napolini, Il Digaditch of Bacteria."[152] As in the Three Stooges *Confusions of a Nutzy Spy,* Hynkel's symbol was the Double Cross. The film marked a clear break with Chaplin's oeuvre because it ended with a soliloquy by the barber impersonating the Phooey, abruptly shattering both the silence and the humor of the film. Critics disagreed about his intentions. Some, such as the members of the Nye-Clark sub-committee on propaganda in motion pictures, argued that the film was warmongering interventionism, while others said that it was an appeal for peace.[153]

British director Alfred Hitchcock emigrated to the United States in 1939 at the behest of producer David O. Selznick. As tensions worsened abroad, he feared that he would be regarded a deserter back home.[154] Wanting to do his part in support of his country, Hitchcock produced a film version of journalist Vincent Sheean's memoir *Personal History*.[155] As the script of *Foreign Correspondent* progressed, so did Hitler's advance across Europe. The script underwent continual revisions to make it more relevant, and by the time it was distributed to movie theaters, the Battle of Britain had begun.

The main character, Johnny Jones, is a brash but naive know-it-all American reporter who slowly recognizes the threat of Nazism. His characterization purposely reflected the style of CBS correspondent Edward R. Murrow, who broadcast harrowing reports from London during the blitz. By the film's end Jones not only appreciates the tenacity of the British people but tries to convince his U.S. editor that Hitler threatens everyone, saying: "You don't keep out of war just by being peaceful while other people are slowly digging away at the ground under your feet. That's not how you keep out of a war. That's how you lose a war."[156] Hitchcock made the connection to Edward R. Murrow more concrete in the last sequence of the film. Broadcasting from a blacked-out London in the midst of an air raid, he informs his listeners:

> Hello, America. I have been watching a part of the world being blown to pieces. A part of the world as nice as Vermont and Ohio, Virginia, California and Illinois, lies ripped up and bleeding like a steer in a slaughter house. . . . You can hear the bombs falling now; falling on the streets, cafes, and homes. . . . It feels like all the lights are out everywhere except America. Keep those lights burning there. Cover them with steel, ring them with guns. Build a canopy of battleships and bombing planes around them. Hello, America. Hang onto your lights. They're the only lights left in the world.[157]

Jones's broadcast is loaded with allusions that a 1940 audience would understand. When World War I erupted, Lord Acton said that "[t]he lights have gone out all over Europe," and the dogs of war were unleashed once more. The situation in 1940 proved different, however, for the lights still blazed in the United States, which should prepare itself for war while at the same time aiding its allies. Hitchcock clearly was asking audiences to aid Britain in its hour of need.

Not everyone was convinced that Britain would prevail against the Nazis, including the American ambassador to England Joseph P. Kennedy. He fully believed that Britain would lose the war; therefore, America, and by extrapolation, the film industry, should prepare to deal diplomatically and economically with Nazi Germany. His jaundiced views later cost him his ambassadorship.[158]

Soon after the release of the Hitchcock film, the studio announced its plans to make a movie about Sergeant York, a film that would turn out to be their most aggressive call to arms in the prewar era. By looking back to World War I and the greatest American hero of the war, the studio could draw direct parallels with current events and drive home the point that Germany and aggressive expansion remained a threat to the globe. Historian Michael T. Isenberg noted that the quasi-historical World War I films produced during the late Depression were

> rekindling the democratic fires of a new generation . . . [and arguing] that democracy was the only political and social system fit for all the peoples of the world.[159]

Warner Bros. wanted to reassure its audience that the Great War had not been in vain and that Americans could not turn a blind eye to the current conflagration. The other six majors, however, continued to waffle concerning the Nazis. In 1940 MGM and Paramount both trumpeted their intentions to make films about Nazism, but they canceled the productions of *I Had a Comrade, Heroes, Invasion,* and *Heil America.*

The timing for a film about Alvin C. York was propitious and topical. York's humble beginnings, his Christian pacifism, and his patriotism held interest for Americans of all walks of life. To understand the difficulties of bringing his story and the interventionist message to the screen, a case study of the creation of the film should prove instructive.

4

A Change of Heart
Alvin York and the Movie Sergeant York

Although the production of *Black Legion* and *Confessions of a Nazi Spy* had produced conflict and controversy both in and outside of the studio, that paled in comparison to the initial furor that came about when Warner Bros. announced that it would produce a film based on the wartime exploits of Sgt. Alvin C. York. Known as the greatest hero of World War I, York avoided profiting from his war record before 1939.[1] On October 8, 1918, Cpl. Alvin Cullum York and sixteen other men under the command of sergeants Harry Parsons and Bernard Early were dispatched to capture the Decauville railroad near Chatel-Chehery in the Meuse-Argonne. After a brief firefight (nine Americans died in the melee), the confused Germans surrendered to what they believed to be a superior force. In all 132 Germans were captured and delivered to U.S. Army headquarters by the seven survivors led by Corporal York. The army singled out York as *the* hero of World War I and presented him with the Congressional Medal of Honor, overlooking the seven others who participated.

Wooed by Hollywood, Broadway, and various sponsors who wanted his endorsement, York turned his back on quick and certain fortune in 1919 and went home to Tennessee to resume private life. According to a personal friend of Alvin York, Guy Williams, a woman in New York offered York fifty thousand dollars to have sex with her in hopes of siring a baby. York turned her down flat, saying, "I've got me a purty little woman back home in the hills."[2]

One could argue, as David D. Lee and J. W. Williamson have, that York's refusal to capitalize on his fame was a well-orchestrated fiction. He used his name to promote his vision for education in Tennessee and was a popular public speaker throughout the 1920s. He used his fame to curry favor with state and federal politicians. To better understand the difficulties surrounding the production of *Sergeant York* and Alvin York's eventual decision to allow a film of his life to be made, an investigation of his life between 1919 and 1939 is necessary.[3]

When the United States declared war on Germany on April 6, 1917, the Wilson administration issued the first wartime conscription act since the Civil War. York received his draft notice on June 5, 1917, and reluctantly reported to Camp Gordon, Georgia, in November. A profoundly religious man, York applied for conscientious objector status at the behest of his pastor, Rosier Pile, but the Fentress County Draft Board denied his request because it refused to recognize the Church of Christ in Christian Union (C.O.C.I.C.U.) as a legitimate Christian denomination.[4] (The federal government deferred to local draft boards concerning exemptions.) Another possible reason for York's failure to receive C.O. status was that as far as the local elites were concerned, York came "from the wrong side of the tracks."[5] It is significant to note that the C.O.C.I.C.U. condemned movies as a sin. According to family folklore, York had seen only one film in his life, and that was while on his honeymoon in Nashville in 1920. York, who took his mother and his pastor with him, accompanied Gov. Albert H. Roberts to see a movie despite Pastor Pile's admonitions. This claim is dubious at best, but is taken as gospel by the family.

As a conscientious objector drafted at age thirty, York typified the underprivileged, undereducated conscript who traveled to France to "keep the world safe for democracy." Possessing only a third-grade education— a subscription-school education that amounted to only nine months' total schooling—York discovered a larger world beyond his ken. Before leaving for Camp Gordon, Georgia, and beyond, York's world consisted of the area within a one-hundred-mile radius of his home. The war introduced him to a mechanized industrial world, and his prolonged exposure to it showed him the important contributions industrialization could make for his friends and relatives at home. Literally a stranger in a strange land, York recognized that he was ill equipped to fully understand or appreciate his foreign surroundings. Initially, he immersed himself in the Bible, hoping that his simple religious faith would see him through, but by the war's end he longed for something more than just his faith.

Yearning to return home and wed his sweetheart, Gracie Williams, and get on with his life, York was taken aback by his New York City hero's welcome—the ticker tape parades, being fawned over by people seeking endorsements, and the like. He prevailed upon Tennessee Congressman and future Secretary of State Cordell Hull to facilitate a hasty retreat to his home. Once he was back in Tennessee, other surprises awaited him. Although the Rotary Club of Nashville, in conjunction with other Tennessee clubs, wanted to present York with a home and a farm, unfortunately not enough money was raised, and they gave him an unfinished home and saddled him with a healthy mortgage to boot. As late as 1922, the deed remained in the hands of the Nashville Rotary Club.[6]

York, who held the office of second elder in his local congregation, fought reluctantly in the Great War and, once it ended, resumed his pacifist stance, often speaking publicly against war. The laconic hero even conducted impromptu prayer meetings on his troopship as it returned home.[7] His heartfelt belief that war represented moral evil never wavered until he began his association with Jesse Lasky and Warner Bros. In a 1937 interview with *Nashville Banner* reporter James Metcalfe, York not only condemned war but even questioned America's involvement in World War I.[8] Like many other Americans who had witnessed the broken lives of veterans, York believed that his country had committed a grave mistake by declaring war.[9] In a Gallup Poll taken in 1937, more than 60 percent of the respondents surveyed believed, like Sergeant York, that the United States had no business getting involved in World War I.

Largely unknown to most Americans was the fact that York returned to America with a single vision. He wanted to provide a practical educational opportunity for the mountain children of Tennessee. Understanding that to prosper in the modern world, people needed an education, York sought to drag Fentress County into the twentieth century. Thousands of like-minded veterans returned from France with similar sentiments, and as a result, college enrollments shot up immediately after the war.[10] Painfully aware of his intellectual limitations, York dedicated the remainder of his life to the improvement of education. York Agricultural and Industrial Institute, north of Jamestown, stands as a monument to his embattled dream.[11]

The very thought of this barely literate veteran launching a campaign for education was fraught with difficulty, for it struck most Fentress County political and social leaders as ludicrous to think that York could serve as an administrator of a school. Because he had no background in education or administration, his intentions, though noble, seemed absurd; his ability to evaluate instructors, curricula, textbooks, and administration was nearly nonexistent. Though regarded as a hero across America, at home York was seen as a threat to the county's Republican party political structure. Celebrity status made it possible for the sergeant to express his *desire* for education to the world at large but gave him little

Fig. 3. After returning home, the most popular hero of World War I, Alvin C. York, turned his back on fame in an attempt to improve education in his native Tennessee. Courtesy of the Alvin C. York collection.

clout when dealing with the old guard Fentress County elite. York came from a poor, isolated community in Fentress County, and local politicians suffered some embarrassment when one they regarded as beneath them socially returned a national hero. Many remembered him as a drunken hell-raiser turned religious fanatic; to add insult to injury, York supported the Democratic party in a staunchly Republican county. They had no intention of including him in the administration of county affairs.

As early as 1920 York formed a nonprofit organization, the York Foundation, and embarked on a series of speaking tours on its behalf. Believing he was on a mission from God, York turned down hundreds of endorsements that capitalized on his war-hero image and tried to make his dream for a "heap o' larnin'" a reality.[12] Just as he had no experience as an educator or administrator, he had no background as a public speaker or in fund-raising. Undaunted, he intended to provide the boys and girls of his native region with "liberating influences and educational advantages which were denied me."[13] His vision was not limited to the education of children from the remote Cumberland plateau region; he wanted to include interested adults as well. A pamphlet issued in 1926 stated:

> [I]t will be the aim of the Institute to afford an opportunity for mature men and women to get an education, regardless of how retarded they may be, and also to send out only such graduates as are prepared to succeed in the work they have chosen to do.[14]

As genuine as York's mission was to the reporters of the *New York Times* and other national media organs, in Tennessee his scheme met raised eyebrows, guffaws, and outright hostility. Parents eking out a living in rural areas needed their children to work on the farms, since few families could afford hired labor. They depended on their children to help plant crops, milk cows, slop hogs, and carry out all the other daily chores that made up farm life. York's proposal for a mandatory eight-month school term angered a host of local farmers, who perceived education as frivolous, impractical, and a waste of hard-earned money.[15]

York's progressive vision fell short of extending that education to African Americans and immigrants. In his pleas for contributions, he consciously endorsed and perpetuated mountain stereotypes. Passing out photos of barefoot, rail-thin kids standing in front of rude cabins, he shamelessly played on people's sympathies. York's deficiencies as a speaker, coupled with his notoriety for showing up late at engagements, eventually took its toll. As word spread that York refused to tell war stories, his popularity diminished. By 1925 the grinding life on the road had garnered only twelve thousand dollars. Twenty-five thousand more had been pledged but went uncollected.[16]

Portraying Tennessee's Upper Cumberland as a haven for white purity was a constant theme in York's pleas for contributions. In 1927 he said that scientists claimed no purer strain of Anglo-Saxon blood existed anywhere in the United States than in York's Tennessee hills. "We have practically no coloured people down there. (We work them too hard and they keep on a going.) We have practically no foreigners"; therefore, his people represented the quintessential Americans.[17] Invoking nativist sentiment, York argued that his region deserved the fruits of education because it was unspoiled and could cultivate and perpetuate religio-patriotic ideals that seemed to be on the wane in middle America.

In an act that would define future behavior, York evaded local politics and took his case to the state legislature. In March of 1925 York asked a joint session of the General Assembly to draft legislation establishing a mountain school near Jamestown.[18] His local ally and representative from Fentress County, George L. Stockton, proposed House Bill 993, requesting a bond issue of $50,000 to undertake the construction of York Agricultural Institute, but lawmakers in the house defeated it by a vote of 41–37. Undeterred, Stockton modified the bill, proposing that Fentress County first float a $75,000 bond issue; once the county raised the funds, the state would then grant the school $50,000. Governor Austin Peay signed the modified bill into law on April 12, 1925.[19]

Floating a bond issue on the Fentress County level did not signal the end of the fight, nor did it ensure the commencement of construction. Since Fentress County bore the burden of raising the initial funds, and since the Republican vanguard, led by O. O. Frogge and W. L. Wright, despised York, they engineered a power play meant to squeeze him out of the picture. Frogge and Wright proposed that Fentress County establish a Board of Trust to administer the funds raised by the bond issue. They created an advisory committee largely composed of York's enemies, whose duties were both to oversee the state-sponsored York Foundation and to stymie the sergeant's efforts.[20]

The preexisting York Foundation, however, had already drafted plans and proposed a site for the school before its endorsement by the legislature and the formation of the Fentress County Board of Trust. The foundation intended to build the school on the old County Poor House site one mile north of Jamestown on newly constructed Highway 127.[21] The Board of Trust, which controlled the funds, proposed a southern location closer to Jamestown. Wright and Frogge wanted the school closer to their own land holdings, believing the school would spawn subsidiary business from which they could profit handsomely. The Board of Trust and the York Foundation came to loggerheads, causing York to overreact and resign in a fit of pique on March 29, 1926.[22]

York made his resignation a media event. Venting his spleen, he accused Wright and Frogge of trying to line their own pockets while politicizing something that could profit the entire county. Petty actions by all participants delayed the school's creation and jeopardized the future of the county's youth.

Taking the twelve thousand dollars he had raised on speaking tours, York called a national press conference and held his own ground-breaking ceremony on May 8, 1926, at the Poor House site before a crowd of two thousand clamoring sympathizers, though Governor Peay was conspicuous by his absence.[23] Although York's reckless action endeared him to many Americans, it weakened his position with county authorities. As a show of good faith, York opened the old Poor House in 1926 and began holding classes with the support of empathetic local educators.

On Sunday, January 16, 1927, the *Nashville Banner* announced the launching of a one-hundred-thousand-dollar fund-raising effort to ensure the school's completion. Supported by the recently organized American Legion, each post promised that it would deliver one dollar per member. University of Tennessee president H. A. Morgan pledged his unwavering support as well.[24]

York's decision to go national with what many considered a local controversy added more fuel to the flames. Irate members of the Board of Trust launched a counterattack and were intent on humiliating him. They decided that York, by holding classes in the old Poor House, was guilty of trespassing since they held the deed for the property. To investigate the matter, they employed attorney L. A. Ligon, who rendered York's action as "unwarranted, unauthorized and illegal."[25] The County Board of Education, headed—not surprisingly—by O. O. Frogge, served York notice to vacate the premises by July 11, 1927, or be forcibly evicted. At 5:15 on Saturday, July 9, 1927, York received the summons.[26] York referred the matter to his attorney, focused his attention upon raising money, rallied supporters to his side, and hit the road again. The 1927 speaking tour deviated radically from his earlier forays. For the first time, York discussed his war record to ensure that he would play to packed houses.[27]

Encountering foreigners and people of other faiths for the first time, York said, his military service had opened his eyes to an entirely new and exciting world. As he sailed to Europe it occurred to him that he "was beginning to understand them there Greeks and Italians and jews [sic]. And they were turning out to be right smart soldiers and pretty good pals too."[28] Dramatically recounting his famous exploit, he told listeners that he had survived the firefight only because of his inerrant belief that God would not allow him to be harmed. He recognized the recent trans-Atlantic flight of Charles Lindbergh, with whom he felt a true kinship.

I felt like Lindy feels today about selling out and I jest couldn't and didn't do it. And let me right here and now salute the flying Colonel. I just love and admire that boy. He's a real hero and a real American.[29]

As he concluded, York said he had survived war and achieved fame because he had been chosen to perform a specific mission:

> When I went out into that big outside world I . . . realized how un-educated I was and what a terrible handicap it were. I was called to lead my people toward . . . the chance to get a sensible modern education. . . . [F]or years I have been planning and fighting to build the school. And it has been a terrible fight. A much more terrible fight than the one that I fought in the war. . . . And so I hed [*sic*] into the frontline and fight another fight. And I couldn't use the old rifle or Colt automatic this time. And it has been a long hard fight.[30]

York's abilities as a speaker had greatly improved, and by finally giving the public what it wanted—exciting war stories—he played to packed houses everywhere. Unfortunately, the speaking tour proved lucrative and costly at the same time. Though pledges came in supporting the mission, York's political capital at home continued to plummet.

The speaking tour proved detrimental in another way; York's decisive action put the construction of the school under way, but the use of private funds raised as a result of the recent fund-raising campaign violated the 1925 legislation. York could get none of the state-proposed fifty thousand dollars, nor any of the money raised by the Fentress County bond issue without the approval of the Board of Trust—and they were in no mood to cooperate. Local papers blistered York while praising the embarrassed Wright-Frogge faction, arguing that York's reckless behavior was indicative of how he would run the school. The children of Fentress County, therefore, would be endangered by his personal ambitions.

York continued speaking engagements throughout 1927 and 1928. New Englanders provided the majority of the financial commitment as well as the greatest interest in his endeavor. On Armistice Day he spoke to a packed audience at Carnegie Hall in New York about the importance of his work and the benighted souls who stood in his way back home, comparing the Fentress County elite to a pair of mules working against each other.[31] Ironically, the appeal to outsiders, especially northern urban industrial outsiders, further alienated York's support at home.

Frazzled and disgusted, York consulted attorney W. A. Garrett for help. On July 25, 1929, Garrett sent a lengthy report to P. L. Harned, Tennessee commissioner of education, and the members of the State Board of Education with his opinion on the matter. He pointed out that the creation of the Board of Trust had been carried out without any investigation of the personalities involved and with total ignorance of Fentress County politics. He accused Frogge, Wright, and company of felonious collusion to personally profit from York's name while undermining his mission.[32] "Why," he wanted to know, did the State Board of Education, which had legislative oversight "let this same crowd who have harassed and annoyed Sgt. York from the beginning continue to do so." He considered their actions a moral outrage, a burden to the people of Fentress County, and an embarrassment to the entire state of Tennessee.

> Again we ask what was the cause of this. . . . Institute being organized, established and now partially built? [W]as it for the purpose of permitting some unscrupulous would-be politicians, schemers and grafters in Fentress County to make money?[33]

On August 6, 1929, members of the Board of Trust, in conjunction with like-minded local authorities, also petitioned the State Board of Education. York's enemies charged him with incompetence and interference with their prescribed duties as board members. The eight signers declared:

> We, the undersigned protest against the request and demand of Sgt. Alvin C. York that he be elected or employed by you as the head or in any way in the control or management of said institution believing that to do so would greatly injure the school, impede its progress, and be against the best interest of the people.[34]

Desperate, York returned to the General Assembly, asking for an amendment to the 1925 law. York won the support of a White County representative and educator, Ransom Isaiah Hutchings, who owned and operated a private "college" in western White County. Hutchings was painfully aware of the inequities inherent in Tennessee education and saw in York's dilemma an opportunity to improve the quality of basic education in the entire state.[35] Because of these efforts, the law was amended, dismantling the onerous Board of Trust. It also set a peculiar precedent by placing York Agricultural and Industrial Institute under the aegis of the State Board of Education. The end results of Hutchings's amendment were the establishment of York Institute and an enlargement of the scope of compulsory education in Tennessee. With free public education available to all Tennessee children ages six to sixteen, private academies and colleges saw their enrollment decline. Hutchings's White County college closed, a victim of its owner's vision.

Unwilling to surrender quietly, the old guard petitioned the state to ban York from any administrative position at the school. They spread baseless rumors that York intended to hire outsiders to run the school and wanted to brainwash the students with fundamentalist doctrine. The obvious truth evaded the locals, for even if York wanted the school staffed entirely by locals, who among them was qualified? After a protracted series of legal challenges, York opened the new school in the fall of 1929.[36]

The school's opening coincided with the onset of the Great Depression, and in 1931 the state ended all appropriations for bus transportation, effectively crippling the struggling institute. The very nature of the school—a mountain school where children could come for a free education—required buses. York went before the County Court and asked for help; the Court refused.[37]

On two occasions, first in 1931 and then in 1935, York secured a mortgage on his farm—received with glee by his political enemy and banker W. L. Wright—to hire drivers, buy buses, and even fund teachers' salaries. As the Depression worsened, Wright badgered York, ultimately declaring him delinquent in his business transactions, and moved to foreclose on his farm. The depth of York's genuine commitment to education was apparent in the selfless act of risking his farm and his family's security for the school's continued operation. Had it not been for his longtime friend and neighbor Susie Williams, York would have lost his farm, for she twice loaned him the money necessary to pay off his note.[38]

Far from crediting York for his selfless efforts, the state never reimbursed York for his altruism. Rather, he was criticized for his behavior, and a fact-finding investigation in 1933 resulted in York's removal from the school. The investigating committee found the school poorly run, the students unmotivated, and nepotism in abundance. York's enemies proposed that the 1927 legislation be annulled and the school turned over to Sergeant York, "to be operated by him as a private institution and supported by donations and endowments."[39] The committee recognized, however, that York was the driving force behind the school and feared its demise if he were removed from the picture. They also acknowledged that if the school were turned over to Fentress County, the situation would be no better. If the county took control, it would limit the scope of the curriculum and abolish the vocational training, which York considered the most important aspect of the school.[40]

Some accusations were legitimate, particularly the charge of nepotism. As president of the school, York surrounded himself with loyal friends and family members who rarely, if ever, questioned his motives. Although not corrupt, they were ill trained to run a school, and their collective incompetence generated inexcusable waste. Regrettably but accurately, the board noted that Alvin York, for all his good intentions, lacked the necessary talents to operate a school.[41] The State Board of Education and Governor Hill McAlister proved reluctant, however, to act on the recommendations. The 1927 legislation placed a significant degree of responsibility on the State Board of Education, which had not provided enough oversight. If it had, many of the problems attested to by the investigating committee could have been circumvented.

York contended, perhaps rightly, that some of the moneys the factfinders carped about came from his own pocket, not from taxes. He reminded the State Board that it had repeatedly deprived the school of necessary operating funds and that the institute had likewise received absolutely no support from the county. The matter came to a head in 1935, when York tried to fire principal H. C. "High Compression" Brier, who refused to give York's brother, Jim York, a school janitor, a pay raise.[42]

To York's chagrin, the State Board backed Brier, so he once again dramatically resigned his position as president. This proved to be a severe miscalculation. York, presuming an outcome like the one in 1927, felt certain that his resignation would bring the State Board to its knees, ensuring the sacking of Brier, a raise for his brother, and his reappointment as president. Instead, they appointed the chairman of the fact-finding team, Robert L. Forrester, as interim president for the remainder of the 1935–36 school year.[43]

On May 8, 1936, a harassed, embittered H. C. Brier tendered his resignation. The State Board responded by granting him an official vote of confidence and then amended the president's job description. The new definition combined the duties of principal with those of business manager. More importantly, it required that the school's president have at least a bachelor's degree, a decision that effectively precluded the possibility of York's ever again being the school's president. In a move toward soothing ruffled feelings, they named York "president emeritus," a title that recognized him as the school's founder but stripped him of any power. Although York made a nominal protest, he realized that his control over the school had ended.[44]

In spite of his loss of position, York continued to promote York Institute, raising private donations for expansion of the school facilities and, when possible, contributing his own money. The irony of York's ouster was that his removal from the school secured its future. With the administration firmly under the control of the State Board of Education, the disputes between York and Fentress County's old guard vanished. Legislation forced the state to have a vested interest in its success, and York's dream of free education for Tennessee's mountain children at last became a reality.[45]

The nature of the United States changed over the course of York's struggle to provide better education for Tennesseans. His campaign began during the flush time of the 1920s, and he fought valiantly to keep the school open as funds dried up during the Depression. As the socioeconomic patterns of the country changed, York shifted political parties. Staunchly antiwet and anti-intervention, York briefly joined the Republican party because FDR promised an end to prohibition if elected president, which alienated York. In 1936 the temperance issue was wounded but not dead, and agents for the reinstitution of the Volstead Act asked York to run for vice president on the Prohibition Party ticket. By the mid-1930s war again seemed imminent, and York, like most Americans, once again embraced pacifism, advocating rigid isolationism. The fear of war led many American legislators, authors, and journalists to remind the public about the disappointments World War I had caused, and such claims created an enormous backlash.[46]

During his battles in Fentress County, York had receded from the national spotlight; he focused his waning political aspirations on the state rather than the local level. Courted by various politicians for his endorsement, York was relegated to an obligatory photo opportunity for aspiring legislators. By the mid-1930s he was practically persona non grata in his own county, so York directed most of his attention to his church, his family, and his farm.

In 1935 York delivered a sermon entitled "Christian Cure for Strife," which argued that vigilant Christians should ignore the potential war in Europe at all costs. Recalling his career as a soldier, York renounced

America's involvement in World War I and echoed the sentiments of North Dakota senator Gerald Nye, when he argued that it was greedy industrialists who enlisted "mothers' boys to help carry out their thirst for life's blood . . . sowing a crop of hatred and malice that will produce of its [own] kind."[47] He implored his listeners:

> [M]an tries to content himself with the thought that war can be stopped by war. . . . When we count up just a little, we find that it [World War I] cost us about 50,000 of the young men of our nation . . . [and] billions of dollars. . . . What did we learn? That war was stopped? NO! [F]or it looms before us today.[48]

With another war brewing, York was enlisted to help in the cause of peace. He joined the Emergency Peace Campaign, led by the eminent churchman Harry Emerson Fosdick, in 1937 and spoke out against American intervention. The Spanish Civil war had no bearing at all on life in the United States and should not be the country's concern, nor should Japanese aggression in China. Speaking on behalf of the Emergency Peace Campaign in Raleigh, North Carolina, in April of 1937, York said the United States should "kiss its old war debts goodbye and stay at home and mind its own business."[49] Though he called for an end to trade with the belligerent Japanese, he predicted:

> I'm a little bit uneasy just now; there's an awful rush for scrap iron over my way. The scrap iron is going to Japan and it could come back in a different form. I'm not saying it will, but it could.[50]

From 1937 to 1939 York spoke often for the Emergency Peace Campaign, arguing that the United States had gained nothing but heartache, political instability, and global depression from the last war. Another war meant potentially greater disaster. As the storm clouds gathered, York spoke more frequently and more adamantly in favor of isolation. America should count itself fortunate, even blessed by God, that two oceans separated it from conflicts in Europe and Asia.

On July 1, 1939, York addressed a Christian rally in San Francisco, urging his listeners not to be alarmed or discouraged by events in Europe but rather to focus attention on this country. The church and the home represented the cornerstones of world peace, and if Americans invested their energies in the success of those two institutions, then the United States would set an example for the rest of the world to emulate and peace would reign throughout. In a revisionist view of America's violent history, he asserted that mothers, especially, played a critical role in the current time of crisis.

> [M]y mother taught me to pray around the old fashioned family altar. She taught me to love peace and hate war. I don't like war now, nor never [*sic*] did like it, because *it* is not the American way to settle trouble.[51]

According to York, then, true Americans were pacific, not belligerent, and isolationists, not interventionists. To promote peace York called for the inclusion of Christian principles in education.[52]

While in San Francisco, York attended the Golden Gate Exposition at Treasure Island. Asked to speak about the success of New Deal programs in Tennessee, he seized the opportunity to promote nonintervention in Europe:

> [A]s I looked at these marvelous exhibits I have been haunted by one thought—all of this would stop if we had to go to war. Worse than that we might even be thrown back a decade or so. . . . If war comes the hands that today are inventing a better light would be forced to assist in pulling down the shades of darkness.[53]

Tennessee had suffered the ravages of war firsthand during the Civil War, he reminded his listeners, and had been slow to recover, lagging behind the rest of the country for decades. Therefore, Tennessee "is a state that believes in the George Washington Doctrine: 'Stay out of foreign entanglements.'"[54]

On Saturday, July 22, 1939, York and Tennessee governor Prentice Cooper spoke at the New York World's Fair Tennessee Day celebration. Using the opportunity to reinforce his position on nonintervention, York took the podium about 2:30 in the afternoon, wet with sweat and short of breath, and spoke about Tennessee's famed Long hunters.[55] While celebrating their frontier spirit, York noted that their attentions had been focused on events at home, not abroad. The frontiersmen created a new life for themselves out of the wilderness, never looking back to the jaded, effete world of Europe. "We in the Tennessee Mountains are not transplanted Europeans; every fibre of our body is American, and every emotion in our heart is American."[56] Clearly, if America wanted continued success, it must look within the confines of its own borders and not be concerned with events overseas.

At the same time, the threat of war had rekindled the interest of some filmmakers, most notably Jesse L. Lasky, into reviving the story of York's wartime heroism. Lasky, having witnessed the famous New York reception of the hero from his eighth-floor office window in May of 1919, had wanted then to tell York's story. Several other studios found interest in York's saga in 1919, but only Jesse Lasky of Famous Players–Paramount (later associated with Twentieth Century–Fox, and finally Warner Bros.) had persistently pursued him since then.[57] In the late 1930s the world once again appeared on the verge of war, and the official stance of the U.S. government was reminiscent of York's initial attitude toward World War I. America (in 1939) and York (in 1917) both had to be convinced that war was not only justifiable, but sometimes necessary.

When York at last relented, he announced that the film would "be a true picture of my life . . . my contributions since the war. It won't be a war picture. I don't like war pictures."[58] He continued:

> Actually it's going to be more a story of our people up there in the mountains than it is of me. It's going to show how education has been taken into the mountains and how we're training our young people now to be good citizens. My part in the war should be presented only as an incident in my life.[59]

Yet the film that bears his name definitely *is* a war picture. The original screenplay presented the war as an epiphany for York that forced him to recognize his own inadequacies but fulfilled his wish to improve himself and his homeland. Unfortunately, that film has not yet been made. The movie that arrived in theaters in July of 1941 not only signaled a profound change in York's pacifism but also sounded the clarion for American involvement in World War II.

York's battlefield feat typified that of the nineteenth-century American hero. He appeared larger than life and was most often compared to three peculiarly American icons: Daniel Boone, Davy Crockett, and Abraham Lincoln. Growing up in a quasi-frontier existence tucked away in a remote Tennessee backwater unscathed by industrialized America, York was born and raised in a log cabin near the Tennessee-Kentucky border—a region that bore no resemblance to the breakneck bustle of New York, Chicago, or Los Angeles. As a result York seemed to belong to a more idyllic time. As late as 1917, he hunted squirrel, raccoon, quail, wild boar, and deer with a muzzle-loader. York's life caught fire in the American imagination not because of who he was but because of what he symbolized: a humble, self-reliant, God-fearing, taciturn patriot who slowly moved to action only when sufficiently provoked and then adamantly refused to capitalize on his fame. George Patullo, the *Saturday Evening Post* reporter who broke the story, focused on the religio-patriotic nature of York's feat. He titled his piece "The Second Elder Gives Battle," referring to York's status in his home congregation.[60]

In 1916 Jesse L. Lasky and his partner Adolf Zukor created Paramount, one of the first viable studios in Hollywood. Both men began in the theater, later branching out into film. Although the theater was Lasky's first love, the mogul exuberantly embraced filmmaking. Director Rouben Mamoulian reminisced, "The greatest aspect of Jesse Lasky was his tremendous enthusiasm . . . he was afire with enthusiasm."[61] A genuinely nice man, he was described by one screenwriter as

> in no way resembl[ing] the stock Hollywood tycoon. He was a gentle, considerate man, blessed with a gracious wife . . . [,] endowed with an almost childlike enthusiasm for his work, and cursed with a total lack of either interest or expertise in financial matters.[62]

His lack of business acumen created a host of problems for the normally ebullient producer. Eugene Zukor, Adolf's son, remembered Lasky as an inveterate dreamer who preferred the company of creative people to that of businessmen.[63] Lasky's chief concern centered on story and talent, and he aggressively pursued and cultivated what he considered quality stories that could be performed by quality actors. Zukor, on the other hand, was an absolutely ruthless businessman who acted as the partnership's financial brains.[64]

Lasky served as Paramount's chief creative producer until 1931, when the Great Depression caused a massive financial overhaul of the studio. Not only was Lasky dismissed, but he also lost his entire personal fortune, including his home.[65] From 1931 to 1938 he bounced from studio to studio in search of employment and even dabbled, unsuccessfully, in radio. Lasky needed a hit movie to revitalize his career because Hollywood, noted for its short memory, considered a person only as good as his most recent picture. So, Lasky remembered, "I began hunting for a story or theme important enough to serve for my second 'comeback' in the picture business."[66]

When Paramount executives called for Lasky's ouster, Harry Warner defended him. Largesse on the part of his competitor/friend could account for Lasky's later affiliation with Warner Bros. Harry even bought the home Lasky lost as a gesture of friendship and loaned Lasky $250,000 to pay off some of his debts. Warner and Lasky enjoyed a long friendship. Both had been involved in the early days of film and had witnessed its evolution. Another link in the chain that held them together was the fact that Lasky introduced the Warner brothers to the man who was to become one of the studio's most successful directors *and* Harry's son-in-law, Mervyn LeRoy, Lasky's nephew.[67]

An RKO executive rekindled his interest in Sergeant York, and Lasky turned once again to the possibility of a biopic based on the mountain hero. The sincerity of Lasky's belief in a movie about York was evident, for since York's return from France in 1919, he had steadily compiled an extensive dossier on the sergeant. In 1938 Lasky turned his notes, the two published biographies of York, the *Liberty* magazine serialization of the sergeant's war diary, and a scrapbook of press clippings over to Gene Fowler, a journalist and screenwriter at Fox Pictures.[68] After Fowler wrote a rough treatment, he and Lasky made their first trip to Tennessee, but York remained uninterested, and there is no available evidence to suggest that York even read Fowler's scenario.[69]

According to the *Sergeant York* press kit, the German invasion of Poland in 1939 rekindled Lasky's interest in a York picture. This explanation is dubious because Lasky contacted York well before the incursion. In his autobiography Lasky stated that York refused to reply to his overtures by mail or by telegram. According to interviews conducted with family members and friends who witnessed Lasky's first trip to Tennessee, York remained uninterested. Guy Williams said that York met Lasky on the front porch of his Pall Mall home, looked the short, sweating man over, and said: "You that movie feller ain't ye? Ain't interested." York then fed Lasky and sent him on his way.[70]

The film community in 1939, perhaps more than any other segment of American society, was anticipating the evil of Adolf Hitler. Anti-Nazi German, Hungarian, Polish, and Jewish artists, musicians, writers, and intellectuals fled to the United States, and by 1939 the list of prominent European expatriates in America included Bertolt Brecht, Theodor Adorno, Heinrich Mann, Thomas Mann, Peter Lorre, Fritz Lang, Marlene Dietrich, Luise Rainier, Billy Wilder, Lion Feuchtwanger, Salka Viertel, Hannah Arendt, Herbert Marcuse, Max Steiner, Bruno Frank, Erich Maria Remarque, Emil Ludwig, Max Horkheimer, Erich Korngold, William Dieterle, Albert Basserman, Franz Werfel, and many more.[71]

Some members of the film community favored American involvement in World War II, though at the same time they were painfully aware that they could not outwardly advocate U.S. intervention.[72]

As the world's political climate deteriorated, York's saga appealed to Lasky even more, and between October of 1939 and March of 1940 he continued undaunted to plot the movie's story line. Lasky wrote, "Germany was again on the loose and President Roosevelt had proclaimed a limited national emergency." So he appealed to York's sense of patriotism to sell his hopes for the movie.[73] A pious, peaceful man, York had fought his country's enemy only after great deliberation and had to be convinced that war was sometimes necessary. His personal struggle in World War I found new resonance in an America at odds over the recent European war, for York personified isolationist-Christian America wrestling with its conscience over whether or not to engage itself in the current war abroad. The finished film "remythologize[d] World War I as a national crusade worthy of admiration and . . . reconcile[d] the conflict between state (patriotism) and church (morality)."[74]

As Lasky's career bottomed out in 1939, York also desperately needed money. A big-hearted but inept businessman, York consistently gave away his money to friends or strangers and rarely demanded repayment.[75] After he lost control of York Institute, he decided to establish a fundamentalist Bible school, but that soon bogged down due to repeated financial irregularities. Failure to get the new school going—which was to train young people for the ministry, to inculcate them with Christian values, and to teach them responsible citizenship—further demoralized him.[76]

Lasky made four arduous treks to Tennessee, including sojourns to York's home in Pall Mall, between the summer of 1939 and the spring of 1940. He had pitched the idea of a York picture to Fox and RKO before settling on Warner Bros. Their politics and his own personal indebtedness to Harry Warner convinced him that Warner Bros. was the logical studio to produce the film. Determined to develop the project, Lasky sought out York's friends and family and conducted interviews.[77] Perhaps the most important person he met was Guy Williams, who had been raised next door to York and knew him better than anyone else. In fact, it was Williams's mother, Susie, who had bailed York out financially on the two critical occasions when he mortgaged his farm. In fact, Margaret Wycherly's portrayal of Mother York was based on Susie Williams rather than York's mother.[78] Williams told Lasky that York's religious denomination condemned movies as a sin, and until that problem could be resolved, it would be impossible to shoot a film. He also warned the producer that once the sergeant signed the contract, he should mete out money to York on a piecemeal basis.[79]

In early February 1940, Lasky, confident that York would finally agree to a movie version of his life, leaked the story to nationally syndicated gossip columnist Louella Parsons. She anticipated the film's casting and wrote that Spencer Tracy should play the famed hero. A few months later she changed her mind, suggesting that James Cagney would make a more convincing mountaineer.[80] Other columnists believed that Henry Fonda or Raymond Massey was perfect for the part; York's personal choice of Gary Cooper was purposely kept from the press.

Lasky's personal trips to Tennessee softened the old warrior, and York grew fond "of the little fat Jew."[81] The press attended their meeting in Crossville, Tennessee, on March 9, 1940, and that face-to-face rendezvous set the stage for a series of discussions over the merits of the proposed movie. Over the course of that month, Lasky's crew followed the sergeant and his friends as they traipsed about the Upper Cumberland, and though often informal, the negotiations proved quite intense. One of the problems surrounding the negotiations stemmed from York's religious beliefs. He had to be convinced that movies were not sinful in and of themselves. He also wanted assurance that "the Devil's tool would be used to do good works."[82]

Another equally serious and related problem concerned York's contemplation of a business partnership with Jews. Tennessee's Upper Cumberland region had been practically devoid of Jews throughout its history. York, due to his insular upbringing, had always regarded Jews as untrustworthy, scheming pariahs whom he perceived as "Christ killers." The Jews, once God's chosen people, had willfully rejected His promises and so were beyond hope of salvation. In interviews York's friends and relatives frequently refer to the fact that the sergeant did business with "a bunch of Hollywood Jews." When I first interviewed Guy Williams, he took a long pull on his cigar and said, "Jesse L. Lasky. He was a Jew, you know. Short too." Lasky was the first Jew these people had ever seen, and he made a deep and positive impression on them. Most people I interviewed who met Lasky remembered him with genuine fondness. Lasky said that York prayed for guidance on the issue, and that is no doubt true. It was not a decision that York made lightly. One cannot overstate the seriousness of this perception when evaluating York's final decision to allow a movie based on his life to be filmed.

Evidence of this problem can be seen in York's private correspondence. In October of 1939, he assumed the role of director of the Cumberland Homesteads near Crossville, Tennessee. The Cumberland Homesteads, part of the New Deal and a pet project of Eleanor Roosevelt's, were engineered to help relieve the onus of homelessness and despair created by the Depression.[83] York had assumed his managerial role at a critical time in the project. Local Cumberland Countians had resented outsiders'—although many were Tennesseans—getting what seemed to amount to free housing and farm land in their own backyard, and they had also resented outside "experts" telling them how to go about their daily lives.[84] York's chief assistant at the project site was Pastor Rosier Pile's brother, O. Proctor Pile. In December of 1939, Pile, with York's approval, sent a three-page letter marked "CONFIDENTIAL" to Tennessee senator Tom Stewart in Washington, D.C., voicing displeasure at the way federal projects were run. The letter illustrates the attitudes of local Tennesseans: their resentment of outsiders and the very real specter of anti-Semitism prevalent in the Upper Cumberland. It foretold the attitudes and difficulties that Lasky would face when trying to win York's confidence. Pile wrote:

> Just thinking things over as they are . . . you know I said . . . I would write you referring to the Yankees and other non-residents holding jobs with both the National and State Government in Tennessee . . . Chas. Poe and his Lieutenant, Sam Brewster, former Commissioner of Conservation under this Browning [former governor of Tennessee], had delegated to Brewster the power to name all the employees . . . and he, being from Texas, naturally has named all of the personnel from his own state (Texas), with the exception of one [man] from Ohio who cannot speak English to a degree that a mountain man can understand what he is talking about.[85]

Pile went on to list the names and origins of people he found offensive. They hailed from Ohio, Michigan, Missouri, Texas, and beyond. Those whose homes he could not identify he simply labeled "Yankee." More alarmingly, the letter displayed anti-Semitism and racism when he wrote, "Miller and Kermit are Texas *Jews*, Hemessee is some kind of *Wop* I am sure, [and] . . . Mr. Garrity [is] a very undesirable Yankee."[86] Pile then defended the local population, whom he felt had been slighted by the unwanted influx of outsiders, and wrote words with which York no doubt agreed:

> You know I was raised in Fentress county and know something of that fine citizenship there; people who are well and truly qualified to handle all state

matters pertaining to their own County Government. To say the least of it, they are not going to be satisfied to have republicans and citizens from other sections of the State to be placed in charge. . . . Neither will they accept leadership from any one other than some of their own citizens. Sgt. Alvin C. York, like myself, . . . we are very much displeased at Yankees and non-residents from Texas and many other states being brought here.[87]

Outsiders posed a distinct problem. York, though more traveled and enlightened than his neighbors, still harbored suspicion of people from outside his community. As Pile's letter clearly expressed, people from different parts of his own home state had no business in the Upper Cumberland. Therefore, Lasky faced a doubly daunting task: he had to win the confidence of the locals, proving he was not a threat to them or their way of life; and he had to convince York that his association with Jews would not damn his soul to hell for eternity. The affable, diligent, and tenacious Lasky eventually accomplished both. If York's anti-Semitism initially created a barrier to the filming of his story, Lasky clearly convinced him that Jews were not unregenerate, that they were worthy of his association, and that the film should be made.

Throughout the month the two men toured various parts of the Upper Cumberland, argued over the movie's emphasis, and developed a genuine admiration for each other. Lasky continued interviews with York's friends but found many of them frustrating because of their taciturn behavior; he noted:

We did manage to supplement our stock of York lore before returning to the Coast, but most of our inquiries about the sergeant's childhood among his backwoods neighbors elicited nothing more helpful than "Alvin, he's a good boy," or "Alvin, he'd never harm nobody."[88]

In spite of those laconic responses, Lasky depended primarily upon four key individuals: Guy Williams, York's close friend; Arthur S. Bushing, York's personal secretary; John Hale, York's attorney; and Prentice Cooper, the governor of Tennessee. Lasky followed Guy Williams's advice regarding proper use of the "Devil's tool" and set up a graduated pay schedule to dole out money to York. Arthur S. Bushing argued that the film could garner national interest in his Bible school and make his noble dream a reality. Governor Cooper, after communications with Lasky and Harry Warner, appealed to York's sense of patriotism, arguing that the movie would instill pride in America for generations to come. Hale echoed their arguments, reinforcing the belief that the time had at last come to put the sergeant's life on the silver screen.[89] On March 24, 1940, York, still skeptical, signed a bogus contract for reporters with Lasky in the governor's office in Nashville.[90]

Lasky agreed to pay York fifty thousand dollars (in measured installments) as well as 2 percent of the box-office gross, something practically unheard of during the Hollywood studio era. York's agreement, though a relief, created a series of complications. The first concerned his desire that Gary Cooper portray him. Although Cooper's contract belonged to Samuel Goldwyn, Lasky did not see that as an insurmountable problem since Goldwyn was married to Lasky's sister, Blanche. Secondly, York had demanded that the actress cast to play Gracie could not drink, smoke, or swear—a hard thing to find at any time in Hollywood. Thirdly, York had wanted editorial control over the screenplay. If the final product demeaned, insulted, or antagonized him in any significant way, York could withdraw his support.[91]

Amazingly, Lasky agreed to York's wishes but explained that, for the sake of dramatization, some events would have to be embellished while others had to be omitted. Lasky initially promised York that the film would not glorify his war years: "I wish to emphasize that this is in no sense a war picture . . . it is a story Americans need to be told today . . . [it] will be a document for fundamental Americanism."[92] Although Lasky had agreed to stick to the facts of York's life, events soon unfolded that made the promise impossible to keep, and, over the course of the next year, the emphasis of the movie and York's attitude toward events in Europe changed significantly. Harry Warner later testified before a congressional subcommittee:

> The script was prepared under the supervision and direction of Sergeant York. The picture was made with Sergeant York constantly on the set. The final result was freely approved by him as an accurate portrayal of his life.[93]

In actuality, York spent very little time on the set because he found the tedious nature of filmmaking boring. York also suffered chronic health problems that exacerbated his feeling of discomfort when visiting the set.[94]

Though Harry Warner's role in persuading York to agree to a movie deal is somewhat hazy, the elder Warner earned the sergeant's respect and friendship. The two men held a number of things in common, for both were unabashedly religious and consulted the Scriptures for comfort and enjoyment. Both had quit drinking and smoking in their youth and con-

Fig. 4. (Left to right: Jesse Lasky, Hal Wallis, Alvin York, and Harry Warner) After twenty-five years Alvin York agreed to a film biography; and, as a result of his relationship with Harry Warner and Jesse Lasky, the pacifist turned interventionist. Courtesy of the Alvin C. York collection.

sidered tobacco and alcohol a detriment to living a full, respectable life. Both recognized the value of an education and regretted that life had not afforded them the opportunity to complete their formal schooling. Both grew up exceedingly poor, understood what it meant to eke out an existence, and were devoted family men. York and Warner considered family the most important thing in their lives other than their devotion to God. Lastly, both York and Warner loved America passionately and zealously advocated the democratic faith.[95] Harry's patriotism and religious zeal impressed York, who came to admire and respect Jews. His empathy for the plight of the Jews, as he became more aware of the situation in Europe, fits squarely within one fundamentalist Christian tradition. His original belief regarded the Jews as perverse and wicked, but he easily rationalized his change of heart by embracing Zionism as a means of heralding the Parousia.[96]

Why York demanded Gary Cooper is shrouded in a mystery of conflicting stories.[97] Some argue that Lasky had planted the seed; others
said that Cooper was the *only* movie star York knew anything about.
Cooper, though he later won an academy award for his portrayal, looked
and acted nothing like the sergeant. York weighed over 300 pounds when
he signed the contract; Cooper weighed 185. They were roughly the
same height, but York had bright red hair and always wore a moustache.[98] Cooper's hair was dark brown and he always went clean shaven.
Cooper was rather taciturn, whereas York had a tremendous sense of
humor and "could talk the ears off a field of corn."[99] York spoke in a
high-pitched tenor voice practically devoid of accent, and Cooper
drawled in a baritone. In spite of their obvious differences, Cooper has
come to embody, for most Americans, the essence of their perceptions
of Sergeant York.

Certain of the success of the picture, Lasky began the task of bringing
the story to the screen. On April 21, Lasky, joined by Harry Chandlee,
Julien Josephson, and Abem Finkel, cultivated friendships with locals by
providing them odd jobs while the writers gathered information to write
the screenplay. One of the oddest hirings was a man named Donoho Hall
from Wartrace, Tennessee, who acted as "interpreter." He translated the
speech of the locals to the Hollywood folk and vice versa; and in light of
Proctor Pile's December 1939 letter, Lasky's crew may very well have been
in need of an interpreter.[100] Albert Ganier, an ornithologist and amateur
photographer from Nashville, shot still photographs of the Pall Mall area
for set and costume crews, and those sixty-seven prints provided the
background necessary for technicians to create the Wolf River Valley on a
Burbank soundstage.[101] Lasky hired Nashville stenographer Agnes Seely
to record the interviews conducted with York's friends, family, and army
personnel. Lasky clearly won the sergeant's trust: York loaned him the
love letters he had penned Gracie while abroad, along with his treasured
war diary. Those interviews, letters, and photographs, in accompaniment
with the Congressional Medal of Honor affidavits, became the key ingre-
dients in writing the screenplay.[102]

Chandlee and Josephson completed a twenty-nine-page rough treatment and submitted it to Lasky on May 8, 1940. It described the general
story line and, more importantly, drew attention to story details requiring fictionalization or alteration. On July 7, Chandlee and Abem Finkel
submitted their revised final treatment, a protoscript titled *The Amazing
Story of Sergeant York,* which York read and approved.[103]

Fig. 5. (Left to right: Julien Josephson, Harry Chandlee, Alvin York, Jesse Lasky, and Jesse Lasky, Jr.) Screenwriters Julien Josephson and Harry Chandlee were instrumental in turning Alvin York's story into a call for intervention in World War II. Courtesy of the Tennessee State Library and Archives, Albert Ganier Collection.

The Amazing Story of Sergeant York emphasized York's days as a hell-raiser and his education at state-line border bars called blind tigers. Everett Delk, York's best friend, was killed in a shoot-out at a blind tiger in Static, Kentucky, in 1915. Because York had maintained that Delk's death profoundly affected him, Chandlee and Josephson detailed the incident in the script but added a curious twist. At York's behest, they transformed Everett Delk into a fictional nemesis named Zeke. After imbibing too much white lightning, York and Zeke wind up in a drunken brawl, during which York accidentally kills him. The change served two purposes: it increased dramatic tension leading to York's religious conversion, and it fulfilled York's desire not to make the Delk family relive the pain of Everett's death.[104]

Another change that York willingly approved was the introduction of the fictional character Pusher, who acted as his foil. A stereotypical Brooklynite who worked in the subway, Pusher functioned as a reference point for the urban audience unfamiliar with mountain people. He also made York's request to take a ride on a subway more understandable. On York's arrival in New York City in 1919, the mayor presented him with a key to the city and assured him that the city would love to grant him some special request. York asked for a ride on the subway because he had never seen one; by making Pusher York's friend, and a subway worker, the film transforms the somewhat comic request into a personal homage to a fallen comrade.

Pusher depicted a nonexistent relationship between York and his former army comrades. Letters received by the studio, and location manager Bill Guthrie's experiences with the survivors, revealed a very different drama from the one Pusher and York lived out on the screen. York had alienated himself from many of the men in his battalion because of his attempt at conscientious objection and his religious beliefs.[105] His best friend in G Company, Murray Savage, died in the October 8, 1918, melee. For York to be designated as the lone hero of the battle of Chatel-Chehery only exacerbated the situation, and even though York, to his credit, *always* willingly gave full recognition to his companions, the army singled him out after George Patullo leaked his version of the story to the press. In a radio address given in 1941, York said:

> [A]lthough I was credited with practically wiping out the whole battalion of 35 machine guns, I was only one of the 17 who did the job. Anyone of the other boys could have done the same thing I did if fate had put them in

my place. *If any of my buddies are listening in tonight I want them and the whole world to know that without their cool courage none of us would be alive today.*[106]

A skeleton film crew arrived in Pall Mall in October of 1940. They shot backgrounds to assist the set painters in replicating Pall Mall. Additional footage of locals going about their daily tasks helped the actors reproduce the mountaineers' mannerisms. Alvin and Gracie recorded their voices on 78 rpm disks to help the cast recreate their patois. In the meantime, back at the studio, future *Dirty Harry* director Don Siegel scoured stock footage and pieced together the movie's montage sequences.[107]

After Cooper signed on, York loaned the actor one of his own muzzle-loaders—a 125-year-old piece that York's Long hunter ancestor Conrad (a.k.a. Coonrod) Pile had brought into the valley. He also gave the actor one of his own floppy Stetsons, which Cooper wore in the film's Tennessee sequences.[108]

The film's problems were not limited to York's personal demands. Because it featured characterizations of people still living, obtaining their written consent was absolutely essential.[109] Bill Guthrie received the assignment of seeking out family, friends, celebrities, and, most importantly, York's fellow survivors from G Company of the 82d Division of the American Expeditionary Force. Secretary of State Cordell Hull, Gen. John J. Pershing, Maj. George Edward Buxton, and other men of rank willingly obliged, but other associates of York's proved frustratingly uncooperative.[110]

Asbury Williams, York's father-in-law, refused to sign a release, even though York's friend and pastor, Rosier Pile, who condemned movies as a sin, willingly gave his permission. Pile, parroting Guy Williams, declaimed that the film's purpose was good and that the Devil's instrument could be used to do God's bidding. No amount of coaxing or coercion could budge York's recalcitrant father-in-law, and the writers were forced to depict Gracie living in the home of Asbury's brother, Elijah ("Lige") Williams. Other friends and family were reluctant to sign as well, including most of York's siblings. Although he was one of eleven children, only his brother George and his sister Lucy appeared in the film, leading the audience to believe that York came from a small mountain family.

The reasons for refusal varied. It appears that Asbury Williams never approved of York, either before or after the war, and abhorred York's marriage to his daughter. Because the writers were well aware of the antipathy between York and his father-in-law, *The Amazing Story of Sergeant York* made that conflict the centerpiece of the story. Lasky said, "[I]n talking to Miss Gracie, who was sixteen when she married York, we discovered that his courtship had stirred up a feud between the two families. Her folks hadn't approved of her keeping company with a hell raiser."[111] Asbury Williams remained unconvinced of the sincerity of York's conversion and felt that the impetus was to allow York to be near his daughter. Gracie's father was a prominent member of the Church of Christ in Christian Union, and York himself said in later years that church was the only place he could legitimately see her before they were married.

York's religious conversion also put him in direct opposition to members of his own family who disagreed with the tenets of the Church of Christ in Christian Union. Raised as Methodists, they saw their brother's conversion to fundamentalism as a move toward fanaticism. York's sister Lucy maintained that Pastor Pile exercised too much influence over her brother and promoted dissension in the family. Nevertheless, many of those recalcitrant family members worked for their famous brother.[112]

A touchier problem arose when Guthrie attempted to get permission from the survivors of Company G: Sergeants Harry Parsons and Bernard Early, Cpl. William Cutting, Percy Beardsley, Joe Konotski, George Wills, Feodor Sok, Michael Saccina, and Mario Mussi. When *Liberty* magazine serialized York's war diary, Cpl. William Cutting (whose real name was Otis B. Merrithew) conducted a personal campaign to discredit York. Cutting/Merrithew (hereafter Merrithew) maintained that it was he, not "Corporal York," who captured the 132 Germans.[113] Wounded during the engagement, Merrithew lay in a first aid station as York marched the Germans into U.S. Headquarters. Feeling robbed of proper credit, he wanted to set the record straight, for he believed that each survivor deserved recognition for heroism. As a result of his unflagging efforts, he and Sgt. Bernard Early were belatedly awarded the Distinguished Service Cross in 1927.[114]

As news of the Warner Bros. plan to make a movie based on York's life became public, Merrithew bombarded the studio with letters. He drafted and notarized an "official version" of his own statement, which came to the attention of Roy Obringer, head of the Warner Bros. legal department.[115] Harry Parsons said of the famous engagement: "York got into a trench and moved around and came upon the troops, and I came face to face with a sniper. My rifle was clogged from sand, and when I fired the barrel opened up and burst. I lay on the ground and fired a pistol at this sniper until I got him . . . *of course, we were firing all the time, and we didn't know what was going on.*"[116] Unaware of the campaign against Sergeant York, however, Guthrie continued his quest to find G Company survivors.

First located was Percy Beardsley, who refused to sign until Guthrie agreed to pay him twenty dollars. This proved a costly mistake, for as Guthrie slowly found the survivors, he discovered none willing to sign a release without compensation—$20 here, $50 there—all of which somehow got back to Merrithew. When Guthrie found Merrithew, he demanded $250, and the location manager grudgingly paid. Promptly contacting his former comrades, Merrithew told them how much money he had received, adding that they had been cheated once again by "Corporal" York. Joining forces, the seven survivors petitioned Warner Bros. to stop production immediately and threatened a lawsuit.[117]

Later, as filming neared completion, Merrithew wrote Guthrie:

> [The seven survivors] never remember signing affidavits for York. *All* of them in recent correspondence are willing to testify that they thought they were signing a 'supply slip' for some article of clothing that was issued to them.[118]

The affadavits Merrithew mentioned were those compiled by the U.S. army officials who investigated the famous October 8, 1918, engagement that led to York's being awarded the Congressional Medal of Honor. Those same affadavits became the foundation of York's international fame. Threatening Guthrie with a supposedly incriminating recording of a conversation that had occurred on October 16, 1940, Merrithew wrote:

> Why doesn't York come out with the true story and give the boys the right recognition that is due them? There is one point in particular that I wish to impress; if the picture shows the German major handing over his pistol to anybody but me as a sign of surrender, Warner Brother's will have a court case on their hands. In handing me that pistol the Major knew that *I* was in command and *not* York.[119]

In spite of these recriminations, the troubles with the survivors appeared minor compared to the byzantine contractual machinations occurring between Warner Bros. and Samuel Goldwyn. York wanted Gary Cooper to portray him; what that meant was Cooper or no film—period. Negotiations went slowly, however, and Lasky was forced to confront the possibility that another actor might have to be substituted. The optimism that originally surrounded the possibility of Cooper portraying York faded when Goldwyn's wife sued him for divorce. Lasky and Wallis believed that if Cooper could not be signed, they might be able to persuade York to endorse another actor. Jack Warner told Lasky that he was "crazy to think that Goldwyn would ever come through for the studio," and to find another actor.[120] Facing the grim possibility that Cooper might be unattainable, on November 15, 1940, they shot a screen test with another actor— Ronald Reagan.[121]

While Harry Warner and Sam Goldwyn parried, Lasky turned to the task of casting the picture's other roles. Always enthusiastic when an idea hit him, Lasky asked Roy Obringer what he thought of Jane Russell's playing Miss Gracie. Obringer replied:

> I agree with you that Jane Russell's very attractive but I hardly think she's the type for 'Sergeant York.' She doesn't look much like the simple backwoods country girl to me.[122]

Undaunted, Lasky examined the screen tests of four actresses who fulfilled York's conditions: Helen Wood, Suzan Carnahan, Linda Hayes, and Joan Leslie. He settled on Joan Leslie and broke the news to her on her sixteenth birthday. York had been thirty years old and Miss Gracie fifteen when he proposed before leaving for France: thus Joan Leslie, at sixteen, closely approximated mountain reality.[123]

Meanwhile, Lasky's ex-brother-in-law kept stalling and further frustrated Warner Bros. by constantly changing the date and conditions of Cooper's availability. Finally on August 16, 1940, in a fit of pique Harry fired off a missive to Goldwyn's liaison, Reeves Espy, demanding that the matter be resolved by one o'clock the following Monday, "or forget the entire transaction."[124] The letter reflected not only the exasperation of the studio but also indicated the way Harry Warner conducted business:

> You and Mr. Goldwyn know me and that when I say 1:00 Monday I don't mean 2:00. It will all be history as far as we are concerned and I wouldn't take Cooper after that for nothing, because with me a deal is a deal.[125]

Goldwyn relented and a contract was hammered out on March 19, 1941, which satisfied both parties.[126] The agreement stipulated that Warner Bros. would lend Jack Carson, Donald Crisp, Lester Cole, and Bette Davis to Metro for one picture each, and Warner Bros. would receive Gary Cooper and his sidekick Walter Brennan for twelve weeks at the prices of $150,000 and $85,000, respectively. If the picture went over schedule,

Warner Bros. agreed to pay an additional $12,500 per week for Cooper's services. Goldwyn demanded that Warner Bros. take Miriam Hopkins at a cost of $50,000 even though the studio had no project for her. As soon as the deal was settled and a shooting schedule established, Jack Warner began looking for loopholes to prevent Bette Davis from going to Metro. To Jack Warner's chagrin, the picture Bette Davis shot at Metro, *The Little Foxes,* earned her a Best Actress Oscar.[127]

The task of actually making the film grew increasingly complex. Because of difficult transportation routes and the lack of hotel or catering facilities and chemical labs for processing film stock, location shooting in remote Pall Mall, Tennessee, proved impossible. The only feasible course of action meant replicating York's Tennessee in Burbank. Set crews painstakingly recreated the Wolf River Valley on a number of soundstages. Photographs and blueprints of Pastor Pile's store, the Wolf River Methodist Church, and the homes of the Yorks and Elijah Williams made it possible to produce strikingly authentic replicas. Exercising selective memory by choosing to forget D. W. Griffith's mammoth sets built for *Intolerance,* the Warner Bros. publicity department touted the sets built for *Sergeant York* as the largest and most elaborate ever constructed for a motion picture.

The finished set consisted of a mountain peak on a carousel that could rotate 360 degrees. It also included a two-hundred-foot mountain spring, three stationary peaks, and a cedar, pine, and oak forest, plus a farmyard, cabins, a church, and a general store. There were 123 sets in all, including eight outdoor locations, and an eighty-acre battlefield on the Calabassas ranch. Only battle scenes were shot on location, and it took a three-hundred-man wrecking crew three weeks to blast the ranch into believable war-torn waste. Crews detonated five tons of TNT, dug two miles of sandbagged, zig-zagged trenches, and placed four hundred denuded trees about the scarred field. In addition, they used 5,200 gallons of paint; actors and extras fired 37,000 rounds of rifle ammunition, 32,000 rounds of pistol ammunition, and 32,000 machine gun rounds.[128]

The film was to be directed by Lasky's long-time associate, independent director Howard Hawks. Drawing an eighty-five-thousand-dollar salary, Hawks began work on *Sergeant York* on December 16, 1940, but filming failed to get under way until January. Like Lasky, York, and Harry Warner, Hawks was accustomed to having things his own way. A perfectionist, he also considered himself something of a writer, and for Hawks a script represented an outline, not a finished product.[129] Hawks regarded the initial York script as a weak story cobbled together by journalists and hacks. It was true that Asbury Williams's refusal to sign a release undercut the central conflict of the original script, and a new plot device was needed. York's war experience seemed the obvious thing to focus on, but both Harry Chandlee and Abem Finkel wanted to stay as true to the original script as possible because York had approved it, so they resisted Hawks's desire to intensify the war sequences. Hawks brought John Huston and his friend Howard Koch on board for the rewrites that Chandlee and Finkel refused to do.[130] Chandlee and Finkel were not totally opposed to focusing on the war story. They wanted the audience to recognize parallels between the current war and World War I, but they preferred the prointerventionist message to be more subtle. They feared that Hawks, Huston, and Koch would blow the war story out of proportion, resulting in the loss of the PCA's seal of approval. Concern about York's reaction to the revamped screen story also worried them.

Howard Koch had undergone a political conversion in the late 1930s. Always politically active, Koch had abandoned his pacifist stance in favor of intervention and had become outspoken in that belief. His screenplay for the Errol Flynn swashbuckler *The Sea Hawk* (1939) preached preparedness against a totalitarian threat. *Sergeant York* (1941) and later *Casablanca* (1942), two of his most successful screen efforts, would tell similar stories. Americans did not generally approve of war, but if the cause was just, they would willingly go to war. Both Alvin York and *Casablanca*'s Rick Blaine would have to be convinced that the war was indeed their fight, and they would reluctantly agree to do battle. The script changes that occurred after Koch and Huston came on board defined the theme of the movie arriving in theaters in 1941, for York and Blaine by then reflected Koch's own politicization.[131]

Initially, the war sequences made up a minimal portion of the story, simply serving as an epiphany for York's educational awakening. The first shooting script involved a serio-comic sequence that followed York and an intellectual northern army buddy as they visited the Louvre. As the screenplay progressed, York grew intellectually and spiritually enlightened, and the film's ending included a montage sequence detailing York's battle to improve education in the mountains of Tennessee. The educational emphasis of the movie, however, was abandoned by the third rewrite.[132]

York's religious faith had to be handled carefully, and everyone agreed that it had to be central to the story. The barroom death of his friend

Everett Delk was presented as an excuse for York to examine his life and condemn all killing. He admitted that the loss prompted him to attend a revival conducted by Rev. M. H. Russell in 1915 and to convert to the Church of Christ in Christian Union.[133] His rapid conversion to an unorthodox faith created a number of issues that required compromise throughout the project. Ostensibly, York joined the church for two reasons: first, because of Everett Delk's death, and second, because it provided the only legitimate way that he could see Gracie Williams. For the movie to suggest that York "got religion to get the girl," even if that was in any way true, might be interpreted as offensive and shallow.[134]

York made the mistake of saying once in an interview that when he converted "it was like being struck by lightning." To attempt to capitalize on this event, the first three scripts remained faithful to the conversion experience by having him repent after the Zeke character's death; that was not how this sequence eventually played on the screen, however, for in the movie Gary Cooper leaves Static, Kentucky, in a drunken stupor during a rain storm and is literally struck by lighting. The lightning bolt sends Cooper and his mule crashing to the ground, twisting the barrel of his smoking muzzle-loader and driving home the message "Thou shalt not kill."[135] A stunned and suddenly sober Cooper looks heavenward and an angelic choir can be heard, signifying the conversion experience.

York hated the sequence, saying Koch and Huston trivialized his religious conversion, and the PCA disliked it as well. After reviewing the sequence, Joseph Breen sent Hal Wallis a terse memo demanding the sequence be reshot because Americans would not stand for mules dying on screen. To satisfy these objections the scene was reshot; in its final version the mule comes miraculously back to life.[136]

York's religion posed other problems. Once he decided to go to war, "he believed that he had received a Divine communication approving his going and assuring him that he would not be killed."[137] Even though press releases informed the public that profits from the picture were earmarked for the creation of an interdenominational Bible school, the religious issue would not abate because York constantly invoked God's name and assured everyone that the movie would be a testament to Christian values. He argued that faith was essential to his story, but the PCA forbade the use of God's name in motion pictures. Chandlee and Josephson informed Lasky, "It is recognized that if York's real religious attitude is included in the picture, there is great danger of his appearing to be merely a religious fanatic and thus lose heavily in audience understanding and sympathy."[138] The screenwriters' problem was how to make York's spirituality convincing without offending audiences or making him look like a lunatic. In their efforts to solve this dilemma, they opted for a balance between godliness and patriotism as a representation of true Americanism. Chandlee and Josephson stated in a memo dated May 8, 1940, "We all realize that this should not be a war picture in the usual sense of the word."[139] That same memo, however, clearly indicated the studio's intention of playing up the war angle in light of the current political situation in Europe, for by that date the American people recognized York as an interventionist. Casting off his pacifist cloak, he called for increased defense spending, a beefed-up air force, military training in the Civilian Conservation Corps (CCC), and American support of Britain. York's most recent conversion was reflected in the script changes that he approved.

Chandlee made two other major alterations in the script. He invented a scene on the rifle range, where York proved his prowess as a marksman. Chandler said, "This scene was put in for its own values and to supply the means for getting York to the interview with his officers."[140] He also concocted the scene where Major Buxton presented York with an American history textbook to help him decide whether or not to fight. Although "[t]his scene never happened in real life," it significantly tempered the perception of York as a religious fanatic.[141] In reality it took months of coaxing by Buxton and Captain Danforth to convince York to fight, but this sequence worked beautifully because it cut to what many considered the symbolic essence of America—the myth of its unique history as the new Eden and the last bastion of Judeo-Christian ethics in the world.[142]

That sequence presented the notion that there were differences between just and unjust wars and that York, the "sword of the Lord," understood the distinction. Buxton asks York specific questions to determine his sincerity and uses his own biblical knowledge to persuade York to interpret the Scriptures in a figurative rather than a literal way. York's first response is, "The book is agin' killin' . . . an' I'm a figgerin' killin' other folks ain't no part o' what He was intendin' fer us to be a doin' here."[143] Like a pair of boxers sizing each other up, Buxton and York swap Scriptures that advocate either aggression or peace. After gaining York's confidence, Buxton clinches the sequence by discussing the uniqueness of America and York's own hero, Daniel Boone, while holding the Bible in one hand and the history text in the other. York, surprised to learn that

Fig. 6. (Left to right: Harry Warner, Jesse Lasky, an extra, and Alvin York) Harry Warner, Jesse Lasky, and Alvin York converse with an extra during a break in the filming of *Sergeant York.* Courtesy of the Alvin C. York Collection.

anyone outside of the Valley of the Three Forks knew anything about Daniel Boone, marvels at the history book. Buxton says:

> [The American history text is] the story of a whole people's struggle for freedom—from the very beginning until now—for we are still struggling. . . . You're a religious man, York. You want to worship God in your own way, plow your fields as you see fit, to raise your own family according to your own lights. Such things are part of our heritage as Americans, *but the cost of that heritage is high. Sometimes it takes all we've got to preserve it—even our lives.*[144]

An overt attempt to convert isolationists to the interventionist cause, it invoked American history and religious practices. The point was further driven home in a sequence in which York, home on furlough, struggles to reconcile God and Country. The sequence depicts York with his hunting dog sitting atop the bluffs known as the "Yellow Doors" overlooking the Wolf River Valley, contemplating the Bible and the American history text. As he struggles with his conscience, voice-overs supplied by Pastor Pile and Buxton plead with York, saying "for God" and "for country." The dilemma is reconciled when York stumbles upon the passage "Render . . . unto Caesar the things which are Caesar's; and unto God the things that are God's" (Matt. 22:21, King James Version).

As tensions mounted around the set, original writers Finkel, Josephson, and Chandlee accused Hawks, Cooper, and the script doctors of an unauthorized rewriting of the picture. The movie was supposed to be a picture of York as he saw himself, not some comic farce or superman story. The fact that York had a degree of veto power, and any aspect of the film that did not meet with his approval could mean financial disaster for Lasky and Warner Bros., sometimes put him at odds with the writers and the studio, whose primary objective was to produce a money-making feature.[145] Hawks's tendency to tamper with the script forced Lasky and the original writers to dole the shooting script out in daily sections in order to reduce his embellishing the story line.[146]

Abem Finkel feared that York and his fellow Tennesseans would be outraged by the final product. Wild improvisations on the battlefield and general disregard for the original intentions of the project had sent him into a frenzy. Hawks and Huston altered the battlefield accounts significantly and played on the myth that York silenced "twenty-five or thirty-five machine guns," when in fact, by York's own admission, he took out only one Maxim gun. (By the time the battle sequences were filmed, York endorsed the changes for what he considered a greater good.) In an agitated memo to Hal Wallis dated January 9, 1941, Finkel made his consternation known, starting with his concerns about the portrayal of the Tennseans. Having accompanied Lasky to Pall Mall, Finkel had developed a genuine affection for the rough-hewn people of the Wolf River Valley. Recognizing their simple dignity, he was concerned about the violence they might inflict if their reputations were impugned. About the potentially offensive treatment of Tennessee he wrote:

> The mass audience knows the mountaineer as an unwashed, unkempt yokel whom it finds amusing. . . . Since we're not making "Coming Round the Mountain" or even an anthropological investigation of primitive American folkways we thought that in order to create understanding, and

therefore sympathy for York it would be best to depict him and his fellow mountaineers as simple human beings with as much common sense as most people. . . . To portray these people as a bunch of oafish clods for the sake of background color or for laughs would certainly antagonize York . . . to him the story of his life is no laughing matter. It took him twenty-five years to make up his mind to let someone put it in a picture.[147]

He elaborated on an issue even closer to York's heart, the manner in which Huston and Koch had revamped the characterization of Gracie.

York still refers to his wife as "Miss Gracie." . . . Their romance was simple and idyllic. . . . The slightest hint that Gracie gave him the "come on" and vamped him into kissing her, even if it were not the tallest kind of corn, York would reach for his rifle gun and come a "shootin." You must remember that York knocked off 25 German machine gunners and he wasn't even sore at them. Can you imagine if he really got mad.[148]

What concerned Finkel most was the real threat of annoying the survivors from Company G. By that time many people at the studio were aware of their attitude, and Finkel saw disaster written all over the movie if Hawks, Huston, and Koch continued to exercise their ideas. Feeling slighted both by history and by the studio, the seven survivors were united in their disdain concerning the project. Finkel continued:

[I]t is not only York that must be considered. . . . You must remember that most of the officers and men involved in York's exploit are still alive. Bill Guthrie can tell you how jealously they guard their contribution to York's exploit . . . they will all yell bloody murder if they are not given their due.[149]

Finkel also tried to defuse a potentially disastrous situation when he discussed the position of the technical director.

I heard it rumored that somebody got the bright idea to bring out a Corporal Cutting . . . to act as tech on the picture. That would really be dynamite! As I understand it Cutting is the guy who claims that York hogged all the credit unjustifiably. While he admits that York did most of the shooting he maintains that he and some of the others helped. He also insists that it was he, not York, that brought the prisoners back and that York pulled a fast one on him by bringing in these prisoners while Cutting was asleep in a shell hole . . . I doubt if you could think of anything that could antagonize York more than to let Cutting anywhere near here.[150]

The screenplay eventually underwent three complete rewrites, the last one taking place while cameras rolled. As a result the project went over schedule and over budget, and the finished film was the first in Warner Bros. history to cost over $2 million.[151]

From the very first day of shooting, February 3, 1941, things went awry. Cooper arrived late, something he was prone to do. Used to being pampered by Goldwyn's studio, Cooper saw no reason to change his behavior for a studio that paid closer attention to the bottom line than to the comfort of its actors. The first sequence involved Cooper and Brennan in a field where Cooper was plowing. The mule got spooked and ran crazily across the set, the plow bouncing behind it leaving torn-up scenery in its wake. Hawks worked at a slower pace than Warner Bros. wanted, compounding the growing anxiety about the picture. An Anglophile, Hawks took afternoon tea and halted production to do so. He also deviated from the storyboards, changing his mind about camera setups, further delaying production. On the last day Hawks simply left and went to the Kentucky Derby, leaving the final shooting to Vincent Sherman.[152]

As world affairs changed during the course of the filming, York, through his close contact with Jesse Lasky and Harry Warner, began to pay closer attention to the international scene.[153] Warner and Lasky convinced York that Hitler represented not only a military threat to the world but evil incarnate and that no one, neither Christian nor Jew, was safe from the barbarity of Nazi Germany.[154] Subsequent changes in the script to place greater emphasis on York's war experiences were made, therefore, with his approval. As a result Lasky could write general sales manager Gradwell Sears:

> We, in the studio sense a great picture in *Sergeant York*, especially in view of present world conditions, and in our treatment of the story we are taking advantage of world events and are making it timely and patriotic to a degree.[155]

Other developments during the period of the filming pushed York toward intervention. On September 16, 1940, President Roosevelt signed a provision calling for the creation of a peacetime draft. Gen. George C. Marshall testified before Congress that the times were such that America needed to be on guard, for history had proved that the United States had been unprepared for the last war, and many lives were needlessly lost as a result. York's conversion to interventionism was so complete that he wholeheartedly agreed with General Marshall.[156] To the chagrin of local political leaders in Fentress County, Governor Cooper approved York's endorsement by naming him chief executive of the Fentress County Draft Board. To his credit, he took the role seriously and did not use it as a forum to settle old scores; with his trusted amanuensis Arthur S. Bushing, he busily set about the task of drafting local men to serve in the peacetime army. York also joined Governor Cooper, Maj. Rutledge Smith, and a number of other prominent Tennesseans in the Tennessee Preparedness Committee, which lobbied for a beefed-up military presence in the state and the nation.[157]

The belief that pacifism could serve as a bulwark against Nazi aggression dissolved in the face of bitter reality. A member of the clergy, Pastor Alfred Grant Walton, observed, "Pacifism is a flight from reality. It has no answer to the needs of the world right now."[158] York agreed with that sentiment. The pastor defended taking action against Nazism by quoting a former British pacifist faced with the reality of Nazi hostility:

> I used to be a pacifist but I would rather go to hell for fighting than have my son brought up to think that it was funny to kick a Jew in the stomach.[159]

Sergeant York premiered on July 2, 1941, at Broadway's Astor theatre. Bill Rice and Charles Einfeld of the Warner Bros. publicity department orchestrated an elaborate opening, including a VFW parade down Fifth Avenue with hordes of veterans marching to the theater. York and Lasky made their triumphal entry in a convertible limousine. Among those in attendance were Wendell Willkie, Gen. John J. Pershing, Prentice Cooper, New York mayor Fiorello LaGuardia, Gary Cooper, and Joan Leslie. Walter Winchell lavished praise on the picture, and Norman Vincent Peale wrote Jack Warner telling him that *Sergeant York* was the most important film of the year and that Warner Bros. may have just saved the country.[160] The reviewer for *Newsweek* praised the picture:

> In such times and in less capable hands . . . [York's story] might have been a jingoistic cross between *Billy the Kid* and *The Fighting 69th.* Instead it is an engrossing and humorous record of the American way of life in a backwoods community, as well as a timely drama of the inner struggle of a deeply religious man who weighs his horror of killing against what he feels is the greater necessity to stop all killing.[161]

York and Lasky spent the next several weeks promoting *Sergeant York*. In Washington, D.C., they held a special screening for President Roosevelt and invited members of the government and the military. FDR noted that the film arrived at a propitious moment but flippantly remarked that he did not approve of so much killing in the film.[162] Lasky cabled the Warners describing the Washington premier: "We came. They saw. We conquered."[163] By July 17, Charles Einfeld was convinced that the movie was "potentially the most important picture ever made in our industry."[164]

The disgruntled seven survivors disagreed, however, and placed a scathing notice in the July 14, 1941, edition of the *Boston Globe*, a portion of which follows:

> I wish to inform you that none of the survivors are in agreement with Warner Brothers or with Sergeant York's version of what really happened "over there" . . . we never recall signing any affidavit . . . that would be against our grain as we always had figured Sergeant York out to be "yellow" and not a conscientious objector; we recall one morning as we were to go over the top, York went stark mad with fear. He jumped up on top of the parapet and started to holler, "I want to go home, for God's sake why isn't this war over?" . . . Sergeant Early rushed up to him and pushed his automatic pistol to his head and said "If you don't shut up I'll blow your brains out."[165]

The irate survivors went on to say that if they signed anything, "we probably thought it was a supply slip for underwear or something."[166] Merrithew further stated that the movie might be a hit in the South but it "wouldn't wash" in the Northeast, where he, Beardsley, Early, and Wills lived.[167] The impact of their protest proved negligible, for the film continued to draw crowds, turned a steady profit, and was popular even in New England.

At least one critic agreed with the seven survivors. Otis Ferguson panned the picture in *The New Republic*. The film was too long, too preachy, and too militant for his taste. Referring with disdain to the controversial peacetime draft, he wrote, "'Sergeant York,'. . . is about the army and arming in a time when people damn well *have* to think about the army."[168] He disliked York's conversion "from hoodlumism to shouting hallelujah," considering the religious aspects of the film extremely uncomfortable; and he wholeheartedly disapproved of York's second conversion to militancy.[169] The film was "nothing but a memorial screed. . . . The keynote is patriotism."[170] Comparing the film to a parade, Ferguson considered it little more than an exercise in jingoism.

Regardless of the negative buzz, the newly politicized York became more outspoken about the war raging in Europe. Convinced by Harry Warner that the United States could not sit idly by while Europe fell beneath the heel of the Axis powers, York grew more strident. Speaking on the *Hello America* radio program in 1941, York told listeners that he had consented to a movie based on his life because he felt that Warner Bros. and Jesse Lasky were the best qualified to produce it. He demonstrated his considerable change of heart when he recalled the Jews, Italians, Slovaks, Swedes, Poles, and Portuguese who made up his unit in World War I and said, "The Old World backgrounds were forgotten . . . we were all Americans united in a common cause."[171] He noted that though they worshiped differently, they were united by a common faith—a faith in "American principles."[172] Now Great Britain alone fought to defend the concepts of freedom and democracy as Hitler spread his totalitarianism across Europe; therefore, Americans owed a debt to England and should be ready to aid if asked. "Yes, we hear it said that our boys won't go to war no more. Don't fool yourself."[173] As he summed up his speech, he quoted his new friend Harry Warner, saying, "Friends let us all fall in line for the defense of our country and do all we can to help put out all 'isms' but Americanism."[174]

Sergeant York proved to be the most important film Warner Bros. made squarely focusing on the intervention debate. Film historians Peter Roffman and Jim Purdy noted,

> *Sergeant York* is one of the least compromised prewar calls to arms. . . . Like other heroes, York finds war a necessary evil: one must kill to prevent killing.[175]

The film accurately captured the atmosphere of the country as it faced the grim reality of another war and its struggle over its world responsibilities. Most Americans in 1941 were familiar with York's World War I heroism. The film dramatically presented York's transformations from backwoods hellion to pacifist Christian zealot to Christian soldier fighting in order to achieve the Christian ideal of peace.[176]

Sergeant York stood at the forefront of a group of films playing at theaters in the summer of 1941 that heightened awareness of the world's political situation, marking a new phase in the struggle over preparedness.[177] They asked Americans to consider their heritage and to appreciate the danger of the Nazi menace threatening the common cultural threads that bound England and America. Like Harry Warner, the films begged American audiences to assume responsibility for their actions and not to turn a blind eye to the current conflict. *Sergeant York* appealed to all Americans because the story of York's life embodied the belief that all "average" Americans are potential heroes. Nick Roddick argued that *Sergeant York* and the wartime films that followed stressed the notion that an individual owes a tremendous debt to society. Each individual must pull his share of the load through "positive physical action," or the underpinnings of the republic will collapse. Alvin York, like *Casablanca*'s Rick Blaine, epitomizes "heroic conservatism and quiet despair" because the individual must not indulge in selfish, self-centered action with the world on the brink of total destruction.[178]

Film historian Michael T. Isenberg considers *Sergeant York* more than simply a biopic and preparedness film; rather, it represents American mytho-cultural shorthand. *Sergeant York* was "Leatherstocking in khaki . . . the most profound of all motion pictures of the warrior-democrat."[179] York's saga reconciled the frontier myth with the modern age, arguing that bucolic simplicity can peacefully coexist with urban-industrial complexity as long as the individual/society is rooted in Judeo-Christian/Jeffersonian-American values.

Throughout its entire length, *Sergeant York* constantly denounced war yet recognized that there were times when war was necessary; York "the sword of the Lord," fought to save lives and preserve peace. The film trod a very fine line between deglamorizing war and urging its audience to be vigilant and prepared to make the supreme sacrifice. A film score subtly blending patriotic music and Christian folk hymns was intended to persuade its audience to practice their Christian principles and follow York into battle. Composer Max Steiner interwove two leitmotifs that underscored the religio-patriotic nature of the film. Strains of "My Country 'Tis of Thee" and "Give Me That Old Time Religion" function as counterpoints linking the two themes. Interspersed with less frequency are "When the Roll is Called Up Yonder," "In the Sweet By and By," "You're in the Army Now," "The Star-Spangled Banner," and "Yankee Doodle Dandy."

It was York's second conversion, the conversion to interventionism, that Americans in 1940–41 needed to see in order to be convinced that the war in Europe was indeed their concern, for York realized that he could be dutiful to the state and still maintain his religious convictions in a holy war against an unholy enemy. John Belton described the impact of the film:

> In this way York (and America) can uphold, without rupturing them, the basic isolationist principles that underpin his (our) identity while realizing his (our) obligations to things outside himself (ourselves). Retaining its inherent distaste for European entanglements and war, America could, at the same time, give itself over to the larger historical (and moral) necessity of fighting fascism.[180]

Thus the movie allowed American audiences to respond by claiming to abhor violence and uphold Christian values and at the same time reveling in the vicarious thrill of battlefield action. Audiences could claim pacifism and isolationism while realizing that some conflicts did require American intervention. Intervention demanded sober reflection, however, before a commitment could be made.

Historian Ian Hamilton argued that the film did more than appeal to the capricious whims of fence-sitters who had yet to recognize the Nazi threat:

> Although York in the movie is a Tennessee hillbilly, he could in some respects just as easily have been a certain sort of thirties intellectual, moving from pacifism to a reluctant acceptance of the necessity of fighting this just war.[181]

Sergeant York appealed to large American audiences because of the universality of its message. Given the highly charged political climate of 1941, many could identify in some way with the movie. They might not agree with the course of action York followed, but they could understood the anguish of his decision.

On August 1, 1941, less than a month after its release, the film was abruptly withdrawn and general release was postponed until July 4, 1942. Senators Gerald P. Nye of North Dakota and Bennet Champ Clark of Missouri introduced Senate Resolution 152, calling for a thorough investigation of the film industry by the Committee on Interstate Commerce. In these isolationist senators' opinion, Hollywood had violated America's official neutrality and had tried to incite public opinion in favor of war. *Sergeant York* was one of the movies singled out as prowar propaganda, and it was pulled out of limited release until after the investigation could be completed.[182]

Through his association with Hollywood, Alvin C. York had undergone a profound change of heart. His politics had turned from pacifistic isolationism to advocacy of armed intervention. His association with Hollywood executives had brought about his increasing admiration and respect for the Jewish race; his gradual awakening to the horrors of the present European war reflected the growing trend in America toward intervention. That battle would come to a head in 1940–41 as York became more outspoken in his remarks concerning America's responsibility to war-torn Europe. This change in attitude would pit him against another American idol from the past, Col. Charles A. Lindbergh.

5

Using the Devil's Tool to Do God's Work

Sergeant York, *America First, and the Intervention Debate*

With the release of the film recounting his military exploits, Alvin York had again become one of America's greatest living heroes, a man who had captured the imagination and admiration of millions of Americans. Perhaps the only other living individual who could have equaled his fame was the Lone Eagle, Col. Charles Lindbergh. Their political stances differed widely, however, and by 1939 national opinion had become polarized by the views that these two men symbolized. York called for intervention while Lindbergh preached isolation.[1]

Lindbergh's life, like York's, had not been a charmed one after achieving fame. He hated the cloying attention of the limelight, and his private life had turned tragic in 1932, when his infant son was kidnapped and killed. The ensuing "Trial of the Century," which ended in the conviction of Bruno Richard Hauptmann, prompted Lindbergh and his wife, Anne Morrow Lindbergh, to migrate to England and establish a residence in London.[2]

The U.S. Military Attaché in Berlin, Maj. Truman Smith, invited Colonel Lindbergh to visit Germany in 1936. The Lindberghs accepted his offer, left London on July 22, and traveled for the first time to Nazi Germany. In the course of his visit, Lindbergh became fascinated with Hitler's Germany and its new air force, the *Luftwaffe*. On August 1 the Lindberghs attended the opening-day ceremonies of the Berlin Olympic Games as personal guests of *Luftwaffe* commandant Reichsmarshall Hermann Göring. While in Germany, Lindbergh assessed the accomplishments of the German air force and gathered information that he supplied to American intelligence agencies.

Overall, the aviation advances of the Nazi regime had impressed Lindbergh. He believed that Hitler, though fanatical, had actually accomplished a great deal of good for his people. Lindbergh's initial visit had also convinced him that Hitler posed no threat to France or Great Britain and that if war should occur, it would be against the National Socialists' most hated enemy—the Soviet Union.[3]

Lindbergh returned to Nazi Germany in 1937. On that two-week visit the colonel toured aircraft factories, inspected planes, and "may have been the first American given the opportunity to examine the ME-109 closely."[4] The report Lindbergh crafted for the U.S. military after his sojourn presented an accurate but rather tempered picture of Nazi air power. Though Nazis had come a long way in a very short time, he believed they posed no serious military threat at that juncture.

In October of 1938, the Lindberghs visited Nazi Germany for the last time. On that tour the Lone Eagle became the first American to inspect a new German aircraft, the Junkers JU-88 bomber, and he was allowed to fly an ME-109. The performance of both aircraft impressed the colonel. On October 18, at a party in his honor, Göring presented Lindbergh with the Service Cross of the Order of the German Eagle with the Star, the highest Nazi citation available to a civilian. The medal, Göring told him, was a personal gift from Adolf Hitler, a token of appreciation for his historic 1927 solo flight across the Atlantic, which had furthered the cause of aviation.[5] During the course of that visit, Lindbergh seriously considered moving his family to Germany and establishing permanent residence there. Biographer Joyce Milton argued that part of Lindbergh's admiration for Nazi Germany stemmed from the fact that the press and the *paparazzi* did not hound him there the way they did in Britain and America.[6] But he seemed oblivious to the growing Nazi persecution of the Jews, a situation that expedited the permanent withdrawal of the U.S. ambassador from Germany. In spite of the warning signs, Lindbergh failed to see the Nazis as a grave threat to American security.[7]

Lindbergh's attitude toward the European war also proved peculiar. The aviator, though he felt ill at ease in the company of pacifists, found himself increasingly among them. Lindbergh wrote in his journal in October 1941: "A prosperous country *may not* have a good army, but a demoralized country *cannot* have a good army . . . I shall work against war, but lay plans for one."[8] He saw no inconsistency in preaching nonintervention while at the same time calling for military preparedness. His confused personal assessment of the war caused him to utter strange, even conflicting, pronouncements. In spite of his garbled rhetoric, Lindbergh found a ready and willing audience among American isolationists. He was by no means alone in his sentiments, for over 50 percent of the respondents to a Gallup Poll taken in 1939 said that the United States had no business interfering with the war in Europe.[9]

Lindbergh remained steadfastly convinced that Germany's rearmament threatened only the Soviet Union. Nevertheless, he warned Britain and France to prepare themselves for military conflict. If war should come in the West, it would be up to those two countries to keep Germany in check. At the same time he espoused another contradiction, for he was convinced that neither France nor England could defeat Germany without American aid. This posed another problem, because he maintained that U.S. involvement would upset the world's delicate balance of power, causing democracy to yield to totalitarianism, and would eventually lead to the complete ruination of the American Republic. Therefore, he advocated a curious and illogical solution endorsed by the America First committee: negotiated peace in Europe.[10] After Munich, however, the notion of a negotiated peace with the Nazis seemed ludicrous—doubly so after Hitler invaded the USSR; yet Lindbergh continued to argue that it was the best possible solution for all concerned.

After the war began, Lindbergh grew more adamantly anti-interventionist where America was concerned. His vociferous stance made him a media lightning rod, earning him both praise and disdain. Critics accused him of sophistry; he was chastised for suggesting that Canada could not go to war without first securing the permission of the United States.[11] One of the most vocal critics of Lend-Lease, Lindbergh considered the policy both dangerous and problematic.[12] Although he always maintained that he did not want Germany to win the war, he did not believe Britain capable of defeating the Nazis. He continued to sing the praises of air power and saw an aggressive fleet of long-range bombers with fighter escorts as the salvation of American peace and security.[13] If America were attacked, then by all means it should defend itself, but nothing short of retaliation could justify American intervention.[14]

By the fall of 1939, the feelings of the two heroes had solidified; Alvin York was convinced that intervention was absolutely necessary, whereas Lindbergh advocated isolationism. Before the invasion of Poland, York held views similar to those of Lindbergh. In November 1938, while still claiming to be a pacifist, York sent a lengthy telegram to the city editor of the *New York Journal-American:*

It seems to me the best plan for keeping us out of the war would to be to build up a much stronger national defence on all lines and put at least two hours per day military training in all our C.C.C. Camps and make it compultry [*sic*].[15]

That same telegram stated that if war broke out in Europe, the United States, already burned in one world war, should stay out. The best way to keep America neutral would be to strengthen its defenses. He also advocated a policy Lindbergh endorsed:

We should fortify every foot of coast line and fortify it strong. And we should start our factorys [*sic*] to making planes and build up our Air Forces to fifty thousand fighting planes, twenty thousand bombing planes, five thousand scout planes and we should have two hundred thousand trained pilots.[16]

Years abroad had convinced Lindbergh that the coming fight need not include the United States, and he had spoken against American involvement as early as 1934. In 1939 Lindbergh communicated his intentions—that he meant to use the radio airwaves to combat intervention—to the federal government. President Roosevelt tried to dissuade Lindbergh and even considered creating a special cabinet position for him, Secretary of Air. Lindbergh rejected the offer, and from that point on the Lone Eagle and the chief executive were bitter enemies. By 1939 Lindbergh continued to believe what York no longer held true, and one year later the colonel emerged as a prominent spokesman against U.S. intervention in Europe. Approached by Ed Webster on March 30, 1941, Lindbergh was offered the chairmanship of the newly organized anti-interventionist America First Committee (AFC). Turning it down, Lindbergh said he preferred some other means of supporting the AFC, and he eventually became its most visible and popular speaker.[17]

The America First Committee, launched in 1940 by Yale law student R. Douglas Stuart, Jr., and four friends, sought to keep America out of the European war. Gen. Robert E. Wood agreed to be the AFC's chairman, which gave the committee more visibility and clout as it built up its membership. Among those who joined were Republicans, Populists (primarily from the Midwest), anti–New Dealers, disillusioned former supporters of FDR, isolationists, idealists, World War I combat veterans, college students, and not a few nativists. Politically conservative, the AFC favored protectionism and frowned on internationalism. America had resources aplenty to take care of its own and to maintain a sufficient defensive posture. Interestingly, most members of America First, like Lindbergh, were not pacifists, though the AFC did count among its ranks those with nonbelligerent sympathies. America First claimed that the threat of Nazism had been blown out of proportion and that subversive elements in this country hungered for war. Colluding with those radicals, the AFC claimed, were members of the Hollywood community.[18]

Tensions in Europe continued apace, and on May 16, 1940, FDR asked Congress for an emergency buildup of America's defenses and the immediate construction of fifty thousand planes. Three days later Lindbergh accused him of warmongering. Stung by the aviator's remarks, the president confided in Secretary of War Henry L. Stimson, "What a pity this youngster has completely abandoned his belief in our form of government and has accepted Nazi methods because apparently they are efficient."[19]

York, as a result of his association with Jesse Lasky and the Warner brothers, saw the world situation differently. Like Harry Warner, he called for U.S. aid to Britain and now spoke in a quasi-official capacity for the antithesis of the AFC, the Fight for Freedom Committee (FFF), which advocated American intervention.[20] The FFF was organized in April 1941 by the hard-boiled *Louisville Courier-Journal* reporter Ulric Bell. A World War I veteran, the Kentucky state commander of the American Legion, and press advisor to Secretary of State Cordell Hull at the Montevideo conference, Bell staunchly supported intervention. Once war was declared, he worked with the film industry and the Roosevelt administration as an advisor to the Office of War Information (OWI). An ideological counterpoint to America First, it included in its ranks Wendell Willkie, Ward Cheney, Herbert Agar, Elmer Davis, James P. Warburg, Dean Acheson, Allen Dulles, Walter Wanger, Harry Warner, Robert Sherwood, and James Conant.

Though Lindbergh had many colleagues in the anti-intervention cause, his public statements created a welter of controversy. In a racist article published in the November 1939 issue of *Reader's Digest*, he cautioned that the war threatened the superiority of the white race and could be a harbinger of the end of Western civilization. The United States, as the obvious inheritor of the treasures of the West, owed posterity an avoidance of the fight; otherwise, Americans would drown beneath the "pressing sea of Yellow, Black and Brown."[21] Like William Dudley Pelley, Gerald B. Winrod, and other nativists, Lindbergh called on caucasian

Americans to fortify against the forces that threatened the supremacy of the white race.

Shortly after Paris fell, York knew that America needed to get involved overseas. He cabled Tennessee senator Kenneth McKellar asking if the United States could seize the French fleet and implored him to step up aid to Britain.[22] In the company of Tennessee governor Prentice Cooper, York addressed four hundred Gold Star mothers on October 4, 1940, proposing the course of action the country should take in the current troubled times. He cautioned: "[L]et us *not* close our eyes to the possibilities already on the war horizon. That is not only dangerous, it is downright foolish."[23] Although the country was officially neutral, Americans needed to be vigilant. Peace should be the objective of every American citizen, but given the fact of Hitler's aggression, it might be impossible to maintain. "I believe we can preserve our democracy in peace," he espoused, "[b]ut we will be willing to [go to] war, if war be the only chance [to preserve American traditions]."[24] Empathizing with the Gold Star mothers and their losses in the last war, York referred to his own twenty-year-old son, Alvin Junior:

> He is not anxious to go to the battle-front. But he is ready, if the leaders of this nation call him . . . and as his father, I pray that my wife will never become a Gold Star mother.[25]

York no longer believed that isolation was practicable.

On January 23, 1941, Lindbergh reassured the American people that they had nothing to fear and stressed that an "air invasion across the ocean [was] absolutely impossible at this time, or in any near future."[26] Japan, he added, possessed an air force so technologically inferior that they need not worry about Japanese expansion in China. He later consoled an Oklahoma audience, telling them not to fret over foreign war; rather, they should pitch in and try to settle this country's domestic issues and push the war to the back of their minds.[27]

On April 23, 1941, the Lone Eagle went on national radio, denouncing the interventionists. He said their inflammatory speeches made the Axis stronger and that "in time of war truth is always replaced by propaganda."[28] It was the interventionists, he argued, who had given comfort to the enemy and had drawn England and France into war. The interventionists were actually "defeatists," undermining the strength of America, and in their zealousness they were destroying democracy. They lacked sufficient confidence in their country's ability to defend itself or to operate rationally in a hostile world.[29]

Lindbergh's isolationist stance, his criticism of the Roosevelt administration, and his commendation by the Nazi government conspired against him. He aroused pointed criticism from public spokesmen, interventionist members of the Roosevelt administration, and FDR himself, who called Lindbergh a "Copperhead." Equating the colonel with the infamous Ohio representative to Congress during the Civil War, Clement L. Vallandingham, whom Abraham Lincoln charged with treason and deported to the Confederacy, FDR implied that Lindbergh was a traitor.[30] Convinced that his views and those of the government were irreconcilable, Lindbergh wrote Roosevelt and Secretary of War Stimson, resigning his commission in the Army Air Corps Reserve effective April 28, 1941. Resignation was his moral duty, he claimed, because he could be a more effective critic as a private citizen.[31] Lindbergh pondered his decision, writing:

> What luck it is to find myself opposing my country's entrance into a war I *don't* believe in, when I would so much rather be fighting for my country in a war I *do* believe in. Here I am stumping the country with pacifists and considering resigning as colonel . . . when there is no philosophy I disagree with more than that of a pacifist. . . . If only the United States could be on the *right* side of an intelligent war.[32]

Alvin York began his attack on Charles Lindbergh and America First in a Memorial Day address at the tomb of the Unknown Soldier. As the outstanding hero of World War I, he had attended the soldier's interment ceremonies in 1919 and was invited to return as official spokesman of the Veterans of Foreign Wars in 1941. By openly advocating intervention to a gathering of veterans, York was in no way preaching to the choir. Veterans were among the most divided and outspoken people in the country in regard to the European war, some clamoring for intervention and others for isolation.[33] As he addressed the crowd, which included President Roosevelt, York said:

> The Veterans of Foreign Wars, of which I am very proud to be a member, have kindly invited me to address you today. They could have chosen many far better speakers. There is a famous transatlantic aviator for one. And a United States Senator whose favorite bird must be the ostrich. They would have been glad to come here; but I was invited instead.[34]

Without Lindbergh's name being mentioned, or that of Sen. Burton K. Wheeler, everyone in the audience knew exactly to whom the plump old soldier referred.[35] He then tackled the popular argument that World War I had been for naught. Though the aftermath had proved disappointing, liberty had endured in America because of the sacrifices made between 1914 and 1918. He punctuated the sentiment by saying, "By our victory in the last war, we won a lease on liberty, not a deed to it. Now after 23 years, Adolf Hitler tells us that lease is expiring."[36] Reminding his listeners that American liberty had often required a blood sacrifice, York urged them to stand up to the Nazi threat.

He compared Senator Wheeler to Neville Chamberlain by pointing out that "the Senator ought to know that you can't protect yourself against bullets with an umbrella."[37] He considered isolationism and appeasement to be one and the same, for "France let Germany into the Rhineland because there was a large group of isolationist [*sic*] in the French government."[38] Americans should not feel safe because an ocean separated them from Germany: though the English Channel had separated Germany and Great Britain, Lindbergh's much admired *Luftwaffe* had bombed England virtually unopposed. He accentuated his point:

> I hope the day will never come when our capitol is renamed—Munich, D.C. . . . If I am wrong . . . then let us stop making guns, and let us surrender to Hitler right now while we can still do so on our own terms.[39]

This last statement stingingly criticized Lindbergh's assumption that a negotiated peace was in everyone's best interest. A few months later York would beam proudly when President Roosevelt quoted at length from this same speech during his Armistice Day address.[40]

The disagreements over American involvement, personified by York and Lindbergh, were unique among the nations who were engaged in the conflict. Detlef Junker noted that

> [t]he United States, blessed among the nations of the world, was the only major power to enjoy the privilege of being able to discuss for two years whether its vital interests were threatened by the Axis powers and Japan.[41]

As tensions mounted, so too did the debates over what America's responsibility should be.

Lindbergh continued his attack upon the interventionists when he addressed a huge America First rally in San Francisco nine days after Hitler launched Operation Barbarossa against the Soviet Union. In that July 1 speech he criticized the Roosevelt administration's foreign policy and cautioned strongly against extension of Lend-Lease credit to the Soviets. Countering York's contentions that the isolationists had been instrumental in bringing on the war, Lindbergh argued that "Russia and Germany would have been at each other's throats two years ago had it not been for the interventionist interference of England and France."[42] In other words, England and France had coerced Germany into invading them, deserving all the punishment they had received from the Nazi juggernaut.

On July 3, 1941, the day after *Sergeant York* premiered at the Astor Theatre, Alvin York spoke to the Tennessee Society of New York. Unlike Lindbergh, who hated crowds, York loved being in the company of people, and over the years he had become a moving and compelling speaker. Openly advocating intervention, York cautioned his listeners not to be as smug as Lindbergh was about the recent invasion of Russia:

> Twenty long years have gone by since I came home, and yet if you pick up your newspaper today, the same topic occupies the headlines as blazed across our front pages then. War . . . Russia's record of military success is rivalled only by Hitler's record for honesty.
>
> I will be sorry if Russia is defeated quickly, for a number of reasons. The first is Hitler *must* be stopped. The second is that a long, drawn out war between Russia and Germany would weaken both dictators. The third, and most important reason for my sorrow at a speedy German victory is that it will give fuel to such isolationists and appeasers as Senator Wheeler and ex-Colonel Lindbergh, and ex-President Hoover.
>
> They will burst forth with long, windy statements to the effect that this effort proves that the German Army is the greatest military machine in the history of the world, and that it therefore makes our helping England a little stupid, since no country, no matter how strong, can possibly stand up before the punishment dealt out by the Nazis.[43]

Continuing in the same vein, York said, "No, I am not a warmonger," while stressing the importance of an English victory for American security. "No one can possibly hate war as much as a soldier who has tried to catch his breath with the mud of trenches caked on his face." "No one in his right mind could possibly be in favor of war. . . . But there comes a time in the life of every free people when it was necessary to fight for the preservation of that freedom."[44] As he argued against sending in troops immediately, York passionately implored his listeners to wholeheartedly support British military aid. Proffering sentiments that mirrored Harry Warner's, he declared that Britain represented the cradle of American freedom, and liberty-loving citizens should rally to its support. York lambasted the isolationists, calling them "misguided but sincerely honest citizens who advocate appeasing dictators," and although he hated the Russians and everything they stood for, he said they too would need American support to defeat that personification of evil in the world—Adolf Hitler.[45]

As his speech continued, York's primary target became Charles Lindbergh, who represented to most Americans the ideology of America First. He drew his verbal knife, shoved it deeply into the popular perceptions of Lindbergh, and twisted it:

> Stalin did everything he could to make himself a super–Neville Chamberlain. And before two years of that counterfeit friendship had run its inevitable course, Germany was sending its armed legions across the border to attack its recent strange bed partner.
>
> Can ex-colonel Lindbergh now say that appeasement hasn't been given every conceivable chance to prove itself? . . . I hope that the former Colonel is not too hurt by what I have said here this afternoon and what I will continue to say on other afternoons and evenings. I hope he understands how I feel, and believe me when I say that I have tried to understand how he feels. I have failed in that, but that may be because of the fact that of all the medals I was fortunate enough to get, none of them came with the personal blessings of Adolf Hitler.[46]

York made it clear that he would continue his assault on isolationists in general and Lindbergh in particular. By mentioning the infamous medal that Göring had presented to the aviator in the name of the Fuhrer, York implied that Lindbergh—a man with a German-sounding name—was in fact a Nazi.[47] As evidence York cited the fact that Lindbergh had forsaken America and moved to England. While living there he had traveled to Germany and had rubbed elbows with the Nazi elite. Then once his adopted country—Britain—fell under attack, Lindbergh refused to rally to its aid, but instead turned tail and ran. Clearly, in York's opinion, the "ex-Colonel" was not only a traitor, but also a coward. If Lindbergh was a Nazi, then the AFC represented a fifth column working for the Axis powers.

York was not alone in his belief that America First was a Nazi front. An unattributed editorial in *The New Republic* charged that the AFC was the greatest domestic threat to U.S. security. "It has become the focal point of anti-Semitism; it feeds the disruptive forces of Roosevelt hatred . . . while professing the loftiest patriotic motives." Judging from the stance assumed by America First, anyone who stood firm against Hitler "must be a Red, a Jew, an Anglophile or an Administration rubber stamp."[48] Anglophobia abounded in the rhetoric of many noninterventionists. Lindbergh, like William Randolph Hearst, expressed the anti-British views of those who felt that English imperialism was a greater threat to American security than Nazism.[49]

Both the anti-interventionists and the interventionists believed conspiracies abounded at home. Throughout 1940–41 there was a trenchant fear of fifth column activity afoot in the heartland. Both camps decried the possibility of unchecked subversion in America. On June 5, 1940, Harry Warner called studio employees together, asking them to join him and cooperate with the FBI to ferret out fifth columnists. That same year George Britt wrote an impassioned monograph warning Americans that Hitler had successfully infiltrated the United States.[50]

While in Washington, D.C., in July, during the movie tour, Alvin York appeared on a special radio round-table discussion aired nationally by the Mutual Broadcasting System. The War Department's Bureau of Public Relations arranged, sponsored, and scripted the "conversation." The panel included York's former commander, retired Maj. Gen. George B. Duncan, and Brig. Gen. Lewis B. Hershey, the deputy director of the Selective Service System. The reason for the broadcast was to garner public support for extending the requirements and length of duty for those drafted into the peacetime military.[51] All three panelists praised the positive benefits of military service and boasted about how much better life in uniform was for servicemen in 1941 than it had been in 1918. The generals complimented York for coming to his country's aid once more, this time as director of the Fentress County Draft Board. Since he had three sons of draft age, York understood what he asked the American people to consider that evening and could empathize with the American public's concern about sending their children into battle.[52] The show sounded chatty and informal, but the message was direct and unsubtle: America was going to war and the country had better face that ugly fact now rather than later.[53]

At the same time, Gen. George C. Marshall gave testimony before Congress, asking it to increase the period of conscription. Marshall argued that when the year's service ended, the armed forces would be reduced to a skeleton force. In the event of emergency, America's anorexic military would be too weak to respond. The period of time necessary to bring the U.S. armed service "up to speed" could be devastating to the country.[54]

Fig. 7. Alvin York pledges his support of American intervention with some members of the Hollywood American Legion. Courtesy of the Alvin C. York collection.

The following day York, accompanied by Governor Cooper, spoke at a formal dinner sponsored by the Tennessee Society of Washington, D.C. Alluding to Lindbergh, York called the noninterventionists a bunch of "Munich Men." Regarding the recent Nazi invasion of the Soviet Union, he noted, "Why, not even Hitler's friends can trust him. Russia has tried to be friendly, and now see the trouble it is in. Mussolini tried to be friendly, and now no one even knows what ever became of Italy." York took a shot at the AFC jokingly, saying, "When I hear people talking of keeping the peace with Hitler, I wonder what has happened to those people who say it. Are they for America first?"[55]

The sergeant acknowledged that it must strike many people as odd that a man who had to be "argued" into fighting in 1918 now openly called for war. The cause then had been "to keep the world safe for democracy"; but now America faced an even greater threat.[56] Hitler represented pure evil, whereas the Kaiser had merely symbolized naked aggression. York concluded his speech by endorsing FDR's request for increasing the term of service for draftees to eighteen months, the need for convoys to protect American ships, and immediate mobilization for impending war.[57]

The debate grew more heated after the Nye-Clark Senate subcommittee hearings began, proceedings that accused Hollywood of disseminating propaganda. On August 9 Charles Lindbergh addressed an America First rally in Cleveland, Ohio. Titling his presentation "Government by Representation or Subterfuge?" he accused Roosevelt's administration of being in cahoots with radical fringe groups, working secretly to usurp the Constitution and lead America into war. Among those sinister elements lurked the film industry, which he accused of staging false events to lead the people astray. He stated emphatically:

> The same groups who call on us to defend democracy and freedom abroad, demand that we kill democracy and freedom at home by forcing four-fifths of our people into war against their will. The one-fifth who are for war call the four-fifths who are against war the "fifth-column."[58]

On the evening of September 11, Lindbergh continued in the same vein. He addressed over eight thousand people at an America First rally in Des Moines, Iowa. During that fateful speech, he singled out three groups whom he accused of fomenting hysteria and pushing the country needlessly toward war: the British, the Jews, and the Roosevelt administration. He maintained that the Jews most accountable for interventionist agitation worked in the movie industry:

> Instead of agitating for war the Jewish groups in this country should be opposing it in every possible way, for they will be among the first to feel its consequences. . . . A few farsighted Jewish people realize this and stand opposed to intervention. But the majority still do not. The greatest danger to this country lies in their large ownership and influence in our motion pictures, our press, our radio, and our government.[59]

The speech angered many people, especially Jews, who perceived it not only as anti-Semitic, but also threatening. Lindbergh seemed to indicate that if war came, America would quickly surrender to the crushing superiority of the Nazis. Jews in America, therefore, faced certain doom unless they opposed war. Underneath those assumptions was the implication that Jews, who controlled much of the media in America, had conspired against the U.S. citizenry and had infiltrated the federal government.[60] By making these statements Lindbergh "crossed the line separating legitimate dissent from conspiracy."[61]

Interventionists exploited the speech, citing excerpts to further its cause. The FFF compiled the texts of all of Lindbergh's speeches and articles in a booklet entitled *America's Answer to Lindbergh*. Endorsed by the prominent theologian Reinhold Niebuhr, this work used Lindbergh's own words to condemn him. Likewise, the Friends of Democracy published *Is Lindbergh a Nazi?* which condemned the ex-colonel as a goose-stepping puppet of the Third Reich. The man who had once been the AFC's greatest asset had "by mid-1941 become its major liability," for even John T. Flynn, one of the original founders of the committee, had come to believe that Lindbergh had overstepped the bounds of good taste.[62] Likewise, FDR confided to Henry Morgenthau that he was "absolutely convinced" that Lindbergh *was* a Nazi.[63] Interventionist writer Max Lerner said, "The America First group has become the center of a genuine honest-to-goodness Fascist alignment. Lindbergh has become a real fascist symbol."[64]

Perplexed, Lindbergh appeared to be at a loss over the knee-jerk reaction to his speech:

> I felt I worded my Des Moines address carefully and moderately. It seems that anything can be discussed in America today except the Jewish problem. The very mention of the word "Jew" is cause for a storm.[65]

He claimed he had intended his address as an appeal to reason for the Jewish community and an expression of his personal concern for their welfare. The fact that quasi-Nazi groups in America praised him brought no comfort, while those who accused him of Jew-baiting disturbed him because they failed to comprehend his intentions. Because of the Des Moines speech, Lindbergh received a torrent of hate mail and his reputation suffered. William Allen White castigated the aviator, saying, "Shame on you, Charles Lindbergh, for injecting the Nazi race issue into American politics."[66] Wendell Willkie, speaking on behalf of the FFF and the MPPDA, accused him of being un-American. Others compared him to Father Coughlin.[67]

After York addressed an American Legion meeting in Jamestown, Tennessee, on September 13, reporters asked for his reaction to the recent allegations by Lindbergh and the Nye-Clark subcommittee regarding pro-

Fig. 8. "Throw Lindbergh square in jail, today not tomorrow," York said as he continued his fight with Lindbergh and America First. Courtesy of the Alvin C. York collection.

paganda in film. Although he was accused along with Hollywood of warmongering, York saw no reason to investigate. Instead, he interjected his belief that the isolationists endangered America by refusing to recognize Hitler for what he was—the Antichrist. Although the senators and the aviator might have had the best intentions, they were busily at work paving America's road to hell. Later that day York issued a statement:

> Lindbergh and Gerald P. Nye ought to be shut up by throwing them square in jail—today, not tomorrow. We can't risk our whole freedom, our country, listening to them when we know full well that they're either looking at

the world through rose-colored glasses or they're downright Nazi-inclined—and one is about as dangerous as the other. . . . I'm anti-Nazi and I'm proud of it, and I'll be glad to tell that to the Senate committee investigating what they call "war propaganda" from Hollywood if they want me to. But personally, I don't think anyone is howling about anti-Nazi propaganda from any source except those who are definitely Nazi-inclined themselves. . . . I think it's just as much the duty of the people in Hollywood to tell us the truth about Hitler's outfit as it is the newspapers to tell us the truth. So far as I'm concerned, I don't think they've pictured the conditions in Germany as bad as they could truthfully have done.[68]

Sergeant York threw down the gauntlet, and in doing so he broadened his attack on the isolationists by insinuating that the Nye-Clark subcommittee was a Nazi front. The Nazis, it seemed, had successfully infiltrated the halls of Congress, and the committee, composed of several men who were openly isolationists and seemingly anti-Semitic, appeared to be anti–First Amendment as well.

Traveling to Milwaukee on September 14 to preside over the opening of the annual American Legion convention, York enlarged upon his Jamestown remarks, adding to his pointed criticism of Lindbergh, Nye, and Wheeler. His public condemnation of them had created controversy and had drawn personal attacks from anti-interventionist reporters. So when he took the podium, York humorously let it be known that the attacks had not fazed him. He found it absurd that Nye had not seen half the films he considered propaganda, and he regarded the subcommittee hearings as hypocritical:

Maybe I shouldn't have come here to speak to you today. Maybe I should go into hiding and not speak to anyone. I say that because I see where Senator Nye says that the picture which bears my name is propaganda. I don't think it is, but perhaps I shouldn't say that, for I have an unfair advantage over Senator Nye. I saw the picture. If our lives are propaganda, then Senator Nye should start immediately tearing up all the history books in the country. . . . just as Hitler made a bonfire of great literature in Germany.[69]

Nye, like the Nazis, had wanted to keep the truth from the American people, he contended, and every time Nye supporters endorsed isolationism, they did the bidding of the Third Reich. He accused Senator Wheeler of being out of touch with his constituency.[70] Defending the movie industry, he stated, "[I]t seems to me that Harry Warner, Jesse Lasky and Louis B.

Mayer are being persecuted, not because they hate Hitler, but because they are being unfair to him."[71]

York consciously mentioned the two men who had persuaded him that Jews were humans—without horns and tails—and the mogul who perhaps best represented the film industry in many Americans' eyes—Louis B. Mayer. York, the Christian soldier, now stood firmly beside his new Jewish friends. Harry Warner had opened his eyes to the horrors of Nazi Germany, convincing York that Hitler's regime was the purest manifestation of evil on the planet. In a New York radio address during a promotional appearance for his film, York cautioned: "Any American who reads the words of Hitler from the days when he penned *Mein Kampf* to his latest diatribe . . . must realize that here at last is the Anti-Christ of prophecy."[72] In later remarks he added the biblical allusion that "Nye and the other isolationists are throwing Christians to the lions."[73] Failure to understand the menace of Hitler was tantamount to biblical destruction. York criticized Flynn as well:

> John T. Flynn . . . said that there were 130 million people in this country, and that he supposed 129 million of them are against Hitler. That still leaves one million who aren't against Hitler. I didn't know the America First Committee had so many supporters.[74]

Proof that York's fundamentalist worldview had undergone profound changes shone through when he spoke about a tolerant, Godly America that represented *all* the moral virtues of the world:

> Let any Protestant, Catholic, Jew or Mohammaden [*sic*] live, . . . so long as he believes firmly and undyingly that this American way of living is the right way. . . . May Almighty God help us to continue to believe that freedom of mankind, whatever his race, color, or creed, is the most desperately important thing in our lives.[75]

York had come a long way from much of his earlier, provincial way of thinking. America represented the last bastion of salvation for a world engulfed in evil, so it must take the offensive and fight the good fight, regardless of the initial sacrifice.

As he continued the oration in Milwaukee, he argued that most people that he came in contact with wanted American involvement in the war. York took potshots at the anti-interventionists, questioned their patriotism, and made his distrust of Lindbergh well known. "Our preamble calls on us to defend the American Constitution, and I think we ought to

Fig. 9. Gary Cooper in *Sergeant York.* Courtesy of the Alvin C. York collection.

be ready to defend it against anybody, even against Lindbergh and Wheeler."[76] Then York went on to say that he knew he could trust his fellow veterans in the American Legion and that when America did get involved in the war, Legionnaires would be four-square behind it.

> I can't hike like I did in the World War, but I can drive a tank just as far into the front lines as a young man . . . I think Hitler has gone just about far enough and it's time to give him a licking.[77]

Ironically, that very same day, Charles Lindbergh went to the movies. The man who stood at the forefront of the battle against intervention and considered Hollywood a domestic threat decided to see some of the purportedly sinister propaganda himself. The picture he opted to see was *Sergeant York.* Later he wrote in his journal:

Thought the acting much above average. It was, of course, good propaganda for war—glorification of war, etc. However, I do not think a picture of this type is at all objectionable and dangerous.[78]

Although Lindbergh recognized the movie for what it was—propaganda veiled as entertainment—he perhaps saw in it many of the values he espoused, deeming it safe for the American public's consumption.

In response to his September 13 and 14 remarks, York received a flurry of angry letters. Mrs. Norine Crosby of Swartz Creek, Michigan, felt pity for him and expressed the odd sentiment that the real enemy to America was England, "our worst enemy," not "our friends the Germans." She continued in a vein reminiscent of Winrod, Pelley, and Shepard: "In the first carnage we had that dreaming fool of a Wilson for president, now we have that egotistical Jew at our head. . . . If you wish more about Roosevelt's Jewry I can furnish it to you." Mrs. Crosby declared that Churchill was also Jewish and accused the prime minister of saying, "England will fight until the very last *American* [is dead]." She concluded her friendly though erratic letter by saying,

> What asses we are made of with the help of our administration. I Hear rumors of impeachment. Dear Mr. York, if you need hospitalization make the ones who look after this give it to you, and I hope success for you.[79]

The tone of Mrs. Crosby's letter was reminiscent of a grandmother gently scolding a mischievous child. She exhibited genuine compassion for the sergeant, but unlike his detractors, who wanted to inflict pain on him, she thought he needed to see a doctor, as if intervention were some sort of disease.

Several other people also voiced their displeasure. Walter Camp of Trenton, New Jersey, wrote:

> You say you allowed your picture to be made because you wanted to encourage patriotism in the youth of America. Well you skunk and ignoramus, you got fooled yourself in the last war, and now for a few dirty dollars that you are getting, you are betraying millions of young men. . . . You ought to kiss every step the Hon. Chas. Lindbergh and that Champion of Men, Mr. Nye is [*sic*] making, just to stop others from getting into the same stupid conditions as you are at the present time. It's a shame that such people as you came back, it would have been a blessing if you were shot to pieces. May you break your neck right now as you and others like you are a menace to civilization.[80]

It was clear the ex-pacifist had struck a raw nerve. The issue of intervention was sharply dividing Americans in the fall of 1941, and thousands felt exactly the same as Mr. Camp. The bitterness caused by the memory of World War I had convinced many that America had nothing to gain from another war and, furthermore, that it simply "wasn't our fight."[81]

An anonymous letter signed "Just an Average American citizen" arrived from Minneapolis. The author addressed the letter to "Hero" York followed by a question mark and maintained that the "Average American Citizen" believed York to be "spouting off at the instigation of your motion picture sponsors." His bald declaration,

> I have not seen your picture (Sergeant York); nor do I intend to do so, as I imagine it is a bit of juicy warmongering propoganda [sic] put out by those interests who apparently bought your soul with the deal.[82]

echoed the sentiments of propaganda hearing sponsors Nye and Clark. This vitriolic comment touched on the familiar theme of what constitutes true Americanism, for which this "Average American Citizen" had an answer:

> Maybe you think I am biased and jumping at conclusions in not even seeing your picture before condemning it; but that is just what you would do by condemning such real American Patriots as Lindbergh and Nye to jail without listening to what they have to say . . . it seems to me that at one time or another you admitted to someone that you were just "an ignorant mountaineer," so let's just leave it that way. . . . Thank God for such clear-sighted, realistic 100% Americans as Lindbergh, Nye and Wheeler.[83]

The nativism apparent in the author's letter reflected the feelings of many isolationists, America Firsters, and various "Shirt" organizations: that 100 percent Americans should concern themselves only with America—period.

York received several more letters that criticized his interventionist stand, claimed that he was a warmonger, and held that he was a dupe of the Anglo-Jewish conspiracy bent on undermining American liberty. Lindbergh, on the other hand, was described as a man who had had the good sense to leave England after having lived there for years and clearly could not be considered a fawning Anglophile.

Other critics, such as retired Col. J. V. Kuznik of New York, accused the sergeant of being a disgrace to his war record by endorsing a movie based on his life:

Heretofore, I have merely deplored your showmanship, but your insulting and unwarranted condemnation of a group of real American patriots cannot help but arouse indignation and resentment that you too should allow yourself to become debauched by a warmongering press and its No. 1 ally, the movies.[84]

Kuznik defended Lindbergh for his contributions to aviation, science, and the military and reiterated the allegations made against York by the seven survivors: that the Tennessean did not deserve the title of the greatest hero of World War I and, further, that the real heroes lay in military cemeteries in Belgium and France. Though Kuznik stopped short of accusing York of cowardice, he chastised him for profiting from his war record and hoped he would renounce interventionism and embrace the cause of isolationism.[85]

What is interesting about all these letters is the level of savagery in them. The invective they display exhibits just how sensitive the intervention issue had become. Most wanted York to break his neck, die at the hands of a firing squad, suffer some other bodily injury, seek medical attention, or at the very least go to jail. It is curious that many labeled York a coward, for if anything his public stance on the intervention issue had attested to his courage. Finally, the bizarre association of York with Wall Street in some letters perhaps demonstrates that Senator Nye's committee and the popular press had been successful in maintaining claims that American entry in World War I had been plotted by greedy bankers.[86]

Lindbergh received similar hate mail from his detractors, and a common theme in both sets of letters was un-Americanism.[87] One of the worst accusations a U.S. citizen could suffer was to be labeled un-American; yet no standard for judgment existed upon which everyone could agree. To level charges of un-Americanism at two men with opposing views, when millions of Americans had perceived one or the other as the epitome of everything America represented, further increased confusion over what America's course of action should be.

That debate over who or what constituted "100 percent Americanism" fueled the creation of a dangerous and insidious Senate subcommittee chaired by Representative Martin Dies of Texas. Originally created as an organ to ferret out Nazi saboteurs and spies, it degenerated in the late 1940s and early 1950s into the House Committee on Un-American Activities (HUAC), which has been more commonly associated with the Cold War witch hunts. Hollywood also found itself at the center of those hearings, but it did not fare as well then as it did with the Nye-Clark subcommittee.[88]

In the midst of the heated debate between the two heroes, interventionist columnist Walter Winchell jumped into the fray. Celebrating York's outspoken criticism of the colonel, Winchell summed up the situation in this way:

> Here is a thumbnail portrait of two famous American citizens that tells its own story. . . . One is Sergeant York, America's outstanding World War Hero; the other is Charles Lindbergh. York fought in the World War and was ready to sacrifice his life for his country, Lindbergh is ready to sacrifice his country for his life. . . . When Lindbergh returned from Europe a hero, he accepted a fat salary for the use of his name on an airline. When York returned from Europe, he received offers totaling more than a million dollars, but he turned them down because he didn't want to commercialize his heroism. . . . When York finally accepted a film company's offer to film his life, he took the money to finance building schools in Tennessee. Sergeant York, America's No. 1 hero, is for all out help to England. Lindbergh, whether he realizes it or not, is for all out aid to Hitler. York was decorated with a medal by the American government; Lindbergh by the Nazi. Lindbergh says he is for America first. Sergeant York says it a lot more convincingly when he offers his life once again in the cause of Liberty.[89]

Speaking at a Red Cross conference in Knoxville, Tennessee, on October 8, 1941, the twenty-third anniversary of his famous exploit in the Argonne, York praised the courageous work done by the Red Cross in providing relief for the war victims in England. He accused Lindbergh and his "fellow travelers" of undermining their humanitarian work in hope of assuring a Nazi victory over Great Britain.[90] The anti-interventionists sought to torpedo the very ideals all Americans held dear, while at the same time accusing York, Hollywood, and others of "War Mongering" to divide the American polity.[91] Countering those who said he wanted to spread war fever, York reminded his audience that having witnessed the horrors of war, he hated it; however, given the current conditions, war was inevitable. Americans must prepare themselves; otherwise, thousands would suffer unnecessarily.

In his last public address for America First, six weeks before Pearl Harbor, Lindbergh continued his accusations against the Roosevelt administration and the film industry. He told a Madison Square Garden audience of around forty thousand: "The most fundamental issue today is not one of war or peace, but one of integrity. . . . There is no danger to this nation from without. The only danger lies from within."[92] He urged listeners to join him and take the fight to Washington. Something must be done about a rogue administration that was dead set on the destruction of all American principles and ideals.

At the American Legion's annual Armistice Day dinner held in Evansville, Indiana, York criticized the alarming level of unpreparedness apparent in America. He argued that Americans were too soft, too complacent, too smug, and too apathetic. Once again he chose the opportunity to wag a scolding finger at Lindbergh. He criticized the ex-colonel's unwillingness to recognize the threat that Hitler posed for the U.S. Good Americans needed to prepare themselves for the inevitable conflict and put America First out of business. He cautioned his listeners:

> The type of speeches Mr. Lindbergh [makes deludes Americans, and] unless we wake up, we'll be easier for Hitler than France was. . . . Charles Lindbergh, Senator Wheeler, Senator Nye and every other leader in the America First movement is [*sic*] an appeaser of Adolf Hitler. That is not an accusation. That is a simple statement of fact . . . we cannot avoid this new war, unless, like Lindbergh, we value our present security more than we value liberty, freedom, and democracy. . . . If we are defeated our children will grow up reading *Mein Kampf* instead of the *Family Bible*. I'm against the isolationists because I stand willing to make some sacrifices now—to insure that the children of this nation will grow up and be able to read that the Cherry Tree was chopped down by George Washington, not Charles Lindbergh. . . . America will defeat both Hitler and Lindbergh.[93]

By the time York presented the speech, he was convinced that America needed to declare war immediately. He doubted the Soviets could hold on much longer, and though he detested Communism, he said it represented the lesser of the two evils. U.S. isolation soon ended, for in just twenty-six days the Japanese bombed Pearl Harbor.

York's fight with Lindbergh played itself out across headlines and the airwaves in America on the eve of war. Likewise, Harry Warner fought valiantly against entrenched isolationists in Congress who tried to stifle his attempts to inform Americans about Nazism. Singled out as one of the worst warmongerers in Hollywood, Warner stormed off to Washington to defend his studio and the industry.

6

Hollywood under the Gun
The Senate Investigation of Propaganda in Motion Pictures

On August 1, 1941, Senators Gerald P. Nye of North Dakota and Bennett Champ Clark of Missouri introduced Senate Resolution 152, drafted largely by America First's true believer, John T. Flynn, calling for a thorough investigation of the film industry.[1] The investigation would be carried out by a subcommittee of the Interstate Commerce Committee directed by isolationist Sen. Burton K. Wheeler. The subcommittee was chaired by D. Worth Clark of Idaho and included Homer T. Bone of Washington, Charles W. Tobey of New Hampshire, and Ernest McFarland of Arizona. Though Nye and Clark, who sponsored the bill that led to the hearings, were not members of the subcommittee, they were the first to testify, and the subcommittee was generally referred to as the "Nye-Clark Committee." Nye, Clark, and many of the subcommittee's members hailed from the country's interior; their politics had been shaped by Populism, and they belonged to or were sympathetic with the America First Committee (AFC).[2] Staunchly isolationist, they were generally suspicious of foreigners and held some of the same views as the cryptofascist organizations that flourished in America during the Depression. They resented Hollywood and the license they associated with it and tended to be Anglophobic. All these resentments emerged once the hearings were under way.

The subcommittee leveled several charges against Hollywood, saying that it was dedicated to warmongering, that it constituted a Jewish-controlled monopoly, and that it was engaged in covert dealings with the Roosevelt administration. In their isolationist—and some would argue anti-Semitic—opinion, Hollywood had willingly violated the official neutrality of the United States and spread war fever among a gullible public.[3] The eight movies they found particularly reprehensible were

154

Confessions of a Nazi Spy, The Great Dictator, Dive Bomber, Flight Command, That Hamilton Woman, Escape, Underground, and *Sergeant York.*[4]

Nye and Clark were neither the first nor the only people intent on curbing the power of Hollywood. On February 24, 1941, Rep. Lyle H. Boren of Oklahoma called for a thorough investigation of the film community because he argued that Hollywood studio heads were ignoring the consent decree they had signed in 1940. His bill got nowhere at the time but proved damaging to Hollywood in 1948 and played a critical role in destroying the studio system.

The proposed hearings launched by Nye and Clark immediately drew attention from several quarters. Not surprisingly, some people, like Silver Shirt Legionnaire William Dudley Pelley, praised the proposal. Others, such as reporter Michael Straight, criticized them and their intention. He accused Nye and Clark of being the toadies of isolationist Sen. Burton K. Wheeler of Montana. The subcommittee was established because "its sponsors, Senator Nye and Senator Clark, did not command enough votes to bring a resolution *for a proper Senate investigation* to the floor of the Senate."[5]

Gerald P. Nye had long harbored bad feelings toward the film industry. He had called for the creation of a government regulatory agency in 1934 to screen and classify movies. Filmmakers rejected such direct governmental intervention and opted to police the industry more rigidly through PCA.[6] Bennett Champ Clark loathed Hollywood as well; both men were convinced the movie industry was undermining the morality of the country and Jewish moguls were bent on turning America into a country lusting for war. Delivering a national radio address from Saint Louis the same day Clark entered the resolution, Nye declared: "Go to Hollywood. It is a raging volcano of war fever. The place swarms with refugees [and] . . . with British actors"; he said it was ruled by foreigners and Jews.[7] The movie colony represented "the most potent and dangerous Fifth Column in our country," and the danger America needed to confront immediately was not the external Nazi threat but the international Jewish conspiracy.[8] "[T]hese men with the motion picture films in their hands, can address 80,000,000 people a week, cunningly and persistently inoculating them with the virus of war."[9] Hollywood Jews, the modern-day equivalent of Typhoid Mary, spread their deadly contagions among a defenseless public. Nye insinuated that the federal government had prodded them to produce prowar propaganda, saying: "I am informed that there are Government men on every moving-picture lot in Hollywood."[10]

His remarks earned plaudits from hosts of noninterventionists, among them Father Charles Coughlin, who welcomed the investigation.

In his recent reappraisal of America First, Bill Kauffman applauded Nye's efforts to muzzle Hollywood, referring to the filmmakers who called for intervention as the "Merchants of Death on Sunset Boulevard."[11] Though he overlooks the fact that Jews in the film community who spoke out against Nazism were in the minority, he insinuates, like Nye, that they constituted a real threat to American security. Displaying latter-day xenophobia, he considers them un-American because they were foreign born; he alleges, "It is a curiously forgotten fact that before Pearl Harbor most 'real' writers . . . were antiwar."[12] Though Kauffman rightly asks for a more sober reappraisal of the AFC, his own prejudices interfere with its effectiveness.[13]

At least forty million people went to the movies each week.[14] In addition to the advertised first-run feature they paid to see, audiences watched short features, trailers, cartoons, and newsreels. Many isolationists believed that the interventionists purposely edited the news in such a way as to promote war hysteria.[15] Senator Wheeler distrusted the film community because he believed the foreigners who dominated it threatened the country and impugned its reputation. He called interventionist moguls by the wildly inappropriate term "Hollywood Hitlers."[16] Noninterventionists claimed that motion pictures excluded their viewpoints, denying any opportunity to present an antidote to the war fever they purportedly spread. The movies, therefore, posed a sinister threat to a generally unsophisticated audience that fell prey to its manufactured misinformation.[17] The implicit accusation that the American viewing public was stupid and unable to think for itself only added more tension to an ever-deteriorating situation.

It could be argued that the Nye-Clark hearings represented a pitched battle between America First and the Fight for Freedom Committee (FFF). The subcommittee, backed by America First, had intended to bridle what they regarded as the Jewish- controlled, British-loving film industry, whereas the film industry, supported by interventionist editor Ulric Bell's FFF, wanted to prove to the world that America First was an insidious cabal packed with fifth columnists, spies, and cowards. Dorothy Thompson, wife of Sinclair Lewis and an outspoken interventionist, declared that America First was "Quislingism, the last and most grotesque form of fascism."[18] The isolationists, however, believed that they were protecting the best interests of American society by closing the country off from the realities of the world situation.[19]

Members of the Motion Picture Producers and Distributors of America (MPPDA) met on August 4, 1941, to plan their defense against the charges. Harry Warner, eager to vindicate the industry, offered to personally pay for a nationwide radio campaign extolling the patriotic virtues of the film industry. MPPDA members declined his generous offer, opting instead to defend themselves collectively at the hearings. Chief strategist Ulric Bell, argued that the film industry should take the offensive and appoint an advisory committee to hire a high-profile, prestigious attorney to defend them.[20] In a somewhat surprising move, they chose Wendell Willkie. Selecting the former Republican presidential candidate, an avowed internationalist, to serve as the film industry's defense counsel rankled Nye, who saw Willkie as a traitor to his party.[21]

The MPPDA followed the announcement of Willkie as their counsel by launching an offensive salvo with the aid of the FFF. Representatives sent an open letter to Congress signed by scores of individuals, including Alvin York, Edward G. Robinson, Dorothy Thompson, and "Wild Bill" Donovan. In the missive they criticized the intentions, insinuations, and isolationist posture of the Nye-Clark subcommittee. They took umbrage with the committee's including *Sergeant York* among the accused films and were convinced that the subcommittee wanted to muzzle the film industry and gut the First Amendment in the process.[22] *Sergeant York* the movie, and Alvin York the man, both stood accused of violating America's neutrality. York argued that the subcommittee was guilty of a conflict of interest and derided the investigation as one-sided and its membership as isolationist, with the single exception of freshman senator Ernest McFarland of Arizona. Likewise, Walter Winchell criticized the goals of the committee and called the AFC the "Hitler First–America Last" committee.[23]

Wendell Willkie followed their lead by sending a letter to the subcommittee's chair, D. Worth Clark, which was printed in its entirety in the *Hollywood Reporter*. It made no bones about the fact that the film industry stood solidly against everything Hitler represented and said they need not apologize for their sentiments. Segments of the industry had criticized the Nazi regime out of moral courage, not because of some imagined clandestine pact with the Roosevelt administration, but because they were good Americans. Willkie ridiculed the accusation that Hollywood

Fig. 10. Wendell Willkie, who defended Hollywood at the Senate Propaganda hearings, at the premier of *Sergeant York.* Alvin York is on the left, Willkie is on the right. Courtesy of the Alvin C. York collection.

produced anti-Nazi films out of greed, saying that if money were the prime motivator, Hollywood would appease Hitler, not criticize him. He promised that émigrés would be called to testify about the bestial nature of Hitler's regime. The concluding remarks articulated an argument that many accepted: If the hearings succeeded, the First Amendment meant nothing, and the collapse of the remainder of the Bill of Rights would follow, resulting in an American fascist state.[24] Unimpressed, Clark dismissed Willkie's dispatch as both insignificant and irrelevant. Willkie later requested that the letter be read into the record of the propaganda hearings, where it sits sandwiched in the middle of Nye's testimony.[25]

While Willkie wrangled with Clark over the subcommittee's focus, Lowell Mellett, presidential aide and future head of the Office of War Information's Bureau of Motion Pictures, published an article in *The Atlantic Monthly* entitled "Government Propaganda."[26] Writing in response to the hearings, he attempted to distance the Roosevelt administration from the film industry. Filmmakers had taken it upon themselves to exercise their right of free speech to tackle current European affairs, he argued, doing so without any governmental coercion or collusion. Mellett claimed that he was sick and tired of people screaming "propaganda" every time a controversial film went into release. He noted the irony that no public furor had erupted when the peacetime draft went into effect, that "the American people took it in their stride, for the American people did understand what was happening in the world and . . . were prepared in mind and heart to do their part."[27] Both Nye and Clark dismissed his article during their testimonies, arguing that the denial of any relationship between the Roosevelt administration and movies was tantamount to a confession of guilt.

Opening on September 9, 1941, the hearings almost immediately took on an ominous tone, when "in an astonishing move, the committee denied Willkie the right to cross-examine or call witnesses; McFarland cast the only dissenting vote."[28] The Arizona senator alone argued against swearing in senators before allowing them to testify. He said, "I think that a United States Senator should have the privilege of appearing before a Senate committee without being sworn," because "he was sworn in before he took his seat in the Senate."[29]

Taking the stand as the prosecution's first witness, Sen. Gerald P. Nye insisted that he be sworn in. He dismissed anti-Semitic charges leveled against him by offering up the most callous of defenses, saying, "I have splendid Jewish friends in and out of the moving-picture business."[30] He was obviously no anti-Semite since some of his best friends were Jews.[31]

Nye startled the proceedings when he put forward the argument that the motion picture industry deserved no First Amendment protection. As he understood the Constitution and legal precedent, the First Amendment protected free speech, not entertainment; therefore, Willkie's and the industry's opposition to the hearings as a violation of the First Amendment was meaningless, for it in no way protected the rights of movie makers to express themselves.[32]

Nye charged that "[t]hose primarily responsible for the propaganda pictures were born abroad."[33] Being foreign born, he implied, made their loyalty to the United States suspect. Nye believed that British undercover agents roved freely in Hollywood and that Tinsel Town was a hotbed of espionage. Though the senator meant to counter Willkie's intention of producing eye-witnesses to the horrors of Nazi persecution, his clumsy comments only seemed to confirm the anti-Semitic charges that had been leveled against him.[34] In his view it was the Jews, not Hitler, who posed the greatest threat to America, because filmmakers had willingly promoted a state of fear and anxiety in order to incite war hysteria. Nye wanted to determine how many of the alleged propaganda pictures "were the work in part or in full of refugee or alien authors [and] . . . how many immigration visas have been arranged for motion-picture executives and by them."[35] Jews represented an insidious fifth column that undermined American liberty, harbored a blood-lust, and loved war; therefore, Americans should gladly welcome the committee's desire to curb their control over the motion picture industry.[36]

Nye argued that the American people sat unprotected from the propaganda onslaught attacking them weekly in movie theaters. Cinema, in his opinion, posed a unique menace because of its captive audience. Radio listeners could change channels if they disliked a program. Newspapers and magazines also made their prejudices known so that discriminating readers could chose what they wanted to read.[37]

As he concluded his testimony, Nye singled out Harry Warner as the worst of the Jewish propagandists. He believed that Warner carried on secret correspondence with FDR, prodding the president toward war. Little did he know that Warner had only recently mended fences with Roosevelt and they corresponded only on rare occasions. Nye alleged that Warner and FDR illegally provided Britain with battleships *before* the "Destroyers for Bases" deal was negotiated and even accused him of blocking the appointment of Joseph Breen's replacement at the PCA when the chief censor chose to accept a position at RKO.[38] Although Warner, as well as every other studio head in the industry, had cared deeply about who replaced Joe Breen, he had little control over the choice of the successor. Lastly, Nye said that Harry Warner wanted to see Ireland bombed into oblivion and would produce evidence proving all his accusations.[39]

Oddly enough, it was Senator McFarland who assumed the role as the chief antagonist against the subcommittee. Since the senators denied Willkie the right to cross-examine witnesses, McFarland accepted the role of chief inquisitor for the defense. "You know," he joked, "I'm a pretty good Democrat and I did not want to have to defend a Republican; I just preferred to let him defend himself by asking his own questions."[40] Under the Arizona senator's questioning, Nye admitted that he had seen only two of the eight films he had labeled propaganda and could not remember for certain which ones they were.[41]

McFarland countered Nye's rather dubious claim that the public was hostage to film propaganda. Movie audiences, he argued, exercised the same freedom of choice afforded those of radio and print media, for patrons could walk out of the theater or educate themselves beforehand about current releases and make their voices heard at the box office. McFarland offered this as evidence because Nye's earlier statement indicated that the studios that made anti-Nazi pictures did poorly at the box office. If so, he argued, patrons did exercise the same kind of freedom of choice afforded by radio and print media. Chairman Clark entered the fray and offered a possible solution: create legislation requiring equal time for controversial issues in movies, as did existing radio laws.[42]

McFarland requested a special screening of the offending films, but Sen. Kenneth Tobey of New Hampshire objected because he feared that exposure to them would leave the subcommittee "punch drunk."[43] While Willkie sat silently frustrated, McFarland chipped away at the case of the subcommittee. As reporter Jack Moffitt quipped, "McFarland worked on Nye like a censor working on *Lady Chatterly's Lover*."[44]

Testifying the next day, Sen. Bennett Champ Clark echoed Nye's arguments that the First Amendment did not protect motion pictures and that a terrible Jewish conspiracy had unleashed thousands of mind-poisoning pictures upon a defenseless public. He spoke of movies in almost pathological terms:

> At the present time they [Jewish moguls] have opened those 17,000 theaters to the idea of war, to the glorification of war, to the glorification of England's imperialism, to the creation of hatred of the people of Germany and now of France, to the hatred of those in America who disagree with them. . . . In other words, they are turning these 17,000 theatres into 17,000 . . . mass meetings for war. . . . [Movies] are used to infect the minds of their audiences with hatred, to inflame them, to arouse their emotions and make them clamor for war. Not one word on the side of the argument against war is heard.[45]

Like Nye, Clark harbored special antipathy toward Warner Bros. He singled out that studio, charging that it made more "hate producing films than any other company in America."[46] He boasted,

> I, for one, pledge that if the industry does not end this propaganda for war, I shall do everything in my power to bring about once and for all the utter destruction of the monopolistic grasp of this little handful of men.[47]

When McFarland asked him if he had seen any of the so-called propaganda movies, Clark responded, "No, I have not seen any of them. I am not going to see any of them."[48] He went on to proudly declare that he had seen only one film in the past six years. Like his cosponsor, Clark found movies in general objectionable as an entertainment; he rarely set foot in a theater and based his case solely upon hearsay evidence.[49]

When Clark's testimony ended, Senator McFarland once again voiced his objections. He expressed faith in the average citizen, saying, "I have confidence in the American public to be able to distinguish between propaganda and facts," and he condemned the notion that Hollywood was involved in a conspiracy bent on "infect[ing] the minds of Americans":

> I should further like to say with regard to all these pictures that have been named here that one could tell they are war pictures by the titles. And references and statements have been made to the fact that you could cut off a person upon the air if you did not want to listen to him. You know its going to be a war picture by the title of it, and if you do not want to go and see it, you do not have to go and see it.[50]

His level-headed assessment of the situation perturbed the senator from Missouri. Lacking McFarland's faith in the American public, Clark hotly protested that film titles purposely misled viewers.

On September 11 John T. Flynn, the subcommittee's star witness and self-professed film expert, vehemently condemned the film industry. Hollywood was a hotbed of subversive activity and intent on dragging America into war. Like Nye and Clark, Flynn was rankled most by Warner Bros., which he denounced as jingoistic and an embarrassment to the American public. Flynn objected to the Warner Bros. patriotic short features because he feared they radicalized audiences. The so-called film expert showed his ignorance about the impetus behind the shorts when he attributed their creation to Jack instead of Harry Warner. "Mr. Jack Warner's idea of Americanism may turn out to be very fine. I do not know what it is."[51]

Senator McFarland again took the defensive, asking that the committee be allowed to view the movies under attack; he requested an immediate adjournment. Flynn professed to have seen the movies in question, and his testimony, McFarland argued, tainted the inquiry because the subcommittee had no firsthand knowledge of the films. How could they, as responsible statesmen, possibly evaluate their merit without seeing them? "The best evidence is the pictures themselves . . . I saw one picture,

Sergeant York, and I thought it was a good picture."[52] Chairman Clark denied McFarland's request.

With Flynn still in the dock, McFarland grilled him about the motives of America First and its ties to pro-Nazi groups in the United States. Sheepishly admitting that the German-American Bund had endorsed the AFC, Flynn denounced the organization.[53] It was the First Amendment issue, however, that comprised the bulk of Flynn's testimony. Echoing the sentiments of Nye and Clark, he went further, arguing that Hollywood films were already under the scrutiny of the PCA. Filmmakers regularly and willingly submitted their products for censorship, Flynn argued, thereby surrendering their protection under the First Amendment. Like those who had testified before him, Flynn committed a serious error that undermined his effectiveness, already alluded to in the previous chapter:

> There are about 130,000,000 people in the United States, and I should say that about 129,000,000 of them are against Adolf Hitler. It does not take any courage to be against Adolf Hitler, particularly if you are above draft age. . . . You do not have to be anti-fascist to hate Hitler, that is the point I'm trying to bring out. I want these people to hate fascism more—go on hating Hitler all you want to, but hate fascism too, because it is that which created Hitler.[54]

Flynn spoke out of both sides of his mouth by asking Americans to despise fascism while remaining uncommitted to action. He further injured his credibility by testifying that he did not find propaganda per se objectionable but believed that both sides should be represented. So, a man who asked people to "go on hating Hitler all you want to" also asked for Nazi propaganda to be given equal time in American theaters. His position weakened the case against Hollywood. After Flynn concluded his testimony, hearings were suspended until Monday.[55]

The subcommittee's hearings resumed on September 15, with the testimony of a shady syndicated movie journalist and purported film industry expert, Jimmie Fidler, who proved embarrassing to the inquiry. More than once Fidler committed perjury while testifying, and, as it turned out, the so-called movie expert knew little more about the films in question than Nye or Clark did. Fidler had a personal ax to grind and accused the industry of attempting "in devious ways" to censor his gossip column and radio show.[56] Fidler, a man whom actor David Niven once described as "a particularly nauseating gossip columnist," tried to discredit the industry because he said the moguls were responsible for the waning popularity of his column and broadcasts.[57] Parroting the First Amendment issue of the former Hollywood detractors, Fidler advocated a double standard. He wanted complete freedom of speech for his stories, while calling for vigorous government-sponsored censorship of movies.[58]

Several quarters of the film industry displayed their contempt that Fidler would be taken seriously by members of the U.S. Congress. During his testimony Fidler attacked publicist Russell Birdwell for the methods he used to promote films, and Birdwell telegraphed a heated response to the committee. He offered to come to Washington to defend his name and asked that his cable be read into the record, calling Fidler "Hollywood's No. 1 liar." Likewise, Howard Dietz said, "I would not accuse Mr. Fidler of perjury, but I would say that Mr. Fidler is a congenital liar and it would be against his conscience to tell the truth."[59]

After Fidler and journalist George Fisher testified, Senator McFarland launched a noisy protest, regarding the proceedings as a time-wasting boondoggle. He criticized the argument that movies were not protected by the First Amendment and chastised fellow subcommittee members about the investigation's lack of merit. Chairman Clark called for a recess, and the hearings were suspended for eight days.[60]

Several journalists looked with great interest at the proceedings. The clear ties to the America First Committee aroused both suspicion and praise. Samuel Grafton, John Roy Carlson, and others excoriated the hearings and their association with America First. An editorial in *The Nation* argued that the hearings were created to bamboozle the American public and make them believe Nazism "was no concern of theirs," merely a "figment of the Jewish imagination." It proposed that, following such ominous logic, "[t]he Senate committee in effect is demanding what Goebbels would never dare ask of the United States."[61]

During the recess the debate over the subcommittee's investigation and its position on intervention raged outside the chamber. Denouncing the hearings at a September press conference, FDR repeated Lowell Mellett's contentions. He denied the charges that the federal government exerted undue influence on the film industry and took the opportunity to read a telegram some wag had sent him, satirizing the hearings:

> Have just been reading book called Holy Bible. Has large circulation in this country. Written entirely by foreign-born, mostly Jews. First part full of war-mongering propaganda. Second part condemns isolationists. That fake story about Samaritan dangerous. Should be added to your list and suppressed.[62]

On the other hand, the German-American Bund praised the hearings, called for further investigation of the film industry, and declared that the "so-called" torments suffered by the Jews in Europe were "a just punishment by God."[63]

In its September 22 issue, *Life* magazine ran a five-page article denouncing the hearings. A large photograph accompanied the lead page, showing Senator Nye staring vacantly at the camera. The most striking feature of the photo, however, was the large Band-Aid that covered the left side of his chin and jowl. The cut-line noted, "The adhesive patch on chin covers a morning shaving cut."[64] Editors at the magazine may well have chosen that somewhat comic photo to add to the growing sentiment that Nye and the subcommittee should not be taken too seriously.

Although journalist Margaret Frakes attempted to strike a balance between the two camps, she favored the noninterventionist cause. Cautioning movie audiences to be more critical in their viewing habits and ponder what they saw, Frakes acknowledged the importance and power of the film industry. She reminded readers that Hitler and Mussolini had both taken over their respective film industries after assuming power and had then used cinema to disseminate their ideologies. She observed,

> Hollywood today is full of these refugees from foreign studios which failed to 'cooperate' quickly enough and completely enough [with fascist regimes]. The lesson can hardly be lost on American producers.[65]

Although the movie producers' impassioned behavior should come as no surprise to savvy viewers, she was bothered by what she deemed their penchant for character assassination rather than a call for vigilance. She pointed out that a recent *March of Time* newsreel depicted a publisher with pro-Axis sympathies speaking in favor of Nazism. Spread before him was a newspaper with a banner headline featuring Lindbergh. Clearly, the casual viewer might conclude, as others had, that Lindbergh was a Nazi.[66]

On Tuesday, September 23, Sen. Sheridan Downey of California and Loews's chief executive officer, Nicholas Schenk, represented the first witnesses testifying in defense of the industry.[67] Senator Downey proved to be surprisingly convincing, even though he was a noninterventionist. An avid filmgoer, he issued a prepared statement eloquently exonerating the motion picture industry. Movies, he argued, "possess the privilege of free speech like the rest of us," but filmmakers must exercise caution and moderation when exercising that right. Concerning the current furor over the movies' role in the intervention debate, Downey argued that "the movies reacted to their public, not the public to its movies."[68]

Downey singled out Charlie Chaplin's *The Great Dictator* as an example of a film that pled for peace and not intervention. The film's only fault, he argued, was that it was lighthearted and not tough enough in its portrayal of the Nazis. Contrary to the accusations of the subcommittee, movies upheld the ideals of noninterventionists and spoke out against American involvement abroad. Downey cautioned the committee against any attempt to censor movies because the film community had been performing a public service by informing Americans about the Third Reich. Echoing Harry Warner and Alvin York, Downey declared that never before had there been an evil force so fully conscious of itself and impervious to the ordinary restraints of civilization unleashed upon the earth. The other side of the intervention argument had enjoyed ample coverage by the media, he argued, for Charles Lindbergh and his followers could be heard on the radio, read in print, and even seen in newsreels shown in the same theaters that screened the films under investigation. In typical fashion, Chairman D. Worth Clark dismissed Downey's testimony as an effort to build a "straw man" that he then set out to demolish.[69]

Nick Schenk of Loews-MGM received the committee's roughest treatment. Hostile senators criticized the way the film industry was run and cast aspersions on his abilities as a businessman. The bulk of the questioning centered on the practice of block booking and studio-owned theater chains. Though the charges of monopoly were secondary to the proceedings, Schenk's 1941 testimony helped to eventually undo the studio system. That was accomplished by the *United States v. Paramount* decision of 1948, which ordered the studios to divest themselves of their theaters.[70]

Undeterred, Schenk accused the senators of trying to trip him up by asking irrelevant questions. When queried about specific pictures, he replied, "I am going to always say it's not propaganda."[71] Chairman Clark naively asked him, "Don't you think the atrocities committed in Germany are actually committed by only a handful of very mean men.?"[72] Filmed depictions of the fascist menace were, in Schenk's opinion, "nowhere near as bad as actually happens," and as a result the American public was exposed to only about one-hundredth of "what we know is happening in Europe."[73] Senator McFarland interrupted Schenk's testimony, pronouncing again that the hearings were irrelevant and counterproductive. He stressed that "Downey is the only Senator who has come here who claims to have seen the pictures. . . . Let us see the pictures."[74]

Harry M. Warner took the stand on Thursday, September 25, and was allowed to read a prepared statement before the subcommittee without interruption.[75] Denying the charges aimed at his studio, he dismissed them as malicious gossip. He denounced Nazi Germany, remaining unapologetic in his criticism of Hitler's regime. Nazis, he argued, represented a totalitarian global revolution intent on undoing all democratic principles in the world. Warner defended the Roosevelt administration and applauded the president's efforts to aid Britain. At the same time, he assured the assembled senators that Warner Bros. had received no secret orders from FDR or his administration about what movies to make or not to make. Claiming sole responsibility for the studio's anti-Nazi posture, he said: "If Hitler should be the victor abroad, the United States would be faced with a Nazi-dominated world . . . I want to avoid such a catastrophe."[76]

Advocating preparedness, Warner articulated his belief that the isolationists had refused to recognize that war might well be inevitable, and he defended the production of *Sergeant York:*

> *Sergeant York* is a factual portrayal of the life of one of the great heroes of the last war. If that was propaganda, we plead guilty. . . .
>
> So it is with each and every one of our pictures dealing with the world situation or with the national defense. These pictures were carefully prepared on the basis of factual happenings and they were not twisted to serve any ulterior purpose.
>
> In truth the only sin Warner Bros. is guilty of is that of accurately recording on the screen the world as it is or as it has been. . . .[77]
>
> If Warner Bros. had produced no pictures concerning the Nazi movement, our public would have had good reason to criticize. . . . Today 70 percent of the nonfiction books published deal with the Nazi menace. Today 10 percent of the fiction novels are anti-Nazi in theme. Today 10 percent of all material submitted to us for consideration is anti-Nazi in character. . . . Today there is a war involving all hemispheres except our own and touching the lives of all of us.[78]

Recounting a brief history of the studio, Harry Warner pointed out that it had garnered a reputation for topical films in the past; thus, the public had expected Warner Bros. to continue to do so in light of the present emergency. He produced case histories of *Confessions of a Nazi Spy, International Squadron, Underground,* and *Sergeant York* to buttress his argument and read into the record with pride a May 16, 1939, newspaper article from the German-American League for Culture, which had praised the studio for its courage in exposing the horrors of Nazism.

Warner informed the subcommittee that his studio was the first in Hollywood to curtail its business with the Nazis, unlike most other studios that had cravenly continued to carry out commerce with the Third Reich until the summer of 1940. Warner Bros. had suffered a considerable financial loss initially but could not justify doing business with anti-Semitic butchers. "When we saw Hitler emerge in Germany, we did not try, nor did we ask our Government to appease him," he said proudly. "We voluntarily liquidated our business in Germany."[79] If the studio could continue competing with other Hollywood studios without the German market, it could likewise do the same without the British market. Warner Bros. was pro-Britain not because it needed the English box office, but because it supported the cause of freedom. Ensuring Britain's success was in every American's best interest because, "Now I believe that Great Britain is fighting our battle, and I think that if we can help her we can keep war away from these shores." Warner maintained his belief that he owed something to Britain: "I said publicly then, and I say today, that the freedom which this country fought England to obtain, we may have to fight with England to retain."[80]

Issuing words that echoed Sergeant York's, Warner said that he wanted only to ensure the welfare of future generations of Americans by making sacrifices today. Like York, he would rather see his grandchildren dead than living under a fascist-controlled regime. "[T]he American people" must take a stand, Warner argued,

> because we have just this choice: Either we help the people over there and give them the material with which to fight, or our children are going to have to fight. What I am interested in is preventing our children from fighting.[81]

Regarding the film *Underground,* Warner declared that he could verify the accuracy of its portrayal of the Gestapo. He could call witnesses who had personally been brutalized by Hitler's thugs, and "[w]e can easily prove to you that the picture understates, rather than overstates, the treatment given suspects by the secret police of Hitler."[82] The studio had acted in good faith as it tried to inform the general public about the war; the non-interventionists, in his view, opposed the people's right to know what was happening abroad.

Warner then leveled his remarks directly at the current proceedings. He pointed out that every public media organ in America routinely presented stories about the Nazis, from news to novels. Singling out the film industry for doing so was illogical and vindictive. He condemned the hearings, saying, "I believe that every speech that is made, every investigation of this kind, only helps the enemy."[83] When Chairman Clark criticized Warner for the brutality depicted in *Underground,* Warner quipped, "Yes; well, do you think we should have made a picture that showed the Nazis kissing them or in love with them, or what?"[84]

Warner then shook up the committee when he produced a curious "smoking gun." He presented a telegram from none other than Sen. Gerald P. Nye dated May 11, 1939. One of those movies that Nye could not remember seeing turned out to be *Confessions of a Nazi Spy,* which the senator attended during its initial release. The telegram read:

> The picture is exceedingly good. . . . The plot may or may not be exaggerated, but is one that ought to be with every patriotic American. As for myself, I hope there may be more pictures of a kind dealing with propaganda emanating from all foreign lands. Anyone who truly appreciates the one great democracy upon this earth will appreciate this picture.[85]

In the cable Senator Nye had not only glowingly endorsed one of the films he referred to as insidious and warmongering, but had called for *more* films like it. Visibly flustered, Nye did not deny sending the telegram and found it difficult to extract himself from this awkward situation. His own shaky credibility as a qualified judge of propaganda suffered even more, and the shocking revelation proved embarrassing for the entire subcommittee. Not surprisingly, the press had a field day with the disclosure. The afternoon session deteriorated further when senator Tobey informed Warner, "I have seen the picture *Dive Bomber,* and I cannot imagine how under the wildest stretch of anyone's imagination it could be construed as propaganda."[86]

Chairman D. Worth Clark scrambled to restore the subcommittee's flagging reputation and called for a recess following the next day's scheduled testimony. Because subcommittee members felt the need to regroup and revise strategy, they scheduled the hearings to resume on October 6. In an attempt to save face, several senators decided they should at least see some of the movies they had so readily condemned.

Judgment on *Sergeant York* came on the same day as Warner's testimony, when two men associated with the subcommittee, Wayland Brooks and Resolution 152 sponsor Bennett Champ Clark, informed Harry Warner that they had recently seen the film. Brooks, like Lindbergh before him, believed that *Sergeant York* might glorify a war hero but posed no threat to national security. He even offered to testify before the subcommittee on the movie's behalf.[87] Praising the picture, Brooks declared:

> I want to tell you I do not think there is any propaganda in it at all, unless it is propaganda for allegiance to this country and to glorify a great hero. . . . If none of the other pictures have any more propaganda in them than that one has, then I think the hearing in itself will prove to be a cleansing of any charges made against you for your conduct.[88]

An equally enthusiastic Clark declared *Sergeant York* "a grand picture and . . . not war propaganda."[89] After such an endorsement Senator McFarland once again protested, arguing that the hearings had wasted the taxpayers' money and the senators' time and had served no real purpose. On September 24, Chairman Clark exhibited reservations about some of the films that had been singled out. Given the recent string of embarrassing developments, he said, "Unfortunately *Sergeant York* crept into this discussion."[90]

Friday, September 26, wound up being the last day of the hearings. Former Warner Bros. employee and Twentieth Century–Fox chief Darryl F. Zanuck charged the committee with undue attempts at censorship, which, if successful, "would leave the American motion pictures as worthless and sterile as those made in Germany and Italy."[91] Zanuck ridiculed the popular belief that Hollywood suffered under the evil influence of an immigrant-Jewish-Anglophilic conspiracy by pointing out that he was born and raised a Methodist in Wahoo, Nebraska. He noted sarcastically, "I usually find that when someone produces something that you do not like, you call it propaganda."[92] Like Senator Downey, Zanuck argued that movies sold the American way of life to the world and made the United States the envy of every other country. Film reinforced the values Americans held dear while promoting them to international audiences.[93]

President of Paramount Pictures Barney Balaban testified after Zanuck, also defending the industry. Like Twentieth Century–Fox, Paramount had been one of the last studios to discontinue its business interests in Nazi-occupied territories. The studio finally gave up after Nazi regulations made film distribution abroad unprofitable. Balaban noted that the film situation in Europe had deteriorated completely since the

Nazi occupation of Paris and that Paramount's production manager, who had been stationed there, was now a prisoner in a concentration camp somewhere. The committee would be hard pressed, Balaban professed, to find anyone in the industry sympathetic to the Nazi cause, and it should encourage filmmakers to be more aggressive in their condemnation of Nazism.[94]

Even though the October 6 scheduled hearings failed to materialize, heated attacks against the film industry by the die-hard critics continued unabated. Sen. Burton K. Wheeler denounced the film industry at an America First rally in Los Angeles on October 2. Speaking on his enemy's turf, he declared that in the future the film industry would be known as "the modern Benedict Arnold" because of its interventionist stance.[95] Hollywood propaganda threatened the very life of the Republic as it spread its tentacles throughout the heartland, choking off the public's capacity for reason. He defended Charles Lindbergh, declaring that the colonel was the hapless victim of character assassination on the part of the bloodthirsty movie industry.

Subcommittee Chairman D. Worth Clark concurred. Speaking on a national radio broadcast on October 11, he enlarged upon Wheeler's Los Angeles address. The subcommittee, like the Lone Eagle, was the victim of a well-orchestrated smear campaign. Although Wendell Willkie and the FFF called for an immediate halt to the investigation, the subcommittee remained committed to its cause. After numerous postponements, Chairman Clark announced on October 28 that even though several other issues demanded immediate attention, the investigation would indeed continue. Accordingly, the committee rescheduled its hearings to resume in January of 1942, but when America declared war on December 8, 1941, the hearings were canceled.[96]

7

"This Isn't What We Had in Mind"

The U.S. declaration of war in December of 1941 brought an end to the Nye-Clark subcommittee hearings.[1] What was ironic about those hearings was that the Nye-Clark subcommittee *could* have proven their allegations of warmongering against Warner Bros. if they had followed John T. Flynn's advice and had conducted a formal investigation. If they had subpoenaed studio records, production files, interoffice memoranda, or other documents currently housed at the Warner Bros. Archives, the committee would have had all the evidence it needed to prove that Warner Bros.—if not the whole industry by 1941—supported intervention. In the lengthy May 8, 1940, memo that Julien Josephson and Harry Chandlee sent to Jesse Lasky, they openly discussed the propaganda elements inherent in *Sergeant York*. They wanted not only to fill audiences with patriotic pride, but also to illustrate the fact that war is sometimes necessary if liberty is to prevail. They wrote, "On the abovementioned point of flag waving, object will be not to wave any flags ourselves, but when the picture is over to have made the audience wave flags."[2]

Though the subcommittee wanted to find fault with Hollywood, the way they conducted the hearings proved haphazard. The senators on the subcommittee were ill informed and operating on hearsay. John T. Flynn appropriately advised the subcommittee about the best means to investigate the film industry, but his recommendations fell on deaf ears. He implored them to

> [g]et the original story. Get the report from the Hays Producers Association, what they said you could not put in, what they said you could put in. Get the report of the cutout. In other words, see every process in the production of those films.[3]

Instead, from the outset the subcommittee's conduct was incompetent, and its findings were both arbitrary and unsubstantiated. It is doubtful, given the eventuality of Pearl Harbor, that even if they had conducted a thorough and logical investigation, Warner Bros. would have been adversely affected for very long. At worst the studio might have been publicly censured, fined, and warned to avoid producing potentially controversial films under pain of further penalties.

There is another irony, which in the long run proved to be a vindication of Harry Warner's prewar stance against Nazism. The selfsame Washington establishment that had called movies the product of a fiendish Jewish plot turned to those same Jews immediately after Pearl Harbor, begging for their much needed assistance in mobilizing a nation for war.[4] Jewish moguls now found the government wooing them for their cooperation in the war effort, and as a result Hollywood and Washington entered into a formal business partnership that would forever change the film industry. Warner Bros. willingly and enthusiastically cemented its partnership with the government and turned its studios over wholeheartedly to the war effort. Not only did movies help instruct soldiers and civilians about life in wartime, but they also unified America in new and unprecedented ways, preaching community sacrifice, individual honesty, and integrity, thereby helping ease the pain of war for both the civilian and the military population. To accommodate audiences involved in wartime production, American movie theaters operated twenty-four hours a day, providing escape and moral support for a nation at war.[5]

Ironically, this cooperation ultimately proved to be detrimental to the life of classical Hollywood because the partnership with Washington soon turned sour, and the film industry has never recovered from that relationship. Beginning in 1947 the House Committee on Un-American activities (HUAC), which Harry Warner had supported in its efforts to uncover Nazi provocateurs, turned its attention on Hollywood. During those hearings in the formative years of the Cold War, the debate over who or what constituted "One-hundred-percent Americanism" breathed new life into the subcommittee formerly chaired by Representative Martin Dies of Texas before World War II. HUAC had looked for both Nazi and Communist subversives before the war, but as the Cold War descended upon the United States, the fear of a monolithic Stalinist takeover gripped the nation. This time HUAC's only culprits were Communists and Communist sympathizers, and once again Hollywood found itself at the center of a federal investigation; but this time it would not fare as well as it had with the Nye-Clark subcommittee on warmongering propaganda.[6] Wendell Willkie's open letter to Chairman D. Worth Clark during the War Propaganda hearings proved incredibly prescient. The counselor noted:

> If your committee . . . insists on proceeding, our only legal relief can come after the committee has heard reckless and unwarranted charges repeated and widely publicized throughout the country. We know that after the damage is done, if we are to protect our rights as citizens, one of our witnesses must refuse to testify and then run the risk of being prosecuted or being cited for contempt by the United States Senate.
>
> . . . By that time the unfounded charges will be on the record; the damage will be done; the inference will be then drawn that he who refuses to testify has something to hide, something of which he is ashamed.[7]

That, of course, is exactly what happened in the paranoid climate that gripped the country and the industry during the early days of the Cold War and during the McCarthy era. Hollywood, which had aided the federal government in its attempts to depict the Soviets as our friendly allies, was now regarded as a hotbed of Communist activity. Though there were some true believers who operated in the film capital, after their politicization because of the socioeconomic turmoil created by the Great Depression, the majority of Hollywood writers and actors who would be called to testify had flirted with Marxism because it seemed fashionable.

In its cooperation with the federal government, Warner Bros. agreed to make films humanizing the Soviets. In 1947, however, Warner Bros. found itself at the center of the witch hunt. The studio was accused of promoting Communistic propaganda in *Mission to Moscow* (1943), and anyone associated with the film found himself or herself tainted and considered a Red. The studio, which had produced the film in response to a personal request from President Roosevelt, stood accused of producing harmful propaganda by the federal government once again. In those oppressive times, Warner Bros. acted less courageously than it had prior to World War II. *Sergeant York* screenwriter Howard Koch, who wrote the bulk of *Mission to Moscow*, became the studio's sacrificial lamb. As the principal writer on the film and an avowed leftist, Koch was blacklisted by both the studio and the industry. The HUAC hearings of 1947–48 caused many employees at Warner Bros. to lose faith in the studio that had once willingly encouraged its workers to become politicized.

In the second round of Washington hearings, it was Jack Warner who testified. Though he defended the production of *Mission to Moscow* as a film that reflected wartime cooperation between allies, he promised

HUAC that he would go after Communist sympathizers in Hollywood. Jack proved to be as virulently anti-Communist as his brother Harry had been antifascist. Agreeing to work with the government to ferret out Reds, Pinkos, and Commies—real and imagined—earned him the enmity of many friends and coworkers. The studio that had stood at the forefront of political activity in Hollywood now turned upon itself. Among those who were forced to testify or sell out their friends were former members of the Anti-Nazi League that Harry and Jack had enthusiastically supported, including Edward G. Robinson and Humphrey Bogart.[8]

To make matters worse, the Justice Department reopened its investigation of possible monopolistic practices on the part of the film industry. In 1948 the courts handed down the decision in *United States v. Paramount*. It forced the studios to divest themselves of their theater chains, paving the way for the destruction of the studio system. To add insult to injury, Warner Bros. and the rest of the industry suffered a crushing blow when actress Olivia De Havilland successfully sued Warner Bros. and won release from her seven-year contract.[9] In De Havilland's case the court declared the industry's standard seven-year contract tantamount to indentured servitude. It was indeed significant that willful cooperation with the federal government would lead eventually to the end of Hollywood's golden age and close the book on a significant period in film history.[10]

Additionally, Alvin C. York and Charles Lindbergh had offered a personal window into the emotions of the time. They represented not only two distinct philosophical viewpoints concerning America's responsibilities to a world at war, but two different personalities and class strata as well. Both men had had fame thrust upon them and both suffered in their adjustment to celebrity status.[11] Whereas Lindbergh hated the limelight, did not like the company of strangers, and was ill at ease speaking, York was just the opposite. Like Will Rogers, he had "never met a stranger." A gregarious bear of a man, York genuinely liked people, loved being surrounded by them, and cared little about his privacy. He so enjoyed the company of strangers that he often arrived late to speaking engagements because he "would stop and talk to anybody."[12] The overweight old soldier possessed a marvelous, somewhat raw sense of humor and over the course of time had become an effective public speaker. Politically, York was an optimistic Wilsonian Democrat, with high ideals and a belief in the common man. Lindbergh, however, relished his privacy, disliked people who showed up unannounced, felt ill at ease with "the common man," and believed that the Republican party provided the best leadership for the country.[13] Lindbergh came from a prominent family that traveled in the circles of high society; York had grown up exceedingly poor. In their varied backgrounds, they personified the drama surrounding intervention for the entire nation and took their roles seriously. Both sincerely believed themselves participants in a moral crusade to defend and preserve American values.[14]

The movie that York had waited so long to endorse brought him mainly grief. Though it made him popular once more, and he played a prominent role in recruiting efforts for the war through an association with the Signal Corps and a weekly syndicated column "Sergeant York Says," it also led to a raft of lawsuits. The Bible school, which the proceeds from the movie were supposed to support, closed after one year's operation. By 1961 York was a penniless invalid hounded by the IRS for over one hundred thousand dollars in back taxes linked to the movie's production.

Finally, one last irony surrounds domestic fascism. Unlike Communism, which has gone the way of the dinosaur, fascism is back with a vengeance. Recent events—the Waco debacle, Ruby Ridge, the Oklahoma City bombing, the Freemen of Montana, the Luddite rantings of the Unabomber, and myriad modern militia movements—mirror the cryptofascist impulse of the 1930s. Their enemies are the same—Jews, Catholics, immigrants, the federal government, and Hollywood. They too wrap themselves in the flag, announcing themselves as true representatives of Americanism and Christian family values. Like Pelley, Winrod, and Dr. Shepard, the neofascists scapegoat rather than look for viable solutions to their problems, they promulgate violence rather than discussion, and they demonize what they do not understand.[15]

Hollywood has changed substantially since the days when Harry Warner wanted to make movies that were unabashedly patriotic, uplifting, instructive, *and* entertaining. In the 1990s filmmaking with a social conscience has been largely left up to independent producers, who struggle to get their movies distributed. In the post–Cold War era few films are being made celebrating what is good about America or what makes this country and its liberties unique. Though Harry's desire for what film could be struck some in the film community as mawkish or provincial, he tried to make a difference, and for that the history of Hollywood is much the richer.

Postscript

In the years since the Depression, filmmakers have often looked back at that era with a degree of nostalgia. Movies like *Bound for Glory* and *Honky Tonk Man* merely used the Depression as a backdrop for the celebration of the human spirit during times of national and personal crisis. Woody Allen's endearing portrait of folks coping in *Purple Rose of Cairo* displays the importance of movies as a refuge in the 1930s, while making audiences yearn for a simplistic, idealized past. One of the best attempts at examining the pain of the Depression is John Sayle's independent film *Matewan;* however, it deals primarily with the problems associated with unionization before FDR's administration made collective bargaining possible. Most post–World War II films about the Depression, however, sentimentalize the 1930s, making the decade appear to have been a time of relative calm in spite of economic hardship. Even films that attempt to show the privations of the Depression tend to be upbeat, almost in the tradition of the Andy Hardy series.

Although the rise of Nazism abroad has been the subject of a number of films, from *Cabaret* to *Swing Kids*, little has been done concerning domestic fascism in the 1930s. Foreign films have dealt with the evil of Nazism much better than post–studio era Hollywood. *A Soldier of Orange, Europa, Europa,* and *The Nasty Girl* have examined Nazism and its legacy in extremely effective ways. John Boorman's delightfully sentimental memoir about life in England during the blitz, *Hope and Glory,* has no Hollywood counterpart. Though Mel Brooks's remake of the Jack Benny comedy *To Be or Not to Be* addressed America's stance before involvement, the best film about the agonizing decision of the United States regarding involvement is still Warner Bros.'s classic film *Casablanca.* In Hollywood's decidedly short memory, World War II has been glamorized as the good war, the fun war; the difficult episodes leading up to America's entry are glossed over or ignored.

Films about the American Nazi movement and its various counterparts are nonexistent. Though there have been made-for-TV movies about Waco, Randy Weaver, and the Oklahoma City bombing, nothing has yet been done with the likes of William Dudley Pelley or Father Charles Coughlin. Currently, the only screen investigation of people in a democratic country toying with the possibility of fascism focuses on Britain before the war, not America. In the BBC dramatizations of P. G. Wodehouse's *Jeeves and Wooster* stories, there is a recurring character, Roderick Spode, based on Sir Oswald Mosley, the British fascist who headed the Nazi-inspired Black Shirts. Yet that character is reduced to a caricature full of bombast instead of a threat.

Movies concerning the Holocaust have become almost a cottage industry, from documentaries—*Night and Fog, The Sorrow and the Pity, Hotel Terminus,* and *Shoah* among the best—to feature films and television miniseries including *Holocaust, Seven Beauties, Sophie's Choice, Escape from Sobibor,* and Stephen Spielberg's "feel good" holocaust movie, *Schindler's List.* Even so, America's role in the event has received little attention. An installment of the PBS *American Experience* series, "Holocaust, Deceit, and Indifference," capitalizing upon David Wyman's *Abandonment of the Jews* exposed the role the State Department played in denying Jews safe haven during the 1930s and on into the war. It, however, is the exception rather than the rule.

One thing endures, though. Nazis continue to be depicted in film in the same way that Warner Bros. pioneered. The officious, sadistic, malevolent Nazi who blindly obeys orders, no matter how repulsive they might be, has become ingrained in the popular culture. The hundreds of portrayals of Hitler share two things: the absolute ubiquity of the available footage of the Fuhrer, with which they can mimic his mannerisms, and the Warner Bros. concretization of the Nazi as evil incarnate.

Notes

NOTES TO THE INTRODUCTION

1. Among the best books yet written is Nick Roddick's, but his encyclopedic look at the studio examines hundreds of films irrelevant to the issue at hand. Aljean Harmetz's fascinating reconstruction of the making of *Casablanca* in *Round Up the Usual Suspects: The Making of Casablanca—Bogart, Bergman, and World War II* makes excellent use of the studio's records, providing insight about how the studio operated once war had been declared. The Warner Bros. prewar anti-Nazi activity has been mentioned in passing in a number of books and articles, often erroneously or superficially because the authors relied too heavily on the dubious memoirs of Hollywood celebrities. The best single work on the subject is Christine Ann Colgan's ambitious dissertation "Warner Brothers' Crusade against the Third Reich: A Study of Anti-Nazi Activism and Film Production, 1933–1941." Though an excellent place to start, it is unwieldy and attempts to cover every movie the studio ever made or considered making that might be construed to have an anti-Nazi bias. Her work also has a greater industrial emphasis than this study.

2. Jack Warner with Dean Jennings, *My First Hundred Years in Hollywood* (New York: Random House, 1965), 248–49.

3. Pat McGilligan, ed. *Backstory: Interviews with Screenwriters of Hollywood's Golden Age* (Berkeley: University of California Press, 1986), 346.

4. James W. Loewen, *Lies My Teacher Told Me: Everything Your American History Textbook Got Wrong* (New York: New Press, 1995), 9.

5. David D. Lee, *Sergeant York: An American Hero* (Lexington: University Press of Kentucky, 1985), xi.

6. The papers, which I am cataloging for the Sergeant York Historical Association, will soon be available to other scholars. Microfilmed copies of the documents will be housed at the Tennessee State Library and Archives in Nashville. The recent biography of York by John Perry, though it claims to make use of some of these documents, lacks depth and is basically another in a long line of hagiographic works about York.

NOTES TO CHAPTER 1

1. Jack Warner with Dean Jennings, *My First Hundred Years in Hollywood* (New York: Random House, 1965), 15, 25; Harry M. Warner, "Speech concerning Christian Refugees from Nazi Germany," American Committee for Christian Refugees Folder, Jack L. Warner Collection University of Southern California, Los Angeles (hereafter cited as JLWC), 8–9; Christine Ann Colgan, "Warner Brothers' Crusade against the Third Reich: A Study of Anti-Nazi Activism and Film Production, 1933–1941," Ph.D. diss., University of Southern California, 1985, 111.

2. Nick Roddick, *A New Deal in Entertainment: Warner Brothers in the 1930s* (London: British Film Institute, 1983), 17. Concerning the Edison Trust, see "*Edison V. American Mutoscope Company* (1902)" and "*Mutual Film Corp. V. Industrial Commission of Ohio* (1915)" in Steven Mintz and Randy Roberts, eds., *Hollywood's America: United States History through Its Films* (St. James, N.Y.: Brandywine Press, 1993), 74–75, 81–84; Robert Sklar, *Movie-Made America: A Cultural History of American Movies* (New York: Random House, 1975), 18–47; J. Douglas Gomery, *Movie History: A Survey* (Belmont, Calif.: Wadsworth, 1991), 6–8, 24–40.

3. Roddick, 17.

4. John Davis, "Notes on Warner Brothers Foreign Policy, 1918–1948," *Velvet Light Trap* 4 (spring 1972): 23; Michael T. Isenberg, *War on Film: The American Cinema and World War I, 1914–1941* (Rutherford, N.J.: Fairleigh Dickinson University Press, 1981), 153.

5. Bob Thomas, *Clown Prince of Hollywood: The Antic Life and Times of Jack L. Warner* (New York: McGraw-Hill, 1990), 40. The book, basically a rehash of Jack Warner's autobiography, is unreasonably critical of Harry Warner.

6. Warner with Jennings, 17, 186; Thomas, 23; and Cass Warner Sperling and Cork Millner with Jack Warner, Jr., *Hollywood Be Thy Name: The Warner Brothers Story* (Rocklin, Calif.: Prima, 1994), 175–78 (hereafter, *Hollywood Be Thy Name*). Novelist and screenwriter William R. Burnett considered Harry "[t]he biggest bore who's ever lived in the history of the world! . . . All he talked about were his charities and his horses." See "W. R. Burnett: The Outsider," interviewed by Ken Mate and Pat McGilligan in Pat McGilligan, *Backstory: Interviews with Screenwriters from the Golden Age of Hollywood* (Berkeley: University of California Press, 1986), 75 (hereafter, *Backstory*).

7. Neal Gabler, *An Empire of Their Own: How the Jews Invented Hollywood* (New York: Crown, 1988), 125, 195.

8. "Warner Brothers," *Fortune,* December 16, 1937, 111.

9. *Hollywood Be Thy Name,* 174; Gabler, 120–23.

10. *Hollywood Be Thy Name,* 176–77.

11. Ibid., 175–78.

12. Warner with Jennings, 185.

13. Rudy Behlmer, *Inside Warner Bros. (1935–1951)* (New York: Simon and Schuster, 1985), 64; Thomas, 30; "Warner Brothers," 110–14.

14. Leonard Dinnerstein, *Antisemitism in America* (New York: Oxford University Press, 1994), 124–25; Garson Kanin, *Hollywood* (New York: Viking, 1974), 138–45; Gabler, 2, 4–6, 14–15, 46, 80–81, 91, 119, 147–50, 167.

15. Quoted in David Niven, *Bring on the Empty Horses* (New York: Dell, 1975), 323.

16. Quoted in Aljean Harmetz, *Round Up the Usual Suspects: The Making of Casablanca—Bogart, Bergman, and World War II* (New York: Hyperion, 1992), 21.

17. John Huston, *An Open Book* (New York: Ballantine, 1980), 81.

18. *Hollywood Be Thy Name*, 195.

19. Gabler, 246.

20. *Hollywood Be Thy Name*, 196–98, 207, 214–16, 266–68, 297–300.

21. Gabler, 120–21; Harmetz, 20–21, Thomas, 225–26.

22. Warner with Jennings, 168.

23. Ibid., 169.

24. Thomas Schatz, *The Genius of the System: Hollywood Filmmaking in the Studio Era* (New York: Pantheon Books, 1988), 58–66.

25. Warner with Jennings, 208.

26. Ibid., 216, 224; *Hollywood Be Thy Name*, 161.

27. Warner with Jennings; "22 Ambulances Donated," *New York Times*, December 14, 1940, 4; Peter Colli to Harry M. Warner, June 20, 1940, June 5th Meeting Folder, JLWC, 3.

28. *Hollywood Be Thy Name*, 160.

29. Robert Gustafson, "The Buying of Ideas: Source Acquisition at Warner Brothers 1930–1949," Ph.D. diss., University of Wisconsin, 1983, 26, 112–15.

30. Thomas, 110.

31. "Warner Brothers," 110–14; *Hollywood Be Thy Name*, 212.

32. Russell Campbell, "Warners, the Depression, and FDR: Wellman's *Heroes for Sale*," *Velvet Light Trap* 4 (spring 1972): 34–38; Andrew Bergman, *We're in the Money: Depression America and Its Films* (New York: Harper Torchbooks, 1971), 27.

33. Gabler, 196.

34. Jerker Erikkson, "American Film in Finland," *Publications of the Institute of History* (University of Turku, Finland) 10 (1983): 73; Schatz, 135–55, 199–227; Richard Sheridan Ames, "The Screen Enters Politics: Will Hollywood Produce More Propaganda?" *Harper's*, March 1935, 475.

35. See George F. Custen, *Twentieth Century's Fox: Darryl F. Zanuck and the Culture of Hollywood* (New York: Basic Books, 1997), 67–172 passim; Darryl F. Zanuck Papers and production reports, 1930–1933; Schatz, 135–58; Marlys J.

Harris, *The Zanucks of Hollywood: The Dark Legacy of an American Dynasty* (New York: Crown, 1989), 11–50.

36. Russell Campbell, "Warner Brothers in the Thirties: Some Tentative Notes," *Velvet Light Trap* 1 (June 1971): 3; Brian Neve, "The Screenwriter and the Social Problem Film, 1936–1938: The Case of Robert Rossen at Warner Brothers," *Film and History* 14, no. 1 (June 1984): 4.

37. Gabler, 197.

38. Behlmer, 56; Ralph A. Brauer, "When the Lights Went Out—Hollywood, the Depression, and the Thirties," *Journal of Popular Film and Television* 8, no. 4 (1981), 18–29.

39. Davis, 23. His argument is flawed; Harry Warner is conspicuously absent and too much credence is placed on Jack Warner's often inaccurate memoir. Davis overstates his case and assumes that Warner Bros. enjoyed a special relationship with the Roosevelt administration prior to America's entry into World War II.

40. Will H. Hays, *Self Regulation in the Motion Picture Industry: Annual Report to the Motion Picture Producers and Distributors of America, May 28, 1938* (New York: Motion Picture Producers and Distributors of America, 1938); Gregory D. Black, *Hollywood Censored: Morality Codes, Catholics, and the Movies* (Cambridge: Cambridge University Press, 1994); J. Douglas Gomery, "Hollywood and the National Recovery Administration, and the Question of Monopoly of Power," *Journal of the University Film Association* 31, no. 2 (spring 1979): 47–52; Richard Maltby, "The Production Code and the Hays Office," in *Grand Design: Hollywood as a Modern Business Enterprise, 1930–1939,* Tino Balio, ed. (Berkeley: University of California Press, 1993), 31–72.

41. Warner with Jennings, 184.

42. Thomas, 128–32.

43. Roddick, 65–67, 119.

44. Bernard Dick referred to Warner Bros. as "the Roosevelt Studio," overstating the ties between the studio and the president; likewise, John Davis argued that Warner Bros. doggedly pursued FDR's foreign policy and were staunch supporters, which is also exaggerated. See Bernard F. Dick, *The Star Spangled Screen: The Hollywood World War II Film* (Lexington: University Press of Kentucky, 1985), 66; Davis, 25.

45. Ames, 481; Lawrence W. Levine, "Hollywood's Washington: Film Images of National Politics during the Great Depression," *Prospects* 10 (1985): 169–71; E. Francis Brown, "The American Road to Fascism," *Current History,* July 3, 1933, 392–98.

46. For the hegemonic nature of American cinema, see Robert Ray, *A Certain Tendency of the Hollywood Cinema, 1930–1980* (Princeton, N.J.: Princeton University Press, 1985), 25–69; David Bordwell, Janet Staiger, and Kristin Thompson,

The Classical Hollywood Cinema: Film Style and Mode of Production to 1960 (New York: Columbia University Press, 1985).

47. Erikkson, 71.

48. Ibid., 63–80.

49. Jan-Christopher Horak, "G. W. Pabst in Hollywood or Every Modern Hero Deserves a Mother," *Film History* 1 (1987): 53–64.

50. Margaret Farrand Thorp, *America at the Movies* (New Haven, Conn.: Yale University Press, 1939), 189.

51. Thomas J. Saunders, *Hollywood in Berlin: American Cinema and Weimar Germany* (Berkeley: University of California Press, 1994), 63–83; Kristin Thompson, *Exporting Entertainment: America in the World Film Market, 1907–1934* (London: British Film Institute, 1985).

52. Thompson, 148–58.

53. Saunders, 221–40.

54. "Warner's German Plans," *Variety,* January 19, 1932, 13; Harry M. Warner, "Speech concerning Christian Refugees from Nazi Germany," 9–11.

55. Harry M. Warner, "Speech concerning Christian Refugees from Nazi Germany," 9–11; Colgan, 32.

56. Waldo Frank, "Should the Jews Survive?" *New Republic,* December 13, 1933, 121–25.

57. Ibid., 125.

58. Quoted in Johan J. Smertenko, "Hitlerism in America," *Harper's,* November 1933, 660.

59. William Orbach, "Shattering the Shackles of Powerlessness: The Debate Surrounding the Anti-Nazi Boycott of 1933–1941," *Modern Judaism* 2 (1982): 154.

60. Leland Stowe, *Nazi Means War* (New York: Whittlesey House, 1934), 101.

61. Ibid., 16, 66–78 passim.

62. Alton Frye, *Nazi Germany and the American Hemisphere, 1933–1941* (New Haven, Conn.: Yale University Press, 1967), 25–26; William Troy, "Tarzan and Hitler," *Nation,* May 16, 1934, 573–74.

63. Regarding Nazi intimidation of the foreign press see Ernest K. Bramsted, *Goebbels and National Socialist Propaganda, 1925–1945* (East Lansing: Michigan State University Press, 1965).

64. Gabler, 338.

65. Colgan, 73, 97.

66. Niven, 280–84.

67. William Troy, "Fascism over Hollywood," *Nation,* April 26, 1933.

68. Ibid., 482–83.

69. Levine, 174–75; Black, 137–44, 244–45.

70. Gustafson, 203–5.

71. Quoted in Gabler, 338.

72. A vast literature cautioned against war. See for example George Seldes, "The New Propaganda for War," *Harper's,* October 1934, 540–54; George Seldes, *Iron, Blood, and Profits: An Exposure of the World-Wide Munitions Racket* (New York, 1934); Helmuth C. Engelbrecht and Frank C. Hanighen, *Merchants of Death* (New York: Harper, 1934); Walter Millis, *The Road to War* (New York, 1935); William Dudley Pelley, *The Dupes of Judah: The Inside Story of Why the World War Was Fought* (Asheville, N.C.: Pelley Publishers, 1938); Nancy Schoonmaker and Doris Fielding Reid, eds., *We Testify* (New York: Smith and Durrell, 1941); Elmer Davis, "Is England Worth Fighting For?" *New Republic,* February 15, 1939, 35–37. See also Geoffrey Smith, "Isolationism, the Devil, and the Advent of the Second World War: Variations on a Theme," *International History Review,* 4 no. 1 (February 1982): 60–71; Justus D. Doenecke and John E. Wilz, *From Isolation to War, 1931–1941,* 2d. ed. (Arlington Heights, Ill.: Harlan Davidson, 1991).

73. Stephen J. Whitfield, "Our American Jewish Heritage: The Hollywood Version," *American Jewish History* 75, no.3 (1986): 322–31.

74. Quoted in Lester D. Friedman, *Hollywood's Image of the Jew* (New York: Frederick Ungar, 1982), 85; Whitfield, 326–31.

75. Whitfield, 327.

76. Warner with Jennings, 248–49. Reinhardt directed the successful Warner Bros. prestige picture *A Midsummer Night's Dream* (1935) starring James Cagney, Joe E. Brown, Olivia de Havilland, and Mickey Rooney.

77. Colgan, 8–9, 40–41. The myth of Joe Kauffman refuses to die. Competent scholars continue to parrot Jack's account of the event that prompted the studio to confront Nazi Germany. The facts undermine the story's plausibility. To their credit, Christine Anne Colgan, Aljean Harmetz, and Thomas Doherty have attempted to set the record straight. See Thomas Doherty, "An Elusive Factoid: World War II Motivation at Warner Bros.?" *Film and History* 27, nos. 1–4 (1997): 120–23. For retellings of the myth, see Gabler, 342; John Davis, 28; Dick, 55–56; Tom Dewe Matthews, *Censored: What They Didn't Allow You to See and Why; The Story of Film Censorship in Britain* (London: Chatto and Windus, 1994); Ina Rae Hark, "The Visual Politics of *The Adventures of Robin Hood,*" *Journal of Popular Film* 5, no. 1 (1976): 4; *Hollywood Be Thy Name,* 232–33.

78. Colgan, 8–9, 40–41.

79. "Nazis Oust U.S. Film Men," *Variety,* April 11, 1933, 13; and "Kaufman [*sic*], Warner European Manager, Dies in Stockholm," *Motion Picture Herald,* December 9, 1933, 30; Colgan, 34.

80. For a discussion of Nazi film production and its intended influence in the United States, see Jan-Christopher Horak, "Luis Trenker's *The Kaiser of California*: How the West Was Won, Nazi Style," *Historical Journal of Film, Radio, and Television* 6, no.2 (1986): 181–88; Bramsted, 57, 65–68, 74, 217–18.

81. Colgan, 170–72.

82. "Nazis Try to Curb Film Ideas Abroad," *New York Times,* February 19, 1934, 6.

83. Eric Rentschler, *The Ministry of Illusion: Nazi Cinema and Its Afterlife* (Cambridge, Mass.: Harvard University Press, 1996) 104.

84. "Anschluss Shifts Austrian Film Biz under Berlin Office Direction," *Variety,* March 30, 1938, 5.

85. Helen Zigmond, "Hollywood and the European Apple Cart," *Jewish Telegraphic Agency,* December 25, 1938, 4.

86. Colgan, 40.

87. "Nazis Oust U.S. Film Men."

88. "U.S. Film Yields to Nazis on Race Issue," *Variety,* May 9, 1933, 13.

89. "WB First U.S. Co. to Bow Out of Germany," *Variety,* July 17, 1934, 1.

90. "WB's Hitler Yarn Search," *Variety,* March 28, 1933, 1.

91. Michael S. Shull and David E. Wilt, *Doing Their Bit: Wartime Animated Short Films, 1939–1945* (Jefferson, N.C.: McFarland, 1987), 23.

92. Bruce Reynolds, *The Mad Dog of Europe* (New York: Veritas, 1938); Colgan, 54–62.

93. Darryl F. Zanuck, who ran Twentieth Century–Fox, was born in America in Wahoo, Nebraska, and was a Methodist.

94. Harmetz, 67.

95. "Warner Bros.," 114.

96. "To Show Hitler Film," *New York Times,* April 22, 1934, sec. 2, p. 6; "Ban Urged on Film of Nazi Activities," *New York Times,* April 29, 1934, 26; "Are We Civilized?" *New York Times,* June 14, 1934, 28; "Loews Cancels Anti-Nazi Pic; and Squawks," *Variety,* September 2, 1936, 7; Dick, 46–51, 61–64.

97. "Lewis Says Hays Bans Film of Book," *New York Times,* February 16, 1936, 1.

98. "Berlin and Rome Hail 'Ban' on Film," *New York Times,* February 17, 1936, 21.

99. Levine, 171.

100. Black, 39, 70, 157, 159, 170, 244–88 passim.

101. Josephine Herbst, "Behind the Swastika (1935)," reprinted in *Massachusetts Review* 27, no. 2 (1986); Dorothy Thompson, *I Saw Hitler* (New York: Houghton-Miflin, 1940); Stowe.

102. Douglas V. Churchill, "Hollywood's Censor Is All the World," *New York Times,* March 29, 1936, sec. 7, p. 3.

103. "Americas Adopt Neutrality Pact," *New York Times,* December 20, 1936, 36; Black, 31–34, 40–46; Ames, 475.

104. David G. Haglund, *Latin America and the Transformation of U.S. Strategic Thought, 1936–1940* (Albuquerque: University of New Mexico Press, 1984), 54.

105. George Gercke, "Pan-American Pictures," *New York Times,* December 18,

1938, sec. 9, p. 6; Frank S. Nugent, "Hollywood Waves the Flag," *Nation*, April 8, 1939, 399.

106. Haglund, 55–70, 90–98; Frye, 65–79; 101–17, 174–75.

107. Quoted in Frye, 174–75.

108. *Report of the Delegate of the United States of America to the Meeting of the Foreign Ministers of the American Republics held at Panama, September 23–October 3, 1939* (Washington, D.C.: GPO, 1941), 33–44, 53–64 (hereafter, *Panama Conference Report*); Haglund, 148–49.

109. Detlef Junker, "The Impact of Foreign Policy on the United States Domestic Scene, 1939–1941," *Storia Nordamerica* 6, nos. 1–2 (1989): 17–34.

110. Nathan Miller, *War at Sea: A Naval History of World War II* (New York: Oxford University Press, 1995), 29–51; Len Deighton, *Blood, Tears, and Folly: An Objective Look at World War II* (New York: Harper-Perennial, 1993), 34–39; Haglund, 48–49; *Panama Conference Report*, 53–64.

111. Leo Rosten, *Hollywood: The Movie Colony, the Movie Makers* (New York: Harcourt Brace, 1941), 154.

112. Lucy S. Dawidowicz, *The War against the Jews, 1939–1945* (New York: Bantam Books, 1986), 368–71.

113. David Shipman, *The Story of Cinema: A Complete Narrative History from the Beginnings to the Present* (New York: St. Martin's, 1982), 621, 624, 626–28; James Hay, *Popular Film Culture in Fascist Italy: The Passing of the Rex* (Bloomington: Indiana University Press, 1987); and Marcia Landy, *Fascism in Film: The Italian Commercial Cinema, 1933–1943* (Princeton, N.J.: Princeton University Press, 1986).

114. "U.S. Pix Stay out of Italy," *Variety*, October 21, 1936, 21.

115. "Film's Victory in Italy," *Variety*, December 30, 1936, 5; "U.S. Companies to Quit Italy by Jan. 1 Unless Rome Changes Its Totalitarian Film Ideas," *Variety*, November 9, 1938, 13; "WB Out of Italy," *Variety*, November 9, 1938, 13.

116. Harry Warner Speeches and Correspondence Files, JLWC; "Film Folk Aid War Orphans," *Hollywood Now* 4 (August 1939): 2; "141 Orphans 'Adopted,'" *New York Times*, July 30, 1939, 18.

117. Harold Rodner correspondence with H. M. Warner, Nazi Data Files, folder 3, JLWC.

118. Harry Warner Speeches File, JLWC; "More Patriotism," *Variety*, February 15, 1939, 6; Colgan, 53–54, 245–48.

119. John Davis, 25.

120. Elizabeth Dalton, "Old Glory: Notes on Warner Shorts," *Velvet Light Trap* 8 (1973): 7–8; Rosten, 152.

121. "WB's Patriotism Costly, Shorts Lost $1,250,000," *Variety*, March 13, 1940, 46.

122. The fourteen shorts were *Song of a Nation* (1936), *Give Me Liberty* (1936), *Under Southern Stars* (1937), *The Man without a Country* (1937), *Ro-*

mance of Louisiana (1938), *Declaration of Independence* (1938), *Lincoln in the White House* (1939), *Sons of Liberty* (1939), *The Bill of Rights* (1939), *The Monroe Doctrine* (1939), *Old Hickory* (1939), *Teddy, the Rough Rider* (1940), *Pony Express Days* (1940), and *Flag of Humanity* (1940).

123. "Defense Pictures," *Variety,* June 12, 1940, 3.

124. Elizabeth Dalton, "Bugs and Daffy Go to War: Some Warners Cartoons of WWII," *Velvet Light Trap* 5 (spring 1972): 44; Jerry Beck and Will Friedwald, *Looney Tunes and Merrie Melodies: A Complete Illustrated Guide* (New York: Henry Holt, 1989); Chuck Jones, *Chuck Amuck: The Life and Times of an Animated Cartoonist* (New York: Farrar, Strauss, Giroux, 1989); Chuck Jones, *Chuck Reducks* (New York: Warner Books, 1996); Hugh Kenner, *Chuck Jones: A Flurry of Drawings* (Berkeley: University of California Press, 1994); Joe Adamson, *Bugs Bunny: Fifty Years and Only One Grey Hare* (New York: Henry Holt, 1990); Norman M. Klein, *Seven Minutes: The Life and Death of the American Animated Cartoon* (London: Verso, 1993), 186–99; Shull and Wilt, 3–67 passim; Stefan Kanfer, *Serious Business: The Art and Commerce of Animation in America from Betty Boop to Toy Story* (New York: Scribner's, 1997), 135–55.

125. Shull and Wilt, 25. For a breakdown of war-related cartoon production, see their table on page 161.

126. Larry Ceplair and Steven Englund, *The Inquisition in Hollywood: Politics and the Film Community, 1930–1960* (Garden City, N.Y.: Anchor Press/Doubleday, 1980), 107–8; Charles Maland, *Chaplin and American Culture: The Evolution of a Star Image* (Princeton, N.J.: Princeton University Press, 1989), 162.

127. "Donald Ogden Stewart: Politically Conscious," interviewed by Allen Eyles and John Gillett in *Backstory*, 345–46.

128. Ella Winter, "Hollywood Wakes Up," *New Republic,* January 12, 1938, 276–77; Rosten, 152.

129. Colgan, 161.

130. Harry Warner Speech, December 15, 1937, American Committee for Christian Refugee folder, JLWC; Colgan, 166–69.

131. Neve, 4; Rosten, 174–75. Warner Bros. earned a reputation as a "writer's studio"; many writers (e.g., W. R. Burnett, the Epstein brothers, Howard Koch, etc.) preferred working there to working at any other studio; *Backstory,* 75, 181, 183–87, 295, 296, 298–310.

132. "H'wood Extends Icy Paw to Young Mussolini; Under Heavy Guard," *Variety,* September 29, 1937, 2; "Il Duce's Phone Call to Vittorio in H'wood Climaxed Italo-U.S. Idea; Too Much Opposish to Roach Plan," *Variety,* October 13, 1937, 5; "H'wood Still Het Up over Mussolini, Jr.; Will Take Rap on Pix Anyway?" *Variety,* October 6, 1937, 2.

133. Winter, 277; Rosten, 141.

134. Quoted in Colgan, 144.

135. "U.S. Film Industry May Pull Out All Distrib from Italy due to Severe

Restrictions; Decree Hits All Nations," *Variety,* September 21, 1938, 11; "WB Out of Italy," 13.

136. Guy Stern, "The Burning of Books in Nazi Germany, 1933: The American Response," *Simon Wiesenthal Center Annual* 2 (1985): 95–113.

137. "Jack Warner's Dinner to Exiled Thos. Mann May Touch Off a Militant Anti-Hitler Campaign in Hollywood," *Variety,* March 23, 1938, 2; Colgan, 226.

138. Colgan, 227.

139. Nazi Data, folder 3, JLWC.

140. "Declaration of Democratic Independence," *Hollywood Now,* December 23, 1938, 1.

141. Ibid.

142. Colgan, 228–32. Assembling on December 21, 1938, to pen their names before newsreel cameramen were Harry and Jack Warner, Edward G. Robinson, Melvyn Douglas, James Cagney, Bette Davis, Philip Dunne, Paul Muni, Claude Rains, Henry Fonda, Bryan Foy, and Groucho Marx. Carl Laemmele was the only other mogul to sign the declaration.

143. William Weiner and Ephraim Schwartzman to Jack and Harry Warner, November 5, 1938, Nazi Data Files, folder 3, JLWC, 2–3.

144. Ibid., 3.

145. Ibid., 4.

146. Helen Zigmond to Harry Warner, January 27, 1939, Nazi Data Files, folder 3, JLWC.

147. Helen Zigmond, "Features," *Jewish Telegraphic Agency,* December 25, 1938, 1.

148. Marc Eliot, *Walt Disney: Hollywood's Dark Prince* (New York: Birch Lane Press, 1993), 120–21.

149. Thomas Doherty, *Projections of War: Hollywood, American Culture, and World War II* (New York: Columbia University Press, 1993), 21; "Leni Riefenstahl Still Getting Film Business Brushoff," *Variety,* December 7, 1938, 1; Rosten, 141.

150. Leni Riefenstahl, *Leni Riefenstahl: A Memoir* (New York: St. Martin's, 1993), 236–41.

151. Harold Rodner correspondence (1936–38), Nazi Data Files, folders 2 and 3, JLWC; Colgan, 50–51.

152. "WB's Schmeling Ban," *Variety,* July 1, 1936, 1.

153. Johnpeter Horst Grill and Robert L. Jenkins, "The Nazis and the American South in the 1930s: A Mirror Image?" *Journal of Southern History* 58, no. 4 (November 1992): 675.

154. Colgan, 152–53.

155. Doris Warner to Harry Warner, 1938, Nazi Data Files, folder 3, JLWC, 1–2.

156. Colgan, 154.

157. Quoted in Raymond Fielding, *The March of Time, 1935–1951* (New York:

Oxford University Press, 1978), 196. For a full discussion of the newsreel and the subsequent controversy, see his chapter "Inside Nazi Germany--1938," 187–201.

158. Winchell's column was published by Anglophobe isolationist William Randolph Hearst.

159. Quoted in Colgan, 156.

160. Neal Gabler, *Winchell: Gossip, Power, and the Culture of Celebrity* (New York: Vintage, 1995), 281–83; (hereafter, *Winchell*).

161. Quoted in *Winchell*, 289.

162. *Winchell*, 294.

163. Colgan, 177.

164. Errol Flynn, "What Really Happened to Me in Spain," in *From a Life of Adventure: The Writings of Errol Flynn*, Tony Thomas, ed. (Secaucus, N.J.: Citadel Press, 1980), 138–45; Richard Slotkin, "The Continuity of Forms: Myth and Genre in Warner Brothers' *The Charge of the Light Brigade*," *Representations* 29 (winter 1990): 1–23.

165. Jack L. Warner to H. M. Warner, October 5, 1939, Joe Hazen Correspondence File, JLWC, 2.

166. Ibid.

167. Joe Hazen Correspondence File (1938–39), Harry Warner Correspondence Files, and Jack Warner Correspondence Files, JLWC.

168. Ibid.

169. Colgan, 248.

170. Harry Warner to Sam Katz, June 27, 1939, Nazi Data Files, folder 3, JLWC.

171. "Ten Nazi Editors Are Guests at Metro Lot," *Boxoffice*, June 24, 1939, 34; "Metro Studio Secretly Receives Nazi Editors," *Hollywood Now*, June 23, 1939, 1; "Mayer Remains Silent on Nazi Editors' Visit," *Hollywood Now*, June 30, 1939, 1.

172. Gabler, 291.

173. "HM Warner Sails," *Variety*, August 9, 1939, 2; "WB, FN Merge English Sales," *Variety*, August 23, 1939, 12; "English Leading Men in U.S. Would Be Hit by a War," *Variety*, August 23, 1939, 1; "Films a Big Hazard in London," *Variety*, August 30, 1939, 1; C. A. Lejeune, "A Little Light on London," *New York Times*, October 22, 1939, sec. 9, p. 4.

174. Warner with Jennings, 277; "Warners to Distribute London Air-Raid Short," *Variety*, October 23, 1940, 20.

175. Frederic James Krome, "'A Weapon of War Second to None': Anglo-American Film Propaganda during World War II," Ph.D. diss., University of Cincinnati, 1992, 40.

176. Ibid., 46, 84–85.

177. Ibid., 47.

178. Ibid., 65.

179. Ibid., 69–70. See also Anthony Aldgate and Jeffrey Richards, *Britain Can*

Take It: The British Cinema and the Second World War (London: Basil Blackwell, 1985).

180. Ibid., 80–82.

181. Ibid., 84.

182. Ibid., 86–87.

NOTES TO CHAPTER 2

1. Hanna Marczewska, "Controversies around the American Policy of Neutrality, 1935–1939," *American Studies* (Warsaw University, Poland) 9 (1990): 61, 68, 74; Justus D. Doenecke and John E. Wilz, *From Isolation to War, 1931–1941,* 2d ed. (Arlington Heights, Ill.: Harlan Davidson, 1991), 54–69, 81–87.

2. See Harry Warner correspondence and Nazi Files, Jack L. Warner Collection, University of Southern California (hereafter, JLWC); Ronald H. Bayor, "Klans, Coughlinites, and Aryan Nations: Patterns of American Anti-Semitism in the Twentieth Century," *American Jewish History* 76, no. 2 (1986): 181–96; Ronald Modras, "Father Coughlin and Anti-Semitism: Fifty Years Later," *Journal of Church and State* 31, no. 2 (1989): 231–47; Ralph L. Kolodny, "Catholics and Father Coughlin: Misremembering the Past," *Patterns of Prejudice* 19, no. 4 (1985): 15–25. David J. Maurer, "The Black Legion: A Paramilitary Fascist Organization of the 1930s," in *For the General Welfare: Essays in Honor of Robert H. Brenner,* Frank Annunziata, Patrick D. Reagan, and Roy T. Wortman, eds., American University Studies no. 9, History (New York: Peter Lang, 1989), 261.

3. William J. Burns to R. W. Budd, September 8, 1938, Nazi Data Files, folder 3, JLWC.

4. Myriad fascist groups came and went in Depression America. According to *New Republic* there were around eight hundred such organizations operating in the United States in 1939. See "The American Fascists," *New Republic,* March 8, 1939, 118; Johnpeter Horst Grill and Robert L. Jenkins, "The Nazis and the American South in the 1930s: A Mirror Image?" *Journal of Southern History* 58, no. 4 (November 1992): 662.

5. J. B. Matthews and R. E. Shallcross, "Must America Go Fascist?" *Harper's,* June 1934, 9.

6. Leonard Dinnerstein, *Antisemitism in America* (New York: Oxford University Press, 1994), 105–7; Harold Lavine and James Wechsler, *War Propaganda and the United States* (New Haven, Conn.: Yale University Press, 1940), 36–38, 120, 132–40; David H. Bennett, *The Party of Fear: The American Far Right from Nativism to the Militia Movement,* rev. ed. (New York: Vintage, 1995), 238–72.

7. Richard Severo and Lewis Milford, *The Wages of War: When America's Soldiers Came Home—From Valley Forge to Vietnam* (New York: Simon and Schuster, 1989), 229–80, passim; Louis Leibovich, "Press Reaction to the Bonus March of 1932," *Journalism Monographs* 122 (1990): 1–32; William Pencak, *For God and*

Country: The American Legion, 1919–1941 (Boston: Northeastern University Press, 1989), 2–23, 208–77 passim; Thomas A. Rumer, *The American Legion: An Official History, 1919–1989* (New York: M. Evans, 1990), 6–7, 58–59, 138–41, 191–93, 227; David Wyman, *Paper Walls: America and the Refugee Crisis, 1938–1941* (New York: Pantheon, 1985), 10; Leo Ribuffo, "Fascists, Nazis, and American Minds: Perceptions and Preconceptions," *American Quarterly* 26 (1974): 417–32.

8. Johan J. Smertenko, "Hitlerism Comes to America," *Harper's*, November 1933, 663.

9. Geoffrey Smith, "Isolationism, the Devil, and the Advent of the Second World War: Variations on a Theme," *International History Review* 4, no. 1 (1982): 58; Denis Fahey, *The Rulers of Russia*, 3d ed. (Royal Oak, Mich.: Charles A. Coughlin, Social Justice, 1940).

10. Eckard V. Toy, Jr., "Silver Shirts in the Northwest: Politics, Prophecies, and Personalities in the 1930s," *Pacific Northwest Quarterly* 80, no. 4 (1989): 140.

11. Matthews and Shallcross, 9.

12. William J. Burns to R. W. Budd, September 8, 1938, Nazi Data, folder 3, JLWC; "American Fascism: Like Communism It Masquerades as Americanism," *Life*, March 6, 1939, 60 (hereafter, "Masquerades").

13. Sidney H. Kessler, "Fascism under the Cross: The Case of Father Coughlin," *Wiener Library Bulletin* 33, nos. 51–52 (1980): 8; Alan Brinkley, *Voices of Protest: Huey Long, Father Coughlin, and the Great Depression* (New York: Vintage Books, 1982), 91, 95, 97, 101, 191–92.

14. Quoted in Wyman, 18; Dinnerstein, 121.

15. Lucy S. Dawidowicz, *The War against the Jews, 1933–1945* (New York: Dell, 1986), 100–104; Leni Yahil, *The Holocaust: The Fate of European Jewry, 1932–1945*, Ina Friedman and Haya Galai, trans. (New York: Oxford University Press, 1990), 84, 109–21, 134; Kessler, 8; Dinnerstein, 116.

16. James Wechsler, "The Christian Front and Martin Dies," *Nation*, January 27, 1940, 89–91; Alson J. Smith, "Father Coughlin's Platoons," *New Republic*, August 30, 1939, 96–97; Kessler, 10; Wyman, 18–19.

17. Brinkley, 124–26, 245–46, 256–58; Dinnerstein, 108–9; Edward S. Shapiro, "The Approach of War: Congressional Isolationism and Anti-Semitism, 1939–1941," *American Jewish History* 74, no. 1 (1984): 47–49; Henry Schwartz, "The Silver Shirts: Anti-Semitism in San Diego, 1930–1940," *Western States Jewish History* 25, no. 1 (October 1992): 52; Leland V. Bell, "The Failure of Nazism in America: The German American Bund, 1936–1941," *Political Science Quarterly* 85, no. 4 (December 1970): 588; Henry L. Feingold, "'Courage First and Intelligence Second': The American Jewish Secular Elite, Roosevelt, and the Failure to Rescue," *American Jewish History* 72, no. 4 (1983): 430; Leonard Dinnerstein, "Jews and the New Deal," *American Jewish History* 72, no. 4 (1983): 461; Geoffrey Smith, 73; "Masquerades," 59.

18. "The American Fascists," 118; Dinnerstein, *Antisemitism in America,* 109.

19. Schwartz, 57; Lavine and Wechsler, 261.

20. There are many similarities between the cryptofascist groups of the 1930s and recent militia organizations. See James William Gibson, *Warrior Dreams: Paramilitary Culture in Post-Vietnam America* (New York: Hill and Wang, 1994); Philip Jenkins, "Home Grown Terror," *American Heritage* 46, no. 5 (September 1995): 38–47.

21. Leo Ribuffo, *The Old Christian Right: the Protestant Far Right from the Great Depression to the Cold War* (Philadelphia: Temple University Press, 1983), 91.

22. Clara R. Paige, "Any Harm in the Movies?" *Good Citizen* 21, no. 5 (May 1933): 13.

23. Ibid., 14–15.

24. Carolyn Jeanne Tweed, "The Life Cycles of William Dudley Pelley," master's thesis, East Tennessee State University, 1990, 9–10.

25. Christine Ann Colgan, "Warner Brothers' Crusade against the Third Reich: A Study of Anti-Nazi Activism and Film Production, 1933–1941," Ph.D. diss., University of Southern California, 1985, 96.

26. Suzanne G. Ledeboer, "The Man Who Would Be Hitler: William Dudley Pelley and the Silver Shirt Legion," *California History* 65 (June 1986): 127–28.

27. Ibid., 128.

28. Ribuffo, *Old Christian Right,* 43–47.

29. Ibid., 25; Tweed, 20; Ledeboer, 127; Toy, 140.

30. Ledeboer, 128; Ribuffo, *Old Christian Right,* 28, 48–53.

31. Ledeboer, 128; Ribuffo, *Old Christian Right,* 53, 59.

32. Ledeboer, 128.

33. Quoted in Smertenko, 664.

34. Ledeboer, 128; Schwartz, 53.

35. Ledeboer, 127.

36. Toy, 141; Tweed, 32; Ribuffo, *Old Christian Right,* 64.

37. Alvin C. York Papers, uncatalogued, Pall Mall, Tenn.

38. William Dudley Pelley, *The Dupes of Judah: The Inside Story of Why the World War Was Fought* (Asheville, N.C.. Pelley Publishers, 1938), 58 (his emphasis; hereafter, *Dupes of Judah*).

39. Ibid., 59.

40. Ibid., 3, 20, 36, 51; Wyman, 16. Hull's wife was Jewish, but he downplayed that fact throughout his career. See Irwin F. Gellman, *Secret Affairs: Franklin Roosevelt, Cordell Hull, and Sumner Welles* (Baltimore: Johns Hopkins University Press, 1993).

41. *Dupes of Judah,* 5.

42. Ibid., 53 (his emphasis).

43. Ribuffo, *Old Christian Right,* 60.

44. Toy, 141; Tweed, 37.

45. Tweed, 35.

46. Gregory D. Black, *Hollywood Censored: Morality Codes, Catholics, and the Movies* (Cambridge: Cambridge University Press, 1994), 39, 41–42, 62–63, 70, 111, 122, 132, 137, 145, 157, 159, 167, 170, 181, 240, 253, 256, 293.

47. Ribuffo, *Old Christian Right,* 61–63.

48. Quoted in ibid., 62; Stephen J. Whitfield, "Our American Jewish Heritage: The Hollywood Version," *American Jewish History* 75, no. 3 (1986): 323.

49. Both Nathanael West and Sinclair Lewis set their exposés of American fascism in Pelley's home state of Vermont.

50. Lawrence W. Levine, "Hollywood's Washington: Film Images of National Politics during the Great Depression," *Prospects* 10 (1985), 177.

51. Colgan, 120–21, 150–52.

52. Grill and Jenkins, 667–69. Though the KKK was anti-Semitic, southern Klansmen despised the German-American Bund. Hitler, however, admired the South of the "Lost Cause," and *Gone with the Wind* was one of his favorite films; Ray Lewis White, "Wom Winde Verweht: *Gone with the Wind* in Nazi Germany," *Southern Studies* 22, no. 4 (winter 1983): 401–6.

53. Peter H. Amann, "Vigilante Fascism: The Black Legion as an American Hybrid," *Comparative Studies in Society and History* 25, no. 3 (1983): 493–501 (hereafter, "Vigilante Fascism").

54. Michael S. Clinansmith, "The Black Legion: Hooded Americanism in Michigan," *Michigan History* 55, no. 3 (fall 1971): 244.

55. George Morris, *The Black Legion Rides* (New York: Workers Library, August 1936), 5.

56. The specific questions are reproduced in ibid., 5–6.

57. Ibid., 5.

58. "Vigilante Fascism," 497, 518; Maurer, 258.

59. Peter H. Amann, "A 'Dog in the Nighttime' Problem: American Fascism in the 1930s," *History Teacher* 19, no. 4 (August 1986): 566 (hereafter, "American Fascism in the 1930s").

60. "Crime: Mumbo-Jumbo," *Time,* June 8, 1936, 11 (hereafter, "Mumbo-Jumbo"); Maurer, 255.

61. "Vigilante Fascism," 502.

62. Ibid., 503.

63. Maurer, 257.

64. "American Fascism in the 1930s," 566; "Vigilante Fascism," 512.

65. Quoted in "Vigilante Fascism," 497.

66. "American Fascism in the 1930s," 566–67; "Vigilante Fascism," 501, 509, 513–22.

67. Ibid.

68. Morris, 8–9; "Vigilante Fascism," 509.

69. "Vigilante Fascism," 520; Colgan, 102; Morris, 32–33.
70. Morris, 35–36.
71. Ibid., 12–13, 16–17.
72. Morris, 19, 21; "Vigilante Fascism," 520; Clinansmith, 257.
73. Morris, 18; "Vigilante Fascism," 510–11, 519.
74. "Vigilante Fascism," 512.
75. Morris, 20.
76. Morris claims that Poole worked for the PWA rather than the WPA.
77. Morris, 3; Maurer, 255, 261. Maurer presents different details, arguing that the reason for Poole's murder was that he had claimed to know Legion members and their secrets. Peter Roffman and Jim Purdy provide yet another explanation for Poole's murder: that Poole led a political campaign against a candidate supported by the Black Legion; Roffman and Purdy, *The Hollywood Social Problem Film: Madness, Despair, and Politics from the Depression to the Fifties* (Bloomington: Indiana University Press, 1981), 177.
78. "Vigilante Fascism," 520–21; Colgan, 101.
79. "Vigilante Fascism," 521.
80. "Mumbo Jumbo," 11; Colgan, 101.
81. Clinansmith, 244.
82. Colgan, 103.
83. Ibid.
84. Brian Neve, "The Screenwriter and the Social Problem Film, 1936–1938: The Case of Robert Rossen at Warner Brothers," *Film and History* 14, no. 1 (1984): 5–6; Nick Roddick, *A New Deal in Entertainment: Warner Brothers in the 1930s* (London: British Film Institute, 1983), 116–17.
85. "Inside Stuff—Pictures," *Variety,* October 28, 1938, 7.
86. "Kluxers Sue WB on 'Black Legion' Insignia," *Variety,* August 18, 1937, 4; "Klan Argues WB's 'Black Legion' Pic Libeled the KKK," *Variety,* March 16, 1938, 5.
87. Ann M. Sperber and Eric Lax, *Bogart* (New York: William Morrow, 1997), 80.
88. Colgan, 115–17.
89. Quoted in Black, 269.
90. *Black Legion,* dir. Archie Mayo, Warner Bros., 1936.
91. David Kennedy, *Over Here: The First World War and American Society* (New York: Oxford University Press, 1980), 12, 24, 67–69, 81–83, 87, 165–66, 363; Geoffrey Perrett, *America in the Twenties: A History* (New York: Touchstone/Simon and Schuster, 1982), 51–88.
92. *Black Legion.*
93. Ibid.
94. Ibid.

95. Ibid.

96. Ibid.

97. Ibid.

98. "Inside Stuff—Pictures," *Variety,* February 3, 1937, 6.

99. Roddick, 157.

100. Otis Ferguson, "Truth in Fiction," *New Republic,* February 17, 1937, 48.

101. Ibid.

102. "Black Legion," *Time,* February 23, 1937, 46.

103. Ibid.

104. "Hollywood Blasts 'Black Legion': Warner Brothers Factual Film Is Powerful and Intelligent," *Literary Digest,* January 16, 1937, 23.

105. Ibid.; *New York Herald Tribune,* January 16, 1937, 14.

106. "Hollywood Blasts 'Black Legion.'"

107. Colgan, 110.

108. Roddick, 73.

109. Black, 252–60.

110. Roddick, 171–74.

NOTES TO CHAPTER 3

1. For more on the film industry under Mussolini, see James Hay, *Popular Film Culture in Fascist Italy: The Passing of the Rex* (Bloomington: Indiana University Press, 1987); Marcia Landy, *Fascism in Film: The Italian Commercial Cinema, 1933–1943* (Princeton, N.J.: Princeton University Press, 1986).

2. Jack Warner with Dean Jennings, *My First Hundred Years in Hollywood* (New York: Random House, 1965), 261.

3. Ibid.

4. For a history of the Bund, see Sander A. Diamond, *The Nazi Movement in the United States, 1924–1941* (Ithaca: Cornell University Press, 1974).

5. Warner with Jennings, 262.

6. Justus D. Doenecke and John E. Wilz, *From Isolation to War, 1931–1941,* 2d ed. (Arlington Heights, Ill.: Harlan Davidson, 1991), 57.

7. Otto D. Tolliscus, "Hitler Demands Colonies, Riches for Japan and Italy; Tells U.S. Not to Meddle," *New York Times,* January 31, 1939, 1.

8. Christine Ann Colgan, "Warner Brothers' Crusade against the Third Reich: A Study of Anti-Nazi Activism and Film Production, 1933–1941," Ph.D. diss., University of Southern California, 1985, 414.

9. Warner with Jennings, 262.

10. For more about *Blockade,* see Matthew Bernstein, *Walter Wanger: Hollywood Independent* (Berkeley: University of California Press, 1994), 129–38.

11. Bruce F. Ashkenas, "A Legacy of Hatred: The Records of a Nazi Organiza-

tion in America," *Prologue* 17, no. 2 (1985): 93–106; Alton Frye, *Nazi Germany and the American Hemisphere, 1933–1941* (New Haven, Conn.: Yale University Press, 1967), 15–80, 131–51 passim.

12. Johnpeter Horst Grill and Robert L. Jenkins, "The Nazis and the American South in the 1930s: A Mirror Image?" *Journal of Southern History* 58, no. 4 (November 1992): 681.

13. Charles Angoff, "Nazi Jew-Baiting in America," *Nation,* May 1, 1935, 501–3; "Dangerous Nazi Campaign in America," *Business Week,* September 28, 1935, 40.

14. Quoted in Angoff, 503.

15. Johan J. Smertenko, "Hitlerism Comes to America," *Harper's,* November 1933, 668.

16. Leland V. Bell, "The Failure of Nazism in America: The German American Bund, 1936–1941," *Political Science Quarterly* 85, no. 4 (December 1970): 586.

17. Charles E. Blake, "Speech for H. M. Warner at the Dinner of the Patriotic Foundation of Chicago, May 21st 1939," Harry Warner Speeches and Interviews Folder, (Jack L. Warner Collection, University of Southern California (hereafter, JLWC), 2.

18. "Footlights and Flickers," *Memphis Commercial Appeal,* December 8, 1938, 11.

19. Cass Warner Sperling and Cork Miller with Jack Warner, Jr., *Hollywood Be Thy Name: The Warner Brothers Story* (Rocklin, Calif.: Prima, 1994), 220; "Remembering a Jewish American Patriot," *Christian Century,* December 17, 1941, 1565.

20. *Hollywood Spectator* 13, no. 22 (November 26, 1938): 3–5.

21. All quotations found in ibid., 3–4.

22. Ibid., 4.

23. Harry Warner Nazi Files, folder 3, JLWC.

24. For information concerning the 1936 Olympics, see George Eisen, "The Voices of Sanity: American Diplomatic Reports from the 1936 Berlin Olympiad," *Journal of Sports History* 11, no. 3 (winter 1984): 56–78; Wendy Gray and Robert Knight Barney, "Devotion to Whom? German-American Loyalty on the Issue of Participation in the 1936 Olympic Games," *Journal of Sports History* 17, no. 2 (summer 1990): 214–31; Alice Hellerstein, "The 1936 Olympics: A U.S. Boycott That Failed," *Potomac Review* 21 (1981): 1–9; Peter Levine, "'My Father and I, We Didn't Get Our Medals': Marty Glickman's American Jewish Odyssey," *American Jewish History* 78, no. 3 (1989): 399–424; Carolyn Marvin, "Avery Brundage and American Participation in the 1936 Olympic Games," *American Studies* (UK) 16, no. 1 (1982): 81–106; Edward S. Shapiro, "The World Labor Athletic Carnival of 1936: An American Anti-Nazi Protest," *American Jewish History* 74, no. 3 (1985): 255–73; Stephen R. Wenn, "A Suitable Policy of Neutrality? FDR and the Ques-

tion of American Participation in the 1936 Olympics," *International Journal of the History of Sport* (London) 8, no. 3 (December 1991): 319–35; and Stephen R. Wenn, "A Tale of Two Diplomats: George S. Messersmith and Charles H. Sherrill on Proposed American Participation in the 1936 Olympics," *Journal of Sport History* 16, no. 1 (spring 1989); 27–43. Regarding Hollywood and the Spanish Civil War, see Bernard F. Dick, "The War That Dared Not Speak Its Name," in *The Star Spangled Screen: The American World War II Film,* by Bernard Dick (Lexington: University Press of Kentucky, 1985), 10–40.

25. G. Reimann, "Morale and the Nazis," *New Republic,* November 17, 1937, 34–35.

26. For more about Leo Frank and the Scottsboro Boys, see Joel Williamson, *A Rage for Order: Black-White Relations in the American South since Emancipation* (New York: Oxford University Press, 1986), 151, 240–44, 246; John Henry Hammond, Jr., "The South Speaks," *Nation,* April 26, 1933, 464–66.

27. *They Won't Forget,* dir. Mervyn LeRoy, Warner Bros., 1937; Peter Roffman and Jim Purdy, *The Hollywood Social Problem Film* (Bloomington: Indiana University Press, 1981), 167–70; Colgan, 181–83.

28. Roffman and Purdy, 170.

29. Brian Neve, "The Screenwriter and the Social Problem Film, 1936–1938: The Case of Robert Rossen at Warner Brothers," *Film and History* 14, No. 1 (1984): 2–13.

30. Nick Roddick, *A New Deal in Entertainment: Warner Brothers in the 1930s* (London: British Film Institute, 1983), 154–55.

31. "Cinema: *They Won't Forget*," *Time,* July 26, 1937, 22.

32. "Screen: Bigotry vs. Justice, a Tragedy in the Deep South," *Newsweek,* July 10, 1937, 23.

33. "Movies: They Won't Forget," *Literary Digest,* July 24, 1937, 29.

34. Ibid.

35. Roddick, 153.

36. For more about the Dreyfus Affair, see Jean-Denis Bredin, *The Affair: The Case of Alfred Dreyfus* (New York: G. Braziller, 1986); Richard Griffiths, *The Use of Abuse: The Polemics of the Dreyfus Affair and Its Aftermath* (New York: Oxford University Press, 1991); and Louis Leo Snyder, *The Dreyfus Case: A Documentary History* (New Brunswick, N.J.: Rutgers University Press, 1973).

37. Colgan, 185–90.

38. *The Life of Emile Zola,* dir. William Dieterle, Warner Bros., 1937.

39. Mark Van Doren, "The Novelist as Hero," *Nation,* September 4, 1937, 246; "Movies Worth Seeing: *The Life of Emile Zola,*" *Literary Digest,* August 14, 1937, 31.

40. Colgan, 140, 252. Diamond, 206–11.

41. "War Scare Palaver Has Show Biz Checking Up on Itself All Over," *Variety,* September 28, 1938, 1.

198 | *Notes to Chapter 3*

42. *Dawn Patrol,* dir. Edmund Goulding, Turner Home Video, 1995. Rathbone, Niven, and Crisp belonged to the reserves.

43. Lucy Dawidowicz, *The War against the Jews, 1933–1945* (New York: Bantam Books, 1986), 88–106; Leni Yahil, *The Holocaust: The Fate of European Jewry,* Ina Freidman and Hanna Galai, trans. (New York: Oxford University Press, 1990), 104–14.

44. William Pencak, *For God and Country: The American Legion, 1919–1941* (Boston: Northeastern University Press, 1989), 231–33, 303–8.

45. "A Tribute to the American Legion: An address delivered by Harry M. Warner, President of Warner Bros. Pictures, Inc., at a studio luncheon tendered to the American Legion officers and other distinguished guests, September 19, 1938," Harry Warner Speeches and Interviews File, box 56, folder 1, JLWC.

46. *Confessions of a Nazi Spy,* dir. Anatole Litvak, Warner Bros., 1938.

47. David Lawrence, "'Trade' U. S. Nazis for Jews," *Nashville Banner,* 1938 (clipping from the York Papers).

48. Ibid.

49. Regarding Jews and quotas, see David Wyman, *The Abandonment of the Jews: America and the Holocaust, 1941–1945* (New York: Pantheon Books, 1984).

50. Colgan, 286, 297.

51. Harry Warner, "Hollywood Obligations in a Producer's Eyes," *Christian Science Monitor,* March 16, 1939, 3.

52. "WB to Unloose Flood of Anti-Nazi Pix, Market Lost to Them Anyway," *Variety,* December 7, 1938, 15.

53. Harry Warner, 3.

54. Ibid.

55. Quoted in Ina Rae Hark, "The Visual Politics of *The Adventures of Robin Hood," Journal of Popular Film* 5, no. 1 (1976): 4.

56. Ibid., 9.

57. Mary S. Lovell, *The Sound of Wings: The Life of Amelia Earhart* (New York: St. Martin's Press, 1989), 314

58. Ibid., 314.

59. Joe O'Neill, "Remarks of H. M. Warner at St. Patrick's Day Dinner at Royal Palms Hotel, March 17, 1939," Harry Warner Speeches and Interviews File, box 56, folder 1, JLWC, 3 (his emphasis).

60. Ibid., 5–6.

61. Ibid.

62. Colgan, 307 (emphasis added).

63. Warner with Jennings, 262. "Our own man in Germany" refers to the story of the death of the fictitious employee, Joe Kauffman, discussed in chapter 1.

64. Rudy Behlmer, *Inside Warner Brothers, 1935–1951* (New York: Simon and Schuster, 1985), 82 (his emphasis).

65. Colgan, 312.

66. "Of Spies and Bund Men," *Nation,* July 2, 1938, 6; "The Cabinet: Snoop, Look, and Listen," *Time,* July 4, 1938, 9.

67. "Of Spies and Bund Men," 6.

68. "Inside Stuff—Pictures," *Variety,* December 21, 1938, 10; Colgan, 314.

69. "Of Spies and Bund Men."

70. Douglas V. Churchill, "Hollywood Looks for the Rainbow," *New York Times,* June 16, 1940, sec. 9, p. 3; Colgan, 316–17.

71. Detlef Junker, "The Impact of Foreign Policy on the United States Domestic Scene, 1939–1941," *Storia Nordamerica* 6, nos. 1–2 (1989): 26. See "U.S. Closing Coast Exchange Scrutiny, Prowl WB Books," *Variety,* August 3, 1938, 6; "Gov't Suit Is All Embracing: It Looks as If Any Moves for Self-Regulation Are Futile," *Variety,* August 10, 1938, 2; "Threat of Theatre Divorcement Is a Subject of Much Concern to Execs Long Trained to Chain Op," *Variety,* September 21, 1938, 15; Nick Browne, "System of Production/System of Representation: Industry Context and Ideological Form in Capra's *Meet John Doe,*" in *Meet John Doe: Frank Capra, Director,* Charles Wolfe, ed. (New Brunswick, N.J.: Rutgers University Press, 1989), 269–88; Michael Conant, "The Paramount Case and Its Legal Background (1961)," in *The Movies in Our Midst: Documents in the Cultural History of Film in America,* Gerald Mast, ed. (Chicago: University of Chicago Press, 1982), 594–604; and Giuliana Muscio, "The Paramount Case," in *Hollywood's New Deal* (Philadelphia: Temple University Press, 1997), 143–95.

72. Colgan, 318–19, 322–23.

73. Hal Wallis with Charles Higham, *Starmaker: The Autobiography of Hal B. Wallis* (New York: Macmillan, 1980), 79; Douglas V. Churchill, "Espionage in Hollywood," *New York Times,* February 5, 1939, sec. 9, p. 5; Colgan, 324–25.

74. Leon Turrou, "Hollywood Does Something about the Nazis," *TAC,* May 1939, 6.

75. Colgan, 320.

76. Quoted in Ibid., 319.

77. Leon G. Turrou, "G-Man Turrou's Own Account of the Spy Situation," *Hollywood Spectator,* April 15, 1939, 18.

78. Thomas M. Pryor, "Miss Lys and the Lingerie," *New York Times,* April 23, 1939, sec. 10, p. 6.

79. *Confessions of a Nazi Spy* production files, Warner Bros. Archives, Special Collections, University of Southern California.

80. Eric J. Sandeen, "Anti-Nazi Sentiment in Film: *Confessions of a Nazi Spy* and the German-American Bund," *American Studies* 20, no. 2 (1979): 69, 73.

81. The Bund's controversial Madison rally had occurred on Monday, February 20, 1939, and approximately seventeen thousand people crammed into the Garden to hear the pro-Nazi rhetoric.

82. *Confessions of a Nazi Spy* (hereafter, *COANS*); Roddick, 164.

83. COANS

84. Ibid.

85. Ibid.

86. Ibid.

87. Ibid.

88. Ibid.

89. Ibid.

90. Colgan, 323.

91. Dick, 59; Roffman and Purdy, 213.

92. Roffman and Purdy, 213.

93. "Confessions of a Nazi Spy," *Variety,* April 28, 1939, 16.

94. James E. Combs and Sara T. Combs, *Film Propaganda and American Politics: An Analysis and Filmography* (New York: Garland, 1994), 43.

95. Quoted in Colgan, 407.

96. "Tempestuous Career of 'Nazi Spy,'" *New York Times,* June 2, 1940, sec. 9, p. 4; "K.C. Beef on 'Nazi Spy,'" *Variety,* May 10, 1939, 1; "Slashed Seats during 'Nazi' Engagement," *Variety,* June 21, 1939, 2.

97. Sandeen, 74.

98. Ibid.; Combs and Combs, 43; Colgan, 408.

99. Warner with Jennings, 263.

100. "Exhibs of 'Nazi Spy' in Poland Hanged by Nazis," *Variety,* April 24, 1940, 3; "Nazis Jail Pole over Spy Film," *New York Times,* November 28, 1939, 10; "WB Fears for Safety of Its Rep in Warsaw due to 'Nazi Spy' Pic," *Variety,* October 4, 1939, 19; Combs and Combs, 43. Sandeen's account disagreed, saying that the distributors received twenty-one years in prison. His essay is riddled with errors, repeatedly saying that it was Jack Warner who testified before the Nye-Clark committee instead of Harry.

101. Franz Hoellering, "Films," *Nation,* May 20, 1939, 596.

102. Ibid., 595.

103. Otis Ferguson, "They're Down! They're Up!" *New Republic,* May 10, 1939, 20.

104. Ibid.

105. "Totem and Taboo," *Time,* May 15, 1939, 58–59.

106. Grill and Jenkins, 667–94 passim; Edward S. Shapiro, "The Approach of War: Congressional Isolationism and Anti-Semitism, 1939–1941," *American Jewish History* 74, no. 1 (1984): 54–59.

107. "Confessions of a Nazi Spy," *Variety,* May 3, 1939, 6.

108. Colgan, 426.

109. "Latin Uproar," *Time,* February 10, 1940; "WB in Challenge to Brazil on 'Nazi' Film," *Variety,* June 12, 1940, 1.

110. James G. Stahlman, "This Should Be Stopped," *Nashville Banner,* September 13, 1939; James G. Stahlman political correspondence in James G.

Stahlman papers, housed at Vanderbilt University Special Collections; *Propaganda in Motion Pictures: Hearings before a Senate Subcommittee on Interstate Commerce, United States Senate (Seventy-Seventh Congress, First Session) on Senate Resolution 152; A Resolution Authorizing an Investigation of War Propaganda Disseminated by the Motion Picture Industry and of any Monopoly in the Production, Distribution, or Exhibition of Motion Pictures, September 9 to 26, 1941* (Washington, D.C.: GPO, 1942), 150–52, and Stahlman's testimony at said hearings, 395–408.

111. "Complete Tabu on War Films, Radio, and Newsreels, but Not the Press, Advocated in D.C.; Strict Neutrality," *Variety*, October 4, 1939, 2.

112. Michael S. Shull and David E. Wilt, *Doing Their Bit: Wartime American Animated Short Films, 1939–1945* (Jefferson, N.C.: McFarland, 1987), 91.

113. The Three Stooges, *They Stooge to Conga: Also Includes You Nazty Spy!* and *I'll Never Heil Again* (Columbia Pictures Home Video, 1993). The disclaimer at the beginning of *I'll Never Heil Again* (released 1941) read: "The characters in this picture are all fictitious. Anyone resembling them is better off dead."

114. *You Nazty Spy!*

115. Ibid.

116. Ibid.

117. Ibid.

118. Ibid.

119. Joe Hazen correspondence files, 1938–1939, JLWC.

120. "Rigid Economy Program Grips Studio; WB, 20th-Fox Lead," *Boxoffice*, May 25, 1940, 23; "Sh! Not Here," *Variety*, May 29, 1940, 2.

121. "U.S. Pic Firms Evacuate Paris," *Variety*, June 12, 1940, 12; "Entire French Market for U.S. Films Gets Wiped Out by Spread of War; Norse Countries Restore Operations," *Variety*, June 12, 1940, 12; "Nazi U-Boats Take Toll on U.S. Pix Shipped Over," *Variety*, October 2, 1940, 3; "U.S. Film Offices Seized," *New York Times*, April 17, 1941, 2.

122. "U.S. Not Being Panicked out of Prod. in England Despite Blitzkrieg," *Variety*, May 15, 1940, 4; "U.S. Companies Map Suspension of British Production for Duration; 20th Seen Joining Metro Wash-Up," *Variety*, June 12, 1940, 12.

123. "British Exhibitors Ask Jack Warner to Refrain from Maxwell Theatre Buy," *Variety*, July 23, 1941, 19; "Max Midler Would Head Warner Interest in Maxwell Theatre Buy; British Deal Remains Unconfirmed," *Variety*, July 16, 1941, 16; "WB in England Maps 50-Week Production Yr.," *Variety*, September 17, 1941, 18.

124. Colgan, 511, 574.

125. *The Fighting 69th*, dir. William Keighly, Warner Bros., 1940 (aired on American Movie Classics, September 1995).

126. Michael T. Isenberg, *War on Film: The American Cinema and World War I, 1914–1941* (Rutherford, N.J.: Fairleigh Dickinson University Press, 1981), 94.

127. Daniel J. Leab, "*The Fighting 69th:* An Ambiguous Portrait of Isolationism/Interventionism," in *Hollywood's World War I: Motion Picture Images,* Peter C. Rollins and John E. O'Connor, eds. (Bowling Green, Ohio: Popular Press, 1997), 101–20.

128. Behlmer, 105.

129. Quoted in Colgan, 534 (emphasis added).

130. Ibid., 536.

131. Quoted in Colgan, 545.

132. Ibid.

133. Stephen Vaughn, "Spies, National Security, and the 'Inertia Projector': The Secret Service Films of Ronald Reagan," *American Quarterly* 39, no. 3 (1987): 355. *Murder in the Air,* though shot in 1939, was not released until 1940.

134. Colgan, 532.

135. Vaughn, 362.

136. Harry M. Warner, "United We Survive, Divided We Fall!" Harry Warner Speeches and Interviews, box 56, folder 1, JLWC, 6, 7.

137. "H. M. Warner asks Studio to Cooperate with F.B.I.," Harry Warner Speeches and Interviews, box 56, folder 1, JLWC.

138. Harry M. Warner, "June 5, Meeting File," JLWC, 3.

139. "Mass Meeting of Warner Bros. Employees, Patriotic Speech by H. M. Warner," Harry Warner Speeches and Interviews, box 56, folder 1, JLWC, 13, 17.

140. Harry M. Warner, "United We Survive; Divided We Fall!" Harry Warner Speeches and Interviews, box 56, folder 1, JLWC, 5; Aljean Harmetz, *Round Up the Usual Suspects: The Making of Casablanca—Bogart, Bergman, and World War II* (New York: Hyperion, 1992), 68.

141. E. Phillips to Harry M. Warner, June 28, 1940, "June 5, 1940 Meeting File," JLWC.

142. Peter Colli to Harry M. Warner, June 20, 1940, "June 5, 1940 Meeting File," JLWC, 1, (his emphasis).

143. Ibid.

144. Helen Zigmond, "Hollywood and the European Applecart," *Jewish Telegraphic Agency,* December 25, 1939, 2.

145. "H. M. Warner Gives Ambulances," *New York Times,* June 6, 1940, 15.

146. "WB Helps Evacuate Kids of Its British Employees; Guarantees U.S. Home," *Variety,* August 7, 1940, 2; "40 WB British Children Now in U.S.," *Variety,* October 16, 1940, 1.

147. "Warner Yacht Given to Navy," *New York Times,* September 16, 1941, 2.

148. "Hope for $400,000 B. O. from Messerschmitt," *Variety,* June 18, 1941, 3.

149. "M-G-M, 20th Barred from Nazi Nations," *Variety,* August 7, 1940, 3.

150. Quoted in Margaret Farrand Thorp, *America at the Movies* (New Haven, Conn.: Yale University Press, 1939), 190–91.

151. "Hollywood Waves the Flag," *Nation,* April 2, 1939, 399.

152. Charles Maland, *Chaplin and American Culture: The Evolution of a Star Image* (Princeton, N.J.: Princeton University Press, 1989), 171.

153. For a more detailed discussion of *The Great Dictator,* see Maland, 159–86, and Richard H. Pells, *Radical Visions and American Dreams: Culture and Social Thought in the Depression Years* (Middletown, Conn.: Wesleyan University Press, 1973), 284–87

154. John Rossi, "Hitchcock's *Foreign Correspondent* (1940)," *Film and History* 12, no. 2 (1982): 26.

155. Ibid., 27. The film was produced by independent producer Walter Wanger and released through United Artists.

156. *Foreign Correspondent,* dir. Alfred Hitchcock, Walter Wanger/UA, 1940.

157. Ibid; Ann M. Sperber, *Murrow: His Life and Times* (New York: Freundlich Books, 1986), 101–294 passim.

158. Mark Lincoln Chadwin, *The Warhawks: American Interventionists before Pearl Harbor* (New York: Norton, 1970), 126–27.

159. Isenberg, 92.

NOTES TO CHAPTER 4

1. Michael E. Birdwell, "The Making of the Movie *Sergeant York:* A Journey from Reality into Myth," master's thesis, Tennessee Technological University, 1990, 36–51. For reports of York's feat, see George Patullo, "The Second Elder Gives Battle," *Saturday Evening Post,* April 26, 1919, 3–4, 71–73; David D. Lee, *Sergeant York: An American Hero* (Lexington: University Press of Kentucky, 1985), 27–48; Theodore Roosevelt II, "The Sword of the Lord and of Gideon," in *Rank and File: True Stories of the Great War* (New York: Scribner's, 1928), 32–59; John Bowers, "The Mythical Morning of Sergeant York, *MHQ: The Quarterly Journal of Military History* 8, no. 2 (winter 1996): 38–47; "Die Entstehung von Kriegslegendon Feststellungen ueber die Angebliche Holdentat des Amerikanischen Sergeanten York an 8. 10. 18," ("The origin of war legends, an investigation of the alleged feat of Sgt. York, October 18, 1918) Sgt. F. W. Merten and W. C. Koenig, trans. (Washington, D.C.: National Archives, 1936).

2. Personal interview with Guy Williams, January 21, 1987.

3. Lee, 69–91; Jerry W. Williamson, "The Mama's Boys," in *Hillbillyland: What the Movies Did to the Mountains, And the Mountains Did to the Movies* (Chapel Hill: University of North Carolina Press, 1995), 173–224.

4. For a discussion of local draft boards, see David Kennedy's *Over Here: The First World War and American Society* (New York: Oxford University Press, 1980), chaps. 2 and 3.

5. Williams interview.

6. Edgar M. Forster, Business Manager of the *Nashville Banner* to York, February 26, 1922, Alvin C. York Papers, uncataloged, (Pall Mall, Tenn. (hereafter, YP); Lee, 64–65.

7. Alvin C. York to Susie Williams, en route from France, 1919. From the collection of Guy Williams, Allardt, Tenn.

8. James Metcalfe, "Never to Fight Overseas," Alvin C. York File, *Nashville Banner* Library, Nashville, Tenn. 1937.

9. Richard Severo and Lewis Milford, *The Wages of War: When America's Soldiers Came Home—From Valley Forge to Vietnam* (New York: Simon and Shuster, 1989), 229–80; Edward S. Shapiro, "The Approach of War: Congressional Isolationism and Anti-Semitism, 1939–1941," *American Jewish History* 74, no. 1 (1984): 49; Geoffrey Smith, "Isolationism, the Devil, and the Advent of the Second World War: Variations on a Theme," *International History Review* 4, no. 1 (February 1982): 59.

10. Dixon Wecter, *When Johnny Comes Marching Home* (Cambridge, Mass.: Houghton-Miflin, 1944), 269; *The Mountaineer* 1, no. 1 (April 1926): 2.

11. York Institute and Department of Education Records, YP.

12. Tom Skeyhill, *Sergeant York: Last of the Long Hunters,* (St. John, Ind.: Larry Harrison Christian Book Gallery, 1992), 232; York Institute papers, Tennessee Department of Education Files, Tennessee State Library and Archives, Nashville, Tenn. (hereafter, TSLA).

13. Quoted in the *Nashville Banner,* Sunday, January 16, 1927, 1.

14. Arthur S. Bushing, secretary to the president, *This Booklet Contains Information about the Alvin C. York Industrial Institute,* YP, 1926, 9.

15. See Lee, chap. 5, "The Hero at Home"; Jeanette Keith, chap. 8–10 in *Country People of the New South: Tennessee's Upper Cumberland* (Chapel Hill: University of North Carolina Press, 1995); Tennessee Department of Education Files, TSLA; York Institute Files, YP.

16. YP.

17. Ibid.

18. York and Stockton drafted a charter on March 31; Alvin York et al., "The Alvin C. York Industrial Institute," YP, 1–2.

19. Private acts of Tennessee, chap. 809, bill 933, 1925.

20. YP.

21. L. A. Ligon, letter to O. O. Frogge, July 10, 1927, YP.

22. Department of Education Files; Attorney General Frank M. Thompson to O. O. Frogge and J. T. Wheeler, April 3, 1926, YP.

23. Alvin C. York to Austin Peay, May 18, 1926, Austin Peay, Governors' Papers, TSLA.

24. Originally, the campaign was to begin on December 14, 1926, in Boston (YP).

25. Summons to Alvin C. York from the County Board of Education, Fentress

County (O. O. Frogge, W. A. Garrett, and P. S. Beaty) and Ray S. Ward, July 9, 1927, YP.

26. Ibid., 2.

27. Alvin C. York, "Speech: York's Own Story," YP, 1927, 1–7.

28. Ibid., 11.

29. Ibid.

30. Ibid., 26–27.

31. Alvin C. York, "Let's All Pull Together," speech delivered at Carnegie Hall, Manhattan; Town Hall, New York; and Boston, Massachusetts, YP.

32. W. A. Garrett, *"Re: Alvin C. York and the Alvin C. York Agricultural Institute,"* presented to the Honorable P. L. Harned, commissioner and members State Board of Education, Nashville, Tennessee, July 15, 1929, YP, 4.

33. Ibid., 13, 18.

34. "To the Board of Education of the State of Tennessee," August 6, 1929, YP. The signers were H. N. Wright, county judge; C. A. Norman, sheriff; Joe Mullinix, county tax assessor; D. O. Beaty, county trustee; W. L. Wright, president of the Bank of Jamestown; C. A. Williams, county court clerk; O. O. Frogge, county superintendent; Porter S. Beaty, chairman of the County Board of Education, and J. N. Clark, county coroner.

35. Private acts of Tennessee, 1927; interviews with the children of Ransom Hutchings, Tillman Hutchings, Treva Hutchings Miller, and Emily Miller in Sparta and Murfreesboro, Tennessee, June 1988; YP.

36. York Institute Files, Tennessee Department of Education Files.

37. YP.

38. Personal interviews with Andrew York, Betsy Ross York Lowry, George Edward Buxton York, Guy Williams, and Leo Hatfield, conducted 1987–1998.

39. Robert L. Forrester, chairman of the Fact Finding Committee, Department of Education Report, November 10, 1933, YP and TSLA.

40. York Institute Files, Department of Education Files, TSLA.

41. Ibid.

42. Interviews with Ernest Buck, former school teacher and principal of York Institute, and Noel Norman, former student and teacher at York Institute Norman was interviewed in Jamestown, Tennessee, July 7, 1998. Norman said, "They sent Brier here to straighten us out, and whooweee, it sure was some fight before it was all over."

43. York Institute Files, Department of Education files, YP and TSLA.

44. Ibid. Brier was given the opportunity to stay on, but he refused.

45. Ibid.

46. Some works, such as C. Hartley Grattan's *Why We Fought* and Walter Millis's *The Road to War,* blamed U.S. intervention on British propaganda, fueling a rising tide of Anglophobia. Other works, such as George Seldes's *Iron, Blood, and Profits* and H. C. Englebrecht and F. C. Hanighen's *Merchants of Death,* claimed

that a cabal existed among Jewish Wall Street Bankers and the munitions industry, who sacrificed the youth of America simply to line their pockets.

47. Alvin C. York, "Christian Cure for Strife: Sgt. York Address to a Babtist [*sic*] Convention at Charlestown, West Virginia, 1935," YP, 3.

48. Ibid., 3–4.

49. "Sergeant York Urges U.S. to 'Stay Home, Mind Its Own Business,'" Associated Press Release, April 30, 1936, YP.

50. Ibid.

51. Alvin C. York, Untitled address delivered in San Francisco, July 1, 1939, YP, 2.

52. On July 25, 1939, York appeared on Richard Maxwell's radio broadcast from the Hotel McAlpin and announced his intentions of creating an interdenominational Bible school.

53. Alvin C. York, "York Radio Speech—Golden Gate Exposition," YP, 1.

54. Ibid., 5.

55. Ibid.

56. Ibid.

57. Jesse L. Lasky with Don Weldon, *I Blow My Own Horn* (Garden City, N.Y.: Doubleday, 1957), 252–53.

58. "Sergeant York Surrenders," *Time,* April 1, 1940, 70.

59. David D. Lee, "Appalachia on Film: The Making of *Sergeant York,*" *Southern Quarterly* 19, nos. 3–4 (spring–summer 1981): 211–12; (hereafter, "Appalachia on Film."

60. Patullo, 3–4, 71–73.

61. Quoted in Neal Gabler, *An Empire of Their Own: How the Jews Invented Hollywood* (New York: Crown, 1988), 203.

62. Philip Dunne, *Take Two* (New York: Random House, 1980), 26.

63. Gabler, 203.

64. Ibid., 34–35.

65. Thomas Schatz, *The Genius of the System: Hollywood Filmmaking in the Studio Era* (New York: Pantheon Books, 1988), 71–81; Rudy Behlmer, *Inside Warner Bros., 1935–1951* (New York: Simon and Schuster, 1985), 185; Gabler, 239, 246, 256; "Appalachia on Film," 209–10; Jesse L. Lasky, Jr., *What Ever Happened to Hollywood?* (New York: Funk and Wagnalls, 1975), 73–74, 77–78.

66. Lasky with Weldon, 253.

67. Gabler, 287.

68. Two biographies of York were written in the 1920s: *Sergeant York and His People,* by Sam K. Cowan, and *Sergeant York: The Last of the Long Hunters,* by Tom Skeyhill. Skeyhill also helped York edit his war diary for serialization in *Liberty* magazine in 1928.

69. *Sergeant York* Files, box A–52, Warner Bros. Archives, Special Collections, University of Southern California (hereafter, *Sgt. York*).

70. Ibid.; personal interviews with Guy·Williams and Leo Hatfield.

71. Leo Rosten, *Hollywood: The Movie Colony, The Movie Makers* (New York: Harcourt, Brace, 1941), 133–62.

72. Bernard F. Dick, *The Star Spangled Screen: The American World War II Film* (Lexington: University Press of Kentucky, 1985), 66–100; David Niven, *Bring on the Empty Horses* (New York: Dell, 1975), 103; Martin Jay, "Adorno in America," *New German Critique* 31 (1984): 157–82; Bruce Cook, *Brecht in Exile* (New York: Holt, Rinehart, Winston, 1982), 17–18, 30–32, 113–17; Richard Lingeman, *"Don't You Know There's a War On?" The American Homefront, 1941–1945* (New York: Putnam's, 1970), 170–80.

73. Lasky with Weldon, 253.

74. Nick Roddick, *A New Deal in Entertainment: Warner Bros. in the 1930s* (London: British Film Institute, 1983), 211; Thomas Doherty, *Projections of War: Hollywood, American Culture, and World War II* (New York: Columbia University Press, 1993), 100.

75. Williams interview.

76. YP.

77. Wide discrepancies exist between Lasky's version and the story the records housed in Los Angeles and Tennessee reveal.

78. Harry Chandlee to Jesse Lasky re: script changes, *Sgt. York,* October 15, 1942, 4.

79. Williams interview; *Sgt. York.*

80. Parsons's column ran April 20, 1940.

81. YP; Williams interview.

82. Ibid.

83. The Subsistence Homesteads Projects were launched in 1934, as a part of the National Industrial Recovery Act. The projects operated in conjunction with several federal agencies, which sometimes worked at cross purposes and were under the aegis of the Department of Interior, the Resettlement Administration, the Farm Security Administration, and the Public Housing Authority.

84. York replaced a controversial Major Oliver. For more on the Cumberland Homesteads, see Ann Malanka, "The Homesteader Experience at Cumberland Homesteads, Tennessee," Department of Conservation and Environment, Nashville, Tenn. 1992, typescript; Paul Conkin, *Tomorrow a New World: The New Deal Community Program* (Ithaca: Cornell University Press, 1959); Russell Lord and Paul H. Johnstone, *A Place on Earth: A Critical Appraisal of Subsistence Homesteads* (Washington, D.C.: USDA Division of Agricultural Economics, GPO, 1942).

85. Confidential letter to Honorable Tom Stewart from O. P. Pile, December 29, 1939, YP. Governor Cooper was instrumental in getting York the job as manager of the Homesteads.

86. Ibid., 2 (emphasis added).

87. Ibid., 2–3.

88. Lasky with Weldon, 258.

89. YP, Williams interview, and interview with Prentice Cooper's widow, Hortense Cooper, November 20, 1988.

90. Ibid; Lasky with Weldon, 256; "Appalachia on Film," 211.

91. YP and *Sgt. York*. Robert Brent Toplin argues that the reason the studio agreed to give York so much say in the production was due to the novelty of a screen biography about a living person, which represented uncharted film territory. See Robert Brent Toplin, *History by Hollywood: The Use and Abuse of the American Past* (Urbana: University of Illinois Press, 1996), 85.

92. "Appalachia on Film," 211. Lasky gave York a personal check for twenty-five thousand dollars as a sign of good faith.

93. *Propaganda in Motion Pictures: Hearings before a Senate Subcommittee on Interstate Commerce, United States Senate (Seventy-Seventh Congress, First Session) on Senate Resolution 152; A Resolution Authorizing an Investigation of War Propaganda Disseminated by the Motion Picture Industry and of any Monopoly in the Production, Distribution, or Exhibition of Motion Pictures, September 9 to 26, 1941* (Washington D.C.: GPO, 1942), 348.

94. YP and *Sgt. York*.

95. Bob Thomas, *The Clown Prince of Hollywood: The Antic Life and Times of Jack L. Warner* (New York: McGraw-Hill, 1990), 36.

96. William R. Glass, "Fundamentalism's Prophetic Vision of the Jews: The 1930s," *Jewish Social Studies* 47, no. 1 (1985): 63–76.

97. Controversy surrounds the choice of Cooper. Lasky said it was his idea; Hal Wallis argued that the inspiration belonged to Jack Warner and himself; and York claimed credit as well. See YP; *Sgt. York*; Lasky with Weldon, 258–59; Hal Wallis with Charles Higham, *Starmaker: The Autobiography of Hal Wallis* (New York: Macmillan, 1980), 69.

98. York began wearing a moustache as early as 1912 and wore one until he died.

99. Williams interview. John Huston admired York and found him to be quite humorous; see Todd McCarthy, *Howard Hawks: The Grey Fox Of Hollywood* (New York: Grove Press, 1997), 307.

100. *Sgt. York*.

101. The Ganier photos are housed in the Albert Ganier Photographic Collection, MSS 89–114A, TSLA. Lasky's son accompanied him and brought along a sixteen-millimeter movie camera. The footage the young Lasky shot influenced the construction of the sets, too.

102. *Sgt. York*; Wallis with Higham, 68.

103. Ibid., 69.

104. Harry Chandlee and Julien Josephson to Jesse Lasky, May 8, 1940, *Sgt. York*, 4.

105. Guthrie worked for the FBI before joining Warner Bros., and he organized the studio's security. His FBI contacts made him invaluable, earning him the promotion to location manager.

106. Transcript of *We The People* broadcast from 1941, YP, 2 (emphasis added).

107. *Sgt. York.*

108. Ibid.; Department of Conservation files, TSLA.

109. Robert Gustafson, "The Buying of Ideas: Source Acquisition at Warner Brothers, 1930–1949," Ph.D. diss., University of Wisconsin, 1983, 219–24.

110. Copies of the consent forms are housed in both the Warner Bros. Archives in Los Angeles and the York papers in Pall Mall.

111. Lasky with Weldon, 258.

112. Personal interviews with Lucy York Rains, Leo Hatfield, George Edward York, Betsy Ross York Lowry, Andrew Jackson York, Elaine Williams, and Guy Williams. Elaine Williams was interviewed in Pall Mall, Tennessee, September 23, 1987.

113. I have been unable to ascertain why Merrithew changed his name.

114. *Sgt. York.*

115. Ibid.

116. See Harry Parsons file, YP (emphasis added).

117. *Sgt. York.*

118. Otis B. Merrithew to Bill Guthrie, March 11, 1941, *Sgt. York* (his emphasis).

119. Ibid. (his emphasis).

120. Lasky with Weldon, 258.

121. *Sgt. York.*

122. Ibid.

123. Ibid. See also York love letters, YP.

124. *Sgt. York.*

125. Ibid.

126. Ibid.

127. Ibid.

128. *Sergeant York* Press Kit, *Sgt. York.*

129. McCarthy, 300.

130. John Huston, *An Open Book* (New York: Ballantine Books, 1980), 90–91.

131. Ian Hamilton, *Writers in Hollywood, 1915–1951* (New York: Harper and Row, 1990), 130–31, 214, 225–26, 242–45. Aljean Harmetz, *Round Up the Usual Suspects: The Making of Casablanca—Bogart, Bergman, and World War II* (New York: Hyperion, 1992), 50–52, 57, 238.

132. Harry Chandlee and Abem Finkel, *The Amazing Story of Sergeant York,* 68–105, *Sgt. York.*

133. Russell came from Indiana and was succeeded as pastor by a long-time

210 | *Notes to Chapter 4*

friend of York's, R. D. Brown. Pastor Pile was only two years older than York, not the wizened old sage that he appears to be in the movie. Pile had been a fellow hell-raiser with York, and it was York who converted Pile to the C.O.C.I.C.U.

134. Harry Chandlee and Julien Josephson to Jesse Lasky, May 8, 1940, *Sgt. York,* 40.

135. Howard Koch wrote in his memoirs: "How the real Alvin York felt about the flamboyant version of his religious conversion I never heard." Howard Koch, *As Time Goes By: Memoirs of a Writer* (New York: Harcourt Brace Jovanovich, 1979), 74–75.

136. *Sgt. York.*

137. Chandlee and Josephson to Lasky, 10.

138. Ibid., 25.

139. Ibid.

140. Harry Chandlee to Jesse Lasky, October 15, 1942, *Sgt. York.*

141. Ibid., 3.

142. This coincides with Richard Slotkin's thesis about American mythology and the role of the frontier in its creation. See his magisterial trilogy *Regeneration through Violence: The Mythology of the American Frontier, 1600–1869* (Middletown, Conn.: Wesleyan University Press, 1973); *The Fatal Environment: The Myth of the Frontier in the Age of Industrialization, 1800–1890* (New York: Atheneum, 1985); and *Gunfighter Nation: The Myth of the Frontier in Twentieth-Century America* (New York: Atheneum, 1992), 144. Harry Chandlee and Abem Finkel, *Sergeant York,* part 1, Temporary Script, October 17, 1940, Warner Bros. Archives, 270; Harry Chandlee, Abem Finkel, John Huston, and Howard Koch, *Sergeant York,* part 1, Revised Final Draft, January 31, 1941, Warner Bros. Archives, 107.

143. Ibid., 108.

144. Chandlee et al., 109–10 (emphasis added).

145. Lasky later credited Huston with the lion's share of the script, saying that Huston wrote the scene where York went off to war. Lasky, 258, 261.

146. Howard Koch wrote that he and Hawks disagreed politically; even so, both supported intervention. Whereas Koch was an avowed socialist, "he [Hawks] was closer to John Wayne's position than mine." Koch, 74.

147. Abem Finkel, "The Sad Story of Sgt. York," *Sgt. York,* 1–2.

148. Ibid., 2–3; Koch, 73.

149. Finkel, "The Sad Story of Sgt. York," 6.

150. Ibid., 7–8.

151. *Sgt. York.*

152. Ibid.

153. Eugene Lyons, "Hitler's Blueprint for a Slave World," *American Mercury* 50, no. 200 (August 1940): 391–400.

154. Leonard Dinnerstein, *Antisemitism in America* (New York: Oxford University Press, 1994), 113.

155. *Sgt. York.*

156. Franklin Roosevelt, "Statement on the Adoption of Peacetime Selective Service," in *The Essential Franklin Delano Roosevelt,* John Gabriel Hunt, ed. (New York: Random house, Gramercy Books, 1995), 190–93. One provision of the peacetime draft allowed the Signal Corps to produce training films. Harry Warner donated the Vitagraph studio to the Signal Corps for that purpose. During World War II, Alvin York was attached to the Signal Corps in its recruiting efforts. See YP; "U.S. Okays 250G for Military Training Pix, *Variety,* October 30, 1940, 6.

157. YP.

158. Alfred Grant Walton, "Pacifism—A Flight from Reality: There Are Some Things More Sacred Than Life," *Vital Speeches of the Day,* August 15, 1941, 660.

159. Ibid.

160. *Sgt. York.*

161. "Sergeant York," *Newsweek,* July 14, 1941, 61–62.

162. "Sergt. York Visits with the President," *New York Times,* July 31, 1941, 13. *Sergeant York Movie Scrapbook,* YP.

163. *Sgt. York.*

164. Ibid.

165. Ibid.

166. Ibid.

167. Ibid.

168. Otis Ferguson, "In the Army, Aren't We All," *New Republic,* September 29, 1941, 404 (his emphasis).

169. Ibid., 405.

170. Ibid.

171. Alvin C. York, "Sgt. York's Speech, Veterans of Foreign Wars, 'Hello America' Program," YP, n.d., version A–1, 2. There are three versions of this speech, containing subtle differences. It is unclear which version York read on the air.

172. Ibid., version A–1, 3.

173. Ibid., version A–2, 3.

174. Ibid., version A–2, 4.

175. Peter Roffman and Jim Purdy, *The Hollywood Social Problem Film: Madness, Despair, and Politics from the Depression to the Fifties* (Bloomington: Indiana University Press, 1981), 215; Tom Perlmutter, *War Movies* (Secaucus, N.J.: Castle Books, 1974), 22.

176. James E. Combs and Sara T. Combs, *Film Propaganda and American Politics: An Analysis and Filmography* (New York: Garland, 1994), 42.

177. Raymond W. Steele, "The Great Debate: Roosevelt, the Media, and the Coming of the War, 1940–1941," *Journal of American History* 71, no. 1 (June

1984): 81. Other films included *A Yank in the R.A.F., Caught in the Draft, Foreign Correspondent, Buck Privates,* and *International Squadron.*

178. Roddick, 87.

179. Michael T. Isenberg, *War on Film: The American Cinema and World War I, 1914–1941* (Rutherford, N.J.: Fairleigh Dickinson University Press, 1981), 95.

180. John Belton, *American Cinema/American Culture* (New York: McGraw-Hill, 1994), 175.

181. Hamilton, 214.

182. Other films singled out as fifth column movies included *Convoy,* Charlie Chaplin's *The Great Dictator, Flight Command, Escape,* Laurence Olivier and Vivien Leigh's *That Hamilton Woman, Man Hunt, Confessions of a Nazi Spy,* and *Underground.*

NOTES TO CHAPTER 5

1. For a historiographical overview of the complex and often contradictory anti-interventionist stance, see Justus D. Doenecke, "The Anti-Interventionist Tradition: Leadership and Perceptions," *Literature of Liberty* 4, no. 2 (summer 1981): 7–67.

2. Joyce Milton, *Loss of Eden: A Biography of Charles and Ann Morrow Lindbergh* (New York: Harper Collins, 1993), 84–359 passim. Leon Turrou, whose story was dramatized in *Confessions of a Nazi Spy,* was one of the key FBI agents involved in investigating the Lindbergh baby kidnapping.

3. Wayne S. Cole, *Charles A. Lindbergh and the Battle against Intervention in World War II* (New York: Harcourt Brace Jovanovich, 1974), 31–35.

4. Ibid., 36.

5. Ibid., 42. Hitler and Lindbergh never met.

6. Milton, 356.

7. Cole, 41–46; Geoffrey Smith, "Isolationism, the Devil, and the Advent of the Second World War: Variations on a Theme," *International History Review* 4, no. 1 (1982): 72.

8. Charles A. Lindbergh, *The Wartime Journals of Charles A. Lindbergh* (New York: Harcourt Brace Jovanovich, 1970), 403–4 (his emphasis). See also 300–301, 392 (hereafter, *Wartime Journals*); Charles Lindbergh, "We Cannot Win This War for England," *Vital Speeches of the Day,* May 1, 1941, 424–26. Peter Roffman and Jim Purdy argued that the "pacifist avoids war for humanitarian reasons, the isolationists out of a sense of national priority." Roffman and Purdy, *The Hollywood Social Problem Film: Madness, Despair, and Politics from the Depression to the Fifties* (Bloomington: Indiana University Press, 1981), 201.

9. "Gallup Poll," *New York Times,* September 22, 1939, 34.

10. Charles A. Lindbergh, "We Are Not Prepared for War," *Vital Speeches of the Day,* February 15, 1941, 266–67.

11. "Unlucky Lindy," *New Republic,* October 25, 1939, 323.

12. *Wartime Journals,* 72, 76, 85; Charles Lindbergh, "Our Air Defense: I Do Not Believe There Is Any Danger of Invasion," *Vital Speeches of the Day,* February 1, 1941, 241–42.

13. Ibid.

14. Elmer Davis considered Lindbergh's assessment naive because the Western Hemisphere depended upon the British navy for its security. See Elmer Davis, "The War and America," *Harper's,* April 1940, 458.

15. Handwritten telegram by Sergeant Alvin York, November 1938, Alvin C. York, uncataloged, Pall Mall, Tenn., 3 (hereafter, YP).

16. Walter L. Hixson, *Charles A. Lindbergh: Lone Eagle* (New York: Harper Collins, 1996), 100.

17. For a fuller discussion of the history and effectiveness of America First, see Wayne S. Cole, *America First: The Battle against Intervention, 1940–1941* (Madison: University of Wisconsin Press, 1953) (hereafter, *America First*), and his biographies of Lindbergh and Nye: *Senator Gerald P. Nye and American Foreign Relations* (Minneapolis: University of Minnesota Press, 1962); and *Charles A. Lindbergh and the Battle against Intervention in World War II* (hereafter, Cole, *Lindbergh*); Mark Lincoln Chadwin, *The Hawks of World War II* (Chapel Hill: University of North Carolina Press, 1968); Justus D. Doenecke, ed., *In Danger Undaunted: The Anti-Interventionist Movement of 1940–1941 as Revealed in the Papers of the America First Committee* (Stanford, Calif.: Hoover Institution Press, 1990).

18. Doenecke, *In Danger Undaunted,* 2–51 passim.

19. Quoted in Smith, 81.

20. Chadwin, 43–73, 159–262 passim. To promote the FFF message, they employed a raft of celebrities and public speakers. Among the speakers for the FFF were Rex Stout, Alexander Woolcott, Lewis Mumford, Harry Warner, William "Wild Bill" Donovan, Carl Sandburg, Dorothy Parker, Harold Ickes, Burgess Meredith, and Alvin York.

21. Quoted in Hixson, 102.

22. Handwritten text of telegram to "Hon. Senator Kenneth D. McKellar, Washington D.C.," YP, May 17, 1940.

23. Alvin C. York, transcript of "Sergeant York's Speech, Wednesday, October 4th, 1940," YP, 3.

24. Ibid., 7.

25. Ibid., 9.

26. Lindbergh, "Our Air Defense," 241.

27. The Oklahoma City rally occurred August 29, 1941.

28. Lindbergh, "We Cannot Win This War for England."

29. Ibid., 425.

30. Smith, 83.

31. Cole, *Lindbergh,* 131.

32. *Wartime Journals,* 478 (his emphasis).

33. Dumas Malone and Basil Rauch, *War and Troubled Peace, 1917–1919* (New York: Appleton-Century-Crofts, 1960), 281–302; Justus D. Doenecke and John E. Wilz, *From Isolation to War, 1931–1941,* 2d. ed. (Arlington Heights, Ill.: Harlan Davidson, 1991), 70–119.

34. Alvin C. York, "Speech by Sergeant Alvin C. York at Arlington on May 30, 1941," YP, 1.

35. Concerning Senator Wheeler's character and his dissatisfaction with Roosevelt and the interventionists, see Richard L. Neuberger, "Wheeler of Montana," *Harper's,* May 1940, 609–18; and Edward S. Shapiro, "The Approach of War: Congressional Isolationism and Anti-Semitism, 1939–1941," *American Jewish History* 74, no. 1 (1984): 49–52; "Fuzzy-Wuzzy and Mr. Wheeler," *New Republic,* August 11, 1941, 188.

36. York, "Arlington Speech," 1–2. Close examination of York's extant speeches indicates that he often had someone dress up or in some cases completely write his orations. In fact, York wrote the majority of his speeches longhand, and there are generally three versions among his papers. First is the handwritten speech, then a typed draft that he marked up, and finally a reading copy that he approved. In his earliest career as a public speaker, the bulk of his rather hokey speeches were written by his factotum, Arthur S. Bushing; *Nashville Tennessean* journalist Hugh Walker also took credit for writing some speeches during the late 1940s and 1950s. Warner Bros. effectively used clips from the Arlington speech in the movie's advertising campaign. See John Davis, "Notes on Warner Brothers Foreign Policy, 1918–1948," *Velvet Light Trap* 4 (spring 1972): 29.

37. York, "Arlington Speech," 2.

38. Ibid.

39. Ibid., 2–3.

40. David D. Lee, *Sergeant York: An American Hero* (Lexington: University Press of Kentucky, 1985), 109.

41. Detlef Junker, "The Impact of Foreign Policy on the United States Domestic Scene, 1939–1941," *Storia Nordamerica* 6, nos. 1–2 (1989): 17.

42. Cole, *Lindbergh,* 97.

43. Alvin York, "Speech to Be Made by Sergeant Alvin C. York at Luncheon of Tennessee Society at Hotel Astor, July 3, 1941," YP, 1 (his emphasis).

44. Ibid., 2.

45. Ibid.

46. Ibid., 2. Harold Ickes was outspoken in his derision of the aviator and the medal. See Harold Ickes, *The Secret Diaries of Harold Ickes.* Vol 2, *Inside the Struggle, 1936–1939* (New York: Simon and Schuster, 1954), 534–53.

47. Lindbergh is a Swedish name.

48. "Smoke Out 'America First,'" *New Republic,* October 6, 1941, 422.

49. In 1941 the sentiments of some of America's most important noninterventionists and Anglophobes were collected in *We Testify*. Among the writers were Herbert Hoover, Harry Emerson Fosdick, Charles and Anne Morrow Lindbergh, Henry Noble MacCracken, Gen. Hugh Johnson, Gen. Robert E. Wood, Amos Pinchot, John T. Flynn, Burton K. Wheeler, Norman Thomas, Robert A. Taft, Oswald Garrison Villard, and William Henry Chamberlain. See Nancy Schoonmaker and Doris Fielding Reid, eds., *We Testify* (New York: Smith and Durrell, 1941).

50. George Britt, *The Fifth Column Is Here* (New York: Wilfred Funk, 1940).

51. For the noninterventionist reaction, see Gerald P. Nye, "No A.E.F.: We Must Not Go Hunting for War," *Vital Speeches of the Day*, August 15, 1941, 650–52.

52. For information about York's sons and their military experience, see Michael E. Birdwell, "Not by Grace Alone: Alvin C. York's Sons and World War II," unpublished typescript, Tennessee Technological University, Cookeville Tennessee, 1993.

53. Radio Branch, Bureau of Public Relations, War Department, Script of "Broadcast—Mutual Broadcasting Systems through WOL Washington, July 30, 1941, 7:45–8:00 p.m., Willard Hotel: Round Table Discussion between Sgt. Alvin C. York, Outstanding American World War Hero; Brigadier General Lewis B. Hershey, Deputy Director of the Selective Service System; and Major General George B. Duncan, U.S. Army Retired, Who Was Commanding Officer of the 82nd Division during the World War and Who Decorated Sgt. York with the Congressional Medal of Honor," YP, 1–13.

54. Doenecke and Wilz, 107–108.

55. Alvin C. York, "Prepared Copy of Address of Alvin C. York at Dinner of Tennessee Society, Thursday evening, July 31, 1941," YP, 1–3.

56. Ibid.

57. Ibid, 4. Harry Warner promised Warner Bros. employees affected by the peacetime draft that their jobs would be waiting for them at the studio when their term of service ended.

58. Cole, *Lindbergh*, 190–91.

59. Quoted in Chadwin, 210, and in Cole, *America First*, 144.

60. The speech haunted Lindbergh long after the United States entered the war and he returned to the Air Corps. In 1942 he testified in the sedition trial of William Dudley Pelley, further damaging his reputation. The prosecution specifically referred to Lindbergh's caustic comments about Jews uttered in Des Moines and accused him of fomenting anti-Semitic rhetoric as Pelley had done regularly by printing his pro-Nazi publications. Lindbergh said it was the only time that he ever made remarks of that nature and that he was misunderstood. See Suzanne G. Ledeboer, "The Man Who Would Be Hitler: William Dudley Pelley and the Silver Shirt Legion," *California History* 65 (June 1986): 136; Leo P. Ribuffo, *The Old*

Christian Right: The Protestant Far Right from the Great Depression to the Cold War (Philadelphia: Temple University Press, 1983), 79.

61. Smith, 72.

62. Ibid., 83; Cole, *America First*, 146–47; Cole, *Lindbergh*, 176–77; Christine Ann Colgan, "Warner Brothers' Crusade against the Third Reich: A Study of Anti-Nazi Activism and Film Production, 1933–1941," Ph.D. diss., University of Southern California, 1985, 701–2; Milton, 401–2; Stephen J. Sniegoski, "Unified Democracy: An Aspect of American World War II Interventionist Thought, 1939–1941," *Maryland Historian* 9 (spring 1978): 40; Nazi Files, Harry Warner Papers, Jack L. Warner Collection, University of Southern California. Cole insists that Lindbergh was not an anti-Semite and that the adverse reactions to his remarks were unfounded.

63. Cole, *Lindbergh*, 128.

64. Quoted in Sniegoski, 40.

65. *Wartime Journals*, 539.

66. Quoted in Leonard Dinnerstein, *Antisemitism in America* (New York: Oxford University Press, 1994), 130.

67. Milton, 394–402; Cole, *Lindbergh*, 142–53, 172–73; "Smoke Out 'America First,'" 422–23.

68. "Top World Hero Raps Nye, Lindbergh," UPI release, September 13, 1941, YP.

69. Alvin C. York, "Speech by Sergeant Alvin C. York at Milwaukee, on Sept. 14, 1941," YP, 1.

70. Ibid., 2.

71. Ibid., 1.

72. Alvin C. York, "Radio Address to Be Delivered under the Auspices of the Laymen's National Committee, 112 Park Avenue, New York City," YP, n.d., 2.

73. Ibid.

74. Ibid., 3.

75. Ibid., 4.

76. Ibid.

77. Ibid.

78. *Wartime Journals*, 538–39.

79. All quotations from Mrs. Norine Crosby to York, September 15, 1941, YP (her emphasis).

80. Walter Camp to Alvin C. York, September 14, 1941, YP.

81. Ibid.

82. Just an Average American Citizen, letter to Sergeant Alvin C. York, September 14, 1941, YP.

83. Ibid.

84. Colonel J. V. Kuznik (Ret.) to Alvin York, September 16, 1941, YP.

85. Ibid.

86. Regarding the munitions hearings, see Cole, *Senator Gerald P. Nye;* Matthew W. Coulter, "The Franklin D. Roosevelt Administration and the Special Committee on Investigation of the Munitions Industry," *Mid-America* 67, no. 1 (1985): 23–36; Doenecke and Wilz, 14–15, 56–59; and John E. Wiltz, *In Search of Peace: The Senate Munitions Inquiry, 1934–1936* (Baton Rouge: Louisiana State University Press, 1963).

87. Cole, *Lindbergh,* 142–53; Dinnerstein, 129.

88. See Eric Bentley, ed., *Thirty Years of Treason: Excerpts from Hearings before the House Committee on Un-American Activities, 1938–1968* (New York: Viking, 1971); Larry Ceplair and Steven Englund, *The Inquisition in Hollywood: Politics and the Film Community, 1930–1960* (Garden City, N.Y.: Anchor Press/Doubleday, 1980); Smith, 76.

89. Walter Winchell, "York vs. Lindbergh," Clippings Files, YP, n.d.

90. Alvin York, "For God and Country: Speech of Sergeant York at a Red Cross Conference Held at Knoxville, Tennessee, October 8, 1941, and Broadcast over Radio Station WNOX," YP, 3.

91. Ibid.

92. Cole, *Lindbergh,* 191–92.

93. Alvin C. York, "Armistice Day Address Delivered by Sergeant Alvin C. York at Evansville, Indiana, 11 November 1941, YP, 1.

NOTES TO CHAPTER 6

1. Wayne S. Cole, *Senator Gerald P. Nye and American Foreign Relations* (Minneapolis: University of Minnesota Press, 1962), 186.

2. Unlike Burton K. Wheeler and Lindbergh, Nye never held a position of authority in America First. See Cole, *Gerald P. Nye,* 179.

3. *Propaganda in Motion Pictures: Hearings before a Senate Subcommittee on Interstate Commerce, United States Senate (Seventy-Seventh Congress, First Session) on Senate Resolution 152; A Resolution Authorizing an Investigation of War Propaganda Disseminated by the Motion Picture Industry and of any Monopoly in the Production, Distribution, or Exhibition of Motion Pictures, September 9 to 26, 1941* (Washington, D.C.: GPO, 1942), 1–64 passim (hereafter, *Propaganda Hearings*). Lindbergh held similar sentiments; see Charles A. Lindbergh, *The Wartime Journals of Charles A. Lindbergh* (New York: Harcourt Brace Jovanovich, 1970), entry for Thursday, May 1, 1941, 481 (hereafter, *Wartime Journals*). See also *Sergeant York* Files, box A–52, Warner Bros. Archives, Special Collections, University of Southern California; "Senate Isolationists Run Afoul of Willkie in Movie 'Warmonger' Hearings," *Life,* September 22, 1941, 21; Christine Ann Colgan, "Warner Brothers' Crusade against the Third Reich: A Study of Anti-Nazi Activism and Film Production, 1933–1941," Ph.D. diss., University of Southern California, 1985, chap. 6, "Mr. Warner Goes to Washington: Hollywood versus the

Non-Interventionists"; James E. McMillan, "McFarland and the Movies: The 1941 Senate Motion Picture Hearings," *Journal of Arizona History* 29, no. 3 (1988): 278; chap. 2 of Clayton R. Koppes and Gregory D. Black's *Hollywood Goes to War: How Politics, Profits, and Propaganda Shaped World War II Movies* (Berkeley: University of California Press, 1987); Edward S. Shapiro, "The Approach of War: Congressional Isolationism and Anti-Semitism, 1939–1941," *American Jewish History* 74, no. 1 (1984): 45–65.

4. Over the course of the hearings, many films came under discussion. A few defy logic, stretching the parameters of what could be regarded propaganda. They included *International Squadron, Dispatch from Reuters, Murder in the Air, Convoy, Man Hunt, Caught in the Draft, The Man I Married* (a.k.a. *I Married a Nazi*), *Buck Privates, The War in the Desert, Men of Lightship 61, Four Sons, One Night in Lisbon, Mystery Sea Raider, I Wanted Wings, North Sea Patrol, Nurse Edith Cavell, Sky Murder, Escape to Glory, Mad Men of Europe, Missing Ten Days, Phantom Submarine, They Dare Not Love, So Ends Our Night, Ski Patrol, In Love Again, Pastor Hall, The Mortal Storm, A Voice in the Night, The Devil Commands, Night Train, Blackout, Foreign Correspondent, So Ends Our Night, Grapes of Wrath,* and *All Quiet on the Western Front.*

5. Michael Straight, "The Anti-Semitic Conspiracy," *New Republic,* September 22, 1941, 362 (emphasis added).

6. Cole, *Gerald P. Nye,* 186; Leonard J. Leff and Jerold L. Simmons, *The Dame in the Kimono: Hollywood, Censorship, and the Production Code from the 1920s to the 1960s* (New York: Grove Weidenfeld, 1990), 3–54, 281–92.

7. Gerald P. Nye, "War Propaganda: Our Madness Increases as Our Emergency Shrinks," *Vital Speeches of the Day,* September 1, 1941, 721; Shapiro, 49.

8. Nye, "War Propaganda," 720–23; Propaganda Hearings 48; McMillan, 286.

9. Nye, "War Propaganda," 721; *Propaganda Hearings,* 45–47.

10. Nye, "War Propaganda," 722.

11. Bill Kauffman, *America First! It's History, Culture, and Politics* (New York: Prometheus Books, 1995), 85–98.

12. Ibid., 90.

13. Kauffman omits the fact that many of those people he so despises found themselves in the pillory of the Cold War HUAC witch hunts. They lost their liberty because of their prewar attempts to preserve it.

14. A study published in 1939 argued that eighty million people went to the movies weekly; the study referred frequently to "the eighty million." That being so, many of those were "repeaters," who attended movies more than once a week. One could posit that at least forty million different people attended weekly, keeping repeaters in mind. See Margaret Farrand Thorp, *America at the Movies* (New Haven, Conn.: Yale University Press, 1939).

15. *Propaganda Hearings,* 37.

16. Ibid., 50.

17. Raymond W. Steele, "The Great Debate: Roosevelt, the Media, and the Coming of the War, 1940–1941," *Journal of American History* 71, no. 1 (June 1984): 72, 78, 81. Steele argues that the isolationists had a legitimate gripe and that their side of the debate lacked adequate representation in the public forum. I disagree with his claim because several newspapers, magazines, columnists, and radio personalities routinely preached nonintervention. Some, like Father Charles Coughlin, were strident, while others, like Oswald Garrison Villard, presented sober, principled arguments against intervention. Nor can one overlook the popularity of America First's star spokesman, Charles Lindbergh. Geoffrey Perrett disagrees with Steele as well. See Geoffrey Perrett, *Days of Sadness, Years of Triumph: The American People, 1939–1945* (Baltimore: Penguin, 1973), 17–18, 55–56, 279–80.

18. Quoted in Stephen J. Sniegoski, "Unified Democracy: An Aspect of American World War II Interventionist Thought, 1939–1941," *Maryland Historian* 9 (spring 1978): 40.

19. Harold Lavine and James Wechsler, *War Propaganda and the United States* (New Haven, Conn.: Yale University Press, 1940), 92.

20. Mark Lincoln Chadwin, *The Hawks of World War II* (Chapel Hill: University of North Carolina Press, 1968), 210–25; Colgan, 687–91; McMillan, 280–82.

21. Willkie testified in favor of Lend-Lease, which distanced him from fellow Republicans, who considered expelling him from the party. His relationship with the party further deteriorated when he went on a junket to London for FDR in January 1941. Charles Lindbergh had doubts about him; during the 1940 election he wrote, "Vandenburg says that if Willkie is elected, the Republicans 'will have a problem child on their hands.' He feels as I do, that Willkie is inexperienced politically and that he has almost no understanding of foreign affairs." *Wartime Journals,* 390. See also David A. Bathe, "Wendell L. Willkie: A Political Odyssey from Realism to Idealism," Ph.D. diss., Illinois State University, 1991, 154–93; Sarah Chapman Thompson, "Wendell Willkie: A Hoosier Liberal," Ph.D. diss., Ball State University, 1980; and Detlef Junker, "The Impact of Foreign Policy on the United States Domestic Scene," *Storia Nordamerica* 6, nos. 1–2 (198): 23.

22. Colgan, 692.

23. Leo P. Ribuffo, *The Old Christian Right: The Protestant Far Right from the Great Depression to the Cold War* (Philadelphia: Temple University Press, 1983), 185.

24. *Propaganda Hearings,* 21. Willkie offered to arrange a special screening of any of the films for the committee, thereby allowing the movies to speak for themselves.

25. Ibid., 18–22.

26. Mellett headed the Office of Government Reports after having worked as a journalist for sixteen years prior to joining the Roosevelt administration. See

David Lloyd Jones, "Measuring and Mobilizing the Media, 1939–1945," *Midwest Quarterly* 26, no. 1 (1984): 36.

27. Lowell Mellett, "Government Propaganda," *Atlantic Monthly,* September 1941, 311.

28. McMillan, 282; *Propaganda Hearings,* 4–5. It was a move reminiscent of the way the Scopes Trial (1925) was conducted, and reporters noted the similarities. By the second day of testimony Senator Brooks confessed a change of heart, saying that cross-examination of witnesses should be allowed. Chairman Clark denied the motion; *Propaganda Hearings,* 87.

29. *Propaganda Hearings,* 5–6, 65.

30. Ibid., 17.

31. Wayne S. Cole argues forcefully that Nye was not an anti-Semite, but that his critics twisted his words and in turn warped the senator's image and tarnished his reputation.

32. *Propaganda Hearings,* 8, 24–26; McMillan, 284; and Colgan, 697. Nye used as the basis of his argument the dubious 1915 Supreme Court verdict *Mutual Film Corporation v. Ohio Industrial Commission,* which denied films protection under the First Amendment. The case helped pave the way for the creation of the industry's self-censorship organ, the Hays Office, under the MPPDA in 1922. Films lacked First Amendment guarantees until the 1952 *Miracle* decision reversed the *Mutual* case. See Leff and Simmons, 180–81, 187, 196, 203, 235; Garth Jowett, "A Capacity for Evil: The 1915 Supreme Court Mutual Decision," *Historical Journal of Film, Radio, and Television* 9 (1989): 59–78.

33. *Propaganda Hearings,* 11.

34. Ibid., 12, 16.

35. Ibid., 54.

36. Both camps labeled their enemies fifth columnists. They accused each other of similar crimes and misdemeanors and used like tactics to discredit their opponents.

37. Ibid., 47–55.

38. Ibid., 47. The bizarre accusation stunned many people, especially Harry Warner.

39 Ibid., 49; Colgan, 698; Thomas Doherty, *Projections of War: Hollywood, American Culture, and World War II* (New York: Columbia University Press, 1993), 41.

40. *Propaganda Hearings,* 79.

41. Ibid., 57–60.

42. Ibid., 33–35, 61–63.

43. Ibid., 57.

44. Quoted in "Hollywood in Washington," *Time,* September 22, 1941, 13.

45. *Propaganda Hearings,* 71.

46. Ibid., 73, 81.

47. Ibid., 78.

48. Ibid., 81, 389. See also newspaper clippings in *Sergeant York* scrapbook, Alvin C. York Papers, Pall Mall, Tenn.; *Sergeant York* Files, box A–52, Warner Bros. Archives; McMillan, 286–87.

49. *Propaganda Hearings,* 83–87. McFarland argued that any film based on the Bible could be categorized as religious propaganda and people rarely agreed about religion; so, one man's interpretation is another man's propaganda.

50. Ibid., 86–87.

51. Ibid., 89, 110–12, 131–32.

52. Ibid.

53. Ibid., 93.

54. Ibid., 105.

55. Ibid., 129–30.

56. Ibid., 142.

57. David Niven, *Bring on the Empty Horses* (New York: Dell, 1975), 117.

58. Ibid., 190–93.

59. Ibid., 167–69, 213–15, 295.

60. Ibid., 203.

61. "Propaganda or History?" *Nation,* September 20, 1941, 241–42. See also Samuel Grafton, "The America First Party," *New Republic,* September 22, 1941, 368–69; John Roy Carlson, "Inside the America First Movement," *The American Mercury* 54, no. 217 (January 1942): 7–25.

62. Quoted in Colgan, 703.

63. Ibid., 704. The piece was written in German as "Die Staatsfiende," *Free American and Deutscher Weckruf,* September 18, 1941.

64. "Senate Isolationists Run Afoul of Willkie in Movie 'Warmonger' Hearings," *Life,* September 22, 1941, 21.

65. Margaret Frakes, "Why the Movie Investigation?" *Christian Century,* September 24, 1941, 1173.

66. Ibid.

67. Loews was the parent company of MGM.

68. *Propaganda Hearings,* 208.

69. Ibid., 209–11.

70. Giuliana Muscio, "The Paramount Case," in *Hollywood's New Deal* (Philadelphia: Temple University Press, 1997), 143–95 passim.

71. Ibid., 275.

72. Ibid., 331.

73. Ibid., 325–26.

74. Ibid., 278, 292.

75. Ibid., 337–48; McMillan, 293.

76. *Propaganda Hearings,* 338–40.

77. Ibid., 339.

78. Ibid., 346
79. Ibid., 347.
80. Ibid., 354.
81. Ibid., 364.
82. Ibid., 350.
83. Ibid., 363.
84. Ibid.
85. Ibid., 345.
86. Ibid., 352.
87. Ibid., 368; Colgan, 707.
88. *Propaganda Hearings,* 366.
89. *Sergeant York* Files, box A–52, Warner Bros. Archives; *Propaganda Hearings,* 368; and John T. Moutoux, "Senators See York Movie and Say It's Grand Film,' *Knoxville News-Sentinel,* September 29, 1941, 1.
90. *Propaganda Hearings,* 333.
91. Ibid., 411.
92. Ibid., 421.
93. Ibid., 423. This is, of course, an exaggeration. Fox continued doing business with the Nazis until 1940.
94. Ibid., 428.
95. Quoted in Colgan, 709.
96. Colgan, 710–11.

NOTES TO CHAPTER 7

1. America's entry into the war ended the political careers of many isolationists. Senators Gerald P. Nye, Burton K. Wheeler, Bennett Champ Clark, and D. Worth Clark saw their political capital plummet. Lindbergh, though he made a degree of peace with the Roosevelt administration and reenlisted, never regained his reputation as America's golden boy. His perceived empathy with Nazism tainted his public reputation for years to come.

2. *Sergeant York* Files, box A–52, Warner Bros. Archives, Special Collections, University of Southern California.

3. *Propaganda in Motion Pictures: Hearings before a Senate Subcommittee on Interstate Commerce, United States Senate (Seventy-Seventh Congress, First Session) on Senate Resolution 152; A Resolution Authorizing an Investigation of War Propaganda Disseminated by the Motion Picture Industry and of any Monopoly in the Production, Distribution, or Exhibition of Motion Pictures, September 9 to 26, 1941* (Washington, D.C.: GPO, 1942), 115.

4. Ronald Brownstein, *The Power and the Glitter: The Hollywood-Washington Connection* (New York: Vintage, 1990); Leonard Dinnerstein, *Antisemitism in America* (New York: Oxford University Press, 1994), 130.

5. Numerous books and articles have been written on the film industry in World War II. See Brownstein; Clayton R. Koppes and Gregory D. Black, *Hollywood Goes to War: How Politics, Profits, and Propaganda Shaped World War II Movies* (Berkeley: University of California Press, 1990); Richard Lingeman, *"Don't You Know There's a War On?": The American Homefront, 1941–1945* (New York: Putnam's, 1970); Thomas Doherty, *Projections of War: Hollywood, American Culture, and World War II* (New York: Columbia University Press, 1993); Frank Capra, *The Name above the Title* (New York: MacMillan, 1971); Steve M. Barkin, "Fighting the Cartoon War: Information Strategies in World War II," *Journal of American Culture* 7, nos. 1–2 (1984): 113–17; Bernard F. Dick, *The Star Spangled Screen: The American World War II Film* (Lexington: University Press of Kentucky, 1985); Otto Freidrich, *City of Nets: A Portrait of Hollywood in the 1940s* (New York: Harper and Row, 1986); and K. R. M. Short, "Washington's Information Manual for Hollywood, 1942," *Historical Journal of Film, Radio, and Television* 3, no. 2 (1983): 171–80; "Special Focus: World War II in Film," *Film and History* 27, nos. 1–4 (1997); John Whiteclay Chambers II and David Culbert, *World War II: Film and History* (New York: Oxford University Press, 1996).

6. See Eric Bentley, *Thirty Years of Treason: Excerpts from Hearings before the House Committee on Un-American Activities, 1938–1968* (New York: Viking, 1971); Larry Ceplair and Steven Englund, *The Inquisition in Hollywood: Politics and the Film Community, 1930–1960* (Garden City, N.Y.: Anchor Press/Doubleday, 1980); Geoffrey Smith, "Isolationsim, the Devil, and the Advent of the Second World War: Variations on a Theme," *International History Review* 4, no. 1 (1982): 76.

7. *Propaganda Hearings*, 22.

8. See chap. 8 of Howard Koch's *As Time Goes By: Memoirs of a Writer* (New York: Harcourt Brace, 1979); Victor Navasky, *Naming Names* (New York: Viking, 1980), 79, 104–6, 109, 165–68, 300; Neal Gabler, *An Empire of Their Own: How the Jews Invented Hollywood* (New York: Crown, 1988), 351–72, 374–85; Marc Eliot, *Walt Disney: Hollywood's Dark Prince* (New York: Birch Lane Press, 1993), 172–74; Brownstein, 67–69, 111–20; Ann M. Sperber and Eric Lax, *Bogart* (New York: William Morrow, 1997), 130–34, 355–88, 392–401, 409–12, 447–49.

9. The seven-year contract was standard throughout the industry. An actor would sign on with a studio that would foster and promote his or her career, demanding allegiance in return. The actor was guaranteed work and a substantial salary. Refusal to comply with the contract often resulted in "penalty time" being added to the contract. De Havilland argued that she should have been released from her contract years earlier but had been denied that privilege because the studio deemed her "difficult." The de Havilland decision was handed down in 1948, the same year as the Paramount decision.

10. Nick Browne, "System of Production/System of Presentation: Industry Context and Ideological Form in Capra's *Meet John Doe*," in *Meet John Doe*,

Charles Wolfe, ed. (New Brunswick, N.J.: Rutgers University Press, 1989), 269–88. It could also be argued that the two Supreme Court decisions, though devastating to the Hollywood studio system, forced Warner Bros. to depend more upon the diversification begun by Harry in the late 1920s. As the studio system declined, the Warners' subsidiary interests in book publishing and musical recordings skyrocketed.

11. One could argue that Lindbergh sought fame when he took up the challenge of the solo flight to Paris in 1927. Judging from the material available, it seems clear that Lindbergh was overwhelmed by his sudden international celebrity.

12. Personal interviews with Andrew Jackson York, George Edward York, Lucy York Rains, Robert York, Betsy Ross York Lowry, Arthur S. Bushing, Jr., Leo Hatfield, and Noble Cody. Robert York was interviewed July 11, 1988, and Nobel Cody has been interviewed repeatedly since 1990.

13. Lindbergh, the man who had disliked fame and looked down his nose at movies, also capitulated to the magnetic pull of Hollywood. In 1957 Lindbergh finally agreed (thirty years after his solo flight across the Atlantic) to a biopic, *The Spirit of St. Louis*—also by Warner Bros., with James Stewart playing the Lone Eagle. Jack Warner called it "the most disastrous failure we ever made . . . [we] took a real bath. The exhibitors are still moaning about it." See Jack Warner with Dean Jennings, *My First Hundred Years in Hollywood* (New York: Random House, 1965), 125, 258.

14. Lindbergh, however, did not share his father's concern over the plight of the less fortunate and was not known for his largesse or charity. See Walter L. Hixson, *Charles A. Lindbergh: The Lone Eagle* (New York: Harper Collins, 1996), 85.

15. The best overview currently available is Kenneth S. Stern, *A Force upon the Plain: The America Militia Movement and the Politics of Hate* (New York: Simon and Schuster, 1996).

Bibliography

MANUSCRIPT COLLECTIONS

Cumberland Homestead File. Tennessee State Library and Archives, Nashville, Tenn. (TSLA).

Davis, Lipscomb. Sergeant York Scrapbook, compiled by the Nashville Rotary Club. Private collection of Buzz Davis, Nashville, Tenn.

———. Vertical File. TSLA.

Evins, Joe L. Papers. Special Collections, Tennessee Technological University Archives, Cookeville, Tenn.

Fentress County Historical Society Papers. Public Library, Jamestown, Tenn.

Ganier, Albert F. Photographic Collection, 1900–55. MSS ac. no. 89-114A, TSLA.

Houston, Colonel Herbert. Manuscript Collection. Special Collections, University Archives, Tennessee Technological University, Cookeville, Tenn.

Hull, Cordell. Cordell Hull Papers. Library of Congress, Washington, D.C.

Kefauver, Estes. Papers. Special Collections, Hoskins Library, University of Tennessee, Knoxville, Tenn.

Lasky, Jesse. Papers. Warner Bros. Archives and Uncataloged Alvin C. York Collection, Los Angeles, Calif., and Pall Mall, Tenn.

McAlister, Hill. Governor's Papers. TSLA.

Nashville Banner Library. Nashville, Tenn.

Nashville Tennessean Library. Nashville, Tenn.

Peay, Austin. Governor's Papers. TSLA.

Roberts, Albert H. Governor's Papers. TSLA.

Smith, Rutledge, and Albert Smith. Papers. Uncataloged. Dollie Smith Williams Estate, Malcolm Williams, Jr., executor, Monterey, Tenn.

Swindler, Col. Henry O. "York of Tennessee." RG 165, War Department General and Special Staffs. E 310 B "Thomas File," National Archives, Washington, D.C.

Tennessee Department of Education Files. TSLA.

Tennessee Folklife Collection. Uncatalogued. TSLA.

Tennessee Society in New York Collection. Record Group 93-020, TSLA.

"Tenn. NP-16, Company 3464, Crossville, Tennessee." *The CCC in Tennessee.* CCC in Tennessee, box 2, files 9–11, Special Collections, TSLA.

U.S. Army Draft Records. National Archives Eastpoint Facility, Atlanta, Ga.
Warner, Harry. Correspondence, Speeches, and Assorted Papers. Jack L. Warner
 Collection, University of Southern California (USC).
Warner, Jack. Studio Files. Jack L. Warner Collection, USC.
Warner Bros. Archives. Files Re: Films produced between 1934 and 1942. Special
 Collections, USC.
York Agricultural and Industrial Institute Files. York Institute, Jamestown, Tenn.
York, Alvin C. Papers. Uncataloged. Pall Mall, Tenn.
York, Alvin C. Vertical File. East Tennessee Historical Society, Special Collections,
 Knoxville, Tenn.
Zanuck, Darryl F. Papers and Production Reports. Warner Bros. Archives, USC.

GOVERNMENT DOCUMENTS

"Alvin C. York: Report to Accompany S. 2183." 76th Cong., 1st sess. Calendar 448,
 Report No. 418. May 11, 1939. Washington, D.C.: GPO.
American Battle Monuments Commission. *82nd Division: Summary of Opera-
 tions in the World War.* Washington, D.C.: GPO, 1944.
Ashe, Stephen, ed. *Messages of the Governors of Tennessee.* Vols. 9–10. Nashville:
 Tennessee Historical Commission, 1990.
Bentley, Eric, ed. *Thirty Years of Treason: Excerpts from Hearings before the House
 Committee on Un-American Activities, 1938–1968.* New York: Viking, 1971.
Birdwell, Michael E. "Coal Mining in the Big South Fork Area of Kentucky and
 Tennessee." Cookeville and Nashville, Tennessee: Upper Cumberland Human-
 ities and Social Science Institute in Conjunction with the Center for the Man-
 agement, Utilization and Protection of Water Resources, and the U.S. Army
 Corps of Engineers, Nashville District, 1990.
Bureau of the Census. "Church of Christ in Christian Union." In *Religious Bodies,
 1916. Part II: Separate Denominations; History, Description and Statistics.*
 Washington, D.C.: GPO, 1919.
"Die Entstehung von Kriegslegendon Feststellungen ueber die Angebliche Hold-
 entat des Amerikanischen Sergeanten York an 8. 10, 18 " (The origin of war
 legends, an investigation of the alleged feat of Sgt. York, October 8, 1918) Sgt.
 F. W. Merten and W. C. Koenig, trans. Washington, D.C.: National Archives,
 1936.
"Hearings before the Committee on Military Affairs." House of Representatives.
 74th Cong., 1st sess. Washington, D.C.: GPO, 1935.
Hull, Cordell. "Hearing before the Committee on Military Affairs on H.R. 8599
 Authorizing the President to Appoint Alvin Cullum York a Second Lieutenant
 and Place His Name on the Retired List with the Pay and Allowances of a Sec-
 ond Lieutenant of the Regular Army." 66th Cong., 1st sess. Washington, D.C.:
 GPO, 1919.

Jones, James B., Jr. "The WPA and CCC in Tennessee." Department of Conservation, Nashville, Tenn., 1983. Typescript.

Lord, Russell, and Paul H. Johnstone. *A Place on Earth: A Critical Appraisal of Subsistence Homesteads.* Washington, D.C.: USDA Division of Agricultural Economics, GPO, 1942.

Malanka, Anne. "The Homesteader Experience at Cumberland Homesteads, Tennessee." Department of Conservation and Environment, Nashville, Tenn., 1992. Typescript.

National Education Association of the United States. *Proceedings of the Sixty-Fifth Annual Meeting Held at Seattle, Washington, July 3–8, 1927.* Washington, D.C.: National Education Association, 1928.

Propaganda in Motion Pictures: Hearings before a Senate Subcommittee on Interstate Commerce, United States Senate (Seventy-Seventh Congress, First Session), on Senate Resolution 152; A Resolution Authorizing an Investigation of War Propaganda Disseminated by the Motion Picture Industry and of any Monopoly in the Production, Distribution, or Exhibition of Motion Pictures, September 9 to 26, 1941. Washington, D.C.: GPO, 1942.

Report of the Delegate of the United States of America to the Meeting of the Foreign Ministers of the American Republics held at Panama, September 23–October 3, 1939. Washington, D.C.: GPO, 1941.

Roosevelt, Franklin. "Message from the President of the United States Relating to: Senate Bill 1871, 'An Act to Prevent Pernicious Political Activities.'" August 2, 1939. York Papers, Pall Mall, Tenn.

Short, K. R. M., ed. "Washington's Information Manual for Hollywood, 1942." *Historical Journal of Film, Radio, and Television* 3, no. 2 (1983): 171–80.

United States Army in the World War, 1917–1919. Vol. 9, *Meuse-Argonne Operations of the American Expeditionary Forces.* Washington: Historical Division, Department of the Army, GPO, 1948.

U.S. Military Personnel and Casualties in Principal U.S. Wars: By Branch of Service from the Revolutionary War to the Vietnam War; By Pre-service Home State from World War I to the Vietnam War. Washington, D.C.: Library of Congress, Congressional Research Service.

NEWSPAPERS

Bloomington (Ill.) Daily Pantograph
Boston Globe
Chattanooga News–Free Press
Chattanooga Times
Christian Science Monitor
Defender
Fentress Courier
Fentress Leader-Times
Hollywood Now
Kansas City Times
Knoxville Journal
Knoxville News-Sentinel
Los Angeles Examiner
Los Angeles Times

Louisville Courier-Journal
McCreary County (Ky.) Record
Memphis Commercial Appeal
Milwaukee Journal
Motion Picture Herald
Nashville Banner
Nashville Tennessean

New York Herald
New York Post
New York Times
Sparta Expositor
Variety
Zarepath (N.J.) Good Citizen

PAMPHLETS AND REPORTS

The ADL Anti-Paramilitary Training Statute: A Response to Domestic Terrorism.
New York: Anti-Defamation League, Law Report, 1995.
America First Committee: The Nazi Transmission Belt. New York: Friends of
Democracy, 1941.
American Battle Monuments Commission. *82nd Division: Summary of Opera-
tions in the World War.* Washington, D.C.: GPO, 1944.
Armed and Dangerous: Militias Take Aim at the Federal Government. New York:
Anti-Defamation League, 1994.
Boyd, Dr. Willis Baxter. *The March of Progress in the Upper Cumberland of Ten-
nessee.* Cookeville, Tenn. Privately published, n.d.
Britt, George. *The Fifth Column Is Here.* New York: Wilfred Funk, 1940.
Bushing, Arthur. *This Booklet Contains Information about the Alvin C. York Indus-
trial Institute.* Jamestown, Tenn., 1926.
Butler, Smedley D. *War Is a Racket.* New York: Round Table Press, 1935.
Cohen, Felix S., ed. *Combatting Totalitarian Propaganda: A Legal Appraisal.*
Washington, D.C.: Institute of Living Law, 1944.
Constitution and Bylaws of the Church of Christ in Christian Union. Circleville,
Ohio: Advocate Publishing House, n.d.
Coyle, David Cushman. *America.* Washington, D.C.: National Home Library
Foundation, 1941.
Danger: Extremism; The Major Vehicles and Voices on America's Far Right Fringe.
New York: Anti-Defamation League, 1996.
*Do You Remember This Poster? Stop This from Happening Again; Protect Your Dol-
lars and Save Sons! Keep the United States out of War and Work for World Peace.*
Philadelphia: Emergency Peace Campaign, Harry Emerson Fosdick, chair-
man, 1937.
Father Coughlin: His "Facts" and Arguments. New York: General Jewish Council,
1939.
Halpern, Thomas, and David Rosenberg. *The Freeman Network: An Assault on the
Rule of Law.* New York: Anti-Defamation League, 1996.
Hays, Will H. *Self Regulation in the Motion Picture Industry: Annual Report to the*

Motion Picture Producers and Distributors of America, May 28, 1938. New York: Motion Picture Producers and Distributors of America (MPPDA), 1938.

High, Stanley, ed. *Watchman, What of the Night? Can Christianity Survive? A Compilation of Original German Documents.* New York: Revell, n.d.

Hobson, Henry W., and Bert Johnston. *Rise Up America.* New York: Fight for Freedom, 1941.

Humble, Richard G., ed. *Sgt. Alvin C. York: A Christian Patriot.* Circleville, Ohio: Advocate Publishing House, 1966.

Is Lindbergh a Nazi? New York: Friends of Democracy, 1941.

MacLennon, Stewart. *An Amazing Proposal: Exterminate the Jews.* Hollywood, Calif.: First Presbyterian Church, 1940.

Morris, George, *The Black Legion Rides.* New York: Workers Library, August 1936.

The Mountaineer. Jamestown, Tenn.: Alvin C. York Industrial Institute, April 1926.

Mountain Herald. Harrogate, Tenn.: Lincoln Memorial University, July 1925.

Pelley, William Dudley. *What Every Congressman Should Know.* Asheville, N.C.: Galahad Press, 1936.

———. *The Dupes of Judah: The Inside Story of Why the World War Was Fought.* Asheville, N.C.: Pelley Publishers, 1938.

———. *Nations in Law.* Asheville, N.C.: Pelley Publishers, n.d.

Reynolds, Bruce. *The Mad Dog of Europe.* New York: Veritas, 1938.

Scherger, George L. *Men of the Hour: Mussolini, Gandhi, Stalin, and Hitler.* Chicago: Popular Interest Series, 1933.

Terrorism in the United States, 1995. Washington, D.C.: U.S. Department of Justice, FBI, 1996.

PUBLISHED MEMOIRS AND DIARIES

Bacall, Lauren. *By Myself.* New York: Knopf, 1978.

Baruch, Bernard. *Baruch: The Public Years.* New York: Holt, Rinehart, Winston, 1960.

Capra, Frank. *The Name above the Title.* New York: Macmillan, 1971.

Carlson, John Roy. *Under Cover: My Four Years in the Nazi Underworld of America—The Amazing Revelation of How Axis Agents and Our Enemies Within Are Now Plotting to Destroy the United States.* New York: Dutton, 1943.

Catton, Bruce. *Warlords of Washington.* New York, 1948.

Dies, Martin. *The Trojan Horse in America.* New York: Dodd, Mead, 1940.

Dunne, Philip. *Take Two.* New York: Random House, 1980.

Flynn, Errol. *My Wicked, Wicked Ways.* New York: Berkeley Books, 1959.

———. *From a Life of Adventure: The Writings of Errol Flynn.* Tony Thomas, ed. Secaucus, N.J.: Citadel Press, 1980.

Hays, Will H. *The Memoirs of Will H. Hays.* Garden City, N.Y.: Doubleday, 1955.

Huston, John. *An Open Book.* New York: Ballantine, 1980.

Ickes, Harold. *The Secret Diaries of Harold Ickes.* Vol. 2, *Inside the Struggle, 1936–1939.* New York: Simon and Schuster, 1954.

Johnson, Hugh. *The Blue Eagle: From Egg to Earth.* Garden City, N.Y.: Doubleday, Doran, 1935.

Jones, Chuck. *Chuck Amuck: The Life and Times of an Animated Cartoonist.* New York: Farrar, Strauss, Giroux, 1989.

———. *Chuck Reducks: Drawing from the Fun Side of Life.* New York: Warner Books, 1996.

Kanin, Garson. *Hollywood.* New York: Viking, 1974.

Koch, Howard. *As Time Goes By: Memoirs of a Writer.* New York: Harcourt Brace Jovanovich, 1979.

Lasky, Jesse L., Jr. *What Ever Happened to Hollywood?* New York: Funk and Wagnalls, 1975.

Lasky, Jesse L., with Don Weldon. *I Blow My Own Horn.* Garden City, N.Y.: Doubleday, 1957.

LeRoy, Mervyn, as told to Dick Kleiner. *Mervyn LeRoy: Take One.* New York: Hawthorn Books, 1974.

Levant, Oscar. *A Smattering of Ignorance.* New York: Doubleday, Doran, 1940.

———. *The Unimportance of Being Oscar.* New York: Putnam's, 1968.

Lindbergh, Charles A. *The Wartime Journals of Charles A. Lindbergh.* New York: Harcourt Brace Jovanovich, 1970.

Mann, Thomas. *Thomas Mann Diaries, 1918–1939.* Richard and Clara Wilson, trans. New York: Harry F. Abrams, 1988.

McGilligan, Pat, ed. *Backstory: Interviews with Screenwriters from the Golden Age of Hollywood.* Berkeley: University of California Press, 1986.

Mencken, Henry Louis. *A Mencken Chrestomathy.* New York: Knopf, 1949.

———. *The Diaries of H.L. Mencken.* New York: Knopf, 1989.

———. *A Second Mencken Chrestomathy.* Terry Teachout, ed. New York: Vintage, 1994.

Naumberg, Nancy, ed. *We Make the Movies.* New York: Norton, 1937.

Niven, David. *Bring On the Empty Horses.* New York: Dell, 1975.

Peay, Austin. *Austin Peay, Governor of Tennessee, 1923–1925, 1925–1927, 1927–1929: A Compilation of State Papers and Public Addresses.* T. H. Alexander, ed. Kingsport, Tenn.: Southern Publishing, 1929.

Riefenstahl, Leni. *Leni Riefenstahl: A Memoir.* New York: St. Martin's, 1993.

Roosevelt, Franklin Delano. *The Essential Franklin Delano Roosevelt.* John Gabriel Hunt, ed. New York: Random House, Gramercy Books, 1995.

Schoonmaker, Nancy, and Doris Fielding Reid, eds. *We Testify.* New York: Smith and Durrell, 1941.

Stowe, Leland. *Nazi Means War.* New York: Whittlesey House, 1934.

Turrou, Leon G. *Nazi Spies in America.* New York: Random House, 1938.

Wallis, Hal, with Charles Higham. *Starmaker: The Autobiography of Hal B. Wallis.* New York: Macmillan, 1980.

Warner, Jack, with Dean Jennings. *My First Hundred Years in Hollywood.* New York: Random House, 1965.

York, Alvin C. "The Diary of Sergeant York: A Famous Hero's Own Story of His Great Adventure." *Liberty,* July 14, 1928, 7–10; July 21, 1928, 14–19; July 28, 1928, 26–29; August 4, 1928, 41–46.

York, Alvin C. *Sergeant York: His Own Life Story and War Diary.* Tom Skeyhill, ed. New York: Doubleday, 1928.

INTERVIEWS (ALL CONDUCTED BY THE AUTHOR UNLESS OTHERWISE INDICATED)

Baker, Ira (World War I Veteran). Dry Valley, Tenn.: June 12, 1988.

Brooks, Ola, and Alva Brooks. Pall Mall, Tenn., December 1, 1988.

Buck, Ernest. Pall Mall, Tenn., May 15, 1997.

Bushing, Arthur S., Jr. Maryville, Tenn., June 13, 1988.

Coolidge, Charles Henry (World War II Congressional Medal of Honor Winner). Interview conducted with Steve Gwilt. Chattanooga, Tenn., May 13, 1989.

Cooper, Hortense (widow of former governor Prentice Cooper). Cookeville, Tenn., November 20, 1988.

Davis, Buzz. May 26, 1993–May 1998.

Gribble, Sutton (World War I POW). Interview conducted with W. Calvin Dickinson. McMinnville, Tenn., June 13, 1988.

Hatfield, Leo. Personal Interviews. Jamestown and Pall Mall, Tenn., May 21, 1989–May 1998.

Hooper, Ed. Cookeville, Tenn., May 27, 1989.

Houston, Col. Herbert, Ret. Chattanooga, Tenn., May 13–15, 1989; June 24, 1989.

Hutchings, Tillman. Sparta, Tenn., June 5, 1988.

Lee, David D. Bowling Green, Ky., 1988–October 1996.

Lowry, Betsy Ross York. Bowling Green, Ky., Pall Mall and Nashville, Tenn., May 7, 1986–May 1997.

Miller, Emily. Interview conducted with W. Calvin Dickinson. Murfreesboro, Tenn., June 3, 1988.

Miller, Treva Hutchings. Sparta, Tenn., June 5, 1988.

Ragland, Jeff (World War I veteran). Interview conducted with W. Calvin Dickinson. McMinnville, Tenn., June 13, 1988.

Rains, Lucy York. Personal Interviews conducted between 1988 and 1990 with Andrew Williams, Calvin Dickinson, and Homer D. Kemp. Jamestown, Tenn.

Webb, Bryan (World War I Veteran). Interview conducted with W. Calvin Dickinson. Rock Island, Tenn., June 7, 1988.

Williams, Dollie Smith. Monterey, Tenn., September 25, 1996.

Williams, Guy. Allardt, Tenn., 1988–1991.

York, Andrew Jackson. Pall Mall, Jamestown, Red Boiling Springs, Nashville, and Cookeville, Tennessee. June 28, 1987–May 1998.

York, George Edward Buxton. Pall Mall, Jamestown, Red Boiling Springs, Nashville, and Cookeville, Tennessee. May 7, 1988–May 1998.

York, Gerald. Nashville and Pall Mall, Tennessee. May 7, 1988–March 1997.

York, Woodrow Wilson. Personal Interview. July 14, 1984.

BOOKS

Adamson, Joe. *Bugs Bunny: Fifty Years and Only One Grey Hare.* New York: Henry Holt, 1990.

Aldgate, Anthony, and Jeffrey Richards. *Britain Can Take It: The British Cinema and the Second World War.* London: Basil Blackwell, 1985.

Baird, Jay. *The Mythical World of Nazi Propaganda, 1939–1945.* Minneapolis: University of Minnesota Press, 1974.

Balio, Tino, ed. *Grand Design: Hollywood as a Modern Business Enterprise, 1930–1939.* Berkeley: University of California Press, 1995.

Batteau, Alan W. *The Invention of Appalachia.* Tucson: University of Arizona Press, 1990.

Beck, Jerry, and Will Friedwald. *Looney Tunes and Merrie Melodies: A Complete Illustrated Guide.* New York: Henry Holt, Owl Books, 1989.

Behlmer, Rudy. *Inside Warner Bros. (1935–1951).* New York: Simon and Schuster, 1985.

———. *Behind the Scenes.* New York: Samuel French, 1989.

Bell, Leland. *In Hitler's Shadow: The Anatomy of American Nazism.* Port Washington, N.Y.: Kennikat Press, 1973.

Belton, John. *American Cinema/American Culture.* New York: McGraw-Hill, 1994.

Bennett, David H. *The Party of Fear: The American Far Right from Nativism to the Militia Movement.* Rev. ed. New York: Vintage, 1995.

Bergman, Andrew. *We're in the Money: Depression America and Its Films.* New York: Harper Torchbooks, 1971.

Bernstein, Matthew. *Walter Wanger: Hollywood Independent.* Berkeley: University of California Press, 1994.

Black, Gregory D. *Hollywood Censored: Morality Codes, Catholics, and the Movies.* Cambridge: Cambridge University Press, 1994.

Bogdanovich, Peter. *Fritz Lang in America.* New York: Praeger, 1969.

———. *Who the Devil Made It?* New York: Knopf, 1997.

Borchard, Edwin, and William Potter Lange. *Neutrality for the United States.* New Haven, Conn.: Yale University Press, 1937.

Bordwell, David, Janet Staiger, and Kristin Thompson. *The Classical Hollywood*

Cinema: Film Style and Mode of Production to 1960. New York: Columbia University Press, 1985.

Bramsted, Ernest K. *Goebbels and National Socialist Propaganda, 1925–1945.* East Lansing: Michigan State University Press, 1965.

Bredin, Jean-Denis. *The Affair: The Case of Alfred Dreyfus.* New York: G. Braziller, 1986.

Brinkley, Alan. *Voices of Protest: Huey Long, Father Coughlin, and the Great Depression.* New York: Vintage Books, 1982.

Brownlow, Kevin. *The War, The West, and the Wilderness.* New York: Knopf, 1984.

Brownstein, Ronald. *The Power and the Glitter: The Hollywood-Washington Connection.* New York: Vintage Books, 1990.

Buhite, Russell D., and David W. Levy, eds. *FDR's Fireside Chats.* Norman: University of Oklahoma Press, 1992.

Campbell, Joseph. *The Hero with a Thousand Faces.* Princeton, N.J.: Princeton University Press, 1973.

Carnes, Mark C., ed. *Past Imperfect: History according to the Movies.* New York: Henry Holt, 1995.

Ceplair, Larry, and Steven Englund. *The Inquisition in Hollywood: Politics and the Film Community, 1930–1960.* Garden City, N.Y.: Anchor Press/Doubleday, 1980.

Chadwin, Mark Lincoln. *The Hawks of World War II.* Chapel Hill: University of North Carolina Press, 1968.

Chambers, John Whiteclay. *To Raise an Army: The Draft Comes to Modern America.* New York: Free Press, 1987.

Chambers, John Whiteclay II, and David Culbert. *World War II: Film and History.* New York: Oxford University Press, 1996.

Christensen, Terry. *Reel Politics: American Political Movies from Birth of a Nation to Platoon.* Oxford: Basil Blackwell, 1987.

Churchill, Allen. *Over Here: An Informal Re-Creation of the Home Front in World War I.* New York: Dodd, Mead, 1968.

Coe, Jonathan. *Humphrey Bogart: Take It and Like It.* New York: Grove Weidenfeld, 1991.

Coffman, Edward M. *The War to End All Wars: The American Military Experience in World War I.* Madison: University of Wisconsin Press, 1986.

Cohen, Warren I. *The American Revisionists: The Lessons of Intervention in World War I.* Chicago: University of Chicago Press, 1967.

Cole, Wayne S. *America First: The Battle against Intervention, 1940-1941.* Madison: University of Wisconsin Press, 1953.

———. *Senator Gerald P. Nye and American Foreign Relations.* Minneapolis: University of Minnesota Press, 1962.

———. *Charles A. Lindbergh and the Battle against Intervention in World War II.* New York: Harcourt Brace Jovanovich, 1974.

Cole, Wayne S. *Roosevelt and the Isolationists, 1932–1945.* Lincoln: University of Nebraska Press, 1983.

Combs, James E., and Sara T. Combs. *Film Propaganda and American Politics: An Analysis and Filmography.* New York: Garland, 1994.

Conkin, Paul. *Tomorrow a New World: The New Deal Community Program.* Ithaca: Cornell University Press, 1959.

Cook, Bruce. *Brecht in Exile.* New York: Holt, Rinehart, Winston, 1982.

Cowan, Sam K. *Sergeant York and His People.* New York: Funk and Wagnalls, 1922 and 1941.

Cozic, Charles P., ed. *The Militia Movement.* San Diego: Greenhaven Press, 1997.

Crutchfield, James A. *Tennesseans at War: Volunteers and Patriots in Defense of Liberty.* Nashville, Tenn.: Rutledge Hill Press, 1987.

Custen, George F. *Twentieth Century's Fox: Darryl F. Zanuck and the Culture of Hollywood.* New York: Basic Books, 1997.

Daniels, Jonathan. *The Time between the Wars: Armistice to Pearl Harbor.* Garden City, N.Y.: Doubleday, 1966.

Davis, Kenneth S. *FDR: Into the Storm, 1937–1940.* New York: Random House, 1993.

Dawidowicz, Lucy S. *The War against the Jews, 1933-1945.* New York: Dell, 1986.

Deighton, Len. *Blood, Tears, and Folly: An Objective Look at World War II.* New York: Harper-Perennial, 1993.

Diamond, Sander A. *The Nazi Movement in the United States, 1924–1941.* Ithaca: Cornell University Press, 1974.

Dibbets, Karel, and Bert Hogenkamp. *Film and the First World War.* London: I.B.D. Limited, 1994.

Dick, Bernard F. *The Star Spangled Screen: The Hollywood World War II Film.* Lexington: University Press of Kentucky, 1985.

———. *The Merchant Prince of Poverty Row: Harry Cohn of Columbia Pictures.* Lexington: University Press of Kentucky, 1993.

Dijkstra, Bram. *Evil Sisters: The Threat of Female Sexuality and the Cult of Manhood.* New York: Knopf, 1997.

Dinnerstein, Leonard. *Antisemitism in America.* New York: Oxford University Press, 1994.

Doenecke, Justus D., ed. *In Danger Undaunted: The Anti-Interventionist Movement of 1940–1941 as Revealed in the Papers of the America First Committee.* Stanford, Calif.: Hoover Institution Press, 1990.

Doenecke, Justus D., and John E. Wilz. *From Isolation to War, 1931–1941.* 2d ed. Arlington Heights, Ill.: Harlan Davidson, 1991.

Doherty, Thomas. *Projections of War: Hollywood, American Culture, and World War II.* New York: Columbia University Press, 1993.

Dooley, Roger. *From Scarface to Scarlett: American Films in the 1930's.* New York: Harcourt Brace Jovanovich, 1981.

Dunne, John Gregory. *The Studio.* New York: Touchstone, 1969.

Eliot, Marc. *Walt Disney: Hollywood's Dark Prince.* New York: Birch Lane Press, 1993.

Engelbrecht, Helmuth C. and Frank C. Hanighen. *Merchants of Death: A Study of the International Armament Industry.* New York: Harper, 1934.

Fahey, Denis. *The Rulers of Russia.* 3d ed. Royal Oak, Mich.: Charles A. Coughlin, Social Justice, 1940.

Ferro, Marc. *Cinema and History.* Naomi Greene, trans. Detroit, Mich.: Wayne State University Press, 1988.

Fielding, Raymond. *The March of Time, 1935–1951.* New York: Oxford University Press, 1978.

Freedland, Michael. *The Warner Brothers.* New York: St. Martin's, 1983.

Freidrich, Otto. *City of Nets: A Portrait of Hollywood in the 1940s.* New York: Harper and Row, 1986.

Freidman, Lester D. *Hollywood's Image of the Jew.* New York: Frederick Ungar, 1982.

Frye, Alton. *Nazi Germany and the American Hemisphere, 1933–1941.* New Haven, Conn.: Yale University Press, 1967.

Fussell, Paul. *The Great War and Modern Memory.* New York: Oxford University Press, 1975.

Gabler, Neal. *An Empire of Their Own: How the Jews Invented Hollywood.* New York: Crown, 1988.

———. *Winchell: Gossip, Power, and the Culture of Celebrity.* New York: Vintage, 1995.

Gelernter, David. *1939: The Lost World of the Fair.* New York: Free Press, 1995.

Gellman, Irwin F. *Secret Affairs: Franklin Roosevelt, Cordell Hull, and Sumner Welles.* Baltimore: Johns Hopkins University Press, 1993.

Gomery, J. Douglas. *Movie History: A Survey.* Belmont, Calif.: Wadsworth, 1991.

Grobel, Lawrence. *The Hustons.* New York: Scribner's, 1989.

Haglund, David G. *Latin America and the Transformation of U.S. Strategic Thought, 1936–1940.* Albuquerque: University of New Mexico Press, 1984.

Hamilton, Ian. *Writers in Hollywood, 1915–1951.* New York: Harper and Row, 1990.

Hampton, Christopher. *Tales from Hollywood.* London: Faber and Faber, 1986.

Harmetz, Aljean. *Rolling Breaks and other Movie Business.* New York: Knopf, 1983.

———. *The Making of the Wizard of Oz.* New York: Limelight Editions, 1984.

———. *Round Up the Usual Suspects: The Making of Casablanca—Bogart, Bergman, and World War II.* New York: Hyperion, 1992.

Harris, Marlys J. *The Zanucks of Hollywood: The Dark Legacy of an American Dynasty.* New York: Crown, 1989.

Hay, James. *Popular Film Culture in Fascist Italy: The Passing of the Rex.* Bloomington: Indiana University Press, 1987.

Herzstein, Robert Ewing. *The War That Hitler Won: The Most Infamous Propaganda Campaign in History.* New York: Putnam's, 1978.

Higham, Charles. *Warner Bros.* New York: Scribner's, 1975.

Hirschorn, Clive. *The Warner Bros. Story.* New York: Crown, 1979.

Hixson, Walter L. *Charles A. Lindbergh: The Lone Eagle.* New York: Harper Collins, 1996.

Hoffmann, Hilmar. *The Triumph of Propaganda: Film and National Socialism, 1933–1945.* Oxford: Berghahn, 1995.

Hollander, Anne. *Moving Pictures.* New York: Knopf, 1989.

Holloway, Elma, ed. *Unsung Heroes.* New York: Macmillan, 1938.

Holt, Andrew David. *The Struggle for a State System of Public Schools in Tennessee, 1903–1936.* New York: Bureau of Publications, Teachers College, Columbia University, 1938.

Horak, Jan-Christopher. *Anti-Nazi-Filme: Der Deutschen Emigration von Hollywood, 1939–1945.* 2d ed. Münster, Germany: Maks Publikationen, 1985.

Isenberg, Michael T. *War on Film: The American Cinema and World War I, 1914–1941.* Rutherford, N.J.: Fairleigh Dickinson University Press, 1981.

Kaes, Anton. *From Hitler to Heimat: The Return of History as Film.* Cambridge, Mass.: Harvard University Press, 1989.

Kagan, Norman. *The War Film.* New York: Pyramid Publications, 1974.

Kane, John F., ed. *The Medal of Honor of the United States Army.* Washington, D.C.: GPO, 1948.

Kanfer, Stefan. *Serious Business: The Art and Commerce of Animation in America from Betty Boop to Toy Story.* New York: Scribner's, 1997.

Kauffman, Bill. *America First! Its History, Culture, and Politics.* New York: Prometheus Books, 1995.

Keegan, John. *The Face of Battle.* London: Penguin Books, 1976.

Keith, Jeannette. *Country People of the New South: Tennessee's Upper Cumberland.* Chapel Hill: University of North Carolina Press, 1995.

Kellogg, Paul, ed. *"Calling America": A Special Number of the Survey Graphic on the Challenge to Democracy.* New York: Harper, 1939.

Kennedy, David M. *Over Here: The First World War and American Society.* New York: Oxford University Press, 1980

Kennedy, Joseph P., ed. *The Story of Films: As Told by the Leaders of the Industry to the Students of the Graduate School of Business Administration, George F. Becker Foundation, Harvard University.* Chicago: A. W. Shaw, 1927.

Kenner, Hugh. *Chuck Jones: A Flurry of Drawings.* Berkeley: University of California Press, 1994.

Kern, Stephen. *The Culture of Time and Space, 1880–1918.* Cambridge, Mass.: Harvard University Press, 1988.

Kershaw, Ian. *The Hitler Myth: Image and Reality in the Third Reich.* New York: Oxford University Press, 1987.

Klein, Norman M. *Seven Minutes: The Life and Death of the American Animated Cartoon.* London: Verso, 1993.

Koppes, Clayton R., and Gregory D. Black. *Hollywood Goes to War: How Politics, Profits, and Propaganda Shaped World War II Movies.* Berkeley: University of California Press, 1987.

Landy, Marcia. *Fascism in Film: The Italian Commercial Cinema, 1933–1943.* Princeton, N.J.: Princeton University Press, 1986.

Langer, William L., and S. Everett Gleason. *The Undeclared War, 1940–1941.* New York: Harper, 1953.

Lavine, Harold, and James Wechsler. *War Propaganda and the United States.* New Haven, Conn.: Yale University Press, 1940.

Lee, David D. *Sergeant York: An American Hero.* Lexington: University Press of Kentucky, 1985.

Leed, Eric J. *No Man's Land: Combat and Identity in World War I.* Cambridge: Cambridge University Press, 1979.

Lewis, Richard W. B. *The American Adam: Innocence, Tragedy, and Tradition in the Nineteenth Century.* Chicago: University of Chicago Press, 1955.

Lewis, Sinclair. *It Can't Happen Here.* New York: Signet, 1993.

Liddell-Hart, Capt. Basil H. *The Real War, 1914–1918.* Boston: Little, Brown, 1930.

Lingeman, Richard. *"Don't You Know There's a War On?" The American Home-front, 1941–1945.* New York: Putnam's, 1970.

Lofaro, Michael A., ed. *Davy Crockett: The Man, the Legend, the Legacy, 1786–1986.* Knoxville: University of Tennessee Press, 1985.

Lovell, Mary S. *The Sound of Wings: The Life of Amelia Earhart.* New York: St. Martin's, 1989.

Lyon, James K. *Bertolt Brecht in America.* Princeton, N.J.: Princeton University Press, 1980.

Maland, Charles. *Chaplin and American Culture: The Evolution of a Star Image.* Princeton, N.J.: Princeton University Press, 1989.

Mast, Gerald. *Howard Hawks, Storyteller.* New York: Oxford University Press, 1982.

Mast Gerald, ed. *The Movies in Our Midst: Documents in the Cultural History of Film in America.* Chicago: University of Chicago Press, 1982.

Matthews, Tom Dewe. *Censored: What They Didn't Allow You to See and Why: The Story of Film Censorship in Britain.* London: Chatto and Windus, 1994.

McCarthy, Todd. *Howard Hawks: The Grey Fox of Hollywood.* New York: Grove Press, 1997.

Miller, Nathan. *War at Sea: A Naval History of World War II.* New York: Oxford University Press, 1995.

Mintz, Steven, and Randy Roberts, eds. *Hollywood's America: United States History through Its Films.* St. James, N.Y.: Brandywine Press, 1993.

Moley, Raymond. *Are We Movie Made?* New York: Macy-Masius, 1938.

Montell, Lynwood. *Don't Go up Kettle Creek: A Verbal Legacy of the Upper Cumberland.* Knoxville: University of Tennessee Press, 1985.

Mordden, Ethan. *The Hollywood Studios: Their Unique Styles during the Golden Age of Movies.* New York: Fireside, 1989.

Mosley, Leonard. *Zanuck: The Rise and Fall of Hollywood's Last Tycoon.* New York: McGraw-Hill, 1984.

Muscio, Giuliana. *Hollywood's New Deal.* Philadelphia: Temple University Press, 1997.

Ogden, August Raymond. *The Dies Committee: A Study of the Special House Committee for the Investigation of Un-American Activities, 1938–1943.* Washington, D.C.: Catholic University Press, 1944.

Pells, Richard H. *Radical Visions and American Dreams: Culture and Social Thought in the Depression Years.* Middletown, Conn.: Wesleyan University Press, 1973.

Pencak, William. *For God and Country: The American Legion, 1919–1941.* Boston: Northeastern University Press, 1989.

Perlman, William J. *The Movies on Trial: The Views and Opinions of Outstanding Personalities anent Screen Entertainment Past and Present.* New York: Macmillan, 1936.

Perlmutter, Tom. *War Movies.* Secaucus, N.J.: Castle Books, 1974.

Perrett, Geoffrey. *Days of Sadness, Years of Triumph: The American People, 1939–1945.* Baltimore: Penguin, 1973.

————. *America in the Twenties: A History.* New York: Touchstone/Simon and Schuster, 1982.

Peuckert, Detlev J. K. *Inside Nazi Germany: Conformity, Opposition, and Racism in Everyday Life.* Richard Deveson, trans. New Haven, Conn.: Yale University Press, 1987.

Polenberg, Richard. *War and Society: The United States, 1941–1945.* Philadelphia: J. B. Lippincott, 1972.

Prater, Donald. *Thomas Mann: A Life.* New York: Oxford University Press, 1995.

Ray, Robert. *A Certain Tendency of the Hollywood Cinema, 1930–1980.* Princeton, N.J.: Princeton University Press, 1985.

Rentschler, Eric. *The Ministry of Illusion: Nazi Cinema and Its Afterlife.* Cambridge, Mass.: Harvard University Press, 1996.

Reuth, Ralf Georg. *Goebbels.* Munich, Germany: Piper, 1992.

Ribuffo, Leo P. *The Old Christian Right: The Protestant Far Right from the Great Depression to the Cold War.* Philadelphia: Temple University Press, 1983.

Roddick, Nick. *A New Deal in Entertainment: Warner Bros. in the 1930s.* London: British Film Institute, 1983.

Roffman, Peter, and Jim Purdy. *The Hollywood Social Problem Film: Madness, De-

spair, and Politics from the Depression to the Fifties. Bloomington: Indiana University Press, 1981.

Ross, Stewart H. *Propaganda for War: How the United States Conditioned to Fight the Great War of 1914–1918.* New York: McFarland, 1995.

Rosten, Leo. *Hollywood: The Movie Colony, the Movie Makers.* New York: Harcourt, Brace, 1941.

Rumer, Thomas A. *The American Legion: An Official History, 1919–1989.* New York: M. Evans, 1990.

Saunders, Thomas J. *Hollywood in Berlin: American Cinema and Weimar Germany.* Berkeley: University of California Press, 1994.

Schatz, Thomas. *The Genius of the System: Hollywood Filmmaking in the Studio Era.* New York: Pantheon Books, 1988.

Schwartz, Nancy Lynn, and Sheila Schwartz. *The Hollywood Writer's Wars.* New York: Knopf, 1982.

Seldes, George. *Iron, Blood, and Profits: An Exposure of the World-Wide Munitions Racket.* New York: Harper and Bros., 1934.

Severo, Richard, and Lewis Milford. *The Wages of War: When America's Soldiers Came Home—From Valley Forge to Vietnam.* New York: Simon and Schuster, 1989.

Sherry, Michael S. *In the Shadow of War: The United States since the 1930s.* New Haven, Conn.: Yale University Press, 1995.

Shipman, David. *The Story of Cinema: A Complete Narrative History from the Beginnings to the Present.* New York: St. Martin's, 1982.

Shull, Michael S., and David E. Wilt. *Doing Their Bit: Wartime American Animated Short Films, 1939–1945.* Jefferson, N.C.: McFarland, 1987.

Skeyhill, Tom. *Sergeant York: Last of the Long Hunters.* 1927. Reprint, Shelbyville, Tenn.: Bible and Literature Missionary Foundation, 1993.

Sklar, Robert. *Movie-Made America: A Cultural History of American Movies.* New York: Random House, 1975.

Slotkin, Richard. *Gunfighter Nation: The Myth of the Frontier in Twentieth-Century America.* New York: Atheneum, 1992.

Sperber, Ann M. *Murrow: His Life and Times.* New York: Freundlich Books, 1986.

Sperber, Ann M., and Eric Lax. *Bogart.* New York: William Morrow, 1997.

Sperling, Cass Warner, and Cork Millner with Jack Warner, Jr. *Hollywood Be Thy Name: The Warner Brothers Story.* Rocklin, Calif.: Prima, 1994.

Stern, Kenneth. *A Force upon the Plain: The American Militia Movement and the Politics of Hate.* New York: Simon and Schuster, 1996.

Stillman, Richard J., ed. *The U.S. Infantry: Queen of Battle.* New York: Franklin Watts, 1965.

Strausz-Hupe, Robert. *Axis America: Hitler Plans Our Future.* New York: Putnam, 1941.

Studlar, Gaylyn, and David Desser. *Reflections in a Male Eye.* Washington, D.C.: Smithsonian Institution Press, 1993.

Suid, Lawrence H. *Guts and Glory: Great American War Movies.* Reading, Mass.: Addison-Wesley, 1978.

Swindell, Larry. *The Last Hero: A Biography of Gary Cooper.* Garden City, N.Y.: Doubleday, 1980.

Thomas, Bob. *Clown Prince of Hollywood: The Antic Life and Times of Jack L. Warner.* New York: McGraw-Hill, 1990.

Thompson, Kristin. *Exporting Entertainment: America in the World Film Market, 1907–1934.* London: British Film Institute, 1985.

Thomson, David. *Showman: The Life of David O. Selznick.* New York: Knopf, 1992.

Thorp, Margaret Farrand. *America at the Movies.* New Haven, Conn.: Yale University Press, 1939.

Toplin, Robert Brent. *History by Hollywood: The Use and Abuse of the American Past.* Urbana: University of Illinois Press, 1996.

Ward, Larry Wayne. *The Motion Picture Goes to War: The U.S. Government Film Effort during World War I.* Ann Arbor, Mich.: UMI Research Press, 1985.

Ward, Stephen R. *The War Generation: Veterans of the First World War.* Millwood, N.Y.: Kennikat Press, 1975.

Watt, Donald Cameron. *How War Came: The Immediate Origins of the Second World War, 1938–1939.* New York: Pantheon, 1989.

Wecter, Dixon. *When Johnny Comes Marching Home.* Cambridge, Mass.: Houghton-Miflin, 1944.

West, Nathanael. *A Cool Million* in *Nathanael West: The Day of the Locust and His Other Novels.* Finland: Werner Soderstrom Oy, Landmark Edition, 1983.

White, David Manning, and Richard Averson. *The Celluloid Weapon: Social Comment in American Films.* Boston: Beacon Press, 1972.

White, Robert H. *Development of the Tennessee State Educational Organization, 1796–1929.* Kingsport, Tenn.: Southern, 1929.

Williams, Ben Ames, ed. *Amateurs at War: The American Soldier in Action.* Boston: Houghton-Mifflin, 1943.

Williamson, Joel. *A Rage for Order: Black-White Relations in the American South since Emancipation.* New York: Oxford University Press, 1986.

Wiltz, John E. *In Search of Peace: The Senate Munitions Inquiry, 1934–1936.* Baton Rouge: Louisiana State University Press, 1963.

Wyman, David S. *The Abandonment of the Jews: America and the Holocaust, 1941–1945.* New York: Pantheon, 1984.

———. *Paper Walls: America and the Refugee Crisis, 1938–1941.* New York: Pantheon, 1985.

Yahil, Leni. *The Holocaust: The Fate of European Jewry, 1932–1945.* Ina Friedman and Haya Galai, trans. New York: Oxford University Press, 1990.

ARTICLES

"Aaron L. Sapiro: The Man Who Sued Henry Ford—A Picture Story." *Western States Jewish Historical Quarterly* 13, no. 4 (1981): 303–12.

Ackerman, Carl W. "War Propaganda: The Battle of Public Opinion." *Vital Speeches of the Day,* August 1, 1940, 636–38.

"The Adventures of Robin Hood." *Time,* May 16, 1938, 57–58.

Amann, Peter H. "Vigilante Fascism: The Black Legion as an American Hybrid." *Comparative Studies in Society and History* 25, no. 3 (1983): 490–524.

———. "A 'Dog in the Nighttime' Problem: American Fascism in the 1930s." *History Teacher* 19, no. 4 (August 1986): 559–84.

"American Fascism: Like Communism It Masquerades as Americanism." *Life,* March 6, 1939, 58–63.

"The American Fascists." *New Republic,* March 8, 1939, 117–18.

Ames, Richard Sheridan. "The Screen Enters Politics: Will Hollywood Produce More Propaganda?" *Harper's,* March 1935, 473–82.

Angoff, Charles. "Nazi Jew-Baiting in America." *Nation,* May 1, 1935, 501–3.

"Arming for Armageddon: Colonel James 'Bo' Gritz: Patriot or Extremist?" *ADL Special Edition,* May 1996.

"Arson De Luxe: The Riddle of the Reichstag Fire." *Harper's,* October 1933, 641–49.

Ashkenas, Bruce F. "A Legacy of Hatred: The Records of a Nazi Organization in America." *Prologue* 17, no. 2 (1985): 93–106.

Banks, Dean. "H.L. Mencken and 'Hitlerism,' 1939–1941: A Patrician Libertarian Besieged." *Maryland Historical Magazine* 71, no. 4 (winter 1976): 498–515.

Barkley, Alben W. "What the United States Faces Today: God Grant That We May Not Be Compelled to Unsheathe Our Sword." *Vital Speeches of the Day,* September 15, 1941, 732–36.

Baumgardner, Erbin. "Sergeant York: Tenn's Hero." *Tennessee Magazine* 17, no. 12 (December 1974): 4–5, 16.

Bayor, Ronald H. "Klans, Coughlinites, and Aryan Nations: Patterns of American Anti-Semitism in the Twentieth Century." *American Jewish History* 76, no. 2 (1986): 181–96.

Beaton, Welford. "A Plea to the Jews Who Control Our Films to Use the Mighty Voice of the Screen on Behalf of the Jews Who Are Victims of Maniac of Germany." *Hollywood Spectator* 13, no. 22 (November 26, 1938): 3–4.

Beaumont, Roger. "Images of War: Films as Documentary History." *Military Affairs* 35 (February 1971): 5–7.

Belknap, Michael. "Frankfurter and the Nazi Saboteurs." *Supreme Court Historical Society Yearbook* (1982): 66–71.

Bell, Leland V. "The Failure of Nazism in America: The German-American Bund, 1936–1941." *Political Science Quarterly* 85, no. 4 (December 1970): 585–99.

Bennett, Michael Todd. "Anglophilia on Film: Creating an Atmosphere for Alliance, 1935–1941." *Film and History* 27, nos. 1–4 (1997): 4–21.

Berninger, Dieter. "Milwaukee's German-American Community and the Nazi Challenge of the 1930's." *Wisconsin Magazine of History* 71, no. 2 (1987–88): 118–42.

Birdwell, Michael E. "A Change of Heart: Alvin York and the Movie *Sergeant York.*" *Film and History* 27, nos. 1–4 (1997): 22–33.

———. "'The Devil's Tool': Alvin York and *Sergeant York.*" In *Hollywood's World War I: Motion Picture Images,* Peter C. Rollins and John E. O'Connor, eds. Bowling Green, Ohio: Bowling Green State University Press, 1997.

"Black Legion." *Time,* January 23, 1937, 46.

Borah, William E. "What Our Position Should Be: No American Boy Should Be Sacrificed." *Vital Speeches of the Day,* April 15, 1939, 397–99.

Bowers, John. "The Mythical Morning of Sergeant York." *MHQ: The Quarterly of Military History* 8, no. 2 (winter 1996): 38–47.

Boyle, Peter G. "The Roots of Isolationism: A Case Study." *American Studies* (Great Britain) 6, no. 1 (1983): 41–50.

Braden, Kenneth S. "The Wizard of Overton: Governor A.H. Roberts." *Tennessee Historical Quarterly* 43, no. 3 (fall 1984): 295–315.

Brauer, Ralph A. "When the Lights Went Out—Hollywood, the Depression, and the Thirties." *Journal of Popular Film and Television* 8, no. 4 (1981): 18–29.

Braustein, Baruch. "Anti-Semitism *Is* America's Concern: A Symptom of the Disease That Kills Great Nations." *Vital Speeches of the Day,* April 15, 1940, 405–7.

Brooks, Wayland C. "Revision of the Neutrality Act: Merchant Ships Cannot Sufficiently Arm." *Vital Speeches of the Day,* November 1, 1941, 43–44.

Broun, Heywood. "I Can Hear You Plainly." *New Republic,* October 18, 1939, 298.

Brown, E. Francis. "The American Road to Fascism." *Current History,* July 3, 1933, 392–98.

Browne, Nick. "System of Production/System of Representation: Industry Context and Ideological Form in Capra's *Meet John Doe.*" In *Meet John Doe: Frank Capra, Director,* Charles Wolfe, ed. New Brunswick, N.J.: Rutgers University Press, 1989.

Byrne, James F. "By Aiding Britain, We Aid Ourselves." *Vital Speeches of the Day,* February 15, 1941, 267–68.

Campbell, Russell. "Warner Brothers in the Thirties: Some Tentative Notes." *Velvet Light Trap* 1 (June 1971): 2–4.

———. "Warners, the Depression, and FDR: Wellman's *Heroes for Sale.*" *Velvet Light Trap* 4 (spring 1972): 34–38.

Carlson, John Roy. "Inside the America First Movement." *American Mercury* 54, no. 217 (January 1942): 7–25.

Carpenter, Lynette. "'There's No Place Like Home': *The Wizard of Oz* and American Isolationism." *Film and History* 15, no. 2 (1985): 37–45.

Charles, Douglas M., and John P. Rossi. "FBI Political Surveillance and the Charles Lindbergh Investigation, 1939–1944." *Historian* 59, no. 4 (summer 1997): 831–47.

Chase, Joseph Cummings. "Corporal York, General Pershing, and Others." In *The World's Work*, n.d.: 645–48.

"A Child of Nature and Grace [York of Tennessee]." *Literary Digest,* June 21, 1919, 33-34.

Clark, Susan Canedy. "America's Nazis." *American History Illustrated* 21, no. 2 (1986): 40–49.

Clifford, J. Garry. "A Note on the Break between Senator Nye and President Roosevelt in 1939." *North Dakota History* 49, no. 3 (1982): 14-17.

Clinansmith, Michael S. "The Black Legion: Hooded Americanism in Michigan." *Michigan History* 55, no. 3 (fall 1971): 243–62.

Cole, Wayne S. "America First and the South, 1940–1941." *Journal of Southern History* 22, no. 1 (February 1956): 36–47.

———. "And Then There Were None! How Arthur H. Vandenburg and Gerald P. Nye Separately Departed Isolationist Leadership Roles." In *Behind the Throne: Servants of Power to Imperial Presidents, 1898–1968,* Thomas J. McCormick and Walter LaFeber, eds., 232–53. Madison: University of Wisconsin Press, 1993.

Colodny, Robert G. "The U.S. Political Culture of the 1930s and the American Response to the Spanish Civil War." *Science and Society* 53, no. 1 (spring 1989): 47–61.

Connally, Tom. "Revise the Neutrality Act: We Must Deliver Aid Against Hitler." *Vital Speeches of the Day,* October 15, 1941, 15–17.

"Conquest of Syphilis Filmed." *Newsweek,* January 26, 1940, 30–31.

"Conscience Plus Red Hair Are Bad for Germans." *Literary Digest,* June 14, 1919, 33–48.

Costello, Michael. "The Man Who Hated War." In *A Journey through World War I.* Robert O. Levell, ed. New Castle, Ind.: Dale Printing, 1953.

Coughlin, Charles. "Background of Persecution." *Social Justice,* December 5, 1938, 3–7.

Coulter, Matthew W. "The Franklin D. Roosevelt Administration and the Special Committee on Investigation of the Munitions Industry." *Mid-America* 67, no. 1 (1985): 23–36.

Courvanes, Francis G. "Hollywood, Censorship, and American Culture." *American Quarterly* 44 (December 1992): 509–53.

Crafton, Donald. "The View from Termite Terrace: Caricature and Parody in Warner Bros. Animation." *Film History* 5 (1993): 204–30.

"Crime: Mumbo Jumbo." *Time,* June 8, 1936, 11.

Cudahy, John. "Are We at War?: What I Learned in Germany." *Vital Speeches of the Day,* October 15, 1941, 14–15.

Dalton, Elizabeth. "Bugs and Daffy Go to War: Some Warners Cartoons of WWII." *Velvet Light Trap* 5 (spring 1972): 17, 44–45.

Dalton, Elizabeth. "Old Glory: Notes on Warners Shorts." *Velvet Light Trap* 8 (1973): 7–9.

Dannenbaum, Jed. "Thumbs Down: History and Hollywood in the Forties." *Radical History Review* 44 (1989): 175–84.

Daugherty, Frank. "Hollywood's Foreign Colony." *Christian Science Monitor,* June 3, 1936, 4–5.

Davies, Alan, and Marilyn Felcher Nefsky. "The United Church and the Jewish Plight during the Nazi Era, 1933–1945." *Canadian Jewish Historical Society Journal* 8, no. 2 (1984): 55–71.

Davis, Elmer. "Is England Worth Fighting For?" *New Republic,* February 15, 1939, 35–37.

———. "The War and America." *Harper's,* April 1940, 449–62.

Davis, John. "Notes on Warner Brothers Foreign Policy, 1918–1948." *Velvet Light Trap* 4 (spring 1972): 23–33.

Dies, Martin. "The Challenge to Democracy: Foreign Isms Threaten Us." *Vital Speeches of the Day,* October 1, 1939, 762–65.

———. "Insidious Wiles of Foreign Influence: Have We Forgotten Washington's Advice?" *Vital Speeches of the Day,* December 15, 1939, 152–57.

Dinnerstein, Leonard. "Jews and the New Deal." *American Jewish History* 72, no. 4 (1983): 461–76.

———. "The Historiography of American Antisemitism." *Immigration History Newsletter* 16, no. 2 (1984): 2–5.

Doenecke, Justus D. "The Anti-Interventionist Tradition: Leadership and Perceptions." *Literature of Liberty* 4, no. 2 (summer 1981): 7–67.

———. "The Literature of Isolationism, 1972-1983: A Bibliographical Guide." *Journal of Libertarian Studies* 7, no. 1 (spring 1983): 157–84.

Doherty, Thomas. "An Elusive Factoid: World War II Motivation at Warner Bros.?" *Film and History* 27, nos. 1–4 (1997): 120–23. Donovan, William J. "Is America Prepared for War? Procrastination Now and Improvisation Later." *Vital Speeches of the Day,* December 15, 1939, 155–57.

———, "What Are We Up Against? There Is a Moral Force in Wars." *Vital Speeches of the Day,* April 15, 1941, 386–89.

Draper, Paula Jean. "The Politics of Refugee Immigration: The Pro-Refugee Lobby and the Interned Refugees 1940–1944." *Canadian Jewish Historical Society Journal* 7, no. 2 (1983): 74–88.

"Dr. Ehrlich's Magic Bullet." *Time,* February 19, 1940, 80–83.

Egan, Eileen M. "'War Is Not Holy': The American Student Peace Movement in the 1930s." *Peace and Change* 2, no. 3 (fall 1974): 41–47.

Eisen, George. "The Voices of Sanity: American Diplomatic Reports from the 1936 Berlin Olympiad." *Journal of Sports History* 11, no. 3 (winter 1984): 56–78.

Elsaesser, Thomas. "Film History as Social History: The Dieterle/Warner Brothers Bio-Pic." *Wide Angle* 8, no. 2 (1986): 15–31.

Erikkson, Jerker. "American Film in Finland." *Publications of the Institute of History* (University of Turku, Finland) 10 (1983): 63–84.

"Fascism—And the British Fuhrer." *Literary Digest,* July 24, 1937, 13–15.

"Fascism in America." *Literary Digest,* August 14, 1937, 16–17.

"Fascism in America: Like Communism It Masquerades as Americanism." *Life,* March 6, 1939, 57–63.

Feingold, Henry L. "'Courage First and Intelligence Second': The American Jewish Secular Elite, Roosevelt, and the Failure to Rescue." *American Jewish History* 72, no. 4 (1983): 424–60.

"Fentress Feud." *Time,* May 25, 1936, 26.

Ferguson, Otis. "Truth in Fiction: Black Legion." *New Republic,* February 17, 1937, 47–48.

———. "New Film in a Dry Month: 'They Won't Forget.'" *New Republic,* July 21, 1937, 335.

———. "Bring Them Back Alive." *New Republic,* August 18, 1937, 48–49.

———. "Jack and a Giant Killer." *New Republic,* June 8, 1938, 131–32.

———. "They're Down! They're Up!" *New Republic,* May 10, 1939, 20–21.

———. "Who's the Doctor?" *New Republic,* March 25, 1940, 409.

———. "Before the Cameras Roll." *New Republic,* September 22, 1941, 369–71.

———. "In the Army, Aren't We All." *New Republic,* September 29, 1941, 404–5.

———. "Hollywood Footnote." *New Republic,* November 17, 1941, 670.

Forster, Edward M. "Two Cultures: The Quick and the Dead." *Vital Speeches of the Day,* October 15, 1940, 28–30.

Frakes, Margaret. "Why the Movie Investigation?" *Christian Century,* September 24, 1941, 1172–74.

Frank, Waldo. "Should the Jews Survive?" *New Republic,* December 13, 1933, 121–25.

"Fuzzy-Wuzzy and Mr. Wheeler." *New Republic,* August 11, 1941, 188.

Fyne, Robert. "From Hollywood to Moscow." *Literature/Film Quarterly* 13, no. 3 (1985): 194–99.

Geist, Raymond H. "Masters of Bigotry: Treason against the Human Race." *Vital Speeches of the Day,* July 1, 1942, 547–51.

Genizi, Haim. "American Interfaith Cooperation on Behalf of Refugees from Nazism, 1939–1945." *American Jewish History* 70, no. 3 (1981): 347–61.

Gillman, Catheryne Cooke. "Government Regulations for the Movies." *Christian Century,* August 26, 1931, 1066–68.

Glass, William R. "Fundamentalism's Prophetic Vision of the Jews: the 1930s." *Jewish Social Studies* 47, no. 1 (1985): 63–76.

Glazener, David. "Ballad of Redhead's Day." *Literary Digest,* June 14, 1919, 48.

Gomery, J. Douglas. "Hollywood and the National Recovery Administration, and the Question of Monopoly of Power." *Journal of the University Film Association* 31, no. 2 (spring 1979): 47–52.

Grafton, Samuel. "The America First Party." *New Republic,* September 22, 1941, 368–69.

Gray, Wendy, and Robert Knight Barney. "Devotion to Whom? German-American Loyalty on the Issue of Participation in the 1936 Olympic Games." *Journal of Sports History* 17, no. 2 (summer 1990): 214–31.

Grill, Johnpeter Horst, and Robert L. Jenkins. "The Nazis and the American South in the 1930s: A Mirror Image?" *Journal of Southern History* 58, no. 4 (November 1992): 662–94.

Gunther, John. "Revolt against Hitler." *Nation,* June 7, 1933, 636–37.

Haas, Edward F. "Huey Long and the Communists." *Louisiana History* 32, no. 1 (1991): 29–46.

Hammond, John Henry, Jr. "The South Speaks." *Nation,* April 26, 1933, 464–66.

Hark, Ina Rae. "The Visual Politics of *The Adventures of Robin Hood.*" *Journal of Popular Film* 5, no. 1 (1976): 3–17.

"Harry Warner Guest Speaker at Nobel Anniversary Dinner—Jack Warner Outlines Company's War Effort." *Canadian Motion Picture Digest,* December 22, 1945, 8, 15.

Hart, Jeffrey. "Yesterday's America Tomorrow." *Commentary* 80 (July 1985): 62–65.

Hellerstein, Alice. "The 1936 Olympics: A U.S. Boycott that Failed." *Potomac Review* 21 (1981): 1–9.

Hemingway, Andrew. "Fictional Unities: 'Antifascism' and 'Antifascist Art' in 30s America." *Oxford Art Journal* 14, no. 1 (1991): 107–17.

Herbst, Josephine. "Behind the Swastika (1935)" (introduction to reprint by John Nelson). *Massachusetts Review* 27, no. 2 (1986): 333–62.

Hershan, Stella K. "Rethinking the American Jewish Experience: A Memoir of Nazi Austria and the Jewish Refugee Experience in America." *American Jewish Archives* 43, no. 2 (fall/winter 1991): 180–206.

Hickey, Neil, and Edward Sorel. "The Warner Mob." *American Heritage* 35, no. 1 (1983): 32–39.

High, Stanley. "Termites in America: It's About Time the American People Began to Be Choosey." *Vital Speeches of the Day,* December 1, 1939, 120–22.

Hitler, Adolph. "Germany's Present Position: We Will Wrest the Victory." *Vital Speeches of the Day,* February 15, 1941, 280–83.

"Hitlerism—What Is It?" *Good Citizen* 21, no. 5 (May 1933): 3–4.

Hoellering, Franz. "Films." *Nation,* May 20, 1939, 595–96.

———. "Films." *Nation,* March 9, 1940, 346–47.

"Hollywood Blasts 'Black Legion': Warner Brothers Factual Film Is Powerful and Intelligent." *Literary Digest,* January 16, 1937, 23.

"Hollywood in Washington." *Time,* September 22, 1941, 13–14.

"Hollywood's Clamor Boys." *American Mercury* 54, no. 217 (January 1942): 85–92.

Horak, Jan-Christopher. "Luis Trenker's *The Kaiser of California:* How the West Was Won, Nazi Style." *Historical Journal of Film, Radio, and Television* 6, no. 2 (1986): 181–88.

———. "G.W. Pabst in Hollywood or Every Modern Hero Deserves a Mother." *Film History* 1 (1987): 53–64.

Horowitz, David A. "An Alliance of Convenience: Independent Exhibitors and Purity Crusaders Battle Hollywood, 1920–1940." *Historian* 59, no. 3 (spring 1997): 553–72.

Howard, Roy W. "America's Future Action: Hard-Boiled Reason and Common Sense Is Necessary." *Vital Speeches of the Day,* April 15, 1939, 401–3.

Hull, Cordell. "The Defense of the United States." *Vital Speeches of the Day,* February 1, 1941, 247–49.

Humble, Mrs. Richard G. "Alvin C. York—A Christian Patriot." *Advocate,* August 13, 1964, 8–11.

Humble, Richard, and Virginia Humble. "A Tribute to Our Friends." *Advocate,* October 8, 1964, 3–4, 6–8.

———. "Oct. 8, 1918 Sergeant Alvin C. York: A Hero for 75 Years." *Advocate* 89 (October 2, 1993): 4–5.

Jacobs, Bruce. "The Legend of Sergeant York." *Saga,* January 1957, 22–25, 70–74.

Jacobson, Louis. "Herman Goldberg: Baseball Olympian and Jewish-American." *Baseball History* 3 (1990): 71–88.

Jarvie, Ian. "Dollars and Ideology: Will Hays' Economic Foreign Policy, 1922–1945." *Film History* 2 (1988): 207–21.

Jaunal, Jack W. "Those War Films—Fact, Fiction, Impact." *Periodical Journal of the Council on America's Military Past* 16, no. 2 (1989): 24–35.

Jay, Martin. "Adorno in America." *New German Critique* 31 (1984): 157–82.

Johnson, Ronald W. "The German-American Bund and Nazi Germany, 1936–1941." *Studies in History and Society* 6 (February 1975): 31–45.

Jones, David Lloyd. "Measuring and Mobilizing the Media, 1939–1945." *Midwest Quarterly* 26, no. 1 (1984): 35–43.

Jones, James B., Jr. "Tennessee's World War I Heroes." *Courier,* 27, no. 1 (October 1988): 4–6.

Jowett, Garth. "A Capacity for Evil: The 1915 Supreme Court Mutual Decision." *Historical Journal of Film, Radio, and Television* 9 (1989): 59–78.

Junker, Detlef. "The Impact of Foreign Policy on the United States Domestic Scene, 1939–1941." *Storia Nordamerica* 6, nos. 1–2 (1989): 17–34.

Kaufman, Menaham. "American Zionism and United States Neutrality from September 1939 to Pearl Harbor." *Studies in Zionism* 9, no. 1 (1988): 19–46.

Kennedy, Joseph P. "My Views on Our Foreign Policy." *Vital Speeches of the Day,* February 1, 1941, 227–31.

Kessler, Sidney H. "Fascism under the Cross: The Case of Father Coughlin." *Wiener Library Bulletin* 33, nos. 51–52 (1980): 8–12.

Knapp, Michael G. "A World War I Retrospective." *Prologue* 24, no. 1 (spring 1992): 55–61.

Kolodny, Ralph L. "Catholics and Father Coughlin: Misremembering the Past." *Patterns of Prejudice* 19, no. 4 (1985): 15–25.

Koppes, Clayton R., and Gregory D. Black. "Blacks, Loyalty, and Motion-Picture Propaganda in World War II." *Journal of American History* 73, no. 2 (September 1986): 383–406.

Kramer, William M., and Norton B. Stern. "Mary Pickford: From a Moment of Intolerance to a Lifetime of Compassion." *Western States Jewish Historical Quarterly* 13, no. 3 (1981): 274–81.

Kuczewski, Andre. "From Political Expediency to Moral Neglect: The United States and the Religio-Ethnic Experience, 1933–1945." *American Jewish Archives* 38, no. 2 (November 1885): 309–21.

La Follette, Robert M., Jr. "The Neutrality Issue: This Is Not an Ordinary Debate." *Vital Speeches of the Day,* November 1, 1939, 59–61.

"Latin Uproar." *Time,* February 10, 1940, 12.

Leab, Daniel J. "*The Fighting 69th*: An Ambiguous Portrait of Isolationism/Interventionism." In *Hollywood's World War I: Motion Picture Images.* Peter C. Rollins and John E. O'Connor, eds., 101–20. Bowling Green, Ohio: Bowling Green State University Popular Press, 1997.

Ledeboer, Suzanne G. "The Man Who Would Be Hitler: William Dudley Pelley and the Silver Shirt Legion." *California History* 65 (June 1986): 127–36.

Lee, David D. "Appalachia on Film: The Making of *Sergeant York*." *Southern Quarterly* 19, nos. 3–4 (spring–summer 1981): 207–21.

Lefebvre, Henry. "The Affair of the Hooded Men." *New Republic,* December 15, 1937, 162–64.

Levine, Lawrence W. "Hollywood's Washington: Film Images of National Politics during the Great Depression." *Prospects* 10 (1985): 169–95.

Levine, Peter. "'My Father and I, We Didn't Get Our Medals': Marty Glickman's American Jewish Odyssey." *American Jewish History* 78, no. 3 (1989): 399–424.

Lewis, David L. "Henry Ford's Anti-Semitism and Its Repercussions." *Michigan Jewish History* 24, no. 1 (1984): 3–10.

Lewisohn, Ludwig. "Germany's Lowest Depths." *Nation,* May 3, 1933, 493–94.

"Life of Emile Zola." *Literary Digest,* August 14, 1937, 31–32.

Lincove, David A. "Activists for Internationalism: ALA Responds to World War II and British Requests for Aid, 1939–1941." *Libraries and Culture* 26, no. 3 (summer 1991): 487–510.

Lindbergh, Charles A. "Appeal for Isolation: Let Us Look to Our Own Defense." *Vital Speeches of the Day,* October 1, 1939, 751–52.

————. "What Our Decision Should Be: Our Policy Must Be as Clear as Our Shore Lines." *Vital Speeches of the Day,* November 1, 1939, 57–59.

————. "Our Drift toward War: No People Ever Had a Greater Decision to Make." *Vital Speeches of the Day,* June 15, 1940, 549–51.

————. "Strength and Peace." *Vital Speeches of the Day,* November 1, 1940, 42–43.

————. "Our Air Defense: I Do Not Believe There Is Any Danger of Invasion." *Vital Speeches of the Day,* February 1, 1941, 241–42.

————. "We Are Not Prepared for War." *Vital Speeches of the Day,* February 15, 1941, 266–67.

————. "We Cannot Win This War for England." *Vital Speeches of the Day,* May 1, 1941, 424–26.

————. "Election Promises Should Be Kept." *Vital Speeches of the Day,* June 1, 1941, 42–43.

Lipstadt, Deborah E. "A Road Paved with Good Intentions: The *Christian Science Monitor*'s Reaction to the First Phase of Nazi Persecution of Jews." *Jewish Social Studies* 45, no. 2 (1983): 95–112.

————. "The American Press and the Persecution of German Jewry: The Early Years 1933–1935." *Leo Baeck Institute Yearbook* 29 (1984): 27–55.

Lore, Ludwig. "Nazi Politics in America." *Nation,* November 29, 1993, 615–17.

Lyons, Eugene. "Hitler's Blueprint for a Slave World." *American Mercury* 50, no. 200 (August 1940): 391–400.

MacDonnell, Francis. "'The Emerald City was the New Deal': E.Y. Harburg and *The Wonderful Wizard of Oz.*" *Journal of American Culture* 13, no. 4 (1990): 71–75.

"Major Heroes." *Newsweek,* May 18, 1942, 30.

Mann, Thomas. "The Problem of Freedom: The Crisis of Democracy." *Vital Speeches of the Day,* July 1, 1939, 547–50.

Marcus, Greil. "Myth and Misquotation." In *The Dustbin of History.* Cambridge, Mass.: Harvard University Press, 1995.

Marczewska, Hanna. "Controversies around the American Policy of Neutrality, 1935–1939." *American Studies* (Warsaw University, Poland) 9 (1990): 59–76.

Mariani, John. "Let's Not Be Beastly to the Nazis." *Film Comment* 15, no. 1 (1971): 49–53.

Marvin, Carolyn. "Avery Brundage and American Participation in the 1936 Olympic Games." *American Studies* (UK) 16, no. 1 (1982): 81–106.

Matthews, J. B., and R. E. Shallcross. "Must America Go Fascist?" *Harper's,* June 1934, 1–15.

Maurer, David J. "The Black Legion: A Paramilitary Fascist Organization of the 1930s." In *For the General Welfare: Essays in Honor of Robert H. Brenner,* Frank Annunziata, Patrick D. Reagan, and Roy T. Wortman, eds., 255–69. American University Studies, no. 9, History. New York: Peter Lang, 1989.

McClure, Arthur F. "Hollywood at War: The American Motion Picture and World War II, 1939–1945." *Journal of Popular Film* 1, no. 2 (1972): 125–35.

McCormick, Thomas J. "Walking the Tightrope: Adolf A. Berle and America's Journey from Social to Global Capitalism, 1933–1945." In *Behind the Throne: Servants of Power to Imperial Presidents, 1898–1968*, Thomas J. McCormick and Walter LaFeber, eds. Madison: University of Wisconsin Press, 1993.

McGinty, Brian. "Alvin York: Soldier of the Lord." *American History Illustrated* 21, no. 7 (November 1986): 40–41.

McMillan, James E. "McFarland and the Movies: The 1941 Senate Motion Picture Hearings." *Journal of Arizona History* 29, no. 3 (1988): 277–302.

Mellett, Lowell. "Government Propaganda," *Atlantic Monthly*, September 1941, 311–13.

"Metro Studio Secretly Receives Nazi Editors: But MGM Won't Make 'It Can't Happen Here.'" *Hollywood Now*, June 23, 1939, 1, 4.

Michael, Robert. "America and the Holocaust." *Midstream: A Monthly Jewish Review* 31, no. 2 (1985): 13–16.

Miller, Joan. "Nazi Invasion." *American History Illustrated* 21, no. 7 (1986): 42–49.

Modras, Ronald. "Father Coughlin and Anti-Semitism: Fifty Years Later." *Journal of Church and State* 31, no. 2 (1989): 231–47.

Moley, Raymond. "Indispensable Principles." *Vital Speeches of the Day*, October 15, 1940, 30–32.

Morgan, Edmund S. "Hostages to Fortune." *New York Review of Books*, June 23, 1994, 36–38.

Morton, Desmond, and Glenn Wright. "The Bonus Campaign, 1919–1921: Veterans and the Campaign for Re-establishment." *Canadian Historical Review* 64, no. 2 (1983): 147–67.

"Movies: They Won't Forget." *Literary Digest*, July 24, 1937, 29.

"Mr. Chase and the Sergeant." *New Yorker*, July 12, 1941, 10–11.

Neuberger, Richard L. "Wheeler of Montana." *Harper's*, May 1940, 609–18.

Neve, Brian. "The Screenwriter and the Social Problem Film, 1936–1938: The Case of Robert Rossen at Warner Brothers." *Film and History* 14, no. 1 (1984): 2–13.

Niebuhr, Reinhold. "The Revival of Feudalism." *Harper's*, March 1935, 483–88.

Norris, George W. "American Neutrality. Let Us Keep the Dollar Sign off the American Flag." *Vital Speeches of the Day*, November 1, 1939, 62–63.

"'No War for England' Prophesies Spirit World." *Psychic News*, July 8, 1939, 1.

Nugent, Frank S. "Hollywood Waves the Flag." *Nation*, April 8, 1939, 398–400.

Nye, Gerald P. "Save American Neutrality: Keep Us Out of War." *Vital Speeches of the Day*, September 15, 1939, 723–26.

———. "This Is Our Critical Hour: We Are Being Blitzkrieged into War." *Vital Speeches of the Day*, May 15, 1941, 453–55.

———. "No A.E.F.: We Must Not Go Hunting for War." *Vital Speeches of the Day,* August 15, 1941, 650–52.

———. "War Propaganda: Our Madness Increases as Our Emergency Shrinks." *Vital Speeches of the Day,* September 1, 1941, 720–23.

———. "Asking for Trouble in the Name of Peace." *Vital Speeches of the Day,* October 15, 1941, 29–32.

"Of Spies and Bund Men." *Nation,* July 2, 1938, 6.

"Old Soldiers." *Time,* May 18, 1942, 63.

Orbach, William. "Shattering the Shackles of Powerlessness: The Debate Surrounding the Anti-Nazi Boycott of 1933–1941." *Modern Judaism* 2 (1982): 149–69.

Paige, Clara R. "Any Harm in the Movies?" *Good Citizen* 21, no. 5 (May 1933): 13–15.

Patullo, George. "The Second Elder Gives Battle." *Saturday Evening Post,* April 26, 1919, 3–4, 71–73.

Pisano, Dominick A. "*The Dawn Patrol* and World War I Air Combat Film Genre: An Exploration of American Values." In *Hollywood's World War I: Motion Picture Images,* Peter C. Rollins and John E. O'Connor, eds., 59-68. Bowling Green, Ohio: Bowling Green State University Popular Press, 1997.

Pittman, Key. "Preparedness for Defense: There Is No More Vital Question." *Vital Speeches of the Day,* April 15, 1939, 404–6.

———. "Reply to Lindbergh: He Encourages the Ideology of Totalitarianism." *Vital Speeches of the Day,* November 1, 1939, 61–62.

———. "What Should America's Position Be? A Reply to Col. Lindbergh." *Vital Speeches of the Day,* June 15, 1940, 551–52.

Pollack, J. H. "The Myth of Jewish Unity." *American Mercury,* July 1940, 294–99.

Prasad, Yuvaraj D. "William Randolph Hearst and Pro-Germanism during World War I." *Indiana Journal of American Studies* 17, nos. 1–2 (1987): 93–100.

"Prestige Pictures: The Life of Emile Zola." *Time,* August 16, 1937, 34–35.

Price, Ed. "The Making of a Legend: Alvin Cullum York." *Now and Then* 4, no. 3 (fall 1987): 3–4.

"Propaganda or History?" *Nation,* September 20, 1941, 241–42.

Raimondo, Justin. "John T. Flynn: Exemplar of the Old Right." *Journal of Libertarian Studies* 10, no. 2 (fall 1992): 107–24.

Raskin, Richard. "*Casablanca* and United States Foreign Policy." *Film History* 4 (1990): 153–64.

Reimann, G. "Morale and the Nazis." *New Republic,* November 17, 1937, 34–35.

Reisner, Edward H. "The Case against Intervention: Place American Interests First." *Vital Speeches of the Day,* August 15, 1941, 655–58.

Ribuffo, Leo. "Fascists, Nazis, and American Minds: Perceptions and Preconceptions." *American Quarterly* 26 (1974): 417–32.

"Rigid Economy Program Grips Studio; WB 20th-Fox Lead." *Boxoffice,* May 25, 1940, 23.

"Robin Hood in Color: Errol Flynn Leads Merry Men in Forest of Chico, Calif." *Newsweek,* May 9, 1938, 22–23.

Robinson, Edward G. "The Movies, the Actor, and Public Morals." In *The Movies on Trial,* William J. Perlman, ed., 26–41. New York: Macmillan, 1936.

Roche, W. T. "Warmongers—Then and Now." *Defender* 14, no. 4 (August 1939): 24.

Roosevelt, Theodore II. "The Sword of the Lord and of Gideon." In *Rank and File: True Stories of the Great War,* 31–59. New York: Scribner's, 1928.

Rosenfeld, Stephen S. "Dateline Washington: Anti-Semitism and U.S. Foreign Policy." *Foreign Policy* 47 (summer 1982): 172–83.

Rossi, John. "Hitchcock's *Foreign Correspondent* (1940)." *Film and History* 12, no. 2 (1982): 25–35.

Roth, Mark. "Some Warners Musicals and the Spirit of the New Deal." *Velvet Light Trap* 17 (winter 1977): 1–7.

Rudin, A. James. "A Jewish Perspective on Baptist Ecumenism." *Journal of Ecumenical Studies* 17, no. 2 (1980): 160–71.

Sandeen, Eric J. "Anti-Nazi Sentiment in Film: *Confessions of a Nazi Spy* and the German-American Bund." *American Studies* 20, no. 2 (1979): 69–81.

Sarna, Jonathan D. "Anti-Semitism and American History." *Commentary* 71, no. 3 (1981): 42–47.

Schrank, Joseph. "Facing Zanuck." *American Heritage* 35, no. 1 (1983): 40–44.

Schulte-Sasse, Linda. "The Jew as Other under National Socialism: Veit Harlan's *Jud Suss.*" *German Quarterly* 61, no. 1 (winter 1988): 22–49.

Schwartz, Henry. "The Silver Shirts: Anti-Semitism in San Diego, 1930-1940." *Western States Jewish History* 25, no. 1 (October 1992): 52–60.

"Screen: Bigotry vs. Justice, a Tragedy of the Deep South." *Newsweek,* July 10, 1937, 23–24.

"Screen: Biography Projects Living Portrait of Novelist." *Newsweek,* August 14, 1937, 19.

Seldes, George. "The New Propaganda for War." *Harper's,* October 1934, 540–54.

"Senate Isolationists Run Afoul of Willkie in Movie 'Warmonger' Hearings." *Life,* September 22, 1941, 21–25.

"Sergeant York." *Time,* August 4, 1941, 70.

"Sergeant York: Converted in a Methodist Manner." *Christian Advocate,* April 9, 1942, 5–6.

"Sergeant York's Greatest Fight: Alvin C. York Industrial Institute." *Literary Digest,* July 3, 1928, 26.

"Sergeant York's Own Story." *Literary Digest,* May 13, 1922, 40–42.

"Sergeant York Surrenders." *Time,* April 1, 1940, 69–70.

Shapiro, Edward S. "The Approach of War: Congressional Isolationism and Anti-Semitism, 1939–1941." *American Jewish History* 74, no.1 (1984): 45–65.

———. "The World Labor Athletic Carnival of 1936: An American Anti-Nazi Protest." *American Jewish History* 74, no. 3 (1985): 255–73.

Sinclair, Upton. "The Movies and Political Propaganda." In *The Movies on Trial,* William J. Perlman, ed., 189–95. New York: Macmillan, 1936.

Singerman, Robert. "The American Career of the *Protocols of the Elders of Zion.*" *American Jewish History* 71, no. 1 (1981): 48–78.

Slotkin, Richard. "The Continuity of Forms: Myth and Genre in Warner Brothers' *The Charge of the Light Brigade.*" *Representations* 29 (winter 1990): 1–23.

Smertenko, Johan J. "Hitlerism Comes to America." *Harper's,* November 1933, 660–70.

Smith, Alson J. "Father Coughlin's Platoons." *New Republic,* August 30, 1939, 96–97.

Smith, Geoffrey. "Isolationism, the Devil, and the Advent of the Second World War: Variations on a Theme." *International History Review* 4, no. 1 (February 1982): 55–89.

"Smoke Out 'America First.'" *New Republic,* October 6, 1941, 422–23.

Sniegoski, Stephen J. "Unified Democracy: An Aspect of American World War II Interventionist Thought, 1939–1941." *Maryland Historian* 9 (spring 1978): 33–48.

"Snoop, Look, Listen." *Time,* July 4, 1938, 9.

Squires, James Duane. "The Problem of Propaganda Today: Credulity or Skepticism." *Vital Speeches of the Day,* July 15, 1939, 588–93.

Steele, Richard W. "The Great Debate: Roosevelt, the Media, and the Coming of the War, 1940–1941." *Journal of American History* 71, no.1 (June 1984): 69–92.

Stern, Guy. "The Burning of Books in Nazi Germany, 1933: The American Response." *Simon Wiesenthal Center Annual* 2 (1985): 95–113.

Stimson, Henry L. "We Must Drop Our Isolation: A Totally Novel and Critical Situation." *Vital Speeches of the Day,* April 15, 1939, 399–401.

———. "The Task We Have Undertaken." *Vital Speeches of the Day,* May 1, 1941, 419–24.

Straight, Michael. "The Anti-Semitic Conspiracy." *New Republic,* September 22, 1941, 362–63.

"Ten Nazi Editors Are Guests at Metro Lot." *Boxoffice,* June 24, 1939, 34.

"They Won't Forget." *Time,* July 26, 1937, 22–23.

Thompson, Dorothy. "Let's Face the Facts: There Are No Neutral Hearts." *Vital Speeches of the Day,* March 15, 1941, 345–47.

Thorkelson, Jacob. "The United States Must Avoid War." *Defender* 14, no. 4 (August 1939): 11.

Tobey, Charles W. "Wake Up America! The Hour Is Late: There Is a Conspiracy to Get Us into War." *Vital Speeches of the Day,* October 1, 1941, 748–51.

"Totem and Taboo: Confessions of a Nazi Spy." *Time,* May 15, 1939, 58–59.

Toy, Eckard V., Jr. "Silver Shirts in the Northwest: Politics, Prophecies, and Personalities in the 1930s," *Pacific Northwest Quarterly* 80, no. 4 (1989): 139–46.

Troy, William. "Fascism over Hollywood." *Nation*, April 26, 1933, 86.

———. "Tarzan and Hitler." *Nation*, May 16, 1934, 573–74.

Turrou, Leon G. "G-Man Turrou's Own Account of the Spy Situation." *Hollywood Spectator*, April 15, 1939, 18–24.

———. "Hollywood Does Something about the Nazis." *TAC*, May 1939, 6–7.

"Unlucky Lindy." *New Republic*, October 25, 1939, 323.

Vandenburg, Arthur H. "Peace or War for America: It Is Not Cowardice to Think of America First." *Vital Speeches of the Day*, April 1, 1939, 354–57.

Van Doren, Mark. "Black Is Back." *Nation*, January 30, 1937, 137.

———. "The Novelist as Hero." *Nation*, September 4, 1937, 246.

Vaughn, Stephen. "Spies, National Security, and the 'Inertia Projector': The Secret Service Films of Ronald Reagan." *American Quarterly* 39, no. 3 (1987): 355–80.

———. "Morality and Entertainment: The Origins of the Motion Picture Production Code." *Journal of American History* 77, no. 1 (June 1990): 39–65.

Wagner, Jonathan F. "Nazi Propaganda among North Dakota's Germans, 1934–1941." *North Dakota History* 54, no. 1 (1987): 14–24.

Walsh, David I. "Keep America out of War: Absolute Neutrality Needed." *Vital Speeches of the Day*, May 15, 1939, 450–52.

Walton, Alfred Grant. "Pacifism—A Flight from Reality: There Are Some Things More Sacred Than Life." *Vital Speeches of the Day*, August 15, 1941, 658–60.

"War and Peace: 'What Did It Get You?'" *Time*, June 9, 1941, 21.

Ward, Larry Wayne. "'Official' European War Films in Neutral America, 1914–1917." *Indiana Social Studies Quarterly* 34, no. 2 (1981): 57–68.

Warner, Harry M. "Initiative." *American Magazine*, April 1937, 192.

———. "Hollywood Obligations in a Producer's Eyes." *Christian Science Monitor*, March 16, 1939, 3.

"Warner Brothers." *Fortune*, December 16, 1937, 110–14.

Weber, Timothy P. "Finding Someone to Blame: Fundamentalism and Anti-Semitic Conspiracy Theories in the 1930s." *Fides et Historia* 24, no. 2 (1992): 40–55.

Wechsler, James. "The Christian Front and Martin Dies." *Nation*, January 27, 1940, 89–91.

Welles, Sumner. "Our Foreign Policy and National Defense." *Vital Speeches of the Day*, October 15, 1940, 15–19.

———. "The United States and the World Crisis." *Vital Speeches of the Day*, February 15, 1941, 269–71.

Wenn, Stephen R. "A Tale of Two Diplomats: George S. Messersmith and Charles H. Sherrill on Proposed American Participation in the 1936 Olympics." *Journal of Sport History* 16, no. 1 (spring 1989): 27–43.

———. "A Suitable Policy of Neutrality? FDR and the Question of American

Participation in the 1936 Olympics." *International Journal of the History of Sport* (London) 8, no. 3 (December 1991): 319–35.

"What Did Alvin C. York Do?" *Ladies Home Journal,* October 19, 1919, 64.

Wheeler, Burton K. "Foreign Policy and Neutrality: The Futility of War." *Vital Speeches of the Day,* April 15, 1939, 406–7.

———. "Marching down the Road to War: Peace Time Conscription a Menace to Our Liberties." *Vital Speeches of the Day,* September 1, 1940, 689–92.

———. "America's Present Emergency: Don't Surrender Our Independence to War-Mongers and Interventionists." *Vital Speeches of the Day,* January 15, 1941, 203–5.

Whitaker, Richard W. "Outline of Hitler's 'Final Solution' Apparent by 1933." *Journalism Quarterly* 58, no. 2 (1981): 192–200, 247.

White, Ray Lewis. "*Vom Winde Verweht: Gone with the Wind* in Nazi Germany." *Southern Studies* 22, no. 4 (1983): 401–6.

Whitfield, Stephen J. "'One Nation under God': The Rise of the Religious Right." *Virginia Quarterly Review* 58, no. 4 (1982): 557–74.

———. "Our American Jewish Heritage: The Hollywood Version." *American Jewish History* 75, no. 3 (1986): 322–40.

Whiting, Cecile. "American Heroes and Invading Barbarians: The Regionalist Response to Fascism." *Prospects* 13 (1988): 294–324.

Williams, Gladys. "Alvin Cullum York." York Institute, Jamestown, Tenn., n.d.

"Willkie and the Film Community." *Newsweek,* September 15, 1941, 51.

Willkie, Wendell. "The Living Spirit of American Democracy." *Vital Speeches of the Day,* October 15, 1940, 8–10.

———. "Cooperation but Loyal Opposition." *Vital Speeches of the Day,* December 1, 1940, 103–6.

———. "A Warning on Isolation." *Vital Speeches of the Day,* February 1, 1941, 249–50.

———. "The Cause of Human Freedom: We Cannot Appease the Forces of Evil." *Vital Speeches of the Day,* May 15, 1941, 455–57.

———. "Senate's Threat to Free Speech: Movie Investigation Highlights Danger." *Life,* November 3, 1941, 42–48.

Wills, Gary. "The New Revolutionaries." *New York Review of Books,* August 10, 1995, 50–55.

Winrod, Gerald B. "The Kings of the East." *Defender* 14, no. 4 (August 1939): 14–15.

Winter, Ella. "Hollywood Wakes Up." *New Republic,* January 12, 1938, 276–78.

———. "Hollywood Organized." *New Republic,* August 16, 1939, 49.

Wolfson, Adam. "The Boston Jewish Community and the Rise of Nazism, 1933–1939." *Jewish Social Studies* 48, nos. 3–4 (1986): 305–14.

Y–. "Underground Germany." *Survey Graphic,* March 1939, 219–23.

"York to Uplift Mountaineers." *Literary Digest,* August 30, 1919, 35.

DISSERTATIONS AND THESES

Bathe, David A. "Wendell L. Willkie: A Political Odyssey from Realism to Idealism." Ph.D. diss., Illinois State University, 1991.

Birdwell, Michael E. "The Making of the Movie *Sergeant York*: A Journey from Reality into Myth." Master's thesis, Tennessee Technological University, 1990.

Colgan, Christine Ann. "Warner Brothers' Crusade against the Third Reich: A Study of Anti-Nazi Activism and Film Production, 1933–1941." Ph.D. diss., University of Southern California, 1985.

Gustafson, Robert. "The Buying of Ideas: Source Acquisition at Warner Brothers 1930–1949." Ph.D. diss., University of Wisconsin, 1983.

Krome, Frederic James. "'A Weapon of War Second to None': Anglo-American Film Propaganda during World War II." Ph.D. diss., University of Cincinnati, 1992.

Laurie, Clayton D. "Ideology and American Propaganda: The Psychological Warfare Campaign against Nazi Germany, 1941–1945." Ph.D. diss., American University, 1990.

Thompson, Sarah Chapman. "Wendell Willkie: A Hoosier Liberal." Ph.D. diss., Ball State University, 1980.

Tucker, Douglas Byron. "Preaching to the Choir: U.S. Government Propaganda towards Its Own Citizens in Military Publications." Ph.D. diss., University of California, Santa Cruz, 1983.

Tweed, Carolyn Jeanne. "The Life Cycles of William Dudley Pelley." Master's thesis, East Tennessee State University, 1990.

Williams, Suzanne Hurst. "A Comparison of Cultural Values in Animated Cartoons Produced for the Theatre and Television." Ph.D. diss., University of Wisconsin, 1987.

FILMOGRAPHY

Feature Films

The Adventures of Robin Hood. Dir. Michael Curtiz, Warner Bros., 1938.

All Through the Night. Dir. Vincent Sherman. Warner Bros., 1942.

Black Fury. Dir. Michael Curtiz. Warner Bros., 1935.

Black Legion. Dir. Archie Mayo. Warner Bros., 1936.

Casablanca. Dir. Michael Curtiz. Warner Bros., 1942.

The Charge of the Light Brigade. Dir. Michael Curtiz. Warner Bros., 1936.

Confessions of a Nazi Spy. Dir. Anatole Litvak. Warner Bros.,1939.

Dawn Patrol. Dir. Edmund Goulding. Warner Bros., 1938

Devil Dogs of the Air. Dir. Lloyd Bacon. Cosmopolitan/Warner Bros., 1935.

Dispatch from Reuters. Dir. William Dieterle. Warner Bros., 1940.

Dive Bomber. Dir. Michael Curtiz. Warner Bros., 1940.

Don Juan. Dir. Alan Crosland. Warner Bros., 1926.

Dr. Ehrlich's Magic Bullet. Dir. William Dieterle. Warner Bros., 1940.

The Fighting 69th. Dir. William Keighly. Warner Bros., 1940.

Fire over England. Dir. William Howard. London Films/UA, 1937.

Foreign Correspondent. Dir. Alfred Hitchcock. Walter Wanger/UA, 1940.

Gabriel over the White House. Dir. Gregory LaCava, prod. Walter Wanger. Cosmopolitan/MGM, 1933.

The Great Dictator. Dir. Charlie Chaplin. United Artists, 1940.

International Squadron. Dir. Lothar Mendes. Warner Bros., 1941.

The Jazz Singer. Dir. Alan Crosland. Warner Bros., 1927.

Juarez. Dir. William Dieterle. Warner Bros., 1939.

The Life of Emile Zola. Dir. William Dieterle. Warner Bros., 1937.

Lilac Time. Dir. George Fitzmaurice. Warner Bros., 1928.

Little Caesar. Dir. Mervyn LeRoy, Warner Bros., 1930.

Man Hunt. Dir. William Clemons. Warner Bros., 1936.

Marked Woman. Dir. Lloyd Bacon. Warner Bros., 1936.

Meet John Doe. Dir. Frank Capra. Capra/Warner Bros., 1941.

Miss Pacific Fleet. Dir. Ray Enright. Warner Bros., 1935.

Murder in the Air. Dir. Lewis Seiler. Warner Bros., 1940.

My Four Years in Germany. Dir. William Nigh. Warner Bros, 1918.

Noah's Ark. Dir. Michael Curtiz. Warner Bros., 1929.

The President Vanishes. Dir. William Wellman, prod. Walter Wanger. Paramount, 1934.

Public Enemy. Dir. William Wellman, prod. Darryl F. Zanuck. Warner Bros., 1931.

The Sea Hawk. Dir. Michael Curtiz. Warner Bros., 1940.

Sergeant York. Dir. Howard Hawks. Warner Bros., 1941.

The Singing Marine. Dir. Ray Enright and Busby Berkeley. Warner Bros., 1937.

Sons o' Guns. Dir. Lloyd Bacon. Warner Bros., 1936.

They Won't Forget. Dir. Mervyn LeRoy. Warner Bros., 1937.

Triumph of the Will. Dir. Leni Riefenstahl. UFA, 1934.

Short Subjects and Cartoons

Bosko's Picture Show. Dir. Friz Freleng. Warner Bros./Looney Tunes, 1934.

The Bug Parade. Dir. Fred "Tex" Avery. Warner Bros./Looney Tunes, 1941.

Confusions of a Nutzy Spy. Dir. Norman McCabe. Warner Bros./Looney Tunes, 1943.

Fifth Column Mouse. Dir. Friz Freleng. Warner Bros/Looney Tunes, 1943.

The Fighting 69th 1/2. Dir. Friz Freleng. Warner Bros./Looney Tunes, 1941.

London Can Take It. Dir. Teddington Studio/Warner Bros., 1940.

Meet John Doughboy. Dir. Robert Clampett. Warner Bros./Looney Tunes, 1941.

Oh, You Nazty Spy! Dir. Jules White with the Three Stooges. Columbia, 1940.

The Warner Bros. *Old Glory* Series:

The Bill of Rights. Dir. Crane Wilbur, 1939.

Declaration of Independence. Dir. Crane Wilbur, 1938.

Flag of Humanity. Dir. Jean Negulesco, 1940.

Give Me Liberty. Dir. B. Reeves Eason, 1936.

Lincoln in the White House. Dir. William McGann, 1939.

The Man without a Country. Dir. Crane Wilbur, 1937.

The Monroe Doctrine. Dir. Crane Wilbur, 1939.

Old Hickory. Dir. Lewis Seiler, 1939.

Pony Express Days. Dir. B. Reeves Eason, 1940.

Romance of Louisiana. Dir. Crane Wilbur, 1938.

Song of a Nation. Dir. Frank McDonald, 1936.

Sons of Liberty. Dir. Michael Curtiz, 1939.

Teddy, the Rough Rider. Dir. Ray Enright, 1940.

Under Southern Stars. Dir. Nick Grinde, 1937.

Index

About the Author

Michael E. Birdwell is an assistant professor of history at Tennessee Technological University specializing in cultural history with an emphasis on film. In addition to his teaching duties, Birdwell works in association with the Sergeant York Patriotic Foundation as the curator of the Alvin C. York papers housed in Pall Mall, Tennessee. He acted as consultant and "talking head" for A&E's biography segment about the life of Alvin York. He received his B.S. and M.A. from Tennessee Tech and his Ph.D. from the University of Tennessee at Knoxville. He has published articles in *Literature/Film Quarterly, Film and History, Tennessee Historical Quarterly,* the *Columbia Companion to American Film,* and *Hollywood's World War I: Motion Picture Images.*

When not engaged in scholarly pursuits, Birdwell dabbles in the arts, goes hiking, and spends time with friends who provide some sanity to an otherwise hectic life. He is actively involved as a director of local theater productions. A visual artist whose favorite medium is pen and ink, Birdwell has also had two one-man shows and displays his art in a number of venues.

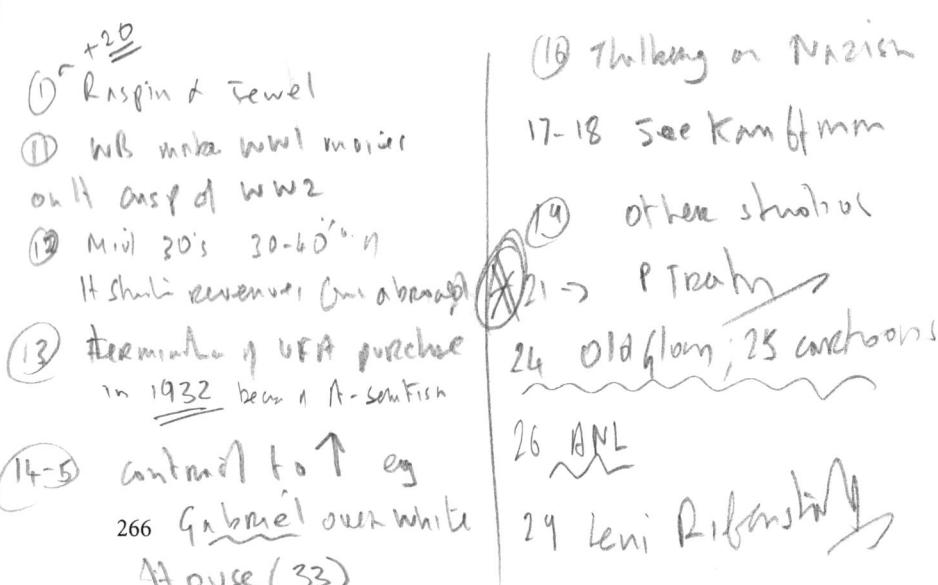